Confucian - Golden Rule

Mozi - Universal love

Mencius - instinct to act morally

Zhuangzi - cognitive Bias

# The Art of Chinese Philosophy

# The Art of
# Chinese
# Philosophy

## Eight Classical Texts
## and
## How to Read Them

## Paul R. Goldin

**Princeton University Press**
**Princeton and Oxford**

Published by Princeton University Press
41 William Street, Princeton, New Jersey 08540
6 Oxford Street, Woodstock, Oxfordshire OX20 1TR

press.princeton.edu

Library of Congress Cataloging-in-Publication Data

Names: Goldin, Paul Rakita, 1972- author.
Title: The art of Chinese philosophy : eight classical texts and how to read them /
    Paul R. Goldin.
Description: Princeton : Princeton University Press, [2020] | Includes bibliographical references
    and index. | English and Chinese.
Identifiers: LCCN 2019029702 (print) | LCCN 2019029703 (ebook) | ISBN 9780691200781
    (hardback) | ISBN 9780691200798 (paperback) | ISBN 9780691200811 (ebook)
Subjects: LCSH: Philosophy, Chinese—To 221 B.C.
Classification: LCC B126 .G655 2020 (print) | LCC B126 (ebook) | DDC 181/.11—dc23
LC record available at https://lccn.loc.gov/2019029702
LC ebook record available at https://lccn.loc.gov/2019029703ISBN (e-book) 9780691200811

British Library Cataloging-in-Publication Data is available

Editorial: Rob Tempio and Matt Rohal
Production Editorial: Sara Lerner
Text and Cover Design: Leslie Flis
Production: Brigid Ackerman
Publicity: Amy Stewart and Alyssa Sanford
Copyeditor: Kathleen Kageff

Cover Credit: Shutterstock

This book has been composed in Minion Pro with Gotham Narrow display

10  9  8  7  6  5  4  3  2  1

In memory of my father

*Ci falt la geste*

# Contents

## Part III. Two Titans at the End of an Age

# Preface

In keeping with the purpose of this book, which is to offer new but rigorous interpretations of some of the most cherished texts in the Chinese tradition, I have aimed to sustain simultaneous and parallel discourses: the main exposition, which is intended to be accessible to all interested readers, and the notes, which are composed for specialists. Consequently I do not provide the same degree of contextual information for the many sources cited in the notes (such as *Guanzi*).

References are abbreviated, as full publication information for each title is found in the appropriate section of the bibliography: the first section, for pre-Tang Chinese texts, and the second section, for Chinese texts from the Tang and later, as well as works in all other languages.

All translations from Chinese sources are my own. Words and phrases that are implied in the original or necessary for clear understanding in English are inserted in brackets; relevant background information, such as the identities and dates of named personages, is inserted in parentheses.

# Acknowledgments

This book is dedicated to my father, who mentioned it on his deathbed. Over the fifteen years that it has occupied me, I have accumulated too many debts to recount, but several colleagues stand out for suggesting improvements that would not have occurred to me otherwise: Ch'i Wan-hsian 齊婉先, Martin Kern, Esther S. Klein, Yuri Pines, Maddalena Poli, Edward G. Slingerland, and Bryan W. Van Norden.

Previous versions of several chapters appeared in the following publications: chapter 1, in *Between History and Philosophy: Anecdotes in Early China*, edited by Paul van Els and Sarah A. Queen (State University of New York Press, 2017); chapters 2, 4, and 8, in Goldin, *Confucianism* (Acumen and University of California Press, 2011; reprint Routledge, 2014); chapter 3, in *How Should One Live? Comparing Ethics in Ancient China and Greco-Roman Antiquity*, edited by R.A.H. King and Dennis Schilling (De Gruyter, 2011); and chapter 9, in *Dao Companion to the Philosophy of Han Fei*, edited by Paul R. Goldin (Springer, 2013). All such material has been thoroughly revised to reflect the latest scholarship and my current thinking. The introduction, chapters 5–7, and the appendix are new.

Thanks, finally, to all the students in "Introduction to Classical Chinese Thought," which I have taught at the University of Pennsylvania since 1997. The need to explain the material to them made me realize that first I needed to explain it to myself. And often *they* explained it to *me*.

# The Art of Chinese Philosophy

# Introduction

## WHAT ARE WE READING?

This book presents interpretations of the eight most important classical Chinese philosophical texts: *Analects* (*Lunyu* 論語), *Mozi* 墨子, *Mencius* (*Mengzi* 孟子), *Laozi* 老子, *Zhuangzi* 莊子, *Sunzi* 孫子, *Xunzi* 荀子, and *Han Feizi* 韓非子. These eight have been chosen both because they continually respond to each other's arguments and because they have exerted outsize influence on subsequent generations. Except for the *Analects*, which purports to record conversations between Confucius (551–479 BC) and his disciples, each text is named after a supposed author, honored by the term Master (*zi* 子). (*Mencius* is merely *Mengzi*, Latinized by Jesuits.) The very titles have fostered considerable misunderstanding.

Although the positions taken in these texts are never identical—the diversity of Chinese philosophy rarely fails to impress—they do address a number of central questions: What obligations do human beings have toward one another, and why? How do we construct an ideal government? What is a life well lived? Hovering over all of these is a rationalist metaquestion that reflects the crisis of the waning of the Bronze Age: How do we answer such questions for ourselves, seeing that gods and spirits, despite our richest devotions, have failed to do so?[1] And with Bronze Age rituals and diplomatic conventions no longer being recognized, at unprecedented cost of human life, what measures can states take to secure their survival?[2] The anxiety of a collapsing society, and the awareness that it will have to be replaced, are palpable throughout. It is no coincidence that the historical period has long been called the Warring States (*Zhanguo* 戰國).[3] It ended with the unification of China under the First Emperor in 221 BC.

One traditional approach to this material has been to divide it into "schools" (*jia* 家): the Confucians said this; the Daoists said that; the Legalists said something else entirely.[4] Sometimes one encounters the

cliché "the contending voices of a hundred schools" (*baijia zhengming* 百
家爭鳴).[5] This conception of Warring States philosophy as a landscape
of warring philosophical factions has a long history in China, where the
term *jia* has been used to group philosophers into a handful of categories,
sometimes in a sincere attempt to understand the complex intellectual
history, but all too often as a device to caricature opposing viewpoints.
In fact, the latter seems to have been the original purpose.

The historical problem with this practice is that only two of these
postulated schools, namely Confucians (*Ruzhe* 儒者) and Mohists
(*Mozhe* 墨者), identified themselves (and each other) as such, and can
be said to have established any institutions. All the others have been reconstructed purely on the basis of their supposed stances, raising a con-
comitant philosophical problem: the division of texts into "schools" has
served to obscure important differences among their supposed members. As I have argued elsewhere,[6] "Legalism" is the most pernicious
label of the bunch, but "Daoism" illustrates similar weaknesses: *Laozi*
and *Zhuangzi*, the two most prominent "Daoist" sources, differ profoundly on the value of government and usefulness (see p. 151), while
*dao* 道 is also one of the most important concepts in *Xunzi*, a Confucian
text (see p. 182). Does this mean that Xunzi was a Daoist too? And if
not, why not?

The sources are simply too rich, and the overall discourse exhibits too
much intertextuality, for the "schools" approach to offer more than a
crude sketch. At its worst, it tends toward reductionism. Hence I prefer
to read each text *as a text*: not necessarily as the manifesto of a school,
nor even necessarily as the work of a single brilliant mind. The modern
world has developed some good methods of reading texts, and they can
help with Chinese philosophy too.

• • •

One of the first questions that readers must ask themselves, regardless of
their hermeneutic framework, is what they are reading. In Chinese philosophy, the question is not often raised, in part because of the long-
standing but specious assumption that the eight classic philosophical
texts were written by the great masters whose names they bear. This approach is congruent with a cardinal tenet of traditional Chinese aesthetics: works of art and literature are produced by talented human beings

as a way of channeling their responses to poignant events.[7] It follows that a great work must have been composed by a great author—and since the texts are undeniably great, each one must have been produced by a magnificently talented human being.

Far from denigrating Chinese philosophy, liberating it from these mythic suppositions only improves our understanding and appreciation of it. As we shall see, not one of the eight texts was written in its present form by the philosopher to whom it is attributed. In some cases, the attribution would not be helpful even if it were valid, since we know virtually nothing about the person who bore the name. This is clearest in the case of Laozi, the mysterious sage whose identity has been disputed since antiquity; but the supposed biography of Sunzi,[8] that is, the great military strategist Sun Wu 孫武, also contains so few credible elements that there remains little reason to assume that he was a real person—other than that traditionalists have long believed it.

More details will be presented in each chapter below; for now, the important point is that such claims do not impugn the stature of *Laozi* or *Sunzi* because it is untrue that great texts must be written by solitary geniuses. Widespread acceptance of the composite authorship of the Bible, for example, has not led anyone to doubt that it is one of the most important texts in Western civilization. By contrast, sustaining the fiction that each classical Chinese philosophical text is the product of a great mind comes with serious interpretive costs. Most patently, it encourages a presumption of philosophical coherence where there may be scant historical warrant for it.[9] More insidiously, it disregards the extent to which transmitters, redactors, and commentators shaped the text for their own audiences and purposes, whether by engineering new implications through new juxtapositions or by foregrounding the passages that appealed to them and mitigating—if not simply excising—those that did not. (Lest there be any doubt about the last possibility, consider that *Mencius* comes down to us in seven chapters because its redactor, Zhao Qi 趙岐 [d. AD 201], excised four others that he deemed unworthy.)[10] A modern reader of classical Chinese texts must strike a fundamental balance: paying due attention to the historical circumstances of each text's transmission without losing sight of its animating ideas—for the ideas are the reason why the texts were transmitted in the first place. It is all too easy for academic interpreters to veer too far in either direction.

Some of the most famous early passages attributing philosophical works to single authors come from the historian Sima Qian 司馬遷 (145?–86? BC):[11]

昔，西伯拘羑里，演《周易》；孔子戹陳蔡，作《春秋》；屈原放逐，著《離騷》；左丘失明，厥有《國語》；孫子臏腳，而論《兵法》；不韋遷蜀，世傳《呂覽》；韓非囚秦，《說難》、《孤憤》；《詩》三百篇，大抵賢聖發憤之所為作也。此人皆意有所鬱結，不得通其道也，故述往事思來者。[12]

In the past, when the Earl of the West (i.e., King Wen of Zhou 周文王, d. 1050 BC) was held captive at Youli, he elaborated on the *Changes of Zhou*; when Confucius was in distress between Chen and Cai, he composed the *Springs and Autumns*; when Qu Yuan was banished, he wrote *Encountering Sorrow*; only when Zuoqiu [Ming] lost his sight was there *Discourses of the States*; when Master Sun (i.e., Sun Bin 孫臏, d. 316 BC) had his legs amputated up to the kneecaps, he expounded on *Methods of War*; [Lü] Buwei (d. 235 BC) was exiled to Shu, and generations have transmitted *Lü's Readings*; when Han Fei (d. 233 BC) was imprisoned in Qin, [he produced] *The Difficulties of Persuasion* and *Solitary Outrage*; and most of the three hundred *Odes* were created when worthies and sages expressed their outrage. All these people had something trammeling their ambition; they were unable to propagate their Way and thus narrated past events, mindful of posterity.[13]

Today we know that this is not how most early Chinese texts were produced; in fact, Sima's own *Records of the Historian* (*Shiji* 史記) was one of the first to have been written by the kind of solitary and brooding author that he described so well. (Sima Qian inherited the grand project from his father, Sima Tan 司馬談 [d. ca. 110 BC], but then seems to have compiled most of the book single-handedly, though relying heavily on preexisting material.)[14] Perhaps the oldest surviving single-authored work is *New Discourses* (*Xinyu* 新語), by Lu Jia 陸賈 (ca. 228–ca. 140 BC), which looks like what it claims to be: a sequence of twelve moralistic essays written in response to a request by Emperor Gao of Han 漢高祖 (r. 202–195 BC).[15] Texts like *Records of the Historian* and *New Discourses* bespeak a sea change in cultural attitudes toward authorship, because no single-authored book is attested before the Han dynasty (206 BC–AD

220), but thereafter it was common for writers to compose in their own name.[16] Yang Xiong 揚雄 (53 BC–AD 18)[17] and Wang Chong 王充 (b. AD 27)[18] are two prominent examples.

Many modern critics have observed that, Sima Qian's lament notwithstanding, pre-Han texts are more typically the product of multiple authors.[19] As we have learned from bamboo and silk manuscripts excavated over the past forty-five years, textual units were originally quite small (sometimes as short as a single episode, maybe even a single artfully crafted sentence); the synthetic texts that come down to us were compiled by weaving together these shorter elements.[20] There are, to be sure, references to writings on bamboo as early as the Bronze Age, but they are rare and usually do not even connote what we would call books.[21]

The composite nature of such texts can explain certain features that would otherwise appear bizarre, such as the conspicuous lack of character development in the longest and most celebrated pre-imperial historical text, the *Zuo Commentary* (*Zuozhuan* 左傳)—a strong indication that the received text was not composed as a single opus, but was pieced together out of smaller exempla. In *Shiji*, much of the same material is recast so as to present believable character arcs,[22] whereas in the older *Zuozhuan*, there is sometimes scant coherence between different episodes, to the point that a character can exemplify the very same errors that, a hundred pages earlier, he or she wisely identified and avoided.[23]

Even more importantly, the role of redactors in the process of transmission is still inadequately appreciated.[24] Much of what we now know about textual formation and redaction was discerned by Yu Jiaxi 余嘉錫 (1884–1955) nearly a century ago;[25] manuscripts from sites like Guodian 郭店 (ca. 300 BC),[26] which he did not live to see, have only confirmed that his model was basically correct.[27]

The preface to a collection called *Springs and Autumns of Master Yan* (*Yanzi chunqiu* 晏子春秋), named after the statesman Yan Ying 晏嬰 (d. 500 BC), though philosophically unremarkable (and hence scarcely read),[28] reveals much about how such texts came into being. The imperial library, it turns out, was a crucial institution in the process, because its bibliographers produced many edited collections in their quest to impose order on the thousands of loose and uncategorized documents all around them. The most celebrated such bibliographer, Liu Xiang 劉向 (79–8 BC),[29] detailed his methods when he submitted his edition of *Springs and*

*Autumns of Master Yan* to the throne. He begins by listing his four main sources (a–d in the translation below):

護左都水使者、光祿大夫臣向言：所校中書《晏子》十一篇，臣向謹與長社尉臣參校讎，太史書五篇，臣向書一篇，參書十三篇，凡中外書三十篇，為八百三十八章。除復重二十二篇六百三十八章，定著八篇二百一十五章。外書無有三十六章，中書無有七十一章，中外皆有以相定。中書以「天」為「芳」，「又」為「備」，「先」為「牛」，「章」為「長」，如此類者多。謹頗略揚，皆已定，以殺青，書可繕寫。

I, your servant Liu Xiang, Supervisor of the Left Commissioner of Waterworks and Counselor of the Palace, say: [a.] the eleven-chapter edition of *Yanzi* in the palace collection, which I carefully edited with your servant [Du] Can (d. AD 24), the Superintendent of Changshe; plus [b.] five chapters in the collection of the Grand Historian;[30] plus [c.] one chapter of my own; plus [d.] thirteen chapters in Can's collection came to thirty chapters in total, comprising 838 episodes. Eliminating twenty-two duplicate chapters with 638 episodes, I fixed the text at eight chapters with 215 episodes.[31] As there were thirty-six episodes not present in the texts from outside the palace and seventy-one episodes not present in the texts from inside the palace, I used both sets complementarily in establishing [the final edition]. In the palace texts, there were many [errors], such as *yue* written as *fang*, *you* written as *bei*, *xian* written as *niu*, and *zhang* written as *chang*. After I had carefully emended each one,[32] the final text was ready; once the strips were heated (a procedure to repel vermin), the book could be copied out.

Liu Xiang then tersely relates Yan Ying's life and achievements, and concludes:

其書六篇，皆忠諫其君，文章可觀，義理可法，皆合六經之義。又有復重文辭頗異，不敢遺失，復列以為一篇。又有頗不合經術，似非晏子言，疑後世辯士所為者，故亦不敢失，復以為一篇。凡八篇，其六篇可常置旁御觀，謹第錄。臣向昧死上。[33]

Six chapters of the book [contain] his loyal remonstrances to his lord. These pieces are worth reading; their righteous principles can serve as a model; they all conform to the principles of the Six Canons. Then there are some repeated pieces whose wording is significantly different; I did not dare to dispose of them and arranged them as a separate chapter. Then there are [pieces] that do not accord with what is narrated in the canons and seem not to be Master Yan's words; I suspect that they were made by polemicists of later generations. Yet I still did not dare to discard them and placed them in a separate chapter [too]. In all, there are eight chapters, of which six can be consistently instituted, relied on, promoted, and observed. Having carefully recorded [the text] in this sequence, I, your servant Xiang, submit it at the risk of my life.[34]

*Pian* 篇, the term translated above as "chapters," denoted a set of bamboo strips sewn together and then rolled open or closed like a sushi mat. In his search for "Master Yan's words," Liu Xiang collected thirty such bundles of lore from diverse sources.[35] A large proportion, he reports, consisted of "duplicates" (*fuchong* 復重).[36] After eliminating these, he corrected certain obvious errors[37] in the remaining episodes and then sorted them by judging how well they "accorded" (*he* 合) with the moral values of the Confucian canons. He does betray the traditional critical bias mentioned above: the episodes that "do not accord with what is narrated in the canons," he says, "seem not to be Master Yan's words," for Master Yan was a great man, and great men do not say unseemly things. But fortunately for posterity, he could not bring himself to delete them. Other redactors were not always so cautious.

This straightforward account explains many features that have perplexed readers for centuries. Once we recognize that what we are reading is not necessarily Yan Ying's own work, but more plausibly what *other people* recorded about him after his death, certain ostensible contradictions immediately become comprehensible: for example, that some episodes present him as an ally of Confucian moralism, others as inimical to Confucius, still others as indifferent.[38] Clearly Yan Ying's approval carried weight—but the fact that his approval was contested implies that there was no authorized repository of his viewpoints and teachings. Liu Xiang's preface also explains why the text frequently attributes to Yan Ying speeches and actions that are elsewhere attributed to other famed personages; why the text often relates multiple versions of the same story;[39] why some episodes take place when Yan Ying would have already been dead;[40] why some parts—but not all—are philosophically consistent;[41] and why some parts—but, again, not all—appear in very similar form in recently excavated manuscripts, notably from Yinque-shan 銀雀山.[42]

Liu Xiang was responsible for editing more classical texts than anyone else, and several of his prefaces to other works (including *Xunzi*) have survived as well. They relate essentially the same editorial process and permit some general inferences. The first is that the *stemma codicum* model, which aims to reconstruct a cladogram of manuscripts, is inapplicable to texts that were assembled as Liu Xiang described, and hence the very concept of an urtext is a chimera. This is not surprising, since stemmatology was pioneered by Karl Lachmann (1793–1851) and others for analyzing classical and medieval European literature,[43] but misapplications of the method to early Chinese texts have endured.[44]

Nor is a model of accretion any more helpful. This theory likens the text to a pearl that grows ever larger within a mollusk's mantle.[45] Accretion is plainly not the method by which *Springs and Autumns of Master Yan* was compiled. Moreover, even when it is possible to demonstrate that some parts are older than others—as is often the case with classical Chinese texts—this alone does not justify a hypothesis of accretion. The varying antiquity of the material might simply reflect the varying sources that lay at the redactor's disposal.

Thus when sections of a received text are found in excavated manuscripts, it is a mistake to use this discovery as "proof" that the entire text must be assigned a very early date. This fallacy has recently been rekindled by China's rich palaeographical inventory. A good case in point is the text called *School Sayings of Confucius* (*Kongzi jiayu* 孔子家語). Most Western scholars—and, until this century, most Chinese scholars too—have considered it a forgery by a zealous teacher and commentator named Wang Su 王肅 (AD 195–256). Because no less than 96 percent of the received text has been shown to consist of passages with parallels in other documents,[46] the truth is not difficult to detect: Wang Su culled a few hundred passages from various sources and passed them off as a book with the pretentious title *School Sayings of Confucius*. (The remaining 4 percent of the text, presumably, was lifted from sources that are now lost.) In his preface to this pastiche,[47] Wang Su asserted that he had received the text from a descendant of Confucius himself, thereby suggesting that it contained authentic Confucian sayings that were never transmitted in the *Analects*. Although the preface was undoubtedly intended to mislead, it is more charitable to think of Wang Su as an irresponsible redactor rather than as a forger, because he probably did not *invent* a single word. (Forgery requires some talent, after all.) Thus it is only to be expected that some sections of the *School Sayings* have been found in manuscripts since the 1970s. Of course, this does not mean that *School Sayings* is an authentic early text;[48] it means only that some of Wang Su's favorite stories were legitimately old. We know that others were not.

A final general inference to be gleaned from Liu Xiang's prefaces is that his compilations are not necessarily works by single authors (whether or not he himself thought they were).[49] But crucially, his prefaces do not preclude that possibility either. When he collected any and all snippets relating to Yan Ying, most of the resulting anthology was apocryphal at best, because nearly five centuries had elapsed since Yan Ying's death in 500. When he collected texts attributed to Xun Kuang 荀況 (d. after 238 BC),[50] however, he had a much better chance of locating authentic documents, because Xunzi was still one of the most influential philosophers in the Han dynasty, with many eminent students.[51] Two further considerations suggest that Liu Xiang's edition of *Xunzi* is of a fundamentally different type from *Springs and Autumns of Master Yan*. First, the percentage of duplicate bundles is noteworthy: 90 percent (290 out of 322) for *Xunzi* as compared to 73.3 percent (22 out of 30) for *Springs and Autumns of Master Yan*. Both the higher percentage of duplicates and the much higher number of reported bundles suggest that the works of Xunzi were more widely circulated and exhibited less variation.[52] Second, the culture and practice of writing had changed profoundly in the centuries between Yan Ying and Xunzi. Whereas the model of instruction in Yan Ying's time was still typically master-to-disciple, Xunzi lived in a much larger society (with a total population in the tens of millions) and consciously wrote for readers whom he would never meet.[53]

In *Xunzi*, therefore, I believe we have a collection of predominantly authentic essays, but once again taken from diverse sources, and certainly not organized in a manner that Xun Kuang himself had authorized.[54] The chapter divisions, in particular, seem unreliable:[55] whereas some chapters read like self-standing essays, others do not. In "Refutation of Physiognomy" ("Feixiang" 非相), for example, only the opening lines deal with physiognomy; the rest of the chapter seems to consist of stray passages that Liu Xiang did not quite know where to insert. There are also some chapters with generic instructional material that seems to have been assembled, in John Knoblock's words, as "a proper curriculum,"[56] as well as poems and rhymed riddles that are rarely studied.[57] As we shall see in chapter 8, one of the consequences of this arrangement is that reconstructing Xunzi's arguments requires reading across chapter boundaries: taken as a whole, the book conveys a distinctive philosophical position, but individual chapters are inadequate, indeed sometimes incoherent, on their own.[58]

*Han Feizi* has a comparable structure and history. Unfortunately, there is no surviving preface to this text, and its redactor is unknown, but formally it looks like *Xunzi*: a posthumous assemblage of memorials, occasional writings, and fragments. It is much longer than *Xunzi*, and for this reason often suspected of including spurious sections, but its philosophical consistency, in addition to its stinging wit, have convinced most modern scholars that, with the exception of a small number of controversial chapters, it was penned by a single author.[59]

Still, we do not know which chapters (if any) were written by Xunzi or Han Feizi in the same way that we know Hume wrote *An Enquiry concerning Human Understanding* and Kant wrote *Critique of Pure Reason*. There is a difference. The works that we call *Xunzi* and *Han Feizi* cannot be interpreted as direct records of a certain philosopher's cogitation. Any claim of coherence has to emerge from the texts themselves and cannot be based on an appeal to their supposed authorship.

Despite their vast philosophical differences, *Springs and Autumns of Master Yan*, *Xunzi*, and *Han Feizi* have nearly identical textual histories: they were all synthesized out of smaller, heterogeneous units by palace librarians in the Han dynasty, whereafter they were preserved and transmitted, in essentially the same recension, down to the present day. Other cases are more complex because there is both direct and indirect evidence of *multiple* recensions. For example, the received text of *Zhuangzi* is attributed to Guo Xiang 郭象 (d. AD 312),[60] but there were several earlier redactions, including one by Liu Xiang. Though some of these survived for at least a couple of centuries after Guo Xiang, they were all eventually lost, their contents now largely a matter of conjecture.[61] As mentioned above, the received text of *Mencius* was produced by Zhao Qi, whose edition likewise supplanted all others.[62]

*Laozi* presents yet more ramifications, because no single redaction ever reigned supreme. Hence we speak today of the Wang Bi 王弼 (AD 226–49) edition, the Heshanggong 河上公 edition, the *Xiang'er* 想爾 edition, and so on,[63] not to mention the two manuscript editions from Mawangdui 馬王堆 and related smaller anthologies from Guodian. The differences among these versions—both textual and philosophical—are often substantial.[64]

The associated interpretive pitfalls are sometimes underestimated. A text like *Laozi*, by its nature, can hardly be read without "commentary" (*zhu* 注). Many commentaries were supplied by the earliest transmitters of a text, such as Zhao Qi and Guo Xiang. Far more of them existed in antiquity than are extant today, because the commentaries of a small number of transmitters were typically singled out by posterity as authoritative. Editions of the text would thenceforth be published only with the canonical commentaries; other commentaries would survive in fragments, if at all.[65] But ancient commentaries were not neutral. Commentators expressed their personal understanding of the text, which was often idiosyncratic and creative. The commentary could come to represent an entire tradition, with its own glosses and, not infrequently, its own version of the text itself, as one quickly discovers by perusing the spectrum of *Laozi* commentaries—among which *Xiang'er*, which was used by the Celestial Master sect (*tianshi dao* 天師道), is apt to strike modern readers as the most outlandish (p. 77).[66]

Furthermore, the mechanisms of manuscript transmission help explain why received texts were furnished with commentaries. Because early manuscripts were usually produced for audiences that were already familiar with the material and its characteristic formulas, they were written with economical and underdetermined graphs.[67] Insiders, who perhaps learned the texts under the guidance of an authoritative teacher, knew when their community read the graph *dui* 兌 as *shuo/shui* 說 and not, say, *tuo* 脫 (to cite a typical example of graphic underdetermination), but to outsiders, such codicological conventions naturally left the text open to a multiplicity of interpretations. Redactors did their best to eliminate this type of ambiguity by adding, regularizing, or modernizing semantic classifiers (such as 言 in the graph *shuo/shui* 說). In this manner, they made the text intelligible to a larger number of readers, but also inevitably narrowed the range of possible interpretations. As texts circulated ever more widely among readers who, unlike the ancients, had no specialized knowledge or authoritative teacher to guide them orally, explanatory commentaries came to be regarded as indispensable.

Only by ignoring this gnarled background would one dare to distinguish confidently between "the text" of *Laozi* and its "commentaries." A related methodological misstep, when encountering a difficult passage, is to rummage through attested commentaries for a reading that happens to suit one's predilections. A traditional Chinese commentary is a network of interpretations undergirding a discrete worldview; extracted from its context, a commentarial opinion loses its very logic.[68] In the same vein, it makes little sense to speak of "the philosophy" of a constellation of texts like *Laozi* without specifying a particular perspective (or, less honestly, without stating which perspectives one is privileging—and why). *Laozi* has thrived for over two millennia precisely because generations of readers continued to find new meaning in its lapidary verses.

The purpose of highlighting such interpretive challenges is not to diminish the philosophical value of early Chinese texts or to deny that they can be read rigorously and profitably. By no means does a text require single and undisputed authorship to be meaningful: for a quotidian example, consider an ordinary Wikipedia article, but more venerated ones abound, such as the Constitution, the Old Testament,[69] the *Mahābhārata*,[70] or virtually any Mahāyāna sūtra.[71] Conflicting recensions often arise in Western literature as well, particularly in cases where the author died before securing publication.[72] Nor is historicism the only legitimate hermeneutic stance.[73] In the pages that follow, the emphasis will be on ideas, both because this puts the texts in their best light,[74] and because an interest in ideas is probably what prompted anyone to open this book. But philosophical readers accustomed to books unproblematically attributed to Hume or Kant need to be mindful that they are reading works from a different time and place, with radically different conceptions of authorship. *Laozi*, *Zhuangzi*, and *Sunzi* are texts, not people.[75]

The next chapter will take up a hallmark of Chinese philosophy that demands a Western reader's cognizance: its preference for nondeductive argumentation. Then comes the core of the book, eight chapters devoted to the eight philosophical texts; and lastly an explanation of the versatile concept of *qi* 氣, which can be confusing because of its wide range of connotations.

CHAPTER ONE

# Nondeductive
# Argumentation and the
# Art of Chinese Philosophy

One fusty criticism of Chinese thought is that it is not truly "philosophical" because it lacks viable protocols of argumentation.[1] Thus it qualifies at best as "wisdom": Confucius, for example, might provide valuable guidance, or thoughtful epigrams to savor, but nothing in the way of formal reasoning that would permit his audience to reconstruct and reconsider his arguments in any conceivable context.[2] As Hu Shih 胡適 (1891–1962) put it, "China has greatly suffered for lack of an adequate logical method."[3]

Such hand-wringing bespeaks the prejudgment that satisfactory argumentation must be deductive. I have no special definition of "deduction" in mind; it suffices to use that of Aristotle: "a discourse in which, certain things being stated, something other than what is stated follows of necessity from their being so" (*Prior Analytics* 24b18–20).[4] This is often called "syllogism" in older translations, because Aristotle thought that all deductive inference must be syllogistic (*Prior Analytics* 41b1–3)[5]—a notion rejected by modern logicians.[6] Aristotle went on to give some examples of syllogisms, which the medieval tradition organized into types according to their "mood," that is, the nature of their premises and conclusion.[7] The mood *AAA* (sometimes called "Barbara syllogism"), for instance, holds that if all A are B, and all B are C, then all A must be C (*Prior Analytics* 26a1).

All elephants are mammals.
All mammals are animals.
∴ All elephants are animals.

Such reasoning allows inferences that must be valid for every conceivable elephant, regardless of how many discrete elephants one happens to have seen in one's lifetime. Aristotle seems to have believed that such powers of inference were unique to human beings.[8]

China took a different tack.[9] Many of the most famous Chinese philosophical statements are patently nonsyllogistic. For example:

季文子三思而後行。子聞之，曰：「再，斯可矣。」 (*Analects* 5.19)[10]

> Ji Wenzi acted only after thinking three times. The Master heard of it and said: "Twice would have been acceptable."

This could be construed as useful practical advice. The dangers of acting too rashly and too slowly are the subjects of contradictory aphorisms (for example, in our culture, "Look before you leap" and "He who hesitates is lost"). Here, Confucius recommends a prudent middle course. Think twice before acting: not once, but not three times, either. Clearly this is not a matter of deductive inference—nor is the statement applicable in every conceivable situation. One should not think twice about whether to avoid an oncoming car. It is left to us to explore the range of plausible applications, but presumably Confucius is talking about weighty moral decisions: these deserve careful consideration and reconsideration,[11] but as soon as one has made up one's mind, further deliberation only leads to inaction.

Another example from the *Analects*:

子曰：「歲寒，然後知松柏之後彫也。」 (*Analects* 9.27)[12]

> The Master said: "Only after the year has grown cold does one know that the pine and cypress are the last to wither."

This is a memorable meiosis, for pines and cypresses are not merely the last to wither; they almost *never* wither. As anyone in Confucius's society would have known from daily exposure to the living world, pines and cypresses not only remain green throughout the year but also are among the longest-lived organisms on earth. Usually *Analects* 9.27 is understood as a comment on friendship: fair-weather friends may, like beautiful plum or cherry blossoms, seem attractive in times of abundance, but true friends resemble evergreens, maintaining their color in all seasons of the year. But it is also, on a deeper level, a statement about the usefulness of looking to patterns in nature as a guide through the perplexities of life, as well as a reminder that the value of things cannot be gauged by their momentary appeal. At the same time, it is an assertion of the need for experience, and not just reason, in judgment: for if the character of pines and cypresses cannot be appreciated before the year has grown cold, then someone who has never experienced winter cannot possibly comprehend how they surpass the gaudy blooms of springtime. Thus it is not surprising that names bearing the word *song* 松, "pine," were favored by literati in traditional China, and the hardy pine—often shown gnarled and twisted in snowy landscapes—was a mainstay of Chinese nature painting.[13]

One observation is crucial: the statement begs to be taken metaphorically,[14] because no one would have bothered to record and preserve this line if it were really just a remark about pines and cypresses. (The *Analects* is not a manual of forestry.) And metaphors have no place in deductive reasoning. When we say that all elephants are mammals, we are not speaking metaphorically; we *cannot* be speaking metaphorically, or else the very inference would be called into question.[15] (Speakers of English sometimes refer to an obvious problem that no one wishes to address as "the elephant in the room," but that kind of elephant is not a mammal.) Thus Confucius's utterance, however we choose to interpret it, cannot be deductive.

Three general types of nondeductive argumentation in classical Chinese philosophy merit extended discussion: paradox, analogy, and appeal to example.[16]

## PARADOX

Many of the paradoxes[17] of the so-called disputers (*bianzhe* 辯者)[18] can be made to seem veridical,[19] or at least veridical in spirit, if interpreted sympathetically. For example, among the ten paradoxes ascribed to Hui Shi 惠施 (fourth century BC), one finds: "The South has no limit but has a limit" 南方無窮而有窮.[20] We do not know how Hui Shi himself defended this paradox, but there are interpretations that would render it veridical: the quadrant called "South" contains an infinite number of points, but it does not include the entire world; it is distinct, naturally, from the quadrants called "North," "East," and "West." Thus it is both limitless and limited at the same time.[21] Another (possible) example of veridical paradox is "Eggs have hair" 卵有毛:[22] if this is taken to mean "Inside an egg, there is hair"—that is, the hair of the unborn chick inside—then it is an unexpectedly true statement. (The Chinese word *mao* 毛 denotes body hair, such as the pelt of an animal, and could have been stretched to refer to the down of a chick.) One paradox that should have attracted more attention from modern linguists is "Dogs can be sheep" 犬可以為羊,[23] which is veridical if it means "Dogs may be called 'sheep'": the word "dog" is arbitrary and has nothing to do with the nature of the dog itself.[24]

Many of the disputers' paradoxes rely on the technique of exploiting a vulnerable keyword, either by using it in a sense different from what the audience expects, or by using it in one sense in one part of the paradox, and in a different sense in another.[25] (This is similar to the fallacy of equivocation in Western philosophy.)[26] Thus "Tortoises are longer than snakes" 龜長於蛇 if one takes "long" in the sense of "long-lived."[27] Unexpected, but not untrue. The most famous paradox of all, "A white horse is not a horse" 白馬非馬,[28] can be identified as another example of this technique if "white horse" and "horse" are taken to refer not to horses, but to sets of horses: the set of objects fulfilling the requirements "white and horse" and the set of objects fulfilling the requirement "horse" are not identical.[29]

Later Mohist exercises in semiotics attest to an interest in analyzing how such paradoxes could be constructed. A typical example: "The fruit of the peach is the peach, but the fruit of the *ji*-tree is not the *ji*" 桃之實, 桃也; 棘之實, 非棘也,[30] which seems to be predicated on the oddity that the word *tao* 桃 (peach) refers to both the tree and the fruit that it bears (as in English), whereas the word *ji* 棘 refers only to the tree, because its fruit is called *zao* 棗 ("jujube" or "Chinese date" in English).[31] From here it would not be far to a hypothetical paradox like "Peaches are not fruit" (because they are trees).

Not everyone was convinced of the value of such adventures in language—Xunzi rejected them as useless for the enterprise of moral self-cultivation (see pp. 193–94)—but some of the most important statements in the *Laozi* rely on the same technique of using a keyword in two different senses (and therefore probably stem from the same intellectual environment). "The highest virtue is not virtuous; therefore, it has virtue" 上德不德, 是以有德 (*Laozi* 38) is usually not treated as sophistry like "Tortoises are longer than snakes," but it relies on the same rhetorical device. For "The highest virtue is not virtuous" to have any intelligible meaning, the keyword *de* 德 (virtue, inner power) must be taken in two different ways. The first *de*, called *shangde* 上德, or the highest virtue, refers to *de* that is real and potent because it derives from the *dao* 道 itself, whereas the second *de*, merely *de*, refers to the great sham that human society, in its self-induced ignorance, wrongly identifies as *de*. Thus the highest virtue has real virtue precisely because it is not the false virtue that everyone has been trained to venerate. Usually such paradoxes are explained as part of a sustained rhetoric in *Laozi* whose purpose is to shake complacent readers and make them question their unnatural assumptions about the world,[32] like the aesthetic technique of defamiliarization.[33]

## ANALOGY

Reasoning by analogy was a crucial mode of deliberation in traditional China.[34] It was one of the hallmarks of Chinese jurisprudence[35] and also figures prominently in early Chinese poetics, where it was identified by the critical terms *bi* 比 (comparison or juxtaposition) and *xing* 興 (arousal). (The precise meanings of *bi* and *xing* are notoriously difficult to unravel and indeed vary from one authority to another.)[36] In philosophy, one of the best-known examples appears in *Mencius*:

> 孟子曰:「魚,我所欲也。熊掌,亦我所欲也。二者不可得兼,舍魚而取熊掌者也。生,亦我所欲也。義,亦我所欲也。二者不可得兼,舍生而取義者也。生亦我所欲,所欲有甚於生者,故不為苟得也。死亦我所惡,所惡有甚於死者,故患有所不辟也。」(*Mencius* 6A.10)[37]

Mencius said: "I like fish; I also like bear's paw. If I cannot have both, I shall forgo fish and choose bear's paw. I like life; I also like righteousness. If I cannot have both, I shall forgo life and choose righteousness. Although I like life, there are things that I like more than life, and thus I should not keep [my life] indecorously. Although I dislike death, there are things that I dislike more than death, and thus there are some perils that I should not avoid."

As moral philosophy, this passage conveys a certain mindset rather than formulating a definite argument (and as an argument it is obviously not deductive). Just as a gourmet is prepared to sacrifice fish for the sake of a delicacy like bear's paw, a moral connoisseur[38] is prepared to sacrifice his or her life for the sake of righteousness. Naturally, the analogy does not *prove* that righteousness is worth dying for; it merely illustrates Mencius's zeal.

Many such analogies refer to natural phenomena with the unstated supposition that patterns observable in nature cannot be wrong.[39] This conviction underlies arguments that are not always well received today. For example, early in the famed debate between Mencius and Gaozi 告子, the latter presents the view that human nature (*xing* 性) lacks any inherent moral orientation; like a torrent of water, it will rush in whichever direction is laid open for it. Mencius responds by assailing the analogy: water does have an inherent orientation after all, because it always flows downward. Thus human nature is inherently good in the same way that water naturally flows downward (*Mencius* 6A.2). This argument has been harshly criticized in modern times;[40] its power must have been greater in a culture like that of ancient China, where reasoning by analogy was deeply respected.[41]

It must also be acknowledged that appeals to natural phenomena were often used to keep women in their place. In "The Oath at Mu" ("Mushi" 牧誓), King Wu of Zhou 周武王 (r. 1046–1043 BC) justifies his decision to attack the King of Shang on the grounds that the latter listens to his wife:

王曰：「古人有言曰：『牝雞無晨；牝雞之晨，惟家之索。』今商王受惟婦言是用。」[42]

The King said: "The ancients had a saying: 'The hen shall not announce the morning; when the hen announces the morning, it means that the family will wane.' Now King Shou of Shang implements only the words of his wife."

Hens should just keep quiet in the morning, because they threaten the survival of the family when they try to do the rooster's job.[43]

Not infrequently, Chinese authors saw meaningful patterns in nature that we would not recognize today; for example, *Comprehensive Discus-*

*sions from the White Tiger Hall* (*Baihu tong* 白虎通) explains that women should follow their husbands because *yang* sings the lead and *yin* harmonizes (*yang chang yin he* 陽倡陰和).[44] This is the problem with analogizing from nature: all observation of the natural world necessarily passes through one's personal interpretive filter, and therefore different people do not always apperceive the same pattern when they perceive the same set of objects.[45]

## APPEAL TO EXAMPLE

Appeals to example are nearly ubiquitous in ancient Chinese philosophy (the most prominent text not to resort to them is *Laozi*), and it seems fruitful to divide the technique into a number of subtypes. Appeal to history has been regarded as so typical of Chinese philosophy that Jeremy Bentham (1748–1832) derided it as the "Chinese argument."[46] Rarely did Chinese persuaders fail to refer to examples from the past that supposedly bolstered their case—nor did they always feel obliged to recount details accurately.[47]

A more specific category is appeal to the sages of yore and the canonical texts attributed to them, which prompted a backlash in texts such as *Han Feizi*.[48] Teaching people how to build nests in trees or drill flint in order to make fire were crucial advances in prehistoric times, but in later eras they would have been laughable:

> 今有構木鑽燧於夏后氏之世者，必為鯀、禹笑矣。有決瀆於殷、周之世者，必為湯、武笑矣。然則今有美堯、舜、湯、武、禹之道於當今之世者，必為新聖笑矣。(*Han Feizi* 49)[49]

If there were someone who built nests or drilled flint in the Xia dynasty, he would surely be ridiculed by Gun and Yu. If there were someone who cleared water channels in the age of Yin and Zhou dynasties, he would surely by ridiculed by Tang and Wu. Yet today there are those who praise the ways of Yao, Tang, Wu, and Yu as though they were appropriate for today's age; surely they are to be ridiculed by new sages.

What may have been laudable actions by sages of the past are not necessarily appropriate to the very different society of today.

Another productive subtype is appeal to proverbs, such as the one about hens announcing the morning, mentioned above. In a later example, Jia Yi 賈誼 (201–169 BC) wrote: "A rustic proverb says: 'Those who do not forget affairs of the past are teachers of the future'" 野諺曰：「前事之不忘，後之師也」.[50] This is both an appeal to a proverb and an appeal to history at the same time (though Jia Yi goes on to emphasize that methods of the past might have to be adjusted to suit present circumstances). He probably did not make up this proverb, because it appears verbatim in an unrelated item in *Stratagems of the Warring States* (*Zhanguo ce* 戰國策),[51] a text that has preserved many other maxims as well (such as "Three people make a tiger" 三人成虎: everyone will believe that there is a tiger if three people independently claim to have seen it).[52]

Modern readers are seldom impressed by these subtypes of appeal to example. Appeals to history are sometimes deemed persuasive, but not if the circumstances are incommensurate (and certainly not if the examples are distorted), while appeals to canonical texts and proverbs fare even worse, usually being dismissed as *argumentum ad verecundiam*. But one subtype of appeal to example is not necessarily fallacious: appeal to exemplary conduct, both good and bad. This discourse is characteristic of the *Analects*:

子曰：「三人行，必有我師焉：擇其善者而從之，其不善者而改之。」 (*Analects* 7.22)[53]

The Master said: "When I am walking [with others] in a threesome, there must be a teacher to me among them. I select what is good in them and follow it; what is not good in them, I correct."

Like Mencius's comment about fish and bear's paw, this is more of a declaration of a certain attitude than a formal argument; it merely asserts the principle that there is always something to learn, whether positive or negative, from the example of others. The idea that we can learn by emulating other people's strengths and reforming their weaknesses has been central to Chinese philosophy for centuries[54] and has fostered the associated conviction that we must judge people's actions fairly—including our own.[55]

The appeal to an anecdote is a productive subtype of appeal to example: the anecdote is intended to furnish an instructive example highlighting the particular philosophical issue under debate. The inferences gleaned from it are never deductive. Take the example in *Han Feizi* of a lucky farmer who caught a rabbit that happened to kill itself by careering into a stump:

宋人有耕田者，田中有株，兔走，觸株折頸而死，因釋其耒而守株，冀復得兔，兔不可復得，而身為宋國笑。今欲以先王之政，治當世之民，皆守株之類也。 (*Han Feizi* 49)[56]

Among the men of Song there was one who tilled his fields; in his fields there was a stump. A rabbit ran by, crashed headfirst against the stump, broke its neck, and died. Thereupon [the man] set aside his plow and kept watch by the stump, hoping to get another rabbit, but no other rabbit was to be gotten, and he became the laughingstock of Song. Now those who wish to use the governance of the Former Kings to bring order to the people of our time are all of the same type as the stump watcher.

Using "the governance of the Former Kings to bring order to the people of our time" is as foolish as waiting for a *second* rabbit (because it is equally unlikely that virtuous individuals will present themselves in government pro bono).

Such anecdotes are fungible in the sense that they can be adapted to serve different arguments, and thus their ability to convey a priori truths is limited, if not nil. The example of the stump watcher is effectively applied in *Han Feizi* to political philosophy, but it could also be used, say, to argue against wagering one's life savings at the roulette table after winning one spin. (Essentially, its purpose is to emphasize the folly of basing one's plans for the future on the hope that a welcome but extremely rare event might happen again.) In *Han Feizi*, anecdotes are so fungible that one can occasionally find the same one marshaled in support of diametrically opposed positions. In "Ten Missteps" ("Shiguo" 十過), Lord Huan of Qi 齊桓公 (r. 685–643 BC) is criticized for ignoring Guan Zhong's 管仲 (d. 645 BC) deathbed advice to purge three self-interested ministers,[57] while in "Critiques, No. 1" ("Nan yi" 難一), Guan Zhong's deathbed advice is itself criticized, because a lord needs to know how to extract service from self-interested ministers.[58] For if *Han Feizi* teaches us anything, it is that ministers are self-interested yet indispensable (see pp. 204–5).[59]

*Han Feizi* does not worry about whether Guan Zhong *really* said what was attributed to him (what stenographer would have been present at his bedside, after all?); the point is that arguments about how to deal with self-interested ministers could be persuasively praised or criticized, depending on one's perspective. This is why so many appeals to historical events, as noted above, contain unconcealed factual errors. Their veracity was less of a concern than their illustrative power.

It would be unproductive, therefore, to distinguish rigidly between "anecdotes" like that of Guan Zhong's deathbed advice in *Han Feizi* and the unmistakably fictitious stories of *Zhuangzi*, which are more commonly characterized as "parables."[60] (None of these English terms, it should be noted, can be mapped neatly onto Chinese vocabulary.)[61] Consider the famous parable that draws the "Inner Chapters" (*neipian* 內篇) of *Zhuangzi* to a close:

南海之帝為儵，北海之帝為忽，中央之帝為渾沌。儵與忽時相與遇於渾沌之地，渾沌待之甚善。儵與忽謀報渾沌之德，曰：「人皆有七竅，以視聽食息，此獨無有，嘗試鑿之。」日鑿一竅，七日而渾沌死。(*Zhuangzi* 7)[62]

The Emperor of the Southern Sea was named Zig; the Emperor of the Northern Sea was named Zag; the Emperor of the Center was named Blob. Zig and Zag often met each other in Blob's territory, and Blob received them very well. Zig and Zag planned to repay Blob for his kindness, saying: "All human beings have seven holes for seeing, hearing, eating, and breathing. [Blob] is the only one who does not have them. Let us try drilling them for him!" Each day they drilled another hole, and on the seventh day Blob died.

No rational reader would object to this anecdote/parable on the grounds that Zig, Zag, and Blob are not real people.[63] We are invited to ruminate on the story, knowing full well that it must be fictitious, for the philosophical insights that it obliquely conveys—an exercise that remains fruitful to this day, with our urgent new concern for maintaining the integrity of the environment.[64] Thus appeals to history, anecdotes, and parables lie on a continuum of historicity ranging from the generally unexceptionable historical examples offered by nearly every ancient persuader at court; to more questionable historical examples, such as Guan

Zhong's deathbed advice in *Han Feizi*; to parables with no pretense of factuality, such as the tale of Zig, Zag, and Blob in *Zhuangzi*. But fundamentally they are of the same species: devices that aim to clarify a philosophical problem by focusing on a cogent example.

• • •

The foregoing should not be misread as a denial that Chinese philosophers ever engaged in deductive reasoning. There are several important classical Chinese arguments that can be restated in terms of propositional logic[65]—for instance, the Mohist defense of impartial love (*jian'ai* 兼愛):

姑嘗本原若眾害之所自生，此胡自生？此自愛人利人生與？即必曰非然也；必曰從惡人賊人生。分名乎天下，惡人而賊人者，兼與？別與？即必曰別也。然即之交別者，果生天下之大害者與？是故別非也。(*Mozi* 16)[66]

If one were to investigate whence these various harms arise, whence do these things arise?[67] Do these things arise from caring for others and benefiting others? One would have to say that this is not the case; one would have to say that they arise from hating others and despoiling others. If one were to categorize things in the world by means of names, would those who hate others and despoil others [be called] impartial or partial? One would have to say partial. Thus is it not the case that engaging [others] with partiality gives rise to the great harms in the world? For this reason, partiality is wrong.

I take this as an early attempt at a deductive argument (essentially a composite Barbara syllogism):

$p \rightarrow q$
(If one is partial, one hates and despoils others.)

$q \rightarrow r$
(If one hates and despoils others, one causes harm.)

$r \rightarrow s$
(If one causes harm, one is wrong.)

$\therefore p \rightarrow s$
(If one is partial, one is wrong.)

More complex deductive arguments can be found in later texts. Xunzi's elaborate argument against abdication, which he tries to rule out as a method of transferring sovereignty in all possible situations,[68] contains an example of disjunctive elimination.

曰:「死而擅之。」是又不然。......聖王已沒, 天下無聖, 則固莫足以擅天下矣。天下有聖而在後 [子][69] 者, 則天下不離, 朝不易位, 國不更制, 天下厭然與鄉無以異也, 以堯繼堯, 夫又何變之有矣? 聖不在後子而在三公, 則天下如歸, 猶復而振之矣, 天下厭然與鄉無以異也, 以堯繼堯, 夫又何變之有矣? 唯其徙朝改制為難。故天子生則天下一隆, 致順而治, 論德而定次; 死則能任天下者必有之矣。夫禮義之分盡矣, 擅讓惡用矣哉? (*Xunzi* 18.5c)[70]

It is said: "When [the King] is dying, he should cede to someone else." This is also not so. . . . If the sage kings have already fallen, and there is no sage in the world, then there is certainly no one adequate to cede the world to. If there is a sage king in the world, and he is among [the current King's] sons or descendants, the dynasty does not change; the state does not alter its regulations. The world will be satisfied with this; there will be no respect in which this differs from [the situation] prior. If a Yao succeeds a Yao, what change would there be? If the sage is not among his sons or descendants, but among the Three Chief Ministers, then the world will come home to him as though he were restoring and sustaining it. The world will be satisfied with this; there will be no respect in which this differs from [the situation] prior. If a Yao succeeds a Yao, again, what change would there be?

This too is deductive in structure:

$\sim p \vee (q \vee r)$
(Either there is no sage or there is a sage among the King's descendants or the Three Chief Ministers.)

$\sim p \rightarrow \sim s$
(If there is no sage, there is no reason for abdication.)

$q \rightarrow \sim s$
(If there is a sage among the King's descendants, there is no reason for abdication.)

r → ~s

(If there is a sage among the Three Chief Ministers, there is no reason for abdication.)

∴ ~s

(There is no reason for abdication.)

The opening premise is questionable, however: Xunzi does not seem to have envisioned a situation in which there is a sage in the world who is *neither* one of the King's descendants *nor* one of the Three Chief Ministers; nor is it entirely clear why succession by one of the Three Chief Ministers did not, in his mind, constitute the establishment of a new dynasty. (Consider the example of Yu, the sage who succeeded Shun, thereby initiating the dynasty known as Xia 夏.) But otherwise, the reasoning is sound.

Ancient Chinese audiences were so familiar with disjunctive elimination that even jokers could use it in texts intended more for entertainment than edification:

秦宣太后愛魏醜夫。太后病將死，出令曰：「為我葬，必以魏子為殉。」
魏子患之。庸芮為魏子說太后曰：「以死者為有知乎？」
太后曰：「無知也。」
曰：「若太后之神靈，明知死者之無知矣，何為空以生所愛，葬於無知之死人哉！若死者有知，先王積怒之日久矣，太后救過不贍，何暇乃私魏醜夫乎？」
太后曰：「善。」乃止。[71]

Queen Dowager Xuan of Qin [d. 265 BC] loved Wei Choufu.[72] When the Queen Dowager fell ill and was about to die, she issued an order, saying: "When I am buried, Master Wei must accompany me in death."

Master Wei was horrified by this. Yong Rui persuaded the Queen Dowager in Master Wei's behalf, saying: "Do you consider the dead to have consciousness?"

The Queen Dowager said: "They have no consciousness."

[Yong Rui] said: "If your Majesty's godlike numen is clearly aware that the dead have no consciousness, why would you vainly take the person you loved in life, and bury him with the dead, who lack consciousness? And if the dead do have consciousness, the former king has been accumulating his wrath for many days. Your Majesty, you will scarcely have the means to make amends for your transgressions—how would you have leisure for assignations with Wei Choufu?"

Restated in propositional form, this yields:

$p \lor \sim p$
(Either the dead have consciousness or the dead do not have consciousness.)

$p \rightarrow r$
(If the dead have consciousness, having your lover buried with you is a waste.)

$\sim p \rightarrow r$
(If the dead do not have consciousness, having your lover buried with you is a waste.)

$\therefore r$
(Having your lover buried with you is a waste.)

And that is a valid inference.

These few but memorable examples leave no doubt that audiences were aware of principles of deduction and thus suggest that Chinese philosophers crafted nondeductive arguments as a deliberate choice. Arguments that rely wholly on deductive inference, like Xunzi's case against abdication, are not easy to find; one can only surmise that they were not preferred. Why? Two answers come to mind. First, there is a deep conviction in Chinese culture that persuasive speech must be artfully patterned, as in the famous saying attributed to Confucius: "If you do not speak, who will know your will? But if you speak it without *wen*, it will not go far" 不言誰知其志? 言之無文, 行而不遠.[73] The basic meaning of *wen* is "pattern," but—not surprisingly in view of such uses—it has attained many other connotations, including "literature" and "civilization."[74] Philosophers who subscribed to this idea would have been motivated to compose as elegantly as possible; sometimes, classical Chinese philosophy is expressed so beautifully that it verges on poetry. But many of the most prized literary devices in the Chinese tradition, such as meiosis and metaphor, are not readily compatible with the fulsome exposition characteristic of deductive argumentation.

Second, the listener bore an onus of interpretation as well. If you read a book by a contemporary philosopher and find little of value in it, you are likely to blame the author and not yourself. Today, the burden of persuasion is thought to lie with *the author*. But in a culture where the supposed authors of philosophical texts were venerated as sages, expectations would have been reversed: if you read a text like the *Analects* and find little of value in it, this reflects only your own failure, because the burden of understanding lies with *you*. These pressures placed a premium on skillful interpretation.[75]

Thus Chinese philosophy demands a high level of interpretive participation. Perhaps this is what Confucius meant when he said, "I begin with one corner; if [a student] cannot return with the other three corners, I do not repeat myself" 舉一隅不以三隅反, 則不復也 (*Analects* 7.8).[76] If the strength of deductive argumentation is supposed to be that it yields correct inferences regardless of circumstance—*modus tollens* is as valid in Dallas as in Krasnoyarsk—then it follows that deductive argumentation yields the same results regardless of the audience's mood, receptiveness, perspective, and so on. By contrast, an audience presented with a statement like "Only after the year has grown cold does one know that the pine and cypress are the last to wither" must ponder it sympathetically—or else derive little, if any, benefit from it. Nor is the meaning that one discovers necessarily identical at every juncture of one's life. In one's youth, the statement about the pine and cypress could mean one thing; as one matures, gains experience, and compares it to other opinions one has encountered, it could take on previously unimagined dimensions. Chinese philosophy, like literature, painting, or music, requires connoisseurship.[77] If we lack the taste—even more so if we exempt ourselves from the task of developing it—we will miss most of what Chinese philosophy has to offer.

# PART I

# Philosophy of Heaven

# CHAPTER TWO

# The *Analects* of Confucius

Confucius is the most influential thinker in Chinese civilization and the first whose philosophy can be reconstructed to any significant degree. In China, he has been known by many posthumous names and titles, the most revealing being *xianshi* 先師, which can be understood as both "the teacher from the past" and "the foremost teacher." Confucius was, as far as we can tell, the first teacher of his kind and the inaugurator of one of the most glorious philosophical ages of any ancient culture.

There were surely many ritual masters in the generations preceding Confucius. Museumgoers know that, in the bounteous Chinese Bronze Age, kings and elite lineages produced untold numbers of bronze vessels in various typical forms with precise ritual functions. It is clear from assemblages in burials that each type of vessel was necessary for the full concert of rituals, and archaic literature—including the many inscriptions cast on these bronze vessels—tells us that the correct performance of these rites was crucial to securing the blessing of the spirits. Deceased ancestors were thought to perdure after death as spirits who had to be properly cultivated with sacrifices and other ritual obsequies. As early as the Shang dynasty (ca. 1600–ca. 1045 BC), for example, kings would divine about the source of their toothaches; for only after it was determined which ancestral spirit was responsible for the affliction could the appropriate steps be taken to placate him or her. (Ancestresses were no less terrifying in this respect than ancestors.) And the toothache was understood as a warning to rectify whatever wrongdoing or oversight had irked the spirit in question. Toothache today—flood or earthquake or some comparable catastrophe tomorrow.[1]

Doubtless, then, the ritual culture implied by the numerous surviving bronze artifacts required ritual masters who could explain to new generations how each vessel was to be used. And there are hints in ancient texts that some of these ritual masters began to incorporate moral principles into their curriculum. Now it was not enough simply to carry out the appropriate sacrifice correctly; it was necessary also to live up to the right moral standard. What these high ancients really said, however, is for the most part beyond recovery, as there are only the scantest records of their utterances. Confucius was apparently the first to have his teachings documented by his disciples, and, not coincidentally, seems to have emphasized the moral aspect of correct ritual practice to an unprecedented degree. Thus he transformed the ancient role of ritual master, expert in the ways of cauldrons and platters, into something that we would call a moral philosopher.

The prime difficulty facing any reader today is that Confucius did not leave behind any written work. Tradition has ascribed to him the redaction of certain canonical texts, especially the *Springs and Autumns* (*Chunqiu* 春秋),[2] but the attributions are not fully convincing, and in any case no one suggests that he *composed* the texts—only that he arranged preexisting material in a morally revealing way. There are dozens of sources that record this or that saying as having been uttered by Confucius, the most authoritative of which is the so-called *Analects*, but these were all produced after his death.

There are two plausible reasons why Confucius never felt compelled to leave behind a treatise or similar written text. First, in his day, writing was not the most important means of communication. In our world, at least for the past several centuries, the surest way to publish one's ideas has been to put them in writing, and even as today's technology has created useful media besides the old-fashioned book, writing is unlikely to disappear soon—as ubiquitous texting and blogging attest. But Confucius's society was small enough that oral communication sufficed for many more purposes than we might assume. When a wise man advised a king, he would typically say, "Your servant has *heard* . . ." (*chen wen* 臣聞 or *chen wen zhi* 臣聞之), rather than "Your servant has *read* . . ." Any idea worth repeating would be transmitted from one mouth to the next. And as soon as people stopped repeating it, it died. To be sure, writing had already been known for a good millennium by Confucius's time, but its uses seem to have been mostly hieratic.[3] If you needed to communicate with ancestral spirits, you needed a scribe. But if you wished to discuss right conduct with your neighbor, you just started talking. Thus one reason why Confucius never wrote down his teachings is that he never imagined it would be necessary to do so. His legacy would continue through his disciples, who would pass it on, orally, to disciples of their own.

Second, Confucius may have deemed writing incompatible with one of his most important ideas: that people need to think for themselves. To reprise the quote with which we ended the previous chapter: "I begin with one corner; if [a student] cannot return with the other three corners, I do not repeat myself" (*Analects* 7.8). A teacher can be expected to lay down the guidelines, but students must then fill out the rest of the picture on their own.[4] Throughout the *Analects*, Confucius is shown to be uneasy about affirming any universal principle; rightness and wrongness must be judged anew in every situation. Thus, in teaching, it is a mistake to deliver wooden lectures to audiences of students with disparate needs:

子路問：「聞斯行諸？」子曰：「有父兄在，如之何其聞斯行之？」冉有問：「聞斯行諸？」子曰：「聞斯行之。」公西華曰：「由也問聞斯行諸，子曰『有父兄在』；求也問聞斯行諸，子曰『聞斯行之』。赤也惑，敢問。」子曰：「求也退，故進之。由也兼人，故退之。」(*Analects* 11.22)[5]

Zilu (i.e., Zhong Yóu 仲由, 542–480 BC) asked: "Should one practice something after having heard it?"

The Master said: "You have a father and elder brother who are still alive; how would you practice something after having heard it?"

Ran Yóu (b. 522 BC) asked: "Should one practice something after having heard it?"

The Master said: "One should practice something after having heard it."

Gongxi Hua (i.e., Gongxi Chi 公西赤, b. 539 BC) said: "When Yóu (i.e., Zilu) asked whether one should practice something after having heard it, you said: 'Your father and elder brother are still alive.' When Qiu (i.e., Ran Yóu) asked whether one should practice something after having heard it, you said: 'One should practice something after having heard it.' I am confused, and venture to ask about this."

The Master said: "Qiu is withdrawn; thus I urged him forward. Yóu [has the eagerness] of two men; thus I held him back."

This exchange is included in the *Analects* for the insight that two different students should not necessarily be taught the same lesson.[6] But in a *written* document, to be read by strangers not in his presence (or indeed after his death), it would have been impossible for Confucius to adjust his teachings in this manner. His philosophy might then become what he despised most: an authority telling you what is right in all times and places. Writing fixes statements, and Confucius wished his statements to remain fluid.[7] (It is rather like the difference between hearing a great musician in a live performance, where there can be inexhaustible variation, and hearing him or her through a recording, which is the same no matter how many times you play it.)

For this reason, Confucius also avoided full expositions of his thinking. Western philosophers may be disappointed to discover that the *Analects* is not a sustained treatise with fully exposed arguments. Rather, Confucian rhetoric typically uses allusive language—often invoking nature and sometimes waxing poetic—in order to spur students to think through the morals on their own.

After Confucius's death, his disciples knew that they had lost an icon and resolved to select for posterity's benefit the most important sayings and exchanges that they could remember from their encounters with the Master.[8] This is, at any rate, the traditional story behind the text known as *Analects*, whose Chinese title, *Lunyu*, means "selected" (*lún*) "sayings" (*yu*). There are various scholarly theories about the provenance of the received text by that name, which contains twenty chapters and has come to be regarded as the most respected of several repositories of sayings attributed to Confucius. One unavoidable difficulty is that it seems to be unattested before the Han dynasty.[9] But the language is demonstrably older than that,[10] and I do think it is possible to reconstruct a coherent philosophy from its core chapters; therefore, like most (but not all)[11] scholars, I accept the first fifteen chapters as the closest we can come today to reading Confucius's own words. (Chapters 16–20, as has been observed for centuries, are written in a more expansive style and probably contain additions from later times;[12] consequently, they will be cited below only when their testimony can be corroborated by passages in chapters 1–15.) There are many other early texts that attribute sayings to Confucius, but it is always necessary to interpret these critically. *Zhuangzi*, for example, which imparts a philosophy uncompromisingly opposed to that of Confucius, shows him saying all sorts of embarrassing and self-demeaning things, and it would be a mistake to put the same stock in such quotations as in the *Analects* or other material endorsed by Confucian disciples.[13]

Of his life and heritage we know only the barest of details,[14] which eager hands eventually embellished incredibly. Within a few centuries, Confucius was depicted as a demigod with supernatural bodily features and strength.[15] In reality, his ancestry was murky;[16] his father, called Shuliang He 叔梁紇 in most sources, may have been a warrior from a place called Zou 陬/鄒; Confucius may have been conceived outdoors; he may have served his home state of Lu 魯 in a minor capacity (as minister of justice, *sikou* 司寇, according to tradition); he traveled to several states offering his counsel and had audiences with multiple feudal lords; he attracted dozens of disciples, some of whom were among the most influential young men in his community; he probably died at an age above seventy. Confucius's importance lies not in the details of his life, but in the philosophy that he left behind.

● ● ●

A modern reader of Confucius, then, is faced with this task: using the *Analects* and perhaps a handful of other early texts, none of which was written by Confucius himself, to reconstruct the philosophy of a master who would have preferred to teach you personally. Fortunately, careful reading of the *Analects* reveals a unique and consistent philosophical attitude. Confucius himself insists twice that although his teachings may appear disparate, there is "one thing with which to string [everything] together" (*yi yi guan zhi* 一以貫之, *Analects* 4.15 and 15.2).

Let us begin a survey of his philosophy with his views of spirits and the afterlife. He was principally agnostic:

子疾病，子路請禱。子曰：「有諸？」子路對曰：「有之。誄曰：『禱爾于上下神祇。』」子曰：「丘之禱久矣。」(*Analects* 7.34)[17]

The Master was critically ill. Zilu asked leave to pray. The Master said: "Is there such a thing?"

Zilu responded: "There is. The eulogy says: 'We pray for you above and below to the spirits of the upper and lower worlds.'"

The Master said: "My prayer is of long standing."

Notice that Confucius does not go so far as to deny the potential value of prayer; he only questions it, then concludes with the unforgettable instruction that, if it has any value at all, prayer consists not of formulas repeated mechanically from predetermined liturgies, but in one's everyday words and deeds. Throughout the *Analects,* we see Confucius deconstructing received religion and enjoining his disciples to think through an entirely new moral system with *human interaction* as its base,[18] not veneration of ghosts and spirits:

樊遲問知。子曰：「務民之義，敬鬼神而遠之，可謂知矣。」 (*Analects* 6.20)[19]

Fan Chi (b. 515 BC) asked about wisdom. The Master said: "To take righteousness among the people as one's duty, and to revere the ghosts and spirits, but keep them at a distance, can be called wisdom."

Do what you think is right, not what you think the ghosts and spirits want you to do. For we can never know what the ghosts and spirits want anyway (at least not until we become ghosts and spirits ourselves).

Confucius is not an atheist—he concedes that there are ghosts and spirits,[20] and that it is advisable not to offend them—but he believes that pondering the afterlife and the supernatural will impede moral reasoning:

季路問事鬼神。子曰：「未能事人，焉能事鬼？」曰：「敢問死。」曰： 「未知生，焉知死？」 (*Analects* 11.11)[21]

Jilu (i.e., Zilu) asked about the services for ghosts and spirits. The Master said: "You do not yet know how to serve people. How will you be able to serve ghosts?"

"May I be so bold as to ask about death?"

[Confucius] said: "You do not yet know life. How can you know death?"

One last passage in the same vein comes from chapter 17, in other words one of the spurious chapters, but is worth citing here because it anticipates a crucial theme in later Confucianism: we may not be able to read the will of the gods, but we can infer how nature works by observing it. Nature abides by regular and discernible patterns, which we can learn by intelligent observation and then apply to our own lives:

子曰：「予欲無言。」子貢曰：「子如不言，則小子何述焉？」子曰：
「天何言哉？四時行焉，百物生焉，天何言哉？」 (*Analects* 17.19)[22]

The Master said: "I wish to be without speech."

Zigong (i.e., Duanmu Ci 端木賜, 520–456 BC) said: "If you do not speak, then what will we, your children, have to transmit from you?"

The Master said: "What does Heaven say? The four seasons progress by it; the many creatures are born by it. What does Heaven say?"

So much for traditional religion; while most other people in Confucius's day were trying to find moral bearings by worshiping gods and spirits, and attempting to ascertain their mysterious wishes through divination and other questionable ceremonies, Confucius told his students to set aside that credulous mode and focus instead on human relationships in the world of the living. And how do we treat other human beings? This is where the "one thing with which to string everything together" comes into play. First, the best-known passage, in which Confucius addresses his student, Zeng Cān 曾參 (505–436 BC?):[23]

子曰：「參乎！吾道一以貫之。」曾子曰：「唯。」子出，門人問曰：
「何謂也？」曾子曰：「夫子之道，忠恕而已矣。」 (*Analects* 4.15)[24]

The Master said: "Cān! In my Way, there is one thing with which to string [everything] together."

Master Zeng said: "Yes."

The Master went out, and the disciples asked: "What was he referring to?"

Master Zeng said: "The Way of the Master is nothing other than *zhong* and *shu*."

*Zhong* 忠 and *shu* 恕 are difficult terms that need to be unpacked by referring to other passages in the *Analects*, as they have acquired other distracting senses in ordinary Chinese. *Zhong*, for instance, is usually understood today as "loyalty," but that is not even close to what Confucius meant.

*Shu* is the more consequential of the two.[25] Remember that Confucius said there was *one thing* in his Way, and yet Master Zeng explained it to the other disciples as *zhong* and *shu*—two things. In two very similar passages, but this time with Zigong as the interlocutor, Confucius implies that the one thing is not *zhong* and *shu*, but merely *shu*. At the same time, he gives a direct definition:

子曰：「賜也，女以予為多學而識之者與？」對曰：「然，非與？」曰：「非也，予一以貫之。」(*Analects* 15.2)[26]

Confucius said: "Ci, do you consider me one who knows things by having studied much?"

[Zigong] replied: "Yes. Is that not so?"

[Confucius] said: "It is not so. I have one thing with which to string everything together."

子貢問曰：「有一言而可以終身行之者乎？」子曰：「其恕乎！己所不欲，勿施於人。」(*Analects* 15.23)[27]

Zigong asked: "Is there one word that one can practice throughout one's life?"

That Master said: "Is it not *shu* (reciprocity)? What you yourself do not desire, do not do to others."

"What you yourself do not desire, do not do to others" is the cornerstone of Confucian ethics,[28] but an immediate qualification is necessary: in practice, *shu* has to be interpreted as doing unto others as you would have others do unto you *if you had the same social role as they.*[29] Otherwise, *shu* would require fathers to treat their sons in the same manner that their sons treat them—a practice that no Confucian has ever considered appropriate.

The detail that the calculus of *shu* requires us also to take the actors' social status into account may not be clear from the *Analects*, but is unmistakable in another famous statement attributed to Confucius and recorded in the *Application of Equilibrium* (*Zhongyong* 中庸):

忠恕違道不遠，施諸己而不願，亦勿施於人。君子之道四，丘未能一焉：所求乎子以事父，未能也；所求乎臣以事君，未能也；所求乎弟以事兄，未能也；所求乎朋友先施之，未能也。(*Zhongyong* 13)[30]

*Zhong* and *shu* are not far from the Way. What you would not suffer others to do to you, do not do to them. There are four things in the Way of the

Noble Man, none of which I have been able to do. I have not been able to serve my father as I demand of my son. I have not been able to serve my lord as I demand of my servant. I have not been able to serve my elder brother as I demand of my younger brother. I have not been able to do unto my friends first as I demand of them.

To revisit the example of a father and son: in order to apply *shu* correctly, the question for a son to consider is not how his father treats him, but how he would like his own son to treat him. *Shu* is a relation not between two individuated people, but between two social roles. How does one treat one's father? In the same way that one would want to be treated by one's son *if one were a father oneself*.[31]

There are well-known difficulties, not addressed by Confucius in the *Analects*, with ethical systems based on the notion of reciprocity. The most important is the objection that different people can sincerely wish to be treated in different ways, and, as a result, might treat other people in different ways too—without necessarily being wicked or hypocritical.[32] Confucius's silence on this problem is significant. Either he believes that people will always come to the same general conclusions about how they wish to be treated (if they practice *shu* without self-delusion), or he believes that such varying interpretations of the demands of *shu* are permissible as long as people's actions rest on a legitimate basis of moral reasoning. In the past I have leaned more toward the former interpretation (implicitly attributing to Confucius a somewhat rigid conception of human nature),[33] but now I favor the latter. Enslaving others under the pretext that it would be best for slaves to be enslaved would never be acceptable as *shu*. But if we observe a crime while it is being committed and can do something about it, is it better to call the police or intervene personally? Either option would be defensible if we truly believe that it is what would be most helpful. Only the person who does nothing at all would be open to condemnation.

*Shu* is crucial to Confucian ethics, as we shall see presently, but first we must ask what is meant by *zhong*. Confucius never defines *zhong* as straightforwardly as he defines *shu*, and some questionable modern interpretations are based on the Neo-Confucian understanding of *zhong* as "making the most of oneself" (*jinji* 盡己). Thus D. C. Lau, for example, has rendered *zhong* too diffusely as "doing one's best."[34] In my view, *zhong* has an effective meaning of "being honest with oneself in dealing with others"[35] in the *Analects*, and the key passage is, not coincidentally, placed in the mouth of the same Master Zeng:

曾子曰:「吾日三省吾身: 為人謀而不忠乎? 與朋友交而不信乎? 傳不習乎?」 (*Analects* 1.4)[36]

Master Zeng said: "Every day I examine myself on three counts. In planning on behalf of others, have I failed to be *zhong*? In associating with friends, have I failed to be trustworthy? Have I transmitted anything that I do not practice habitually?"

What Master Zeng means by the first of his three tests is whether, in carrying out *shu*, he has done wrong by others by pretending that what is beneficial to *himself* is what *they* would want him to do. *Shu* is instantly perverted if it is applied dishonestly, but self-deception is not always easy to discover and root out if one does not vigilantly review one's own actions. For this reason, *zhong* is frequently paired with *xin* 信, "trustworthiness," in the *Analects*.

To return to *shu*: Confucius's identification of *shu* as "What you yourself do not desire, do not do to others" helps explain several other passages in the *Analects*. Confucius's disciples knew that although he spoke of several different virtues, the most important was called *ren* 仁, "humanity." (The word is homophonous with *ren* 人, "human being," and Confucians have been fond of taking advantage of this aural connection.)[37]

子曰:「知者樂水, 仁者樂山。 知者動, 仁者靜。 知者樂, 仁者壽。」 (*Analects* 6.21)[38]

The Master said: "The wise take joy in rivers; the humane take joy in mountains. The wise are active; the humane are still. The wise are joyous; the humane are long-lived."

Clearly both the wise and the humane are praised in this statement, but a listener attuned to Confucius's suggestive style will recognize that, in this formulation, humanity comes before wisdom in the same way that rivers flow down from mountains. Rivers always move; mountains remain stationary till the end of time. There can be mountains without rivers, but no rivers without mountains.

It must have been frustrating to some of Confucius's disciples that he never defined *ren*; he always talked around it (using metaphors involving mountains and rivers), as he preferred to spur his students to come to their own understanding of it. Thus one finds examples where a disciple will come to Confucius with some overblown statement, and ask whether it would qualify as *ren*:

子貢曰：「如有博施於民而能濟眾，何如？可謂仁乎？」子曰：「何事於仁！必也聖乎！堯舜其猶病諸！夫仁者，己欲立而立人，己欲達而達人。能近取譬，可謂仁之方也已。」(*Analects* 6.28)[39]

Zigong said: "Suppose there is someone who extensively confers benefits on the people and was able to help the multitude. What about that—can one call this humanity?"

The Master said: "Why make an issue of humanity? Would this not have to be *sagehood*? Could even [the sage kings] Yao and Shun find infirmity in someone [like that]? Now as for humanity—what one wishes to establish in oneself one establishes in others; what one wishes to advance in oneself, one advances in others. The ability to take what is near as an analogy can be called the method of humanity."

In other words, Zigong's standard is impossibly high: only sages—whom ordinary people cannot hope to match—could ever do as much as Zigong demands. Humanity is something much simpler: it is the virtue based on the method of *shu*. If we work tirelessly to make *shu* our regular practice, we will be on the path of humanity itself. *Shu* is placing oneself in the position of others, and acting toward them as one imagines they would desire. How can one possibly imagine what someone else would desire? By taking oneself as an analogy.

The definition of *shu* as not doing to others what you yourself do not desire also unlocks an otherwise enigmatic exchange:

子貢曰：「我不欲人之加諸我也，吾亦欲無加諸人。」子曰：「賜也，非爾所及也。」(*Analects* 5.11)[40]

Zigong said: "What I do not desire others to do to me, I do not desire to do to them."

The Master said: "Ci, you have not attained to that."

Here the Master bursts Zigong's self-satisfied bubble. Zigong has obviously heard Confucius define *shu* and emphasize its significance (perhaps in the same dialogue recorded in *Analects* 6.28) and wishes to impress his master by asserting that he will adopt the same principle. Confucius responds that it is more easily said that done. Practicing *shu* is not a matter of making grand announcements, but doing it one's whole life. (Recall "My prayer is of long standing," p. 35.)

Confucius has much more to say about *ren* and links it to the concept of *li* 禮, "ritual," in a dense and easily misunderstood passage:

顏淵問仁。子曰：「克己復禮為仁。一日克己復禮，天下歸仁焉。為仁由己，而由人乎哉？」顏淵曰：「請問其目。」子曰：「非禮勿視，非禮勿聽，非禮勿言，非禮勿動。」顏淵曰：「回雖不敏，請事斯語矣。」 (*Analects* 12.1)[41]

Yan Yuan (i.e., Yan Hui 顏回, 521–481? BC, the Master's favorite disciple) asked about humanity. The Master said: "Overcome the self and return to ritual in order to practice humanity. If you can overcome the self and return to ritual for one day, the world will bring humanity home to you. Does the practice of humanity emerge from the self, or does it arise from others?"[42]

Yan Yuan said: "May I ask for an overview?"

The Master said: "Do not look in opposition to the rites. Do not listen in opposition to the rites. Do not speak in opposition to the rites. Do not move in opposition to the rites."

Yan Yuan said: "Although I am not clever, I beg to live in service of this saying."

The fact that Yan Yuan, Confucius's premier disciple, is asking here about humanity, Confucius's premier virtue, marks this as one of the most important passages in the entire collection. For careful readers, the unstated message is "Pay attention to this one!"

Western interpreters of Confucius have frequently mischaracterized *li* as something like a code of conduct,[43] leading to serious misconceptions about what Confucius means by not looking, listening, speaking, or moving in opposition to the rites. One might think there is a discrete and knowable code, called *li*, which one can rely on for guidance in all matters: if you do not know how to act, cleave to the *li*, and you will never be wrong. This might also have been the standard conception of *li* in Confucius's own day: a practicable code that ambitious young men hoped to learn from experienced ritual masters. The problem is that this under-standing of *li* is inadequate for Confucius, because he explicitly *contrasts* the rites with anything like a predetermined code (and, to this extent, the very translation of *li* as "rite" or "ritual" can be misleading):

子曰：「道之以政，齊之以刑，民免而無恥。道之以德，齊之以禮，有恥且格。」(*Analects* 2.3)[44]

The Master said: "If you guide them with legislation, and unify them with punishments, then the people will avoid [the punishments] but have no conscience. If you guide them with virtue, and unify them with ritual, then they will have a conscience; moreover, they will correct themselves."

Legislation and punishments are not ineffective; on the contrary, they are *highly* effective, because they make people do whatever is necessary to avoid being punished. But what laws and punishments cannot do is effect any moral transformation in the populace, and this (as will soon become clear) is the only legitimate purpose of government. Laws and punishments are like traffic lights at an intersection. Traffic lights are effective at preventing accidents because most people abide by them. And why do we abide by them? For two obvious reasons: we do not want to be fined for going through a red light, and we do not want to cause an accident by driving headlong into traffic. (The former would seem to be the overriding concern, as most motorists stop at red lights even in the middle of the night, when the intersection is empty.) Confucius's point would be that traffic lights do not make anyone a better person. One can be a perfectly wicked person and still stop unfailingly at every red light. Traffic lights simply mold our conduct, not our inner morality. And this, as far as Confucius is concerned, is not enough; what government really needs are not laws and punishments, but virtue and ritual. Only virtue and ritual can aid in moral self-cultivation.

Thus, as tempting as the interpretation may be, *li* cannot refer to a code of conduct, and, therefore, in order to understand *Analects* 12.1—"Do not look in opposition to the rites; do not listen in opposition to the rites;

do not speak in opposition to the rites; do not move in opposition to the rites"—we need to reconstruct the meaning of *li* by examining its usage elsewhere in the text.

The most revealing passage has to do with rituals in a ceremonial hall:

子曰：「麻冕，禮也。今也純，儉，吾從眾。拜下，禮也。今拜乎上，泰也。雖違眾，吾從下。」 (*Analects* 9.3)[45]

The Master said: "A cap of hemp [is prescribed by] the rites, but today [one uses] jet-black silk. This is frugal, and I follow the majority. To bow at the bottom of the hall [is prescribed by] the rites, but today one bows at the top [of the hall]. This is self-aggrandizing, so I oppose the majority; I follow [the tradition of bowing at] the bottom [of the hall]."

In Confucius's day, the ritual cap of hemp was considered more extravagant than one of silk (which was a plentiful material). The passage addresses the question of when it is and is not permissible to alter the received rituals. Substituting a more frugal ceremonial hat for the fancy one prescribed by the rites is acceptable, but bowing at the top of the hall instead of the bottom of the hall is not. It follows, then, that the rites are subject to emendation in practice, but one cannot depart from them capriciously or groundlessly. Rather, they must be practiced in such a way as to convey and reinforce deeper moral principles. Nor can one simply follow the majority. Laudable practice of the rites requires thinking for oneself.[46]

*Li* is best understood, then, as embodied virtue, the thoughtful somatic expression of basic moral principles, without which the ceremonies are void. A disciple named Zixia 子夏 (i.e., Bu Shang 卜商, b. 507 BC) seems to be indicating this point in his subtle analysis of a classical poetic verse:

子夏問曰：「『巧笑倩兮，美目盼兮，素以為絢兮』，何謂也？」子曰：「繪事後素。」曰：「禮後乎？」子曰：「起予者商也！始可與言詩已矣。」 (*Analects* 3.8)[47]

Zixia asked: "'Oh, her artful smile is dimpled. Oh, her beautiful eye is black-and-white. Oh, a plain [background] on which to apply the highlights.'[48] What does this refer to?"

The Master said: "In painting, everything follows the plain [background]."

[Zixia] said: "Does ritual follow [in similar fashion]?"

The Master said: "Shang, it is you who have inspired me. Finally I have someone to discuss the *Odes* with."

Confucius's fascination with the canonical *Odes* is evident throughout the *Analects*. On one occasion (*Analects* 16.13), he is said to have told his son that if he does not study the *Odes*, he will have "nothing with which to speak" (*wu yi yan* 無以言). All early Confucians joined him in regarding the *Odes* as the supreme model of dignified expression.[49] In this particular passage, Zixia presumably means to say that the rituals, significant though they may be, are effective only if practiced by those who have morally prepared themselves for the task. Someone who is morally alive, then, must reassess at every moment how best to perform the rites. The rites prescribe a fine hat? Ah, but a plain one would be more frugal. Choose a plain one. The majority bows at the top of the hall even though the rites call for bowing at the bottom of the hall? Bowing at the top of the hall is self-aggrandizing, and that sends the wrong message, even if it has become customary. Bow at the bottom of the hall instead. Far from a static code of conduct, *li* is the sum total of all the moral calculations that a thinking Confucian must go through before acting. *Li* is in constant flux; it must be constantly reinterpreted and reapplied to suit changing situations.

Thus when Confucius tells Yan Yuan not to look, listen, speak, or move in opposition to the rites, he does not mean that Yan Yuan need only memorize a certain body of accepted conventions and take care always to follow them; rather, using the fuller sense of *li*, he means that Yan Yuan must ask himself how to put the most humane face on the rites in each new situation, and then carry them out conscientiously. What sounds like a deceptively simple instruction is really a demand that Yan Yuan not only act with unflagging moral awareness but also assess *for himself* the right course of action at every moment.[50]

• • •

Confucius's statement that only virtue and ritual satisfy the moral demands of government opens the door to the next major theme in his philosophy. The ruler and his aides are responsible for the moral complexion of the people.

季康子問政於孔子。孔子對曰：「政者，正也。子帥以正，孰敢不
正？」 (*Analects* 12.17)[51]

Ji Kangzi (i.e., Jisun Fei 季孫肥, d. 468 BC) asked Confucius about government. Confucius answered: "To govern is to correct. If you lead with rectitude, who will dare not be correct?"

"To govern is to correct" is a keen paronomasia in Chinese, for the word for "government" (*zheng* 政) is a homophonous derivative of the word for "correction" or "rectitude" (*zheng* 正).[52] While our most prominent political metaphor in the West is the ship of state—the word "governor" originally refers to a steersman—Confucius's metaphor is that government is a project of moral correction. In his pithy response to Ji Kangzi, he makes two fundamental claims: government is inescapably a moral endeavor, and the ruler's behavior has an irresistible influence on his subjects. Confucius returns to these points repeatedly:

子曰：「其身正，不令而行；其身不正，雖令不從。」 (*Analects* 13.6)[53]

The Master said: "If he himself is rectified, [his will] is carried out even if he does not command it; if he himself is not rectified, [his will] is not followed even if he does command it."

The ruler's verbal commands then, are essentially pleonastic: the people will examine his conduct, and adjust their own accordingly. Government is not successful if those at the top abuse their position in order to gratify their desires. If the people see that their ruler is greedy, they will become thievish themselves, but if they see that he has learned how to restrain his desires, they will emulate him in this respect as well.

季康子患盜，問於孔子。孔子對曰：「苟子之不欲，雖賞之不竊。」
(*Analects* 12.18)[54]

Ji Kangzi was concerned about thievery and asked Confucius about it. Confucius responded: "If you were not covetous, they would not steal even if you were to reward them for it."

And immediately another response to the same Ji Kangzi, who now proposes to execute all those who act immorally, eliciting a line that has been treasured for centuries:

孔子對曰：「子為政，焉用殺？子欲善而民善矣。君子之德風，小人之德草，草上之風，必偃。」 (*Analects* 12.19)[55]

Confucius replied: "In exercising government, why do you need to kill? If you desire goodness, the people will be good. The character of the noble man is like wind; the character of the petty man is like grass. When the wind [blows] over the grass, it must bend."

The people will sway in whichever direction their superiors incline them.

Rulers have the power to shape the people's conduct because of another fundamental belief of Confucius: *all* human conduct affects every other person near the actor. Morality spreads: "The virtuous are not orphans; they will have neighbors" 德不孤，必有鄰 (*Analects* 4.25). Indeed, people whom we might consider barbaric are uncultivated only because they have not yet had the benefit of moral guidance. In the presence of the right teacher, they could not help becoming rectified themselves:

子欲居九夷。或曰：「陋，如之何？」子曰：「君子居之，何陋之有？」 (*Analects* 9.13)[56]

The Master wished to dwell among the several barbarians. Someone said: "They are rude; how will you get along?"

The Master said: "If a noble man dwelled there, what rudeness would there be?"

Everyone has a stake in the moral standing of the human community, and at the same time the wherewithal to affect it either positively or negatively. But rulers are uniquely positioned, because of their unparalleled authority, to affect whole nations. A scrupulous gentleman might be able to affect his family and perhaps a few of his neighbors; a sage ruler, by contrast, could conceivably lead all human beings to that ideal Confucian kingdom of universal moral excellence. And with great power comes great responsibility: while a selfish commoner will probably never be more than a local pest, a tyrant could hurl his whole kingdom to perdition. Most rulers, in Confucius's view, do not comprehend the momentous duties that accompany their lofty titles.

A question about politics occasioned yet another famous remark:

齊景公問政於孔子。孔子對曰:「君君, 臣臣, 父父, 子子。」公曰: 「善哉! 信如君不君, 臣不臣, 父不父, 子不子, 雖有粟, 吾得而 食諸?」 (*Analects* 12.11)[57]

Lord Jing of Qi (r. 547–490 BC) asked Confucius about government. Confucius answered: "The lord acts as a lord, the minister as a minister, the father as a father, the son as a son."

The lord said: "Excellent! Surely, if the lord does not act as a lord, nor the minister as a minister, nor the father as a father, nor the son as a son, then although I might have grain, would I be able to eat it?"

Readers are sometimes puzzled by this exchange, not least because Lord Jing's enthusiastic agreement does not seem to shed much further light on Confucius's pithy saying. (The main reason for Lord Jing's presence in the passage is probably to show that Confucius was sought out by some of the loftiest men in the Chinese world for his opinions on government; today's equivalent would be something like "Vice President Pence asked Professor So-and-so about health-care reform." The famous personage was Lord Jing, not Confucius.)

"The lord acts as a lord, the minister as a minister, the father as a father, the son as a son" is beautifully terse in Chinese (*jun jun chen chen fu fu zi zi* 君君臣臣父父子子), because the pliable grammar of the classical language allows any word to function as any part of speech depending on its place in the sentence. Thus *jun jun* means "the lord" (*jun*, noun) "acts as a lord" (*jun*, verb). The saying could conceivably be read as an apology for preexisting power relations—if you are not the lord, you must hold your tongue, because only the lord can be the lord—but this is not how Confucius's words have been understood by the tradition. Rather, "to act as a lord," "to act as a minister," "to act as a father," and "to act as a son" are taken to be moral demands: if a ruler, minister, father, or son are to be reckoned as such, they must act as required by their positions in society. "To act as a lord" means to live up to the moral demands of the position of rulership that we have outlined above. It means to be

vigilant about one's own conduct so as to provide a worthy model for the
people to follow in their quest for moral self-cultivation.

"To act as a lord" does not mean to enforce one's will imperiously and
disregard upright remonstrance.[58] That would be "to act *not* as a lord,"
and indeed lords who act in such a heedless way do not deserve to be
called "lords" at all.[59] Confucius's statement is one of the oldest examples
of a typical theme in early Chinese philosophy: rectifying names (*zhengming* 正名),[60] or making sure that names fit the realities they are supposed to represent. In Confucius's formulation, rectifying names is fundamentally a moral undertaking: appropriate names and titles are
determined by the moral standing of the people who bear them.[61] A lord
is someone who acts like a lord; a tyrant is someone who acts like a tyrant.
In the same fashion, Confucius redefined the old title *junzi* 君子, meaning literally "son of a lord" and denoting a member of the hereditary
aristocracy, in moral terms: a *junzi* is someone who acts as a *junzi* should,
regardless of birth.[62] Defenders of the entrenched social hierarchy would
thus not have been enthusiastic Confucians. (Throughout this book, *junzi*
in this moral sense is rendered as "noble man.")

Confucius's recipe for good government permits some other inferences. First, modern readers can hardly avoid observing that all four
characters—the lord, the minister, the father, and the son—are male. It
was a social reality in Confucius's day that lords and ministers were without exception male, but instead of "the father" and "the son," he might
well have said "fathers and mothers" and "sons and daughters." Readers
must decide for themselves how much to make of this problem. On the
one hand, there is little reason why Confucius's ideas could not be extended today to include women as well; on the other hand, there is also
little reason to suppose that he himself would have thought to do so.[63]
All his disciples were male, and his few comments about women suggest
that he thought most consequential actions were undertaken by men. Or
perhaps Confucius cited male roles merely because he knew that Lord
Jing was male, and he always took the speaker's circumstances into account in his responses.

Another inescapable observation is that the four cardinal roles are all
relative. No one can be a lord without a minister, a minister without a
lord, a father without a son, or a son without a father. By the same token,
it is possible for the same person to play more than one of these roles in

different situations and in relation to different people. All males are sons, and thus any father is not only a father to his son but also a son to his own father. Similarly, a minister may be a lord in his own right, but a minister to a lord higher than he; indeed, in Bronze Age politics, even the highest king, the Son of Heaven, is conceived as a lord to all other human beings but only a vicegerent of Heaven above. These dimensions of Confucius's saying should not be overlooked. All Confucian morality, as we have seen, emerges from relations with other people. It is impossible to practice *shu* except in relation to other people, just as virtue, as Confucius has told us, always has neighbors. (This is why I defined *zhong* earlier as "being honest with oneself *in dealing with others*"; one never finds any sort of action characterized as *zhong* unless it involves another human being.)

Moreover, the stipulation that we must act in accordance with our social role means that the right way to behave depends on our relationship with the person we are presently engaged with. There are no universally valid moral injunctions because no one is in the same social position at every instant of his or her life:

子曰：「君子之於天下也，無適也，無莫也，義之與比。」 (*Analects* 4.10)[64]

The Master said: "In his associations with the world, there is nothing that the noble man [invariably] affirms or denies. He is a participant in what is right."

This confirms our earlier conclusion that for Yan Yuan to look, listen, speak, and move in accordance with the rites, he must analyze each new situation afresh and infer from it the right mode of conduct for that particular moment. If he is in the role of father, he has one set of moral demands to consider; if he is in the role of son, the rites call for a very different pattern of behavior. And it is up to him, through conscientious moral reasoning, to determine all such obligations.

• • •

The last major element of Confucius's political philosophy is that people's obligations to their kin are greater than their obligation to the state.

葉公語孔子曰：「吾黨有直躬者，其父攘羊，而子證之。」孔子曰：「吾黨之直者異於是：父為子隱，子為父隱，直在其中矣。」 (*Analects* 13.18)[65]

The Lord of She said to Confucius: "In our village there is one named Upright Gong.[66] His father stole a sheep, so the son testified against him."

Confucius said: "The upright people of my village are different from this. The fathers are willing to conceal their sons; the sons are willing to conceal their fathers. Uprightness lies therein."

Confucius's response was taken by opponents to mean that he condoned theft (see p. 210), and Mencius went on to discuss the hardships that handling a criminal father can entail (e.g., *Mencius* 7A.35). A son's obligation to his father includes not just protecting him from the arm of the law, but also expostulating with him when he believes his father's conduct is reprehensible. What Confucius means to say by this example is not that the son should welcome his father's misdeeds, but that he is misguided if he thinks he owes more to the faceless state than to the father who reared and raised him. Moral development begins in the family and only then radiates outward to the rest of the world. Moral influence cannot be turned in the other direction. Notice also that the father's crime is mere larceny rather than rape or murder—that is to say, full restitution is still possible.

Confucius recognizes that serving parents can be difficult:

子曰：「事父母幾諫，見志不從，又敬不違，勞而不怨。」(*Analects* 4.18)[67]

The Master said: "In serving your parents, remonstrate slightly. If you see that they do not intend to follow [your advice], remain respectful and do not disobey. Toil and do not complain."

The remonstrance is indispensable: "acting as a son" must include raising controversial issues with one's parents whenever necessary. But imperfect parents are not always persuaded to mend their ways, and Confucius does not accept taking parents' mistakes as grounds for losing one's filial respect. "Toil and do not complain": you may know you are in the right, but if you have done everything you can to make your case, and your parents are intractable, you must endure your lot. No one ever said that life as a committed Confucian would be easy:

子曰：「弟子入則孝，出則弟，謹而信，汎愛眾而親仁。行有餘力，則以學文。」(*Analects* 1.6)[68]

The Master said: "Disciples should be filial at home and courteous when abroad. They should be careful and trustworthy; they should overflow with love of the multitude and be intimate with humanity. If they have energy left over from their actions, then they may use it to study refinements."

"Refinements" are pursuits such as literature and archery that are not directly related to moral practice, and are permissible only if there is time and energy left over for them. One can survive, if necessary, without literature or archery, but no one can live without morality.

• • •

Two final themes before concluding this chapter: First, the opening line of the *Analects* merits comment.

子曰:「學而時習之, 不亦說乎? 有朋自遠方來, 不亦樂乎? 人不知而不慍, 不亦君子乎?」 (*Analects* 1.1)[69]

The Master said: "To study and then practice [what you have learned] at the right time—is this not indeed a delight? To have friends come from distant places—is this not indeed a joy? One who is unknown by others, yet not indignant—is this not indeed a noble man?"

It is only fitting that a philosopher who regards morality as a matter of thinking first but then *acting* appropriately should insist that study is incomplete without timely application. Moral practice cannot exist in isolation from other human beings, and thus self-cultivation that does not demonstrably affect the rest of the world is trivial. Evidently some of Confucius's disciples questioned their teacher on this account, arguing that, by teaching on the sidelines instead of throwing himself into the riotous political field, Confucius was betraying his own tenets. But he had a response:

子貢曰:「有美玉於斯, 韞匵而藏諸? 求善賈而沽諸?」
　子曰:「沽之哉! 沽之哉! 我待賈者也。」 (*Analects* 9.12)[70]

Zigong said: "There is a beautiful jade here. Should we enclose it in a case and store it, or should we seek a good price and sell it?"
　The Master said: "Sell it! Sell it! I am waiting for [a good] price."

Inasmuch as Zigong went on to have a worldly career,[71] he is the right disciple to have asked this question. Confucius means to say that he would relish the opportunity to serve in government, but he will not do so until the regime has become worthy of his support. As long as his services are undervalued, he will keep himself off the labor market.

Moreover, carrying on with equanimity in an unappreciative, if not outright contemptuous, world is a major theme in Confucian philosophy; Confucius returns to it repeatedly,[72] and we shall see Mencius address it as well. The ability to rise above the carping of the unenlightened is borne of the self-assurance that comes of rigorously assessing one's own conduct and satisfying oneself that one has truly lived up to the demands of one's conscience.[73] But Confucius's self-confidence reached a level that may alienate atheist readers, for there are suggestions that he thought Heaven itself supported his didactic mission:[74]

子畏於匡。曰:「文王既沒, 文不在茲乎? 天之將喪斯文也, 後死者不得與於斯文也。天之未喪斯文也, 匡人其如予何?」(*Analects* 9.5)[75]

The Master was terrorized in Kuang. He said: "Since the death of King Wen, has Culture not still been here? If Heaven were about to let This Culture die, then I, a later mortal, would not be able to partake of This Culture. Since Heaven has not let This Culture die, what can the people of Kuang do to me?"

Such statements resonate with Confucius's claim that "at fifty, I knew Heaven's Mandate" 五十而知天命 (*Analects* 2.4). He seems to have been convinced that Heaven put him on this earth in order to teach mankind "This Culture" (*siwen* 斯文). And for most of Chinese history, posterity shared this belief.

# CHAPTER THREE

# *Mozi*

If we know frustratingly little about the historical Confucius, we know even less about Mo Di 墨翟 (d. ca. 390 BC), his first great philosophical rival. Since *mo* can mean "tattoo" (a common punishment in ancient China), it has been suggested that Mo Di may have been a convict, and that Mozi is not a name but an epithet: "The Tattooed Master."[1] *Mo* can also mean "ink-line," and because of the very mechanical and repetitious style of the Mohist writings, as well as their penchant for analogies taken from workmen's experience, others suspect that Mozi and his followers may have originally been artisans or craftsmen.[2] From these obscure beginnings, Mohism quickly burgeoned into an influential philosophical school with a firm hierarchy and organization. Whatever their origins, Mohists soon came to be known first and foremost as thinkers.

One classical text says that Mozi was a disenchanted student of Confucian teachings,[3] and although we do not know the basis of this assertion, it makes some sense. Confucians and Mohists share some striking argumentative conventions;[4] for example, they venerate the same coterie of sages and employ the same scriptures, especially the *Documents* and *Odes*, as proof texts. Although the use of most other texts in *Mozi* is unreliable at best, its quotations from the *Documents* and *Odes* are scrupulous and show that Mohists were working with editions similar to our own.[5] Some Mohist slogans also echo Confucian diction.[6] In addition, *Mozi* contains a section (*Mozi* 46–50), sometimes called the "Mohist Analects," relating discussions between Mo Di and an array of interlocutors consisting of disciples, political figures such as territorial lords, and representatives of various dissenting schools and points of view. The language and composition are reminiscent of the Confucian *Analects*: the text presents one brief episode after the other, with a minimum of details, always culminating in a teaching from the mouth of the master.

Mohists detested Confucian philosophy, however, which they regarded as partisan and conducive to nepotism. Although the tendency is not yet crystal clear in the *Analects*, other early Confucian texts lay out a vision of moral practice as commencing in the family and only then extending to the rest of the world. *Great Learning* (*Daxue* 大學), while short and undatable, is indispensable for two reasons: its authority in later centuries was unquestioned, and it tidily encapsulates a quintessentially Confucian understanding of the connection between self-cultivation and moral governance. The core paragraph reads:

古之欲明明德於天下者，先治其國；欲治其國者，先齊其家；欲齊其家者，先修其身；欲修其身者，先正其心；欲正其心者，先誠其意；欲誠其意者，先致其知；致知在格物。物格而后知至，知至而后意誠，意誠而后心正，心正而后身修，身修而后家齊，家齊而后國治，國治而后天下平。[7]

Because the ancients desired to make their brilliant virtue shine throughout the world, they first ordered their states; desiring to order their states, they first regulated their families; desiring to regulate their families, they first cultivated themselves; desiring to cultivate themselves, they first rectified their hearts; desiring to rectify their hearts, they first made their intentions sincere; desiring to make their intentions sincere, they first brought about knowledge. Bringing about knowledge lies in investigating things. After things are investigated, knowledge is brought about; after knowledge is brought about, one's intentions are sincere; after one's intentions are sincere, one's heart is rectified; after one's heart is rectified, one cultivates oneself; after one has cultivated oneself, one's family is regulated; after one's family is regulated, the state is ordered; after the state is ordered, the world is at peace.

In order to bring about peace in the world: one must go back logically, step by step, to the elemental act of "investigating things"—as the opaque phrase *gewu* 格物 is usually understood. It can also mean "to make things arrive" or "to come to things"; since the stage of *gewu* is obviously pivotal in this text, commentators have been debating its precise meaning for centuries. Confucians of a rationalist bent have held that it means understanding the underlying patterns of the cosmos by studying the rhythms and correspondences of things in nature. Then one attains knowledge, whereupon one can make one's intentions sincere, rectify one's heart, cultivate oneself, regulate one's family, order one's state, and finally bring peace to the world.

*Great Learning* not only affirms that the ultimate end of the Confucian moral project, namely good government in all quarters of the world, can be achieved in this manner but also implies that it cannot be achieved by any other process. The only way to achieve world peace is to begin by cultivating yourself, and then spread your morality outward, through your own family, to your body politic around you and finally the rest of the world. Nothing will be accomplished by going in the other direction. The privileged place of the family in the process of moral development is highlighted by the virtue of *xiao* 孝, "filial piety."

The Mohist objection was that we should love everyone, not just the people closest to us. The Confucian doctrine of caring more for our kin than for strangers, in their view, was a perversion of justice. An example of the kind of attitude that galled Mohists is *Mencius* 4B.29:

今有同室之人鬥者，救之，雖被 [=披] 髮纓冠而救之可也。鄉鄰有鬥者，被髮纓冠而往救之，則惑也。雖閉戶，可也。[8]

If a member of your household is involved in a fight, coming to the rescue would be acceptable even if you were to go out with unbound hair and your chinstraps [dangling from] your cap (i.e., in haste and incompletely dressed). If it is your neighbor who is involved in the fight, then coming to the rescue by going out with unbound hair and chinstraps [dangling from] your cap would be deluded. It would be acceptable to shut your door.

Are we really under no obligation to aid victims of assault if they happen not to be related to us? According to Mencius (in this passage), you do not even need to alert the authorities. Shut your door and mind your own business. This attitude might be particularly difficult for Westerners to accept because of the Christianized expectation that a philosophical text should teach us to love our neighbors.[9]

In a vicious chapter, "Opposing the Confucians" ("Feiru" 非儒, *Mozi* 39), *Mozi* accuses Confucius and his followers of disloyalty and machination, with a barrage of specific historical examples. In one of the most elaborate indictments, we are told that the King of Qi was initially disposed to offer Confucius a benefice but was dissuaded by his renowned minister, Yan Ying, who argued that Confucians (*ru*)—i.e., not just Confucius himself—were unworthy.[10] Confucius's furious response was to unleash a plot that ended in the demise of two states. Scholars commonly dismiss the story as slanderous or lacking documentary "support,"[11] but there are two reasons why this is inadequate: first, it happens to be repeated in other classical texts,[12] but more importantly, to readers of "Opposing the Confucians," the burden of proof was not necessarily on the Mohist side. Interpretations of history portraying Confucius and Zigong as unscrupulous conspirators would have been savored by anyone who was already inclined to believe that Confucians were clannish careerists who would not hesitate to contrive the destruction of their neighbors.

Historically speaking, Mohism failed. (Its *philosophical* value is debated to this day.) By the end of antiquity, it seems, there were no longer any avowed adherents; if Mozi was cited by other philosophers, it was in order to point out the errors of his teachings.[13] Only under the modernist pressures of the nineteenth and early twentieth centuries, when Chinese intellectuals sought to rediscover evidence of logical and scientific reasoning in their patrimony, did *Mozi* recapture their interest.[14] One frequently proposed explanation for this decline is that Mohism alienated ancient rulers, but the same was true of other traditions (such as *Zhuangzi*). Thus there must have been other reasons why Mohist philosophy gradually fell into disfavor,[15] and I have two suspicions: first, it suffered for failing to advance a robust notion of self-cultivation, and second, it was thought to require taking too much on faith. Mohist theodicy, in particular, could not have been deemed fully persuasive. In explicating Mohism, then, philosophers and historians part company: the former tend to ask what aspects can be salvaged and perhaps repurposed today, while the latter try to understand what it stood for in its own time, and why it was ultimately rejected.

• • •

*Mozi*, the sole surviving repository of Mohist teachings, is extensive and is best understood as a school text. It cannot have been written by Mo Di, as it refers to him, as well as some of his disciples, in the third person, as masters. The core of the book is a sequence of what were originally thirty chapters advancing ten basic credos: (1) "Exalting Worthies" ("Shangxian" 尚賢, *Mozi* 8–10); (2) "Upward Conformity" ("Shangtong" 尚同, *Mozi* 11–13); (3) "Impartial Love" ("Jian'ai" 兼愛, *Mozi* 14–16); (4) "Objecting to [Military] Aggression" ("Feigong" 非攻, *Mozi* 17–19); (5) "Moderating Expenditure" ("Jieyong" 節用, *Mozi* 20–22, of which only 20 and 21 survive); (6) "Moderating Funerals" ("Jiezang" 節葬, *Mozi* 23–25, of which only 25 survives); (7) "The Will of Heaven" ("Tianzhi" 天志, *Mozi* 26–28); (8) "Clarifying Ghosts" ("Minggui" 明鬼, *Mozi* 29–31, of which only 31 survives); (9) "Objecting to Music" ("Feiyue" 非樂, *Mozi* 32–34, of which only 32 survives); and (10) "Objecting to Fatalism" ("Feiming" 非命, *Mozi* 35–37).[16] The significance of these triplets remains unclear; possibly they represent three different strands within the Mohist school, or perhaps they reflect evolving Mohist defenses of their positions.[17] Other sections of *Mozi* address topics such as language and logic, optics, and defensive warfare (in addition to the aforementioned "Mohist Analects"). My treatment here will focus on the core chapters, with references from other portions of the text only where they serve to amplify the discussion; otherwise, it would have to exceed the length of a chapter.

One of the many curiosities of Mohist philosophy is that this written corpus might not have come down to us had it not been included in the massive *Daoist Canon* (*Daozang* 道藏).[18] All modern editions of the *Mozi* are derived from or related to this text.[19] There are many consequences of this oddity. For example, the relative ignorance with which premodern literati derided Mohist philosophy—generally speaking of it as though "Impartial Love" were its sole significant tenet—may be explained by their lack of access to a reliable edition. Only after the publication of the *Daoist Canon* in 1447 was *Mozi* likely to have been available to most readers; before this, they would probably have had to rely on the various snippets preserved haphazardly, and often unfairly, in highbrow collectanea.

The question of why the *Mozi* was included in the *Daoist Canon* is a good framing device for a general inquiry into the text and its ideas, for the *Daoist Canon* is an unlikely source indeed. Whatever definition of "Daoist" one wishes to apply,[20] Mo Di cannot be said to qualify. He was, naturally, not a religious Daoist, as he lived centuries before the epoch-making revelation to Zhang Daoling 張道陵 in AD 142. Nor does *Mozi* adopt the concept of the *dao* as a crucial philosophical principle (unlike the traditions to be examined in part 2, below).[21]

Yet Mo Di was canonized, long after his death, as a kind of Daoist demigod, even as he was discarded by every other philosophical current. Some early medieval sources depict him as a master alchemist and an immortal invested with revelations from even higher beings.[22] Why might Mohist beliefs have been regarded as antecedents of the religious Daoist faith? Mohism has many characteristics of a religion:[23] it offers principles of conduct sanctioned by Heaven, delivered to humanity by a sage teacher, and enforced by awesome spirits. In these respects, the texts that most closely resemble the *Mozi* are those of the early Celestial Masters, such as the *Xiang'er Commentary to the Laozi*. These correspondences are not often recognized because of the stubborn consensus that Mohism is a kind of utilitarianism[24]—a hermeneutic prism affording a good understanding of one aspect of Mohism, but scant appreciation of the rest.

••• 

The similarity of certain Mohist arguments to those of Western utilitarianism is undeniable and worth examining here. Some of the most familiar material appears in the "Impartial Love" chapters:

子墨子言曰：仁人之事者，必務求興天下之利，除天下之害。然當今之時，天下之害孰為大？曰：若大國之攻小國也，大家之亂小家也，強之劫弱，眾之暴寡，詐之謀愚，貴之敖賤，此天下之害也。又與為人君者之不惠也，臣者之不忠也，父者之不慈也，子者之不孝也，此又天下之害也。又與今人之賤人，執其兵刃毒藥水火，以交相虧賊，此又天下之害也。姑嘗本原若眾害之所自生，此胡自生？此自愛人、利人生與？即必曰非然也，必曰從惡人、賊人生。分名乎天下惡人而賊人者，兼與？別與？即必曰別也。然即之交別者，果生天下之大害者與？是故別非也。」(*Mozi* 16)[25]

Master Mozi said: The undertaking of a humane person is to try to promote whatever benefits the world and to eliminate whatever harms the world. This being the case, what are the greatest things that harm the world in today's times? I say: When large states attack small states, large lineages dislocate small lineages, the strong extort the weak, the many maltreat the few, the cunning machinate against the foolish, the noble overbear the base—these are things that harm the world. So too the ungenerosity of those who are lords of men, the disloyalty of ministers, the unkindness of fathers, the unfiliality of sons—these are also things that harm the world. So too the base people of today who injure and despoil others by means of weapons, blades, poison, drugs, water, or fire—these are also things that harm the world. If one were to investigate whence these various harms arise, whence do these things arise? Do these things arise from loving others and benefiting others? One would have to say that this is not the case; one would have to say that they arise from hating others and despoiling others. If one were to categorize things in the world by means of names, would those who hate others and despoil others [be called] impartial or partial? One would have to say partial. Thus is it not the case that engaging others with partiality gives rise to the great harms in the world? For this reason, partiality is wrong.

The argument, though verbose, bears scrutiny. It begins with the premise that the "humane person's" (*ren ren* 仁人) task is to advance whatever brings good to the world and oppose whatever brings harm. (By commencing the disquisition with the word *ren*, the text is effectively saying that Confucians do not even understand the virtue that they claim to cherish above all others.) Then the text lists the most important causes of harm and infers that they are all born of "hating and despoiling people" (*wu ren, zei ren* 惡人、賊人), that is, the desire to enrich oneself at others' expense, which, paradoxically, only leads to impoverishment. The conclusion to the paragraph is characteristic of Mohist thinking: because the attitude of "partiality" (*bie* 別) engenders such inclinations, partiality is wrong. "*For this reason*, partiality is wrong." What is right, in other words, is anything conducive to general profit; what is wrong is anything conducive to general harm.

It is on the basis of such passages that Mohism has been so frequently identified with utilitarianism, both in spirit and in argumentation. Compare these paragraphs from Bentham:

By utility is meant that property in any object, whereby it tends to produce benefit, advantage, pleasure, good, or happiness, (all this in the present case comes to the same thing) or (what comes again to the same thing) to prevent the happening of mischief, pain, evil, or unhappiness to the party whose interest is considered: if that party be the community in general, then the happiness of the community: if a particular individual, then the happiness of that individual. . . .

A man may be said to be a partizan of the principle of utility, when the approbation or disapprobation he annexes to any action, or to any measure, is determined by and proportioned to the tendency which he conceives it to have to augment or to diminish the happiness of the community: or in other words, to its conformity or unconformity to the laws or dictates of utility.

Of an action that is conformable to the principle of utility one may always say either that it is one that ought to be done, or at least that it is not one that ought not to be done. One may say also, that it is right it should be done; at least that it is not wrong it should be done: that it is a right action; at least that it is not a wrong action. When thus interpreted, the words *ought*, and *right* and *wrong* and others of that stamp, have a meaning: when otherwise, they have none.[26]

Most of the Mohist doctrines are readily reducible to the notion of doing what is most profitable for human beings as a moral community. Impartial love is enjoined out of the conviction that if everyone were to treat others as well as they treat themselves (and, by extension, treat strangers as well as they treat family members), strife—which harms all—could be avoided. Similarly, offensive warfare is condemned on the grounds that it is nothing more than theft on a grand scale, which hardly brings about the greatest good for the greatest number of people. The Mohists' commitment to dissuading rulers from campaigns of conquest was so deep that, as even non-Mohist sources acknowledge, they became experts in defensive warfare, to whom besieged states could appeal for aid,[27] and accordingly some of the most detailed ancient material pertaining to siege craft is found in a long section of their book (*Mozi* 52–71).[28] The Mohist doctrines of moderating expenditure, moderating funeral expenses, and even opposing lavish musical performances all follow naturally from the assumption that wastefulness is harmful to the overall economy;[29] a lord with enough of a surplus for such frippery would do better to succor the poor instead.[30]

Even the meritocratic ideal of promoting the worthy in government is defended along utilitarian lines: just as a ruler takes care to employ a competent tailor when he desires a coat, or a competent slaughter master when he desires beef or mutton, so too must he select only competent administrators, even if they happen to be ugly or low-born.[31] The "worthy" are described in unabashedly fiscal terms; a worthy administrator is one who knows how to benefit the state and its people through his assiduousness at collecting taxes and managing finances:

賢者之治國者也，蚤朝晏退，聽獄治政，是以國家治而刑法正。賢者之長官也，夜寢夙興，收斂關市、山林、澤梁之利，以實官府，是以官府實而財不散。賢者之治邑也，蚤出莫入，耕稼樹藝，聚菽粟，是以菽粟多而民足乎食。(*Mozi* 9)[32]

When a worthy man governs the state, he arrives at court early and retires late; he hears lawsuits and puts the government in order. Thus the state and its families are orderly, and the penal institutions are correct. When a worthy man heads the bureaucracy, he goes to bed late at night and arises early in the morning; he collects taxes on the profit from passes, cities, mountains, forests, wetlands, and bridges, filling the official treasury. Thus the official treasury is full, and capital is not dissipated. When a worthy man governs a district, he leaves [his residence] early and comes back only after dusk; he [sees to] the plowing and sowing, the planting of orchards, and the harvesting of beans and grain. Thus beans and grain are plentiful, and the people have enough to eat.

The Mohist conception of "worthiness" does include a less readily quantifiable moral dimension: we are told, for example, that the worthy differ from the unworthy, who are unfilial toward their parents, sexually promiscuous, larcenous, and rebellious.[33] But the larger point is that the worthies' administrative successes are laudable as a moral achievement in their own right. Whereas Confucius typically cast the worthy or the noble man as one who responds appropriately to the unique moral demands of each situation (see p. 45), Mohists simplified: a worthy is someone who profits the state and its people—no more and no less. These worthies, moreover, are to be richly compensated and provisioned, for only then will their judgments be respected by the populace.[34] Wealth and finery are thus not intrinsically contemptible; the bitter criticisms in the "Moderating Expenditure" and "Opposing Music" chapters are aimed only at the shameful misuse of such resources. These views clash with those of Confucians, who caution that moral excellence is not necessarily accompanied by social prestige.[35]

Other chapters, however, complicate the picture. Consider "The Will of Heaven" ("Tianzhi" 天志):

然則天亦何欲何惡？天欲義而惡不義。然則率天下之百姓以從事於
義，則我乃為天之所欲也。我為天之所欲，天亦為我所欲。然則我
何欲何惡？我欲福祿而惡禍祟。然則 [lacuna] 我率天下之百姓以從
事於禍祟中也。

　然則何以知天之欲義而惡不義？曰：天下有義則生，無義則死；
有義則富，無義則貧；有義則治，無義則亂。然則天欲其生而惡
其死，欲其富而惡其貧，欲其治而惡其亂，此我所以知天欲義而
惡不義也。 (*Mozi* 26)[36]

This being the case, what indeed does Heaven desire, and what does it hate? Heaven desires righteousness and hates unrighteousness. Thus if we were to lead the Hundred Surnames to pursue their affairs in righteousness, we would be doing what Heaven desires. If we do what Heaven desires, Heaven will surely do what we desire. This being the case, what do we desire, and what do we hate? We desire fortune and lucre, and hate disasters and infestation. If [we were to lead the Hundred Surnames to pursue their affairs in unrighteousness],[37] we would be leading them to pursue their affairs in the midst of disasters and infestation.

This being the case, how do we know that Heaven desires righteousness and hates unrighteousness? I say: Whoever possesses righteousness in the world lives; whoever lacks righteousness dies. Whoever possesses righteousness is wealthy; whoever lacks righteousness is poor. Whoever possesses righteousness is orderly; whoever lacks righteousness is disorderly. Thus Heaven desires life and hates death, desires wealth and hates poverty, desires order and hates disorder. This is how we know that Heaven desires righteousness and hates unrighteousness.

This is a crucial passage for several reasons—and the moment where the hull in the Mohist ship starts to leak. First, it lays out a theodicy that, as other excerpts will confirm, is to be taken absolutely literally. If you are righteous, Heaven will see to it that you flourish; by the same token, if you are unrighteous, Heaven will see to it that you fail. The unwillingness to admit that bad things sometimes happen to good people (and the converse) is one of the hallmarks of Mohist philosophy. Taken together with the equally peculiar Mohist conception of "righteousness" (*yi*), Mohist theodicy will not only prove incompatible with the most familiar forms of utilitarianism but will also lead the way toward a more culturally plausible account of Mohist philosophy.

What is the "righteousness" that Heaven desires? The text offers thick and thin answers. The thin answer is that "righteousness" is simply whatever Heaven desires. Anyone who wishes to investigate the origin of righteousness will look for it among the eminent and wise, and Heaven being the wisest and most eminent agent in the universe, the origin of righteousness must lie with Heaven.[38] But this is tautological: if we are told that Heaven desires righteousness and hates unrighteousness, it does not help us to be informed that "righteousness" refers to whatever Heaven desires. So the text adds a thicker answer, one that immediately connects the discussion of Heaven to the utilitarian moral theories surveyed above: Heaven desires whatever benefits all the people in the world.[39] The text even repeats the same phrases that we have seen in "Impartial Love":[40]

既以天之意以為不可不慎已，然則天之將何欲何憎? 子墨子曰：天之意，不欲大國之攻小國也，大家之亂小家也，強之劫弱，眾之暴寡，詐之謀愚，貴之傲賤，此天之所不欲也。不止此而已，欲人之有力相營，有道相教，有財相分也。又欲上之強聽治也，下之強從事也。上強聽治，則國家治矣; 下強從事，則財用足矣。若國家治，財用足，則內有以絜為酒醴粢盛，以祭祀天鬼; 外有以為環璧珠玉，以聘撓 [=交][41]四鄰，諸侯之冤不興矣，邊境兵甲不作矣。內有以食飢息勞，持養其萬民，則君臣上下惠忠，父子弟兄慈孝。故惟毋明乎順天之意，奉而光施之天下，則刑政治，萬民和，國家富，財用足，百姓皆得煖衣飽食，便寧無憂。」(*Mozi* 27)[42]

If one cannot fail to be cautious about acting in accordance with Heaven's intentions, what does Heaven desire, and what does it detest? Master Mozi says: Heaven's intentions are as follows. It does not desire that large states attack small states, that large lineages dislocate small lineages, that the strong extort the weak, that the many maltreat the few, that the cunning machinate against the foolish, that the noble overbear the base. These are what Heaven does not desire. But it does not end with this. [Heaven] desires that those with energy work for others, that those with the Way teach others, that those with capital distribute it among others.

It also desires that superiors attend to government sedulously, and that inferiors pursue their affairs sedulously. If superiors attend to government sedulously, the state and its lineages will be orderly; if inferiors pursue their affairs sedulously, capital and resources will be sufficient. If the state and its lineages are orderly and capital and resources sufficient, then, within [the state], it will be possible to prepare clean offerings of wine and millet with which to sacrifice to Heaven and its ghosts, while beyond [the state] it will be possible to prepare jade disks and gems with which to sustain ceremonial relations with neighbors in all four directions. The resentment of the territorial lords will not be aroused; weapons and armor will not emerge along the frontier. If, within [the state], it is possible to feed the starving and rest the weary, to support and nurture the myriads of people, then there will be grace and loyalty between lord and minister and between superior and inferior, and kindness and filial piety between father and son and between elder brother and younger brother. Thus if only one is enlightened about following Heaven's intentions, serving them and brilliantly spreading them throughout the world, then laws and government will be orderly; the myriad people will be in harmony; the state and its lineages will be wealthy; capital and resources will be sufficient; the Hundred Surnames will have warm clothes and plenty to eat. They will live in comfort and tranquility, without distress.

In line with "Impartial Love," we are encouraged here to labor tirelessly against the injustices of the world, and to bring about a society of perfect peace and harmony—for that alone provides the greatest benefit to the people, whom Heaven loves generously.[43] But this raises a dilemma similar to the one known from *Euthyphro*: Do we venerate Heaven because it wants us to bring about the greatest benefit for the people, a principle that we recognize independently as just; or do we bring about the greatest benefit for the people because that is what Heaven wants, and we venerate Heaven?

*Mozi* does not resolve this dilemma—indeed, it does not even formulate it—but there is little evidence in the text for the position that we venerate Heaven because it upholds a principle that we recognize independently as just. On the contrary, there are indications in favor of the other horn of the dilemma, as disconcerting as it may be.[44]

First, the text states explicitly that Heaven dictates what is right and wrong in the world:

子墨子言曰：我有天志，譬若輪人之有規，匠人之有矩。輪匠執其
規矩，以度天下之方圓，曰：中者是也，不中者非也。(*Mozi* 26)[45]

Master Mozi said: We have the will of Heaven just as the wheelwright has
his compass and the carpenter his square. The wheelwright and carpenter
wield their compass and square in order to measure what is square and
what is round in the world. They say: Whatever fits [these models] is right;
whatever does not fit is wrong.

Although it is impossible to determine from this one simile whether
Heaven is to be construed as a divine commander who lays down morality by fiat, other evidence bolsters this interpretation. For example, one
cannot ignore the statement in "The Will of Heaven" that the ruler sacrifices to Heaven in order to announce to the public that its power is
supreme:

天子為政於三公、諸侯、士、庶人，天下之士君子固明知；天之為
政於天子，天下百姓未得之明知也。故昔三代聖王禹湯文武，欲以
天之為政於天子明說天下之百姓，故莫不犓牛羊，豢犬彘，潔為粢
盛酒醴，以祭祀上帝鬼神，而求祈福於天。我未嘗聞天下之所求祈
福於天子者也，我所以知天之為政於天子者也。(*Mozi* 26)[46]

The men-of-service and gentlemen of the world surely know clearly that
the Son of Heaven governs over the Three Dukes, the territorial lords, the
men-of-service, and the common people. But the Hundred Surnames of
the world have not yet attained clear knowledge that Heaven governs over
the Son of Heaven. Thus, in the past, the sage kings of the three dynasties,
namely Yu, Tang, and Kings Wen and Wu, wished to explain clearly to the
Hundred Surnames of the world that Heaven governs over the Son of
Heaven. Thus, without exception, they battened their oxen and sheep,
reared their dogs and pigs, prepared clean offerings of millet and wine
with which to sacrifice to the Deity Above and his ghosts and spirits, and
to pray for fortune from Heaven. I have never heard that the world prays
for fortune from the Son of Heaven; from this I know that Heaven governs
over the Son of Heaven.

Such statements make one suspect that if Heaven, with its irresistible
might, favored some principle other than impartial love, the Son of
Heaven would have no choice but to follow it.

Consider next the "Upward Conformity" chapters, which begin with the premise that society cannot survive if everyone is free to abide by his or her personal sense of righteousness. The result would be a war of all against all. What is needed instead is a universal standard of righteousness enforced by leaders in government. Heaven initiates this organization by selecting "the worthiest and most able person" (*xianke zhe* 賢可者)[47] in the world, and anointing him as Son of Heaven. The Son of Heaven thereupon selects the three next-worthiest men and appoints them as Three Dukes, followed by the "territorial lords and rulers of states" (*zhuhou guojun* 諸侯國君), followed at last by the lowest rank in this hierarchy, the officials and local chiefs, known as "directors and elders" (*zhengzhang* 正長). At this point, we read:

正長既已具，天子發政於天下之百姓，言曰：「聞善而不善，皆以告其上。上之所是必皆是之，所非必皆非之。」 (*Mozi* 11)[48]

When the directors and elders had been installed, the Son of Heaven broadcast his government to the Hundred Surnames of the world, saying: "If you hear of good or of evil, you must report it to your superiors. What your superiors affirm, you must all affirm; what they deny, you must all deny."

If you disagree with your superior's ideas of righteousness, you are wrong, because he is your superior and he was chosen for a reason. The warning is repeated at every level of the hierarchy. The village elders tell their subordinates, "What the district elder affirms, you must all affirm; what the district elder denies, you must all deny." The district elders, in turn, tell their subordinates, "What the lord of the state affirms, you must all affirm; what the lord of the state denies, you must all deny." The lords of the states, in turn, tell their subordinates, "What the Son of Heaven affirms, you must all affirm; what the Son of Heaven denies, you must all deny."

Other chapters confirm this hierarchy:

是故庶人不得次 [=恣] 己而為正，有士正之；士不得次己而為正，有大夫正之；大夫士不得次己而為正，有諸侯正之；諸侯士不得次己而為正，有三公正之；三公士不得次己而為正，有天子正之；天子士不得次己而為政，有天正之。 (*Mozi* 28)[49]

Thus the common people cannot institute what is correct on the basis of their own impulses; there are men-of-service to correct them. Men-of-service cannot institute what is correct on the basis of their own impulses; there are grandees to correct them. Grandees cannot institute what is correct on the basis of their own impulses; there are territorial lords to correct them. Territorial lords cannot institute what is correct on the basis of their own impulses; there are the Three Dukes to correct them. The Three Dukes cannot institute what is correct on the basis of their own impulses; there is the Son of Heaven to correct them. The Son of Heaven cannot institute what is correct on the basis of his own impulses; there is Heaven to correct him.

Ever mindful that people may mistakenly place the Son of Heaven at the top of the pyramid and thus forget that he too is only carrying out the august intentions of his superior,[50] the authors add this stern note:

天下之百姓皆上同於天子，而不上同於天，則菑猶未去也。今若天飄風苦雨，溱溱而至者，此天之所以罰百姓之不上同於天者也。(*Mozi* 11)[51]

If the Hundred Surnames of the world all conform upward to the Son of Heaven, and not to Heaven, then catastrophes will be as though unceasing. When, in these days, Heaven causes cyclones and bitter rain, [when these portents] arrive all together, this is Heaven's punishment of the Hundred Surnames for failing to conform upward to Heaven.

It is striking that no effort is made to justify *on its own merits* the standard of righteousness undergirding this tight system. By choosing the particular Son of Heaven that it did, Heaven seems to have declared, once and for all, the standard of righteousness that is to be valid for the entire human race.[52] If Heaven had privileged warlike skill over bringing benefit to the people, it would have selected some other champion as Son of Heaven, and we would have received radically different moral principles to live by. (It would not be hard to formulate the necessary argument: "How do we know that Heaven desires warlike skill? Master Mozi says: 'Because the strong dominate; the weak submit. Hence . . .'") To be sure, Mohists probably did not imagine a power comparable to Heaven but with a different moral orientation; from their point of view, obeying Heaven and practicing impartial love were two different ways of saying the same thing. Perhaps the clearest way to express the foundation of Mohist ethics, then, is to say that we must do what Heaven desires, lest we be punished, and it is a contingent fact that Heaven wants us to bring the greatest benefit to other people[53]—rather as the theological utilitarians argued that we must strive to make people happy because this is God's will.[54]

• • •

Another salient feature of Mohism, already discernible in the passages reviewed so far, might be called "intransigent optimism":[55] the sense that the universe never diverges from its just and beneficent pattern, because Heaven will always prevent undue phenomena from occurring. This is perhaps the most alien aspect of all: in effect, the *Mozi* declares that its arguments cannot be refuted empirically.

The clearest example of this sort of inflexibility is the Mohist theodicy, cited above: "If we do what Heaven desires, Heaven will surely do what we desire." This means that anyone who has contributed to Heaven's project of worldwide peace and prosperity will be rewarded with "fortune and lucre" (*fulu* 福祿), which all human beings desire; anyone who attempts to thwart the same celestial plan will be punished with "disasters and infestation" (*huosui* 禍祟), which all human beings hate. Not even when the text considers various likely rebuttals is there any hint of doubt that Heaven acts fairly and unfalteringly. Rather, the *Mozi* typically dilates on the famous examples of the sage kings Yao, Shun, Yu, Tang, and Wen and Wu, whom Heaven established as Sons of Heaven, and the deposed tyrants Jie, Zhòu, You, and Li, whose downfall Heaven likewise superintended.[56]

If one were to object to this theory by pointing to a good person who has had to endure disasters and infestation, there could be only three Mohist responses: (1) the person is not truly (or sufficiently) good; (2) the person has not truly endured "disasters and infestation"; (3) the suffering is only temporary, and Heaven will see to it that all injustices are redressed in the end. Ning Chen has discovered three such instances in the *Mozi*, and in each case the first argument carries the day: the person in question is found not to be virtuous enough to enjoy Heaven's favor.[57] But in general, the third response, as we shall see more fully below, probably comes closest to the Mohists' understanding of their own theory.

"Intransigent optimism" is also evident in the so-called Three Standards (*sanfa* 三法) or Three Gnomons (*sanbiao* 三表),[58] which I read as an attempt to work out a theory of truth.[59] In the context of an argument attempting to refute Confucianism on the (spurious) grounds that it advocates fatalism, *Mozi* says:

然則明辨此之說，將奈何哉？子墨子言曰：必立儀，言而毋儀，譬猶運鈞之上而立朝夕者也，是非利害之辨，不可得而明知也。故言必有三表。何謂三表？子墨子言曰：有本之者，有原之者，有用之者。於何本之？上本之於古者聖王之事。於何原之？下原察百姓耳目之實。於何用之？廢 [=發][60] 以為刑政，觀其中國家百姓人民之利。此所謂言有三表也。(*Mozi* 35)[61]

This being the case, how does one judge their propositions? Master Mozi said: One must set up a gauge. Speaking without such a gauge would be like determining sunrise and sunset on the basis of a spinning potter's wheel. One could never come to know clearly the difference between right and wrong, benefit and harm. Thus one must speak in accordance with the Three Gnomons. What is meant by the "Three Gnomons"? Master Mozi said: There is "verifying the root," "verifying the origin," and "verifying the utility."[62] How does one "verify the root"? One "verifies the root" in the affairs of the sage kings of old. How does one "verify the origin"? One "verifies the origin" by investigating the things that the Hundred Surnames hear and see. How does one "verify the utility"? Observe the benefit that [the proposition] would bring to the state, its people, the Hundred Surnames, and the populace if it were disseminated by being made into law. This is what is meant by speaking in accordance with the Three Gnomons.

Thus, according to Mohism, a proposition is valid if and only if it satisfies three criteria: (1) the sage kings practiced it in high antiquity; (2) ordinary people have practiced it in more recent times; and (3) it brings benefit to the world when it is made the law of the land. The text proceeds to subject the doctrine of fatalism—again, libelously attributed to Confucianism—to this threefold test and finds that it fails on all three counts. The sage kings did not believe that all things were foreordained; ordinary people do not normally act on such a belief either; and, most importantly of all, fatalism is dangerous because it would lead to moral apathy if people put their faith in it. (If people believed that their lot in life is decreed immutably, they would not strive to improve themselves and attain the manifold fortunes that proper behavior, in this moral system, reliably elicits.)[63] Thus fatalism is false.

Obviously, this theory is defective in many respects, but one of its most noticeable features is the indisposition to entertain the possibility that a proposition may satisfy some, but not all, of the three criteria. Whenever the *Mozi* brings the Three Gnomons to bear, the proposition under scrutiny invariably satisfies or fails all three tests at the same time. To some extent, this felicitous regularity is explained by fact that Mohists could not have conceived of sage kings who would have put false doctrines into practice. If the sage kings sanctioned a certain viewpoint, then, as far as Mohists were concerned, it must certainly have been both true and beneficial to society. Thus any proposition that passes Test 1 will necessarily pass Test 3 as well. But is it really credible that all beneficial notions must be true merely because they are beneficial? One could certainly appreciate the utility of having, say, a superhuman constabulary force monitoring all human action on earth, and indefatigably rewarding the good and punishing the wicked. For most modern minds, however, the utility of such a hypothetical power is hardly sufficient reason to suppose that it must exist.

Mohists, by contrast, were apparently convinced that anything beneficial to the world must exist, or at least be a realistic goal worth striving for. Take that same superhuman constabulary force. Mohists earnestly believed in it.

是故子墨子曰: 嘗 [=當][64] 若鬼神之能賞賢如 [=而][65] 罰暴也, 蓋本施之國家, 施之萬民, 實所以治國家、利萬民之道也。是以[66] 吏治官府之不絜廉, 男女之為無別者, 鬼神見之。民之為淫暴寇亂盜賊, 以兵刃毒藥水火退 [=追][67] 無罪人乎道路, 奪人車馬衣裘以自利者, 有鬼神見之。是以吏治官府不敢不絜廉, 見善不敢不賞, 見暴不敢不罪。民之為淫暴寇亂盜賊, 以兵刃、毒藥、水火退無罪人乎道路, 奪車馬、衣裘以自利者, 由此止,[68] 是以天下治。

故鬼神之明, 不可為幽閒、廣澤、山林、深谷, 鬼神之明必知之。鬼神之罰, 不可為富貴眾強、勇力強武、堅甲利兵, 鬼神之罰必勝之。 (*Mozi* 31)[69]

For this reason, Master Mozi said: If the principle that ghosts and spirits can reward the virtuous and punish the villainous were spread among the state and its families, and among the myriad people, it would surely be a way to put the state and its families in order, and benefit the myriad people. Thus when clerks in charge of the official treasury are not taintless and incorrupt, when men and women are promiscuous in their activities, the ghosts and spirits see these things. When the people practice licentiousness, villainy, brigandage, disorder, robbery, or banditry, whether with weapons, blades, poison, drugs, water, or fire; when they prey on innocent people on the highways; when they take other people's chariots, horses, clothing, or furs for their own benefit; there are ghosts and spirits who see these things. Therefore clerks in charge of the official treasury dare not be anything other than taintless and incorrupt: when they see goodness, they dare not fail to reward it; when they see villainy, they dare not fail to indict it. Practicing licentiousness, villainy, brigandage, disorder, robbery, or banditry, whether with weapons, knives, poison, drugs, water, or fire; preying on innocent people on the highways; taking other people's chariots, horses, clothing, or furs for one's own benefit—these will cease for the above reason and the world will be orderly.

Thus the percipience of the ghosts and spirits cannot be counteracted [by hiding in] dark recesses, broad marshes, mountain forests or deep valleys; the percipience of the ghosts and spirits will certainly know [where you are]. The punishment of the ghosts and spirits cannot be counteracted by means of wealth, rank, manpower, force, bravery, strength, military might, stiff armor, or keen weapons; the punishment of the ghosts and spirits will certainly overcome them.

Enduring cultural attitudes must have had some influence on the Mohist view of ghosts and spirits[70]—as noted above (p. 31), the idea that terrible spirits can exert their will in the sublunary world is traceable all the way back to the oracle-bone inscriptions of the Shang dynasty—but what is noteworthy, for our purposes, is that the belief in ghosts and spirits is defended here solely on the grounds that it is conducive to social justice. If people could be made to believe that their every action is viewed by the unimpeachable spirit police, they would be reluctant to practice evil.[71] A naysayer today might observe that the widespread belief in ghosts and spirits could have the same desired social consequences even if ghosts and spirits do not exist—in other words, that demonstrating the social benefit of such a belief is not sufficient to establish its truth.[72] But

Mohists did not approach logic in this manner. If it is beneficial, it must be true.[73]

The above is not the only argument for the existence of ghosts that the *Mozi* supplies. In accordance with the Three Gnomons, the chapter on ghosts goes on to recount numerous supposedly historical (yet utterly unverifiable) examples of their intervention in human affairs,[74] with the repeated refrain, "Seeing that the story is in several books, one can hardly doubt that ghosts exist" 以若書之說觀之, 鬼神之有, 豈可疑哉. The Mohist authors are confident that, by showing how the belief in ghosts and spirits satisfies all three of their criteria for truth, they have proved its veracity. But by this point, the barrage of appeals to the past comes almost as an afterthought. Readers familiar with the "intransigent optimism" of Mohist philosophy already know to expect detailed historical examples soon after the benefit of an idea is affirmed. Just as the doctrine of fatalism cannot be true because the world is better off when people do not believe in it, ghosts must exist because the world is better off when people do believe in them.

• • •

One last feature of classical Mohism needs to be discussed, a subtle point that is rarely appreciated in modern studies: Mohists must believe that Mohism is part of the celestial plan. Mozi, his teachings, and the work of his followers must all have a role to play in Heaven's dispensation of justice; otherwise the Mohist theodicy is incomplete. We recall that, throughout the core chapters, the text laments the selfish and destructive habits of men in power: "When large states attack small states, large lineages dislocate small lineages, the strong extort the weak, the many maltreat the few, the cunning machinate against the foolish, the noble overbear the base." But how are all these malefactors able to offend repeatedly without incurring Heaven's wrath? If the strong regularly extort the weak, why does Heaven allow them to remain strong?

The Mohist answer must be that people who do bad things are cementing their own doom, which is sure to come eventually. One of the most impressive achievements of Mohist philosophy, after all, is that it shows how exploitation is unprofitable because it ultimately harms even the exploiter. When the strong extort the weak, whatever temporary goods they expropriate will, in the long term, be outweighed by the damage that

they heedlessly bring upon themselves. But that self-inflicted destruction has not necessarily arrived yet. The Mohists may tirelessly recite
historical examples of felons who could not, in the end, avoid their just
deserts, but if there were really no injustice in the world—that is, no
cases where people were not immediately requited for their moral or
immoral behavior—there would be no need for Mohist philosophy in
the first place. Mohists must, therefore, have regarded themselves as
Heaven's instruments, their agenda of social justice as Heaven's way of
bringing about the sublime order in which all human beings are benefited
to the utmost.

While there is no direct evidence of Mozi's self-conception as Heaven's
emissary, the text relates his conviction that his work furthers Heaven's
will:

曰：義正者，何若？曰：大不攻小也，強不侮弱也，眾不賊寡也，
詐不欺愚也，貴不傲賤也，富不驕貧也，壯不奪老也。是以天下之
庶國，莫以水火毒藥兵刃以相害也。若事上利天，中利鬼，下利人，
三利而無所不利，是謂天德。故凡從事此者，聖知也，仁義也，忠
惠也，慈孝也，是故聚斂天下之善名而加之。是其故何也？則順天
之意也。(Mozi 28)[75]

It is asked: What is righteous government? I say: The large do not attack
the small; the strong do not abuse the weak; the many do not despoil the
few; the cunning do not deceive the foolish; the noble are not arrogant
toward the base; the wealthy are not haughty toward the poor; the hardy
do not take from the elderly. Therefore the many states of the world do
not harm one another with water, fire, poison, drugs, weapons, or blades.
When affairs are like this, Heaven is benefited above, the ghosts are benefited in the middle, and people are benefited below. All three are benefited, and no one is not benefited—this is what is known as the virtue of
Heaven. Thus whoever devotes himself to this is sage, wise, humane, righteous, devoted, magnanimous, kind, and filial; he garners the good names
in the world and attaches them to himself. What is the reason for this? He
proceeds along the course of Heaven's intention.

Inasmuch as Mozi teaches the large not to attack the small, the strong
not to abuse the weak, and so on, he is surely "proceeding along the
course of Heaven's intention" (shun tian zhi yi 順天之意).

If Mohists themselves were wary of claiming a Heavenly mission for their master, Mozi's later apotheosis as a Daoist immortal suggests that religious Daoists in the ensuing centuries were prepared to fill the gap.[76] Here is an excerpt from the biography of Mozi in *Biographies of the Spirit Immortals* (*Shenxian zhuan* 神仙傳), a collection attributed to Ge Hong 葛洪 (AD 283–343):[77]

墨子年八十有二，乃嘆曰：「世事已可知矣，榮位非可長保，將委流俗以從赤松遊矣。」乃謝遣門人，入山精思至道，想像神仙，於是夜常聞左右山間有誦書聲者。墨子臥後，又有人來以衣覆之，墨子乃伺之，忽有一人，乃起問之曰：「君豈山嶽之靈氣乎？將度世之神仙乎？願且少留。誨以道教。」神人曰：「子有至德好道，故來相候，子欲何求？」墨子曰：「願得長生，與天地同畢耳。」於是神人授以素書朱英丸方，道靈教戒、五行變化，凡二十五卷，告墨子曰：「子既有仙分緣，又聰明，得此便成，不必須師也。」墨子拜受合作，遂得其效。乃撰集其要，以為五行記五卷，乃得地仙，隱居以避戰國。至漢武帝時，遂遣使者楊遼，束帛加璧以聘墨子，墨子不出，視其顏色，常如五六十歲人，周遊五嶽，不止一處也。[78]

When Mozi was in his eighty-second year, he sighed and said: "From the affairs of the world it can be known that glory and status are not preserved for long. I shall renounce the vulgar rabble, and wander, following Master Red Pine." Thus he came to Mount Zhoudi, where he pondered the methods of the Way discriminatingly, imagining the spirit immortals. That night, there were several times when he heard the sound of someone chanting texts in the mountains to the left and the right. After Mozi had slept [for a while], a man approached, with robes [so long that they] covered his feet. Mozi watched and suddenly saw the man, so he got up and asked: "Sir, are you not the numinous *qi* of mountain peaks? Or a spirit immortal who has passed from this world? I would like you to stay a while, and instruct me in the essentials of the Way."

The spirit man said: "I know that you have superb virtue and fondness for the Way; thus I have come to wait on you. What do you seek?"

Mozi said: "I would like long life, so that I may perish only when Heaven and Earth do!"

Thus the spirit man transmitted to him the silk texts *Recipes for Pills of Vermilion Efflorescence*, *Instructions from the Numen of the Way*, and *The*

*Transformations of the Five Phases*—twenty-five bundles in all. He told Mozi: "You have the bones of an immortal;[79] in addition, you are keen of hearing and sight. Having obtained these [texts], you will be successful; you will not need another teacher." Mozi bowed and received [the texts] and did as they prescribed; having attained this experience, he set down their essentials in *A Record of the Five Phases*. He also obtained a mountain of earth, where he dwelt as a hermit in order to avoid the Warring States. At the time of Emperor Wu of Han (r. 140–87 BC), a herald named Yang Wei wrapped some silk and jade as an offering to Mozi, but Mozi would not come out. If one saw his visage, it was always like that of a man in his fifties or sixties. He wandered among the Five Peaks, never staying in one place.

This hagiography contains many anachronistic elements that disqualify it as a genuine Mohist text or a credible account of the school's founding father.[80] The authors may have admired Mozi, but they were not Mohists themselves in any philosophically meaningful sense. Nevertheless, the tale reveals the willingness of religious Daoists to see in Mozi a forerunner of their own belief system. The "spirit man" (*shenren* 神人—a term that we shall reencounter in *Zhuangzi*) declines to answer Mozi's questions about his origin, but we may infer that he is some kind of celestial emissary; otherwise he could not have possessed the miraculous texts that he transmitted to Mozi, let alone the authority to reveal them to a mortal. Only the purest human beings were ever granted such a theophany. Why would Daoist authors believe that, in the estimation of a "spirit man," Mozi was someone with "superb virtue and fondness for the Way" (*you zhide haodao* 有至德好道)? With the exception of Laozi himself, classical philosophers are rarely accorded such praise in Daoist literature. Nor is this an isolated instance: Daoist scriptures from various sects recognize Mozi as a revered immortal. Perhaps the most striking of these is *Arrayed Annals of the Lord of the Dao, Latter Sage of Shangqing* (*Shangqing housheng daojun lieji* 上清後生道君列紀), where Mo Di is named by the Sage Lord himself (the most elevated being to have any contact with humans)[81] as one of the twenty-four teachers sent down to instruct the chosen followers of the Way.[82] Not even Zhuangzi attained this honor.

A review of the basic Mohist beliefs may help us comprehend why Mozi is treated with such adulation in the *Daoist Canon*. Mohists held that Heaven is the most powerful entity in the universe, and that it exerts its will in the human realm by rewarding those who further its plan and punishing those who obstruct it. Heaven desires a society in which all human beings work for one another's benefit. Under these ideal conditions, there will be no injustice, poverty, or starvation, but hierarchical ranks will remain necessary, inasmuch as people are not equally talented, and a perfectly benevolent ruler needs to make the best use of the best men. Finally, Heaven employs a legion of demonic functionaries who travel unseen throughout the world; they observe all conduct, good or bad, and reward or punish people accordingly.

Is this not remarkably similar to the utopia described in the *Xiang'er Commentary to the Laozi*?

治國法道，聽任天下仁義之人，勿得強賞也。所以者，尊大其化，廣聞道心，人為仁義，自當至誠，天自賞之，不至誠者，天自罰之；天察必審於人，皆知尊道畏天，仁義便至誠矣。[83]

When the state is ordered and the *dao* taken as the standard, when the humane and righteous people of the world are installed in office, there is neither coercion nor reward. This is because people will become humane and righteous when moral transformation is revered and the mind of the *dao* is opened broadly. Those who, of their own accord, possess the utmost sincerity will be rewarded by Heaven; those who do not possess the utmost sincerity will be punished by Heaven. Heaven's scrutiny is surely more extensive than man's. It knows all who revere the *dao* and fear Heaven. Humanity and righteousness will thus be of the utmost sincerity.

As Stephen R. Bokenkamp has observed, "'Heaven,' in this case, is . . . a celestial bureaucracy modeled on the Dao."[84] Although there are many concepts in religious Daoism that find no analogue in *Mozi*—in particular, early Daoist religion espoused an incomparably more complex theodicy[85]—*Mozi* and the *Xiang'er Commentary* imagine the same kind of inegalitarian utopia with a stratified administration, staffed by righteous civil servants, ensuring that no one among the populace is abused or exploited. (It is not very different from the predominant sense of government's role in society in the People's Republic of China today.) Hence, despite our lack of information about the reception of *Mozi* in Han times, it is likely that members of the early Daoist sects regarded Mozi as the classical philosopher whose teachings were most like their own (again, disregarding Laozi, whom they took as a god, not a mere philosopher). Accordingly, they refashioned him as a Heavenly immortal and duly consecrated what they had collected of his writings by incorporating it in their own scriptural canon. Although readers of the *Mozi* today need not be bound by the worldview of Daoist masters, their response to Mohism is still valuable for providing a glimpse of how that philosophy was understood in late antiquity.[86]

In sum, the hermeneutic line that renders Mozi as "China's utilitarian" is a terrible simplification. The original motivation may not necessarily have been malice or chauvinism: the early Western interpreters of Chinese civilization were confronted with an avalanche of sophisticated literature, and they may have found it convenient to begin digesting it all by seeking out cultural elements that seemed to have a straightforward Western analogue.[87] But the deracination that is necessary to recast Mozi as an eccentric old Chinese utilitarian is no longer worth the cost today, when we have enough resources to try to understand what Mohism meant to people for whom it was a real philosophical option, not a relic of the distant past. Coming to grips with Mohism means coming to grips with its ghosts.

CHAPTER FOUR

# *Mencius*

Mencius is said by Sima Qian to have studied with Confucius's grandson, Zisi 子思 (483?–402? BC),[1] but the latter's dates make this unlikely. What is more probable is that Mencius, more than any other Chinese philosopher of the fourth century BC, was thought to have furthered the Confucian mission and thereby inherited the mantle of Confucius himself. In later centuries, Neo-Confucians regarded him as the last sage.

Mencius poses many of the same interpretive problems as Confucius. Mencius did not write the surviving repository of his teachings, the eponymous *Mencius*, which was compiled after his death and edited in its present form by Zhao Qi. Zhao reported that he took a text in eleven sections and eliminated four that he considered inferior, leaving the *Mencius* in seven books that we know today. One can only guess how different our conception of Mencius would be if we could read the parts that Zhao excised. (Throughout imperial history, opportunists tried to present some "newly discovered" text as the four lost books of *Mencius*, but these were always shown to be forgeries.)[2]

And once again there are few external sources that one can use to corroborate details of Mencius's life.[3] Like Confucius, Mencius was known mostly as a teacher who had audiences with some powerful rulers, but did not assume significant office himself. At times, he was criticized for inaction:

淳于髡曰：「男女授受不親，禮與？」

　孟子曰：「禮也。」

　曰：「嫂溺，則援之以手乎？」

　曰：「嫂溺不援，是豺狼也。男女授受不親，禮也。嫂溺援之以手者，權也。」

　曰：「今天下溺矣！夫子之不援，何也？」

　曰：「天下溺，援之以道；嫂溺，援之以手。子欲手援天下乎？」

(*Mencius* 4A.17)[4]

Chunyu Kun (fl. 320–311 BC) said: "Is it ritually correct that, when males and females give and take, they are not to touch each other?"

Mencius said: "That is ritually correct."

[Chunyu Kun] said: "If one's sister-in-law is drowning, does one extend one's hand to her?"

[Mencius] said: "One who does not extend [his hand] when his sister-in-law is drowning is a jackal or a wolf. It is ritually correct that, when males and females give and take, they are not to touch each other, but to extend one's hand to one's sister-in-law when she is drowning—that is *quan* 權 (i.e., disregarding an otherwise binding norm in exigent circumstances)."[5]

[Chunyu Kun] said: "Now the world is drowning; sir, why do you not extend [yourself]?"

[Mencius] said: "If the world is drowning, I extend the Way to it; if my sister-in-law is drowning, I extend my hand to her. Sir, do you want me to extend my hand to the world?"

Chunyu Kun, whom later writers often disparaged,[6] was hardly so barbaric as to suggest that one stand idly by while one's sister-in-law is washed away merely because the ritual codes proscribe physical contact between a man and his brother's wife. Rather, his purpose was to convey that the world is drowning, and that Mencius, who had a reputation as an admirer of ritual, might do well to abandon his devotion to such niceties and take some bold action.

Several statements attributed to Mencius in the book aim to shed light on how he conceived of his mission. First, there is his famous comment about his "flood-like *qi*" (*haoran zhi qi* 浩然之氣):

「敢問夫子惡乎長？」

曰：「我知言，我善養吾浩然之氣。」

「敢問何謂浩然之氣？」

曰：「難言也。其為氣也，至大至剛，以直養而無害，則塞於天地之間。其為氣也，配義與道。無是，餒也。是集義所生者，非義襲而取之也。行有不慊於心，則餒矣。我故曰告子未嘗知義，以其外之也。必有事焉而勿正，心勿忘，勿助長也。無若宋人然：宋人有閔其苗之不長而揠之者，芒芒然歸，謂其人曰：『今日病矣，予助苗長矣！』其子趨而往視之，苗則槁矣。天下之不助苗長者寡矣。

以為無益而舍之者，不耘苗者也。助之長者，揠苗者也。非徒無益，
而又害之。」(*Mencius* 2A.2)[7]

[The disciple Gongsun Chou 公孫丑 said:] "I venture to ask: wherein lie
your strengths, Master?"

[Mencius] said: "I know words. I am good at nourishing my flood-
like *qi*."

"I venture to ask: What do you mean by 'flood-like *qi*'?"

"It is difficult to say. It is the kind of *qi* that is greatest and firmest. If it
is nourished with uprightness and is not damaged, it fills in the space
between Heaven and Earth. It is the kind of *qi* that is the companion of
righteousness and the Way. Without it, [the body] starves. It is engendered by the accumulation of righteousness and is not obtained through
sporadic righteousness. If there is something in one's actions that does
not satisfy the heart, then [the flood-like *qi*] starves. Thus I say: Gaozi
never knew righteousness, because he considered it external. You must
take it as your duty and not let it out of your heart.[8] Do not let it out of
your heart, and do not 'help it grow.' Do not be like the man from Song.
There was a man from Song who was sorry that his sprouts were not
growing and pulled them up. He came home, appearing weary, and said
to his people: 'Today I am worn out; I have helped my sprouts grow.' His
son rushed out and went to look; the sprouts were all withered. There are
few people in the world who do not 'help their sprouts grow.' Those who
abandon them, thinking that they cannot [do anything to] benefit them,
do not weed their sprouts. Those who 'help them grow' pull up their
sprouts; not only are they not [doing anything to] benefit them—they are
also damaging them."

Gaozi was an older contemporary of Mencius, probably a Confucian of
a rival faction, with whom Mencius had an important debate that will be
analyzed further below.

This opaque passage has been the subject of much dispute, and there
can be no definitive interpretation, inasmuch as Mencius himself concedes that "flood-like *qi*" is difficult to explain. *Qi* will be discussed at
length in the appendix. Literally, it means "breath" or "vapor," but it was
used by most ancient philosophers as a generic term for matter: all material in the world is made up of *qi*. Further, *qi* was thought to come in

different qualities: tables or hammers are not capable of the same feats as sentient beings. The highest form of *qi* resides in human beings, but there too grades must vary, for some people seem to be inherently more talented than others.

In this discussion, Mencius departs from his contemporaries' understanding by stating that the method of cultivating *qi* lies in regular moral practice: "it is engendered by the accumulation of righteousness and is not obtained through sporadic righteousness." Before this, tending one's *qi* was usually understood as a bodily activity, such as calisthenics or meditation. For Mencius, by contrast, the secret is to accumulate righteousness day in and day out.[9] Morality is good for your health. In the *Analects*, Confucius does not make any claim remotely resembling this.

Moreover, Mencius's distinction between *engendering* flood-like *qi* by accumulating righteousness and trying *to obtain* it through sporadic acts highlights another characteristic theme in his philosophy: morality has to be made to grow naturally and cannot be seized like an external object. The closing analogy of the foolish husbandman who tried "to help his sprouts grow" drives the point home. We foster our morality by providing it with nourishing conditions and then letting it take root.

Mencius's second informative comment about himself comes in response to his disciple's observation that others deem him "fond of disputation" (*haobian* 好辯). Mencius's response was: "How could I be fond of disputation? I simply cannot avoid it." He saw himself as the defender of the Confucian tradition in the face of new heterodoxies threatening to overwhelm it:

楊朱墨翟之言盈天下，天下之言，不歸楊則歸墨。楊氏為我，是無君也。墨氏兼愛，是無父也。無父無君，是禽獸也。……楊墨之道不息，孔子之道不著，是邪說誣民，充塞仁義也。仁義充塞，則率獸食人，人將相食。吾為此懼，閑先聖之道，距楊墨，放淫辭，邪說者不得作。作於其心，害於其事；作於其事，害於其政。聖人復起，不易吾言矣。(*Mencius* 3B.9)[10]

The words of Yang Zhu and Mo Di swell across the world. [People's] words throughout the world find their home in Mo if they do not do so in Yang. Yang's [credo] is "For Me!"—there is no ruler in that. Mo's [credo] is "Universal Love!"—there is no father in that. To be without ruler or father is to be a beast. . . . If the ways of Yang and Mo are not quelled and the Way of Confucius not made manifest, then these heterodox propositions will delude the people and fully obstruct humanity and righteousness. When humanity and righteousness are completely obstructed, beasts will be led to eat people, and people to eat one another.

I am alarmed by this and defend the Way of the Former Kings. I resist Yang and Mo and banish their obscene statements, so that their heterodox propositions have no opportunity to intrude. If they intrude on [people's] hearts, they will damage affairs; if they intrude on affairs, they will damage the government. When a sage rises again, he will not alter my words.

Yang Zhu was a peripheral figure whose philosophy later scholars tried to reconstruct (mostly unsuccessfully), on the assumption that if Mencius mentioned him as one of the two great heretics in the world, he must have been an important philosopher. Suffice it to say that there are only three or four references to Yang Zhu in the entire surviving pre-imperial literature, all of them in partisan sources. What Mencius meant by "For Me!" as Yang's credo is not entirely clear, but it is usually taken to mean that Yang thought no action is worthwhile unless it benefits the self, and therefore would not help the rest of the world if it caused him any hardship.[11]

Mohism, on the other hand, is well understood, and we know why Mencius anathematized it: the notion that morality lies in denying special relationships among family members repelled him as contrary to nature itself. Mencius's full refutation of Mohist ethics appears in a discussion (through intermediaries) with a Mohist named Yi Zhi 夷之, who was trying to obtain an interview with him.

他日，又求見孟子。孟子曰：「吾今則可以見矣。不直則道不見，我且直之。吾聞夷子墨者，墨之治喪也，以薄為其道也。夷子思以易天下，豈以為非是而不貴也？然而夷子葬其親厚，則是以所賤事親也。」

徐子以告夷子。夷子曰：「儒者之道，『古之人若保赤子』，此言何謂也？之則以為愛無差等，施由親始。」

徐子以告孟子。孟子曰：「夫夷子信以為人之親其兄之子為若親其鄰之赤子乎？彼有取爾也：赤子匍匐將入井，非赤子之罪也。且

天之生物也，使之一本，而夷子二本故也。蓋上世嘗有不葬其親者，
其親死，則舉而委之於壑。他日過之，狐狸食之，蠅蚋姑嘬之。其
顙有泚，睨而不視。夫泚也，非為人泚，中心達於面目。蓋歸反虆
梩而掩之。掩之誠是也，則孝子仁人之掩其親，亦必有道矣。」
(*Mencius* 3A.5)[12]

On another day, [Yi Zhi] sought an audience with Mencius again. Mencius said: "Today I can see him. If I do not correct him, the Way will
not be apparent. So let me correct him. I have heard that Master Yi is a
Mohist. According to the Mohist precepts on funerals, sparseness is their
way. If Master Yi thinks that he can change the world with [such pre-
cepts], would he not consider them correct and would he not honor
them? But Master Yi buried his own parents richly, and thus served his
parents in a way that he considers base."

Master Xu told Master Yi about this, and Master Yi said: "According to
the Way of the Confucians, 'the ancients were as though protecting an
infant.' What does this refer to? To me, it means to love without differences of degree, but the practice [of love] begins with one's parents."

Master Xu told Mencius about this, and Mencius said: "Does Master
Yi really think that a person is as close to his elder brother's child as to his
neighbor's infant? What we can take from his [teachings] is this. If an
infant were crawling around and were about to fall into a well, this would
not be the fault of the infant. Moreover, when Heaven engenders creatures, it gives them one base, but Master Yi has two bases. This is the
cause [of his errors].

"In earliest times, there were those who did not bury their parents.
When their parents died, they carried them away and cast them into a
ditch. On another day, they passed by [and saw] that foxes and wildcats
had eaten [their parents' corpses] and that flies and gnats were gnawing
at them. Their foreheads became sweaty, and they glanced away so as not
to see. Now as for their sweat—it was not that they were sweating for
other people. The [emotions] of their innermost heart reached their faces
and eyes; they went home forthwith, and [came back] to cover [the
corpses] with overturned baskets and shovels. If covering them was indeed right, then, by covering their parents, the filial son and humane
person must also be with the Way."

What is meant by the "two bases" is not directly explained but probably refers to the fact that Yi Zhi espoused one set of views regarding appropriate burial customs, but then went ahead and buried his parents as his conscience guided him, even though this violated Mohist doctrine. In Mencius's view, Yi Zhi was well served by following his unstated impulses, since they were pushing him in the right direction: we love our parents and wish to bury them decorously because that is how human beings ought to feel. But it follows that we must abandon Mohism because it prescribes behavior incompatible with humane instincts.[13]

The notion that the bedrock of morality lies within natural human impulses is typical of Mencius[14] and informs his most important area of departure from Confucius: his theory of human nature. Mencius is famous for having argued that human nature is good, but his position is complex and requires careful unraveling. Mencius believed that all human beings are endowed by Heaven with what he called the "Four Beginnings" (*siduan* 四端)[15] of virtue. These are lodged in the heart (which was, we must remember, also taken to be the locus of mental processes, as we regard the brain today).[16] Mencius's proof is that on occasions where we are presented with a sudden and unforeseen moral crisis, and we have no opportunity to calculate how we should act (or how outsiders will judge us for acting), we unthinkingly act with compassion. His best-known illustration is the analogy of an infant about to fall into a well:[17]

今人乍見孺子將入於井，皆有怵惕惻隱之心，非所以內交於孺子之父母也，非所以要譽於鄉黨朋友也，非惡其聲而然也。由是觀之，無惻隱之心，非人也；無羞惡之心，非人也；無辭讓之心，非人也；無是非之心，非人也。惻隱之心，仁之端也。羞惡之心，義之端也。辭讓之心，禮之端也。是非之心，智之端也。(*Mencius* 2A.6)[18]

Suppose a person suddenly saw a child about to fall into a well. All people [in such a situation] would have a frightened, compassionate heart, not in order to ingratiate themselves with the child's parents, not because they want praise from their neighbors and friends, and not because they would hate to have the reputation [of one who would not save an innocent child].[19] From this we see: Whoever lacks a commiserating heart is not human. Whoever lacks a heart of shame is not human. Whoever lacks a heart of deference is not human. Whoever lacks a heart of right and wrong is not human. The heart of commiseration is the beginning of humanity. The heart of shame is the beginning of righteousness. The heart of deference is the beginning of ritual. The heart of right and wrong is the beginning of wisdom.

Even people with serious moral failings can be capable of impulsive demonstrations of compassion. King Xuan of Qi 齊宣王 (r. 319–301 BC), for example, was a repugnant monarch whom Mencius criticized on many counts, but Mencius pointed out that even he displayed his basic moral orientation at an unexpected moment:

曰：「臣聞之胡齕曰：『王坐於堂上，有牽牛而過堂下者，王見之曰：牛何之？對曰：將以釁鐘。王曰：舍之！吾不忍其觳觫，若無罪而就死地。對曰：然則廢釁鐘與？曰：何可廢也，以羊易之。』不識有諸？」

曰：「有之。」

曰：「是心足以王矣。百姓皆以王為愛也，臣固知王之不忍也。」

王曰：「然。誠有百姓者，齊國雖褊小，吾何愛一牛？即不忍其觳觫，若無罪而就死地，故以羊易之也。」

曰：「王無異於百姓之以王為愛也。以小易大，彼惡知之。王若隱其無罪而就死地，則牛羊何擇焉？」

王笑曰：「是誠何心哉？我非愛其財。而易之以羊也，宜乎百姓之謂我愛也。」

曰：「無傷也，是乃仁術也，見牛未見羊也。君子之於禽獸也，見其生不忍見其死，聞其聲不忍食其肉，是以君子遠庖廚也。」
(*Mencius* 1A.7)[20]

[Mencius] said: "I have heard that Hu He said: 'The King was sitting at the top of the hall. There was someone with a sacrificial ox passing by the bottom of the hall. The King saw him and said: What ox is that? The man answered: We are going to use it for a blood sacrifice with a bell. The King said: Leave it; I cannot bear its fearful expression. It is like that of an innocent person approaching the execution ground. The man answered: Then will you do away with the blood sacrifice and bell? The King said: How could I do away with that? Change it for a sheep.' I am not aware whether that happened."

[The King] said: "It happened."

[Mencius] said: "This type of heart is sufficient for a [true] king. The Hundred Surnames all thought that you begrudged [the expense of the animal], but I know surely that it was because you could not bear the sight."

The King said: "That is so. But there was indeed [an appearance] of what the Hundred Surnames supposed. Although the state of Qi is narrow and small, how would I begrudge one ox? Since I could not bear its frightened appearance—like that of an innocent person approaching the execution ground—I exchanged it for a sheep."

[Mencius] said: "Your Majesty, do not think it strange that the Hundred Surnames thought you begrudged [the expense]. When you exchanged a large [animal] for a small one, how would they know [the real reason]? If you felt compassion on account of its [appearance as] an innocent person approaching the execution ground, then what was there to choose between an ox and a sheep?"

The King laughed and said: "Indeed! What was in my heart? I did not begrudge the expense, but I exchanged it for a sheep. It was appropriate that the Hundred Surnames called me stingy!"

[Mencius] said: "Do not be hurt by it. [Your conduct] was an instantiation of humanity. You saw the ox; you did not see the sheep. With regard to beasts, the noble man [acts] as follows. When he sees them alive, he cannot bear to see them die. When he hears their sounds, he cannot bear to eat their flesh. Therefore the noble man keeps a distance from the kitchen."

Although most observers apparently thought the King merely wanted to economize by sacrificing a sheep instead of an ox, Mencius discerns that he insisted on saving the ox because he could not bear to see his "fearful expression," whereas the sheep, out of sight in its pen, had no direct effect on his emotions. Presumably, if the King had seen the sheep as well, he would have been unable to consign it to the blood sacrifice either.

The King becomes mightily self-satisfied when he hears Mencius's analysis of his conduct, asking how the philosopher could have known that his heart corresponds to that of a true king. Mencius immediately rebukes him:

曰：「有復於王者曰：『吾力足以舉百鈞，而不足以舉一羽；明足以察秋毫之末，而不見輿薪』，則王許之乎？」

曰：「否。」

「今恩足以及禽獸，而功不至於百姓者，獨何與？然則一羽之不舉，為不用力焉；輿薪之不見，為不用明焉；百姓之不見保，為不用恩焉。故王之不王，不為也，非不能也。」(*Mencius* 1A.7)[21]

[Mencius] said: "If there were someone who responded to you, saying: 'My strength is sufficient to lift a hundred *jun* (a unit of weight), but not sufficient to lift a single feather; my keenness of sight is sufficient to detect the tip of an autumn hair (i.e., an animal's new winter coat), but I cannot see a cartload of firewood,' would Your Majesty accept this?"

[The King] said: "No."

"Now your grace is sufficient to reach birds and beasts, but your merit does not extend to the Hundred Surnames—why indeed is this? In such a case, not lifting a single feather is a matter of not using one's strength; not seeing a cartload of firewood is a matter of not using one's keenness of sight. Not protecting the Hundred Surnames is a matter of not using your grace. Thus your Majesty is not a true king because you do not act as one; it is not because you are unable."

In other words, the basic impulse that Mencius has just praised as the foundation of morality is not morality itself. King Xuan has demonstrated not that he is a true king, but that he is capable of *becoming* one. As he is manifestly not a true king, he has failed only because he has not done what is necessary. If he is capable of treating sacrificial oxen with compassion, how much more appropriate would it be for him to treat his subjects with the same grace?

After enumerating the Four Beginnings of humanity, righteousness, ritual, and wisdom, Mencius intones the same warning:

人之有是四端也，猶其有四體也；有是四端而自謂不能者，自賊者也。謂其君不能者，賊其君者也。凡有四端於我者，知皆擴而充之矣，若火之始然，泉之始達。苟能充之，足以保四海；苟不充之，不足以事父母。(*Mencius* 2A.6)[22]

Humans have these Four Beginnings as we have our four limbs. To have these Four Beginnings and say that one is incapable [of developing them] is to make oneself into a brigand; to say that one's lord is incapable [of developing them] is to make one's lord into a brigand. Since we all have these Four Beginnings within ourselves, if we know to broaden them all and make them full, then it is like a fire beginning to blaze, or a spring beginning to rise up. If one can make them full, they will be sufficient to protect the Four Seas; if one cannot make them full, they will not be sufficient [even] to serve one's father and mother.

In line with his understanding of moral self-cultivation as constitutive of physical self-cultivation, Mencius asserts that the Four Beginnings are as fundamental to the human constitution as the four limbs. No one can claim that he or she lacks the Four Beginnings, for Heaven has endowed all of us with them.[23] The most we can say is that we have declined to develop them, and thus have allowed ourselves to devolve into evil.[24] We cannot pretend that we were born as "brigands" (*zei* 賊).[25]

Moral self-cultivation, then, is a matter of "extending" (*da* 達 or *tui* 推) the incipient virtue lying in each person's heart:[26]

孟子曰：「人之所不學而能者，其良能也。所不慮而知者，其良知也。孩提之童，無不知愛其親者；及其長也，無不知敬其兄也。親親，仁也。敬長，義也。無他，達之天下也。」 (*Mencius* 7A.15)[27]

Mencius said: "What people can do without having learned it is their innate ability; what they know without thinking is their innate knowledge. There are no young children who do not know to love their parents; when they have grown, there are no people who do not know to respect their elder brothers. To be intimate with one's parents is humanity; to respect one's elders is righteousness. There is no other [task] but to extend this to the rest of the world."

Thus, as A. C. Graham compellingly argued,[28] when Mencius claims that human nature (*xing* 性) is good, he means not that all people are necessarily good, not even that we are born good, but that we all have *the capacity to become* good—or, more strongly stated, that goodness is the state we are expected to attain if we are provided with the proper nurturing environment. For this is how Mencius consistently employs the keyword *xing*: the ideal state than an organism is expected to attain under the right conditions.

This nuance is crucial, because it underlies the entire discussion of *xing* in book 6A.[29] It begins with an exchange with Master Gao, who had a radically different understanding of the term: *xing* refers to all inborn faculties and impulses in an organism. "[Appetite for] food and sex is the *xing*" 食色, 性也, he said (*Mencius* 6A.4). Mencius objected:

> 告子曰: 「生之謂性。」
>> 孟子曰: 「生之謂性也, 猶白之謂白與?」
>> 曰: 「然。」
>> 「白羽之白也, 猶白雪之白; 白雪之白, 猶白玉之白與?」
>> 曰: 「然。」
>> 「然則犬之性猶牛之性, 牛之性猶人之性與?」(*Mencius* 6A.3)[30]

Gaozi said: "What is inborn is called *xing*."

Mencius said: "Is what is inborn called *xing* in the way that white is called 'white'?"

[Gaozi] said: "It is so."

"Is the whiteness of white feathers like the whiteness of white snow; is the whiteness of white snow like the whiteness of white jade?"

[Gaozi] said: "It is so."

"Then is the *xing* of a dog like the *xing* of an ox; is the *xing* of an ox like the *xing* of a human being?"

It was never clear to traditional commentators what Mencius accomplished in this exchange.[31] The recent discovery of the Guodian manuscripts reveals what was at stake. This corpus includes a text called *The Xing Emerges from the Endowment* (*Xing zi ming chu* 性自命出), which defines *xing* as the set of inborn characteristics shared by all members of a species.[32] The similarity of the Guodian manuscripts to philosophical views that can be tentatively ascribed to Master Gao has led some scholars to postulate a sectarian connection between the two. While this cannot be confirmed with the available evidence, it is clear that Master Gao adopted what must have been a commonplace definition, yet one that Mencius could not accept because of his own peculiar usage of *xing* as the ideal state that an organism should attain in a conducive environment. As far as Mencius was concerned, by asserting that "what is inborn is called *xing*" (*sheng zhi wei xing* 生之謂性), Master Gao effectively denied that there is a fundamental difference between human beings and animals. Animals, after all, desire food and sex as much as humans do, yet it would be intolerable to Mencius to declare their *xing* is the same as ours, because we do not have high moral expectations of animals. The Guodian manuscripts suggest, contrary to all subsequent orthodoxy, that it may have been Mencius's usage of *xing*, not that of Master Gao, that was considered eccentric in ancient times.

In the *Analects*, Confucius rarely discussed *xing*; indeed, according to Zigong, *xing* was one of the concepts that one could never hear Confucius speak of (*Analects* 5.12). In *Analects* 17.2—one of the suspiciously late sections—Confucius declares: "By their nature, people are close to each other. They grow distant from each other through practice" 性相近也, 習相遠也. This seems craftily worded so as not to be easily mapped onto the later spectrum of opinions about *xing*: it could mean, in line with Gaozi, that people are born with essentially the same faculties and desires, but then diverge because of habits and other forms of acculturation; or it could mean, in line with Mencius, that people are born with the same fundamental tendency toward goodness, but that not everybody does the necessary legwork to develop these roots into the flourishing state of goodness that Mencius wanted us to attain.

Thus readers are sometimes puzzled as to why Mencius devoted so much energy to caviling over definitions. Why not simply use uncontested terminology and avoid all the controversy? Two observations are in order. First, Mencius's debate with Gaozi represents a phenomenon that could not have occurred in Confucius's time: rival Confucian camps with mutually incompatible doctrinal stances. In the days of Confucius and his disciples, there was one living and unquestioned authority, whose philosophy each follower struggled to understand. Now, some two centuries later, the sole unquestioned authority was long dead, and opponents like Mencius and Gaozi could regard themselves as authentically Confucian and each other as regrettably misguided.[33]

Second, by redefining *xing* in his peculiar fashion, Mencius was able to cast human beings not as static objects with certain characteristics determined by birth, but as growing organisms constantly tending toward higher planes of moral awareness. He regarded humanity not as a matter of being, but as a matter of becoming, to use a Greek sort of distinction.[34] Mencius may have wanted to convey obliquely that, where moral development is concerned, human beings can never stand still.

The rest of book 6A is devoted to tying up the loose ends of the theory of *xing*. If we are all born with the Four Beginnings of virtue in the same way that we are born with four limbs, one might ask why some people become good and others do not.

孟子曰:「牛山之木嘗美矣。以其郊於大國也, 斧斤伐之, 可以為美乎! 是其日夜之所息, 雨露之所潤, 非無萌蘖之生焉, 牛羊又從而牧之, 是以若彼濯濯也。人見其濯濯也, 以為未嘗有材焉, 此豈山之性也哉? 雖存乎人者, 豈無仁義之心哉? 其所以放其良心者, 亦猶斧斤之於木也。旦旦而伐之, 可以為美乎? 其日夜之所息, 平旦之氣, 其好惡與人相近也者幾希。則其旦晝之所為, 有梏亡之矣。梏之反覆, 則其夜氣不足以存。夜氣不足以存, 則其違禽獸不遠矣。人見其禽獸也, 而以為未嘗有才焉者, 是豈人之情也哉! 故苟得其養, 無物不長; 苟失其養, 無物不消。」 (*Mencius* 6A.8)[35]

Mencius said: "The trees of Ox Mountain were once beautiful. Because it was in the suburbs of a great city, with axes and hatchets chopping at it, could it remain beautiful? With the respite afforded by the nights,[36] and the moisture of the rain and dew, it was not without buds and sprouts growing on it; but then the cattle and goats came to pasture there. That is why it is so bald. People see its baldness and suppose that it never had timber on it. Is this the *xing* of the mountain?

"Even what exists within human beings—are we without a heart of humanity and righteousness? The manner in which we let go of our good hearts is like axes and hatchets with respect to trees. If [the trees] are chopped down every morning, can they remain beautiful? With the respite afforded by the nights, and the [restorative influence] of the morning air, our likes and dislikes are close to those of other people. [But the power of this restorative process] is slight, and it is sequestered and undone by what takes place during the day. When this sequestering is repeated again and again, the [restorative] nocturnal airs are insufficient to preserve [our goodness]. If the nocturnal air is insufficient to preserve [our goodness], then we are not far from being unruly beasts. People see our bestiality, and suppose that there was never any ability[37] in us. Is this human *xing*?

"Thus, if it obtains its nourishment, no creature will fail to grow; if it loses its nourishment, no creature will fail to decay."

Note that, once again, the imagery is taken from the botanical world. Mountains may be lush or bald, just as people may be good or bad, but it is a mistake to assume that the mountain's *xing* is anything other than to be lush, for this is the state it would attain with the right "nourishment." Thus it is no refutation of Mencius's theory to point out that Ox Mountain is currently bald—or that some people are bad; Mencius's response is that Ox Mountain, like a bad person, has been denied its due "nourishment."[38]

But this is not wholly satisfactory as an answer to the question of why some people become bad, because it does not explain how some people are fortunate enough to enjoy a nutritive environment, while others are not. Moreover, unless people bear some responsibility for settling themselves in the right environment, one might wrongly infer from the parable of Ox Mountain that becoming good or bad is just a matter of luck. "I am not to be blamed," a criminal might proclaim; "I am simply a product of my deleterious circumstances." Mencius does not fail to undercut this argument in a discussion with another disciple:

公都子問曰：「鈞是人也，或為大人，或為小人，何也？」
　　孟子曰：「從其大體為大人，從其小體為小人。」
　　曰：「鈞是人也，或從其大體，或從其小體，何也？」
　　曰：「耳目之官不思，而蔽於物。物交物，則引之而已矣。心之官則思，思則得之，不思則不得也。此天之所與我者，先立乎其大者，則其小者弗能奪也。此為大人而已矣。」 (*Mencius* 6A.15)[39]

Gongduzi asked: "We are all equally human. Why is it that some of us become great people, and some become lesser people?"

Mencius said: "Those who follow their greater parts become great people; those who follow their lesser parts become lesser people."

[Gongduzi] said: "We are all equally human. Why is it that some people follow their greater parts, and some follow their lesser parts?"

[Mencius] said: "The organs of the ears and eyes do not think and are blinded by objects. When an object interacts with another object, it simply leads it astray. But the organ of the heart thinks. If it thinks, it obtains its [object, i.e., morality]; if it does not think, it does not obtain [its object]. These are what Heaven has imparted to us; if we first establish ourselves in the greater [parts], then the lesser ones cannot snatch [our attention]. To be a great person is nothing more than this."

The "greater part" is the heart, the "lesser parts" the sense organs (and perhaps other organs as well, such as the genitals). People who become good emphasize the greater part; people who become bad emphasize the lesser parts. But why do some people emphasize the greater part and others the lesser parts? Because those who emphasize the lesser parts are seduced by their own desires. Those who emphasize the greater part use the special function of the heart "to think"—Mencius always understands "thinking" (*si* 思) in a moral sense—and sincerely assess their own conduct. Most people cannot bear this degree of self-scrutiny and simply avoid asking themselves whether their behavior is truly reconcilable with morality; they must know, in their marrow, that the answer is no, but acknowledging this would force them to transcend the urges of their "lesser parts," which have thoroughly led them astray. Thus becoming good is not simply a matter of being born and raised in an environment that fosters our Four Beginnings; for if we find that our Four Beginnings have been devastated, we must, if we are to be honest, admit that we ourselves have had a hand in the devastation. In this respect, we are responsible for our own morality.

Mencius's conception of *xing* is essential to understanding his otherwise enigmatic pronouncements about "destiny" (*ming* 命):

孟子曰:「盡其心者, 知其性也。知其性, 則知天矣。存其心, 養其性, 所以事天也。殀壽不貳, 修身以俟之, 所以立命也。」

孟子曰:「莫非命也, 順受其正。是故知命者不立乎巖牆之下。盡其道而死者, 正命也。桎梏死者, 非正命也。」(*Mencius* 7A.1–2)[40]

Mencius said: "Those who exhaust their minds know their *xing*. If they know their *xing*, then they know Heaven. Preserving one's mind and nourishing one's *xing* is how one serves Heaven. Not being of two minds in the face of premature death or long life and cultivating oneself in order to await [one's fate] is how one establishes one's destiny."

Mencius said: "There is nothing that is not destined. One should compliantly receive one's proper [destiny]. Therefore those who know destiny do not stand by a precipitous wall. To die having exhausted the Way is proper destiny. To die in manacles and fetters is not proper destiny."

Recall that Mohists criticized Confucius and his followers for being fatalists: by declaring that everything was "destined" (*ming* 命), they argued, Confucians abandoned all hope of a theory of personal responsibility (p. 70). What Confucians before Mencius thought about *ming* is difficult to reconstruct (according to the *Analects*, at least, Confucius had little to say about *ming* other than that, as we have seen, his mission was sanctioned by Heaven). If we take Mencius's formulation, however, the Mohist charge is untenable. Mencius hardly agrees that a theory of *ming* has to be one of fatalism. Indeed, the very translation "destiny" can be misleading if we adopt the connotations of that word familiar from romantic literature and film (e.g., "The moment Algernon first mentioned to me that he had a friend called Ernest, I knew I was destined to love you").[41] To Mencius, destiny is not the fate that has been *predetermined* for us, but the exalted state that we are expected *to attain* through our own diligent labor. Our proper destiny is waiting for us, and if we fail to achieve it, we have only ourselves to blame.[42] We may have no control over our longevity or social status, but there is one thing we can do regardless of our lot in life: we can preserve our hearts, nourish our *xing*, and become moral paragons.

• • •

The best-known example of Mencius's belief in the rightness of basic human impulses is the parable of the baby about to fall into a well, but there are several others. In a difficult passage that is rarely discussed (*Mencius* 3B.10), Mencius and a friend consider the case of one Chen Zhongzi 陳仲子, a man so fastidious that he refused to live with his brother because he thought his brother's wealth was ill-gotten, and once even forced himself to vomit a meal that his mother had cooked for him because he considered the meat unclean. Mencius's judgment is that if Chen's principles were pushed to their logical extremes, only an earthworm could live up to them. Human beings, unlike earthworms, have certain natural relationships with one another, and violating them on account of the ideals that one has constructed for oneself cannot possibly be right. However high-minded you may be, if your scruples prevent you from living with your brother, and lead you to vomit your mother's food, you have been waylaid by your specious sensibilities.

Other examples bear on Mencius's political philosophy. A sustained discussion with the aforementioned King Xuan of Qi is centered on the idea that human desires are inescapable. The stage is set by a report by an otherwise unknown Zhuang Bao 莊暴, who tells Mencius that he was unable to respond when the King told him of his fondness for music. What the King meant, presumably, is that talking about morality may be fine for philosophers, but lovers of the good life revel in music and cannot be persuaded to reform themselves. Mencius tells Zhuang Bao that he should have built on this basic human trait of the King's by urging him to share his pleasure with his people. Then they would rejoice whenever they heard the distant strains of his music (*Mencius* 1B.1).[43] Eventually Mencius had his own audience with the King and asked why the King had not put good government into practice, if he applauded it in the abstract.

王曰：「寡人有疾，寡人好貨。」

對曰：「昔者公劉好貨，詩云：『乃積乃倉，乃裹糇糧，于橐于囊，思戢用光，弓矢斯張，干戈戚揚，爰方啟行。』故居者有積倉，行者有裹囊也，然後可以爰方啟行。王如好貨，與百姓同之，於王何有？」

王曰：「寡人有疾，寡人好色。」

對曰：「昔者大王好色，愛厥妃，詩云：『古公亶甫，來朝走馬，率西水滸，至于岐下；爰及姜女，聿來胥宇。』當是時也，內無怨女，外無曠夫，王如好色，與百姓同之，於王何有？」 (*Mencius* 1B.5)[44]

The King said: "I have a weakness; I am fond of wealth."

[Mencius] responded: "In the past, Gong Liu was fond of wealth. It is said in the *Odes*: 'He stocked and stored; he wrapped dry provisions in sacks and bags. Ah, he gathered in order to make [his people] eminent. With bows and arrows nocked, and shields, halberds, and axes brandished—then he commenced his advance.'[45] Those who stayed at home had stocked storehouses; those who advanced [with him] had sacks of wrapped [provisions]—only then could he 'commence his march.' Your Majesty, if you love wealth, but share it with the Hundred Surnames, what [damage] would this cause you?"

The King said: "I have a weakness: I am fond of sex."

[Mencius] responded: "In the past, King Tai was fond of sex and loved his consort. It is said in the *Odes*: 'Ancient Lord Danfu came in the morning, galloping his horse; he followed the banks of the western rivers until he came to the foot of [Mount] Qi. Thither he brought Lady Jiang; he came and tarried there, making it his abode.'[46] At that time, there were no frustrated girls within [the home], no bachelors abroad. Your Majesty, if you love sex, but share it with the Hundred Surnames, what [damage] will this cause you?"

The King cannot use his love of wealth and sex as an excuse not to partake of Mencius's program of moral cultivation; on the contrary, these urges only demonstrate his humanity (who does not love wealth and sex?) and should prompt him to extend his virtue throughout the domain by enabling his people to enjoy the same pleasures. Then he would be a king cherished by grateful subjects! Confucians never argued that desires are objectionable per se because one can hardly be human without desires; what is, however, subject to praise or blame is the manner in which one pursues those desires. King Xuan of Qi monopolizes his enjoyment of music, wealth, and sex, whereas a more enlightened ruler would provide the people with the means to enjoy them alongside him.[47]

Mencius never tolerates false pretexts or mere velleities when it comes to the serious business of moral self-cultivation.[48] If morality is your stated aim, you must pursue it with every ounce of energy; otherwise, you may as well acknowledge that you do not care enough to do more. When King Hui of Liang 梁惠王 (i.e., King Hui of Wei 魏, r. 370–319 BC) complains that he has "exhausted his heart" (*jinxin* 盡心) on behalf of his state, but his power has only decreased, Mencius compares him to a cowardly soldier who flees fifty paces on the battlefield, and looks down on others who fled a full hundred paces (*Mencius* 1A.3). When Dai Ying-zhi 戴盈之 (otherwise unknown) protests that it is bureaucratically inconvenient to reduce taxes before the following year, Mencius replies that this is like asking if it is all right not to stop stealing chickens until next year (*Mencius* 3B.8). And when King Xuan of Qi wishes to reduce ritually mandated mourning periods, and Gongsun Chou is inclined to allow this dereliction on the argument that observing an abbreviated mourning period is better than not observing any mourning period at all, Mencius's response is that this is like saying "Do it gently!" to someone who is twisting his elder brother's arm (*Mencius* 7A.39). Permitting such rationalizations only encourages people to destroy their own hearts, and a loyal minister must be his lord's unflinching moral guide (e.g., *Mencius* 1B.9).

• • •

Mencius's conception of government is similar to that of Confucius; the most important plank of his platform is that the purpose of government is the cultivation of morality—no more and no less. The best-known passage is the opening of the book:

孟子見梁惠王，王曰：「叟不遠千里而來，亦將有以利吾國乎？」
　　孟子對曰：「王何必曰利，亦有仁義而已矣。王曰『何以利吾國』，大夫曰『何以利吾家』，士庶人曰『何以利吾身』，上下交征利，而國危矣！萬乘之國，弒其君者，必千乘之家。千乘之國，弒其君者，必百乘之家。萬取千焉，千取百焉，不為不多矣。苟為後義而先利，不奪不饜。未有仁而遺其親者也，未有義而後其君者也。王亦曰仁義而已矣，何必曰利？」 (*Mencius* 1A.1)[49]

Mencius had an audience with King Hui of Liang. The King said: "Venerable man, you have not considered it [too] far to come here from a thousand *li* away; surely you will have some means to profit my state?"

Mencius responded: "Your Majesty, why must you speak of profit? Indeed, I possess nothing more than humanity and righteousness. If the King says: 'How can I profit my state?' then the grandees will say: 'How can I profit my family?' and the men-of-service and commoners will say: 'How can I profit myself?' Superiors and inferiors will wage war on each other for profit, and the state will be imperiled. In a state with ten thousand chariots, the one who assassinates his lord will be from a family with a thousand chariots; in a state with a thousand chariots, the one who assassinates his lord will be from a family of a hundred chariots. To have one thousand out of ten thousand, or one hundred out of one thousand, is not an inconsiderable [share],[50] but if one were to put righteousness last and profit first, they would not be satiated without snatching more. There has never been one with humanity who yet abandoned his family; there has never been one with righteousness who yet placed his lord last [in his list of obligations]. Surely Your Majesty should say: 'Humanity and righteousness, and nothing more!' Why must you speak of profit?"

When one considers that King Hui may well have been older than Mencius, yet still addresses him honorifically as "venerable man," one can imagine his surprise when Mencius takes him to task for what he presumably intended as a harmless formulaic greeting. But Mencius does

not permit misconceptions about the purpose of government, even for
the sake of courteous rhetoric. Government is about spreading humanity
and righteousness; it is not about profit seeking.[51] To the familiar Confucian affirmations of moral governance, Mencius adds a parallel argument:
it is prudent.[52] As before, the assumption is that ordinary people will
follow the lead set by their superiors, and if the King himself makes profit
seeking his principle of government, his subjects are sure to imitate him,
with hazardous consequences.[53] Who has the most to lose in a society
devoted to profit seeking, if not the King himself? Humanity and righteousness are useful virtues because a populace that has imbibed these
virtues will not depose its sovereign.

Mencius probably did not intend this appeal to prudence as disposi-
tive, but he did not underestimate its value in persuasion. Compare *Mencius* 6B.4, where Mencius objects to Song Keng 宋牼, a philosopher of
uncertain affiliation who intended to convince the Kings of Qin and Chu
to end their war because it would be profitable to do so. The language is
very similar to that of 1A.1:

曰：「先生之志則大矣，先生之號則不可。先生以利說秦楚之王，秦
楚之王悅於利，以罷三軍之師，是三軍之士樂罷而悅於利也。為人
臣者懷利以事其君，為人子者懷利以事其父，為人弟者懷利以事其
兄，是君臣父子兄弟終去仁義，懷利以相接，然而不亡者，未之有
也。先生以仁義說秦楚之王，秦楚之王悅於仁義，而罷三軍之師，
是三軍之士樂罷而悅於仁義也。為人臣者懷仁義以事其君，為人子
者懷仁義以事其父，為人弟者懷仁義以事其兄，是君臣父子兄弟去
利、懷仁義以相接也，然而不王者，未之有也。何必曰利？」
(*Mencius* 6B.4)[54]

[Mencius] said: "Sir, your aspiration is great, but your slogan is unacceptable. If you persuade the kings of Qin and Chu by means of profit, they
will recall the captains of their threefold armies because they are delighted
by profit; then the men-at-arms in the threefold armies will be pleased by
the ceasefire and will be delighted by profit. If you cause ministers to serve
their lords by embracing profit, if you cause sons to serve their fathers by
embracing profit, if you cause younger brothers to serve their elder brothers by embracing profit, then lords and ministers, fathers and sons, and
elder brothers and younger brothers will abandon humanity and righteousness and receive one another by embracing profit. There has never

been [a ruler] in such a case who did not perish. Sir, if you persuade the kings of Qin and Chu by means of humanity and righteousness, they will recall the captains of their threefold armies because they are delighted by humanity and righteousness; then the men-at-arms in the threefold armies will be pleased by the ceasefire and delight in humanity and righteousness. If you cause ministers to serve their lords by embracing humanity and righteousness, if you cause sons to serve their fathers by embracing humanity and righteousness, if you cause younger brothers to serve their elder brothers by embracing humanity and righteousness, then lords and ministers, fathers and sons, and elder brothers and younger brothers will abandon profit seeking and receive one another by embracing humanity and righteousness. There has never been [a ruler] in such a case who did not become a true king. Why must you speak of profit?"

In some respects, however, Mencius differed from Confucius. Whereas Confucius was content to let people die of famine, if necessary, in order to preserve trustworthy government (*Analects* 12.7), Mencius held that rulers need to promote the people's material welfare to a certain minimum standard for moral suasion to be practicable:

曰：「無恆產而有恆心者，惟士為能；若民，則無恆產，因無恆心。苟無恆心，放辟邪侈，無不為已。及陷於罪，然後從而刑之，是罔民也。焉有仁人在位，罔民而可為也？是故明君制民之產，必使仰足以事父母，俯足以畜妻子，樂歲終身飽，凶年免於死亡，然後驅而之善，故民之從之也輕。」(*Mencius* 1A.7)[55]

[Mencius] said: "Only a gentleman can have a constant heart without constant sustenance. In the case of the populace, if they have no constant sustenance, they will accordingly have no constant heart. And if they have no constant heart, they will indulge themselves and veer into intemperance; there is nothing that they would not do. To pursue and punish them after they have fallen into crime would be to ensnare the people. How could a humane man in [the ruler's] position ensnare the people? For this reason, in determining the sustenance of the people, an enlightened lord must cause them to have enough both to serve their father and mother, and to support their wives and children, so that in happy years they are always full, and in inauspicious years they escape untimely death. Only then do you drive them toward goodness, so that the people find it easy to follow you."

Without abandoning the characteristic Confucian concern for moral self-cultivation, Mencius evidently believed that it was ineffective to preach to the people about morality as long as they are routinely starved and mactated.

Lastly, a point that has been frequently miscast by modern readers who wish to portray Mencius as a kind of protodemocrat:[56] whereas Confucius had relatively little to say about the legitimation of rulers—a legitimate ruler is simply one who acts as a ruler should—Mencius had an intricate theory of Heaven's Mandate that also explained why succession did not always proceed from father to son:

> 萬章曰:「堯以天下與舜, 有諸?」
> 孟子曰:「否。天子不能以天下與人。」
> 「然則舜有天下也, 孰與之?」
> 曰:「天與之。」 (*Mencius* 5A.5)[57]

Wan Zhang said: "Yao gave the world to Shun—is this the case?"

Mencius said: "No, the Son of Heaven cannot give the world to another person."

"Then if Shun possessed the world, who gave it to him?"

[Mencius] said: "Heaven gave it to him."

Yao was a sage king who abdicated and handed over the throne to the virtuous commoner Shun, rather than to his own son. But in Mencius's view, Yao did not have the authority to make such a transfer himself; rather, it took place because Heaven sanctioned it. For the ruler does not possess his own kingdom; he is only stewarding it for the true owner, Heaven. Mencius elaborates: "Heaven does not speak but merely reveals itself through actions and affairs" 天不言, 以行與事示之而已矣. The Son of Heaven may recommend a worthy successor, but this candidate will not become the next Son of Heaven unless Heaven endorses him with unambiguous signs.

> 曰:「使之主祭而百神享之, 是天受之; 使之主事而事治, 百姓安之, 是民受之也。天與之, 人與之, 故曰: 天子不能以天下與人。」
> (*Mencius* 5A.5)[58]

[Mencius] said: "If you place him in charge of sacrifices and the Hundred Spirits enjoy them, this means that Heaven has accepted him. If you place him in charge of [terrestrial] affairs and the affairs are all orderly, if the

Hundred Surnames are at peace with him, this means that the people have accepted him. Heaven gave him [the demesne], and the people gave it to him too; thus I have said: 'The Son of Heaven cannot give the world to another person.'"

Although Mencius frequently reminds his interlocutors, as in the above passage, that a ruler's legitimacy is revealed through the approval of the people, failing to perceive that the approval of Heaven is always the true determinant would lead to grave misunderstandings—as in the next section, where Wan Zhang asks why abdication has gone out of favor as a method of royal succession:

萬章問曰:「人有言, 至於禹而德衰, 不傳於賢而傳於子。有諸?」
　孟子曰:「否, 不然也。天與賢則與賢, 天與子則與子。」
(*Mencius* 5A.6)[59]

Wan Zhang asked: "People have a saying, 'In the time of Yu, virtue decayed [as compared to Yao and Shun], for he did not transmit [the throne] to a worthy man, but transmitted it to his son.' Is this the case?"

　Mencius said: "It is not so. If Heaven gives it to a worthy man, it will be given to a worthy man; if Heaven gives it to [the ruler's] son, it will be given to his son."

Once again, Heaven's choice is discernible through the aggregate actions of the populace. As the passage goes on to relate, when Yu died, the people spontaneously paid homage to his capable son, Qi 啓, and not to the successor that Yu himself recommended, a worthy named Yi 益. As the first competent prince in several generations, Qi was not an unwise choice for the people to follow. But it is still necessary to distinguish the roles of Heaven and the people on a theoretical level, even if there are no cases in the *Mencius* where Heaven explicitly overruled the manifest will of the people. For a shortsighted or deluded populace may try to install a defective government that Heaven cannot ordain. Mencius would never contend that Heaven's hand would be forced in such an instance. On the contrary, he took pains to explain that Heaven's will lay behind all these developments:

舜禹益相去久遠, 其子之賢不肖, 皆天也, 非人之所能為也。莫之為而為者, 天也。莫之致而至者, 命也。(*Mencius* 5A.6)[60]

That Shun, Yu, and Yi served as ministers for differing periods, and that the sons [of Yao, Shun, and Yu] were of differing worth—this was all due to Heaven. It was not something that was done by human beings. When something is done though no one does it, it is due to Heaven; if something comes about though no one brings it about, it is due to the Mandate.

The unstated elements of Mencius's argument are at least as important as the explicit ones, for no one in Warring States times could pretend that all crown princes were as capable as Yu's formidable son Qi. Any critical reader would have to ask why Heaven permits petty and inept rulers to accede to the throne. (In *Mencius* 2B.13, the answer is simply: "Heaven does not yet wish to bring peace and order to the world" 夫天未欲平治天下也.)[61] If succession from father to son has become the norm in Mencius's day, that must be because Heaven now wills it. Abdication may have been viable in the past, but—as the disastrous episode involving Zizhi 子之 and King Zikuai of Yan 燕王子噲 demonstrated (*Mencius* 2B.8)—in the present it is mere folly.[62]

In accordance with his theory of Heaven's Mandate, Mencius distinguishes between the hegemon (*ba* 霸), or a warlord who rules by strength, and the true king (*wang* 王), or the Son of Heaven, who attains the genuine submission of the people by conquering their hearts:[63]

孟子曰:「以力假仁者霸, 霸必有大國。以德行仁者王, 王不待大, 湯以七十里, 文王以百里。以力服人者, 非心服也, 力不贍也。以德服人者, 中心悅而誠服也。如七十子之服孔子也。詩云:『自西自東, 自南自北, 無思不服。』此之謂也。」 (*Mencius* 2A.3)[64]

Mencius said: "One who uses force and stints on humanity is a hegemon, but a hegemon must have a large state; one who uses virtue to carry out humanity is a true king, and a true king need not depend on a large [domain]. Tang [became a king] with only seventy square *li*, King Wen with only a hundred. When one makes people submit by force, one does not make them submit in their hearts; [they submit only because] their own force is insufficient. When one makes people submit through virtue, they are delighted in their innermost hearts and truly submit, as the seventy disciples submitted to Confucius. When it is said in the *Odes*, 'From the West, from the East, from the South, from the North—ah, there was none who did not submit,'[65] this is what it refers to."

No one faced with a choice of submitting to a virtuous king or defending a coercive despot will ever choose the latter:

故曰域民不以封疆之界, 固國不以山谿之險, 威天下不以兵革之利。
得道者多助, 失道者寡助。寡助之至, 親戚畔之; 多助之至, 天下
順之。以天下之所順, 攻親戚之所畔, 故君子有不戰, 戰必勝矣。
(*Mencius* 2B.1)[66]

Thus it is said: "One does not confine the people with boundaries such as demarcated frontiers; one does not safeguard the state with escarpments of mountains and valleys; one does not overawe the world with the keenness of one's weapons and armor. One who has attained the Way will have many helpers; one who has lost the Way will have few helpers. The ultimate of having few helpers is to be betrayed by one's own kin; the ultimate of having many helpers is to be obeyed by the whole world. [A true king attacking a tyrant] will be one who is obeyed by the whole world attacking one who is betrayed by his own kin. Thus although there are times when the noble man does not fight, he is sure to win when he does."

In an interview with Lord Wen of Teng (fl. 326 BC), however, Mencius is forced to concede that, in certain extreme situations, even an admirable policy of morality cannot save a state from extinction. Wedged between the mighty states of Qi and Chu, Teng has little hope of survival, and Mencius thus counsels the beleaguered Lord Wen to act as a beacon to later generations:

滕文公問曰:「齊人將築薛, 吾甚恐。如之何則可?」
　孟子對曰:「昔者大王居邠, 狄人侵之, 去之岐山之下居焉。非
擇而取之, 不得已也。苟為善, 後世子孫必有王者矣。君子創業垂
統, 為可繼也。若夫成功, 則天也。君如彼何哉? 彊為善而已矣。」
(*Mencius* 1B.14)[67]

Lord Wen of Teng said: "The men of Qi are about to fortify Xue. I am very fearful; how would it be right to proceed?"

Mencius responded: "In the past, King Tai (the grandfather of King Wen and thus the ancestor of the House of Zhou) dwelled in Bin. The men of Di invaded [Bin], so he left it and dwelled beneath Mount Qi. It was not that he chose to do this, but he had no alternative. If you do good, there will surely be a king among the sons and grandsons of your progeny. In commencing an enterprise, a noble man suspends a thread that can be continued. Whether he succeeds is up to Heaven. My lord, what can you do about [the men of Qi]? You may do no more than exert yourself to do good."

Because it is Heaven, not man, who disposes, most of us do not have an opportunity to become kings. Lord Wen may be doomed, but not his line; if he leaves behind an admirable example, he may yet serve as an inspiration to unborn kings of the future. King Tai himself, after all, was not really a king; we call him "king" because he was a progenitor of kings.

PART II

Philosophy of the Way

# CHAPTER FIVE

# *Laozi*

*Laozi* is one of the few classical Chinese texts for which a theory of accretion might fit the facts. Currently, there is only one set of undisputedly pre-imperial *Laozi* texts: the so-called *Laozi* A, B, and C manuscripts from Guodian, each of which contains a small number of passages that are found, with some variation, in the Wang Bi recension.[1] There is very little overlap among the three Guodian texts, and, even taken together, they represent less than half of the Wang Bi recension, which comprises eighty-one brief chapters. There are two main theories attempting to explain this distribution: some scholars suppose that each of the three Guodian texts represents a set of selections from some larger, currently unknown edition, while others argue that the eighty-one-chapter text must be the endpoint of a long history of accretion, and that shorter texts like the manuscripts from Guodian represent snapshots of that process.[2] To be sure, these hypotheses are not mutually exclusive. The number eighty-one is probably not accidental: it is 9×9 and also the conventional length (in years) of a healthy life.[3] Thus even if the first hypothesis is correct, and the Guodian texts were indeed short anthologies drawn from a larger corpus, it is still likely that some later redactor had a hand in determining the length and organization of the text.[4] Nor do all extant versions share the same section divisions.

There are, in addition to the Guodian manuscripts, two short texts that may or may not be pre-imperial: the "Explaining *Lao*" ("Jie *Lao*" 解老) and "Illustrating *Lao*" ("Yu *Lao*" 喻老) chapters of *Han Feizi*. Chinese literati have long suspected that, despite their transmission, they should not be accepted as the work of Han Fei (whose philosophy will be treated in chapter 9).[5] "Explaining *Lao*" and "Illustrating *Lao*" provide politically minded comments on several passages, and their significance for the textual history of *Laozi* is similar to that of the three Guodian texts: we cannot tell whether they are selections from some longer text, or two further examples of the various shorter texts that eventually coalesced to become the eighty-one-chapter *Laozi*. Regardless of their authorship, "Explaining *Lao*" and "Illustrating *Lao*" survived, unlike similar texts that must have abounded, because of their unique interpretations.

It is frustrating not to be able to say more than the above, yet we can safely dismiss most traditional accounts of the text's genesis. A. C. Graham demonstrated many years ago that the manifold and contradictory tales about the supposed author, Lao Dan 老聃, reveal more about the competition among diverse ideological camps than they do about Lao Dan himself.[6] Like Homer and Hesiod in ancient Greece,[7] Lao Dan was a constructed figure, the details of whose life were tailored to suit later polemicists' intentions. Sometimes the name Laozi is construed as "Old Master," since the normal meaning of *lao* 老 is "old, venerable," but I suspect that Lao is a surname, and a certain Scribe Lao 史老, known as an adviser of King Ling of Chu 楚靈王 (r. 540–529 BC),[8] may be the dimly remembered historical figure (or one of the dimly remembered figures—perhaps there were several) who inspired the world-famous text. Scribe Lao was in the right place at the right time: as a member of King Ling's court, he was from Chu, where Laozi is said to have been born,[9] and he was probably an older contemporary of Confucius, just like Lao Dan. (This is not to say that Scribe Lao was necessarily responsible for any portion of the received *Laozi*.) Some later devotees, not content with attributing the text to a spurious savant of antiquity, held it to be no less than an avatar of Lord Lao (*Laojun* 老君), a god who chose to descend *in the form of a book* in order to spread his sublime doctrines on Earth.[10] Few philosophers believe this.

*Laozi* is placed at the head of part 2 of this volume because its philosophy marks a major turning point: the conceptualization of "the Way" (*dao*) as a cosmic principle. All the texts in part 1 use the word *dao*, but not nearly as frequently, and, crucially, without any cosmic connotations. In these earlier texts, *dao* usually means "right conduct, right course of action,"[11] but sometimes it refers to *any* habitual course of action, right or wrong. (In those contexts, *dao* was not very far from the Hebrew *halakhah*, Greek *hodos*, or Arabic *sharīʿah*, all of which were originally in the semantic domain of "road, path," just like *dao*.) We cannot be sure that *Laozi* was the very first text to use the word *dao* in its radically new sense, but the text is representative of intellectual trends that emerged around the fourth century BC[12] and whose significance was grasped almost immediately. Every subsequent text to be discussed in this book, regardless of its philosophical orientation, displays a deep familiarity with the traditions of *Laozi*. The strategy of this chapter will be to lay out a centrist interpretation of the text on the basis of the Wang Bi recension (though not, in the main, relying on Wang Bi's commentary), and then ask how much of this account needs to be adjusted in view of evidence from the Guodian manuscripts.

• • •

Let us begin with *Laozi* 38, which we saw in chapter 1 (p. 17): "The highest virtue is not virtuous; therefore, it has virtue" 上德不德, 是以有德. My suggestion there was that the keyword "virtue" must be taken in two different ways: "the highest virtue" is real and potent because it derives from the *dao* itself, whereas ordinary "virtue" refers here to the great sham that human society wrongly identifies as virtue. Thus the highest virtue has real virtue precisely because it is not the false virtue that everyone has been trained to venerate.[13]

The passage continues with an indictment of conventional (and conspicuously Confucian) values and self-appointed authorities. A "great man" (*da zhangfu* 大丈夫) conducts himself very differently from such fools:

故失道而後德, 失德而後仁, 失仁而後義, 失義而後禮。夫禮者, 忠信之薄而亂之首。前識者, 道之華而愚之始。是以大丈夫處其厚, 不居其薄; 處其實, 不居其華。故去彼取此。

Thus there is virtue only when the Way is lost; there is humanity only when virtue is lost; there is righteousness only when humanity is lost; there is ritual only when righteousness is lost. Ritual, a thin manifestation of loyalty and trustworthiness, is the fountainhead of disorder. Rash cognizance is but the flower of the Way, the starting point of foolishness. Therefore, the great man abides by the thick and does not dwell in the thin; he abides by the fruit and does not dwell in the flower. Thus he rejects one thing and chooses another.

Teachers advancing the cardinal Confucian virtues of humanity, righteousness, and ritual—we must imagine someone like Mencius[14]—are impugned for their "rash cognizance" (*qian shi* 前識), that is, their failure to comprehend that their ethical system is contrived and unnatural. The "great man" rejects this "thin" dwelling place and chooses instead the most profound source. But in this respect, he walks alone:

眾人皆有餘，而我獨若遺。我愚人之心也哉！沌沌兮！俗人昭昭，我獨若昏；俗人察察，我獨悶悶。澹兮其若海，飂兮若無止。眾人皆有以，而我獨頑似鄙。我獨異於人，而貴食母。(*Laozi* 20)

The multitude have abundance; I alone seem to be at a loss. I have the mind of a fool! Confused! The vulgar are shiny; I alone seem to be dim. The vulgar analyze; I alone am muddled. I bob, as though at sea; I drift as though without stopping. The multitude all have their means; I alone am mulish, like a boor. I am different from others; I value feeding from the Mother.

The Mother, as we will see shortly, is the Way.

The sustained assault on traditional values fuels some searing passages, such as *Laozi* 5:

天地不仁，以萬物為芻狗；聖人不仁，以百姓為芻狗。

Heaven and Earth are not humane; they treat the Myriad Creatures as straw dogs. The Sage is not humane; he treats the Hundred Surnames as straw dogs.

Confucians might be horrified to read that "Heaven and Earth are not humane"—one could scarcely imagine a dictate more antithetical to Confucian norms—but *Laozi* deftly invokes nature's capacity for cruelty to argue that Confucian virtues are not, in fact, immanent in the world around us. Heaven and Earth are not humane because "humanity" is a human concept, not a natural one. The "straw dogs" are probably accouterments at a sacrifice: they have an indispensable role at a certain juncture of the ceremony but thereafter are cast aside, as they have no further use.[15] Anyone who has seen an animal rent by predators in the wild knows what the text is trying to say. *Laozi* turns Confucian and Mohist naturalism on its head: if you really want to be just like Heaven, you will be pitiless.

The celebrated virtues, then, are an indication of *decline*. Only people who fail to grasp the dreadful truth of *Laozi* 5 would try to construct a comforting edifice of virtue upon virtue:

大道廢，有仁義；智慧出，有大偽；六親不和，有孝慈；國家昏亂，有忠臣。(*Laozi* 18)

When the Great Way declined, there were humanity and righteousness; when wisdom and cleverness appeared, there was great dissimulation; when the six cardinal relationships were no longer harmonious, there was filial kindness; when the state and its families were bedimmed and disordered, there were loyal ministers.

絕聖棄智，民利百倍；絕仁棄義，民復孝慈；絕巧棄利，盜賊無有。(*Laozi* 19)

If we abrogate sagacity and cast aside wisdom, the people will profit a hundredfold; if we abrogate humanity and cast aside righteousness, the people will return to filial kindness; if we abrogate craftiness and cast aside profit, there will be no robbers or bandits.

An openly acknowledged expository problem is that "the great man's" thicker source, which he chooses over the delusions of man-made virtue, is too profound to capture in mere words.[16] "Way" is a mere byname.

道可道，非常道；名可名，非常名。(*Laozi* 1)

A way that can be told is not the perduring Way. A name that can be named is not the perduring Name.

The wiseacres of the world may brandish keywords like *dao* and try to name everything under the sun, but they cannot be referring to "the perduring Way" (*changdao* 長道) when they do so, because the perduring Way defies description.

Occasionally one encounters the criticism that, after declaring the Way ineffable, *Laozi* proceeds to expatiate on it incessantly,[17] but this is unfair, as the text never succumbs to the fallacy of trying *to specify* the Way. Rather, its primary tactic is to hammer home the point that most people's beliefs are the opposite of ultimate truth because they thoughtlessly accept the fallacies of their society. Often the theme is the usefulness of "emptiness" (*xu* 虛), and "not having" or "nonexistence" (*wu* 無) as opposed to the more familiar values of "having" or "existence" (*you* 有):

三十輻共一轂，當其無，有車之用。埏埴以為器，當其無，有器之用。鑿戶牖以為室，當其無，有室之用。故有之以為利，無之以為用。(*Laozi* 11)[18]

Thirty spokes share a single hub; it because of the nonexistence (i.e., the hole for the axle) that a carriage is useful. One combines water and clay to make a vessel; it is because of the nonexistence (i.e., concavity) that a vessel is useful. One cuts out doors and windows in order to make a room; it is because of the nonexistence (i.e., the openings furnished by doors and windows) that a room is useful. Thus having something may be profitable, but not having something is useful.

Elsewhere in *Laozi*, the Way is presented as inexhaustible even though it cannot be tasted, seen, or heard. It seems to have no substantiality whatsoever, yet it is the most useful thing in the universe.

道之出口，淡乎其無味，視之不足見，聽之不足聞，用之不足既。 (*Laozi* 35)

When the Way emerges from one's mouth, it is insipid, as though tasteless. One may look for it, but that is not enough to see it; one may listen for it, but that is not enough to hear it; one may use it, but that is not enough to exhaust it.

In multiple chapters, the text revisits standard descriptions of the Way: it is nameless and inexhaustible; it is like a vessel, hollow yet useful; and it exemplifies traits that, in our ignorance, we denigrate rather than esteem:

明道若昧，進道若退，夷道若纇。上德若谷，太白若辱，廣德若不足，建德若偷，質真若渝。大方無隅，大器晚成，大音希聲，大象無形。道隱無名，夫唯道善貸且成。(*Laozi* 41)

When the Way is bright, it is as though dull; when the Way advances, it is as though retiring; when the Way is level, it is as though ragged. The highest virtue is like a valley; the greatest immaculacy seems disdained; the broadest virtue seems inadequate; the firmest virtue seems shiftless; genuine authenticity seems capricious. The greatest square has no corners; the greatest vessel is the last to be brimmed; the greatest tone has the slightest sound; the greatest image has no shape. The Way is hidden and has no name. Only the Way is adept at lending assistance to and perfecting [all things].

大成若缺，其用不弊：大盈若盅[19]，其用不窮。大直若屈，大巧若拙，大辯若訥。(*Laozi* 45)

The greatest accomplishment seems deficient, yet its uses never expire. The greatest fullness seems hollow, yet its uses are never exhausted. The greatest rectitude seems crooked; the greatest skill seems clumsy; the greatest eloquence is like stammering.

信言不美，美言不信；善者不辯，辯者不善；知者不博，博者不知。(*Laozi* 81)

Trustworthy words are not beautiful; beautiful words are not trustworthy. The good are not eloquent; the eloquent are not good. The wise are not learned; the learned are not wise.

In a very important chapter, the text recapitulates these themes and concludes with an inference that, by this point, readers are apt to have noticed on their own: "Correct words seem contrarian":[20]

天下莫柔弱於水，而攻堅強者莫之能勝，其無以易之。弱之勝強，柔之勝剛，天下莫不知，莫能行。是以聖人云，受國之垢，是謂社稷主；受國不祥，是謂天下王。正言若反。(*Laozi* 78)

There is nothing in the world softer and weaker than water, yet for attacking what is brittle and strong (i.e., rock), there is nothing that can surpass it. There is no substitute for it. There is no one in the world who is unaware that weakness overcomes strength and that softness overcomes hardness, but no one can put this into practice. Thus a sage would say: The one who accepts the filth of the kingdom is dubbed the proprietor of its altars; the one who accepts the inauspiciousness of the kingdom is dubbed the King of the World. Correct words seem contrarian.

As is typical of *Laozi*, these assertions are left for readers to interpret according to their own experience. The image of water "attacking" rock could evoke, for example, the unforgettable vista of a mountain canyon or, more mundanely, pebbles that have been flattened and smoothened by a river as perfectly as by the most meticulous sculptor. Both associations would be appropriate. And why is the King the one who accepts "the filth of the kingdom" and its "inauspiciousness"? Is it because filth is what we are taught to detest, yet, because we are learning that we must unlearn everything we have been taught, we must come to appreciate its value? Or is it because only someone who can embrace *all* the attributes of the body politic, whether beautiful or ugly, deserves to be the sovereign? Questions like these are always open for the reader to ponder. But the thrust is clear: the truth is the opposite of what you have been conditioned to accept. Rethink your assumptions.

Water is one of the text's favorite metaphors,[21] not only because it is soft yet potent, but also because it gathers in the lowest spots, which the ignorant rabble predictably misprize. Recall that in Confucius's famous simile, both mountains and rivers are praised, but mountains are unmistakably privileged (p. 40). This text admires water instead.

上善若水。水善利萬物而不爭，處衆人之所惡，故幾於道。(*Laozi* 8)

The highest adeptness is like water. Water is adept at profiting the Myriad Creatures without competing with them and abides in places that the multitude detest. Thus it is close to the Way.

Hence rulers, who have already been advised to accept what everyone else discards, would be wise to imitate the lowly yet inexhaustible rivers and seas:

江海所以能為百谷王者，以其善下之，故能為百谷王。是以聖人欲上民，必以言下之；欲先民，必以身後之。是以聖人處上而民不重，處前而民不害。是以天下樂推而不厭。以其不爭，故天下莫能與之爭。(*Laozi* 66)

Rivers and seas are able to be sovereigns of the hundred valleys because they are adept at placing themselves below them. Thus they are able to be sovereigns of the hundred valleys. Therefore, if a sage wishes to be above the people, he must place himself below them with his words; if he wishes to be foremost among the people, he must place himself behind them with his body. Therefore, a sage abides above the people, but they do not consider him burdensome; he abides in front of the people, but they do not consider him harmful. Therefore, the world takes joy in him and does not tire of him. Because he does not compete, no one in the world is able to compete with him.

If a sage can position himself as the people's waterway, they will love him because he will appear to nourish them without competing with them, and thus, painlessly, they will be induced to accept him as their suzerain.[22]

The political overtones are significant and will be considered in due course. But first it is necessary to review certain other themes in *Laozi*, starting with "nonaction" (*wuwei* 無為), which *Laozi* 43 juxtaposes to the familiar theme of weak water:

天下之至柔, 馳騁天下之至堅, 無有入無閒, 吾是以知無為之有益。
不言之教, 無為之益, 天下希及之。[23]

The softest thing in the world stampedes over the most brittle thing in the world; a thing with no substantiality enters [even where there is] no space. From these examples, we know the benefits of nonaction. Few in the world attain the wordless teaching and the benefits of nonaction.

Presumably, we can infer from previous passages that "the softest thing in the world" refers to water, once again methodically boring through rock. The "thing with no substantiality" (*wu you* 無有), that is, the Way, permeates the entire universe precisely because it is not subject to the ordinary limitations of matter. But what are "the benefits of nonaction" that so few know how to obtain?

Fortunately, other passages shed some light, especially by associating "nonaction" with another keyword, "spontaneity" (*ziran* 自然).

為者敗之, 執者失之。是以聖人無為, 故無敗; 無執, 故無失。民
之從事, 常於幾成而敗之。慎終如始, 則無敗事。是以聖人欲不欲,
不貴難得之貨。學不學, 復眾人之所過。以輔萬物之自然, 而不敢
為。(*Laozi* 64)

One who acts on a thing ruins it; one who holds a thing loses it. Therefore, the Sage does not ruin things because he does not act on them and does not lose things because he does not hold them. When people pursue their undertakings, they usually ruin things just as they are near completion. If one is as careful about the end as the beginning, one will not ruin one's undertakings. Therefore, the Sage desires what is not desired and does not prize rare objects. He studies what is not studied and returns to what the multitude have passed by. Because he assists in the spontaneity of the Myriad Things, he does not dare to act.

As *ziran* has served as a stock translation of the Western word "nature" since the nineteenth century, it is all too easily misunderstood in its original contexts. *Ziran* is indeed similar to "nature" in some respects, but with a fundamental connotation of noncausality.[24] Literally, *ziran* means "to be as it is [*ran*] of its own accord [*zi*]." The implied contrast is with a hypothetical phrase like *taran* 他然, which would mean "being as it is because some other force or entity caused it to be so."[25] We may be inclined to regard most things in the world as *taran*—that wall is the work of a mason; this book is the work of an author—but the Way, in its magnificence, does not rely on any external source.[26] Nor can we hope to create the Myriad Things, as the Way has done for us; from our perspective, they are effectively self-engendering, since we cannot bring them about ourselves. (Who planted the first tree?) Hence the most we can do is "assist" (*fu* 輔) in the cosmic processes.

常有司殺者殺，夫代司殺者殺，是謂代大匠斲。夫代大匠斲者，希有不傷其手矣。(*Laozi* 74)

There is always the Master Executioner to kill things. Killing in place of the Master Executioner is called hacking in place of the Great Carpenter. Of those who would hack in place of the Great Carpenter, few avoid injuring their own hands.

Do not try to do the *dao*'s work because you will be unable to achieve it;[27] worse, you will probably only hurt yourself. Applying this insight to his government of the world, the Sage rules not by trying to act on the world himself, but by being wise enough to foresee how the Way will act on it, and positioning himself accordingly. (As we will see in chapter 7, *Sunzi* applies a comparable approach to battlefield strategy.) In this manner, the Sage "achieves without acting" (*bu wei er cheng* 不為而成, *Laozi* 47). Similarly:

為學日益，為道日損。損之又損，以至於無為，無為而無不為。
(*Laozi* 48)

Those who perform their studies daily increase; those who perform the Way daily decrease. They decrease and decrease again until they reach the point of nonaction. Through nonaction, nothing is left undone.[28]

故聖人云，我無為而民自化。(*Laozi* 57)

Thus the Sage says: I will be without action, and the people will be spontaneously transformed.

是以聖人終不為大，故能成其大。(*Laozi* 63)[29]

Therefore the Sage, to the end, does not do great things, and thus he is able to achieve his great things.

The ideal of nonaction has two important implications: it entails a recognition of one's own limitations, of the fruitlessness of trying to proceed athwart the Way; and it offers the prospect of silently dominating everyone who does not grasp this philosophy.

• • •

Another one of *Laozi*'s characteristic inversions is to exalt "the Mysterious Female":

谷神不死，是謂玄牝，玄牝之門，是謂天地根。緜緜若存，用之不勤。(*Laozi* 6)

The spirit of the valley does not die; it is called the Mysterious Female. The gates of the Mysterious Female are called the root of Heaven and Earth. Filamented, it only appears to exist, yet it is used without exhaustion.

In interpreting this highly allusive passage, it is easiest to start from the end. We know from other passages that insubstantiality and inexhaustibility are two fundamental attributes of the Way, and thus "the Mysterious Female," whatever else it might connote, is, if not a byword for the Way itself, at least a closely related concept. No one really knows what "the spirit of the valley" denotes,[30] but valleys are, strikingly, the opposite of the Confucians' beloved mountains. Given a choice between concavity and convexity, *Laozi* will always choose concavity. And if "the gates of the Mysterious Female" make one think of a vagina, the image is probably apt, in as much as the Way is repeatedly portrayed as the great mother that bore the entire cosmos, including Heaven and Earth:

天下有始，以為天下母。既得其母，以知其子；既知其子，復守其母，沒身不殆。(*Laozi* 52)

The world has a beginning, which is to be considered the Mother of the world. Once you attain the Mother, you will know her children; once you know her children, if you revert to preserving the Mother, you will be without danger to the end of your life.

Accordingly, the famous and enigmatic cosmogony of chapter 42 narrates the generation of the cosmos as a process of miraculous differentiation, with the Way as the ultimate source:

道生一，一生二，二生三，三生萬物。萬物負陰而抱陽。

The Way bore the One; the One bore the Two; the Two bore the Three; the Three bore the Myriad Things. The Myriad Things bear *yin* on their backs and hold *yang* to their breast.

Like so much else in *Laozi*, the meaning of "the One," "the Two," and "the Three" are left entirely for the reader to unravel. Commentators furiously disagree with one another,[31] but my understanding is that "the One" refers to *qi*,[32] "the Two" to *yin* and *yang*,[33] and "the Three" to Heaven, Earth, and human society, with the Sage King at the top.[34] The last line provides a strong hint that all material things are to be conceived as manifestations of *qi* in its two complementary aspects, *yin* and *yang*. (For more on these concepts, see the appendix.) The Way, which exists at a metaphysical level anterior to materiality itself,[35] commences the chain of generation by "giving birth" (*sheng* 生) to the One, or undifferentiated matter. Notably, the Way does not "create" (*zuo* 作) or "fashion" (*zhi* 制) the cosmos; as the Mother, it "gives birth" to the cosmos. The One then begins to split, first into *yin* and *yang*, then into Heaven, Earth, and human society, until, at the endpoint of the progression, all the Myriad Things are produced.[36]

Describing the Way as "female" (*ci* 雌 or *pin* 牝, which normally refer to female birds and beasts, respectively) is a poetic device that serves multiple philosophical ends. First, whereas readers operating within Confucian and Mohist discourse would, as a matter of course, place the very masculine Heaven at the top of the cosmic hierarchy, *Laozi* proposes that Heaven itself was produced by something more mysterious, which we scarcely perceive because its existence is unlike that of any material object. What better method of dethroning Heaven—with all its demands, oppression, and self-assertion—than to present it as the child of a Mother that transcends time and space?

有物混成，先天地生，寂兮寥兮，獨立不改，周行而不殆，可以為天下母。吾不知其名，字之曰道。(*Laozi* 25)

There was something undifferentiated and perfect before the birth of Heaven and Earth. Silent and vast, it stands autonomous and does not change; it revolves without tiring; it is able to be the Mother of Heaven and Earth. I do not know its name; I style it "the Way."

Second, in order to emphasize that this nameless power is unlike anything that the reader is apt to have learned in school, the text resumes its contrarian diction: the greatest thing is not rigid and masculine; it is yielding and feminine. The image of sexual intercourse (implicitly the missionary position: male on top, female below) appears more than once:

天門開闔，能為[37]雌乎？ (*Laozi* 10)

In the opening and closing of the Gates of Heaven, are you able to act the part of the female?

大國者下流。天下之交，天下之牝。牝常以靜勝牡，以靜為下。
(*Laozi* 61)

A great state is a low-lying flow, the crossroads of the world, the female of the world. The female eternally overcomes the male through stillness. She lies below in stillness.

Naturally, such passages should not be misread as feminist in a modern sense.[38] Femininity is merely a productive metaphor. The "great man," whom we encountered above, is a man (*zhangfu* 丈夫).

● ● ●

After "The Way bore the One," chapter 42 takes up another important theme:

強梁者不得其死，吾將以為教父。

Those who are strong like a crossbeam do not attain [a natural] death. I will make this the father of my teaching.

Yet another advantage of being yielding and flexible is that one is likely to live longer. Strength, sturdiness, and rigidity, when subjected to contrarian deconstruction, are recast as harbingers of death:

物壯則老，是謂不道，不道早已。(*Laozi* 30)

When things become stiff, they are senescent. This is called "not in accord with the Way." What is not in accord with the Way comes to an early end.

Readers must think of rigor mortis. The human body is at its stiffest when it is dead.

By contrast, those who know how to accord with the Way seem to have a knack for avoiding predators and living long:

蓋聞善攝生者，陸行不遇兕虎，入軍不被甲兵，兕無所投其角，虎無所措其爪，兵無所容其刃。夫何故？以其無死地。(*Laozi* 50)

I have heard that those who are adept at managing life traverse the continent without encountering rhinoceroses or tigers, and enter battle without donning armor or weapons. Rhinoceroses have no occasion to launch their horns; tigers have no occasion to exercise their claws; soldiers have no occasion to use their blades. What is the reason for this? There is no terrain of death in such people.

Of all the imperfect Myriad Things, the one furthest from death is a newborn, who exemplifies many of the same traits as the Way:

含德之厚，比於赤子。蜂蠆虺蛇不螫，猛獸不據，攫鳥不搏。骨弱筋柔而握固，未知牝牡之合而脧[39]作，精之至也。終日號而不嗄，和之至也。(*Laozi* 55)

The bounty [that comes of] imbibing the power [of the Way] can be compared to an infant. Bees, scorpions, serpents, and vipers do not prick it;

wild beasts do not seize it; predatory birds do not snatch it. Its bones are weak and its sinews soft, yet its grasp is solid. It does not yet know the congress of female and male, yet its member is erect: it is the acme of vital essence. It can cry the whole day and without becoming hoarse: it is the acme of harmony.

Yet although health and long life are invariably praised, *Laozi* is careful not to hold out the prospect of immortality (unlike many later traditions).[40] Being "strong like a crossbeam" is bad because—just like trying to take the place of the Great Carpenter—it leads to an early death, but the proper alternative is *living out one's proper lifespan*, not trying to transcend it, as that too would be a failure to recognize and conform to the Way. (As we will see in the next chapter, the theme of accepting mortality is vividly expanded in *Zhuangzi*.) The goal is "to die without being obliterated" 死而不亡 (*Laozi* 33).[41]

Thus it is important to remember that although there are allusions to macrobiotic practices involving the manipulation of *qi*,[42] these are to be understood as exercises to maintain one's health, not as methods of attaining immortality.

載營魄抱一，能無離乎？專氣致柔，能嬰兒乎？滌除玄覽，能無疵乎？愛民治國，能無知乎？天門開闔，能為雌乎？明白四達，能無為乎？生之、畜之，生而不有，為而不恃，長而不宰，是謂玄德。(*Laozi* 10)

In regulating your *hun* soul[43] and holding the One to your breast, are you able to do it without ceasing? In concentrating your *qi* and bringing about softness, are you able to be a baby? In polishing your dark mirror (i.e., the mind), are you able to be without blemish? In loving the people and governing the state, are you able to be without wisdom? In the opening and closing of the Gates of Heaven, are you able to act the part of the female? In comprehending all within the four directions, are you able to perform nonaction? It bears them and rears them; it bears them without possessing them; it acts without relying [on anything else]; it leads without being masterful. This is called Mysterious Virtue.

• • •

The same chapter that upholds the goal of "dying without being obliterated," that is, immortality in the restricted sense of being remembered after one's death, also emphasizes the importance of knowing content-ment: "To know sufficiency is to be wealthy" 知足者富 (*Laozi* 33). Covet-ing more than one needs only leads to the misery of considering oneself poor.

富貴而驕，自遺其咎。功遂身退，天之道。(*Laozi* 9)

The wealthy and noble become arrogant, bequeathing calamity on them-selves. Retiring when one's work has succeeded is the Way of Heaven.

知足不辱，知止不殆，可以長久。(*Laozi* 44)

Those who know sufficiency are not disgraced; those who know when to stop are not endangered. They can live long.

Yet I do not think *Laozi* is encouraging the reader to become an ab-stemious hermit. The issue, rather, is the impact of social pressures on one's happiness (in modern times, this was brilliantly captured in the syndicated comic strip *Keeping Up with the Joneses*)[44]—and the possibility of manipulating them. "Knowing sufficiency," when conjoined with "eliminating wisdom," acquires troubling political dimensions: if "know-ing sufficiency" means teaching people to make do with whatever one allows them to have, and "eliminating wisdom" means preventing them from discovering more about the world, the result is a chilling political system in which the people are not even aware that their simple lives could be any different.

古之善為道者，非以明民，將以愚之。民之難治，以其智多。(*Laozi* 65)

Those who were adept at practicing the Way in the past did not enlighten the people, but made them ignorant. What makes the people difficult to govern is too much wisdom.

雖有舟輿，無所乘之，雖有甲兵，無所陳之；使民復結繩而用之，甘其食，美其服，安其居，樂其俗。鄰國相望，雞犬之聲相聞，民至老死不相往來。(*Laozi* 80)

Though there may be boats and carriages, there should be no occasion to ride in them; though there may be armor and weapons, there should be no occasion to deploy them. Make the people return to the use of knotted cords (i.e., life before writing) and think their food sweet, their vestments beautiful, their dwellings secure, and their customs delightful. Though they may gaze at the neighboring country and hear the cries of chickens and dogs coming from it, they should have no inclination to go hither and thither, until they grow old and die.

If making the people "think their food sweet, their vestments beautiful, their dwellings secure, and their customs delightful" calls to mind North Korea,[45] where much of the citizenry lives within range of South Korean airwaves, but is too terrified to inquire further, one can only wonder whether *Laozi* has, directly or indirectly, inspired the regime.

People who know better are the greatest danger to such a state, since they are the only ones who could pop the bubble of ignorance. Accordingly, the wise are to be cowed into silence:[46]

不尚賢，使民不爭；不貴難得之貨，使民不為盜；不見可欲，使心不亂。是以聖人之治，虛其心，實其腹，弱其志，強其骨。常使民無知無欲。使夫智者不敢為也。為無為，則無不治。(*Laozi* 3)[47]

If you do not esteem the worthy, you will cause the people not to contend with one another; if you do not value rare goods, you will cause the people not to steal; if you do not show them things they might desire, you will cause their minds to avoid disorder. Therefore, the government of the Sage is to empty their minds, fill their bellies, weaken their wills, and strengthen their bones. Always make the people be without wisdom and without desire; make the wise dare not to act. If you act through nonaction, nothing will fail to be placed in order.

This relentless autocratism is so vital to the worldview of *Laozi* that "the King" is written into the very structure of the cosmos:

故道大，天大，地大，王亦大。域中有四大，而王居其一焉。(*Laozi* 25)

Thus the Way is great; Heaven is great; Earth is great; and the King is great. Within the realm, there are four great things, and the King occupies one place among them.

If the Way produced the world we live in, it determined that there must be a King ruling over us, just as there must be Heaven above and Earth below.[48]

The implied reader of *Laozi* is a literate, solitary, and ambitious lord: the sort of person who might have the vision and wherewithal to put the dark teachings into practice and make himself a Sage King. The pointed lack of allusions to named persons and places—particularly noticeable in the context of classical Chinese literature, which abounds in them—conveys that the method of complying with the Great Carpenter is timelessly effective. The text merely has to wait for the right reader to discover it.

• • •

The foregoing has been, by and large, a mainstream reading of *Laozi*, though perhaps highlighting the political implications more than most, since I believe that whitewashing them would result in distortion.[49] Early imperial movements like Huang-Lao 黃老, which attempted to apply *Laozi*'s teachings to the business of statecraft and conquest, confirm that what most elites wanted out of the text was a handbook of domination. (We will return to Huang-Lao on p. 224.)

What remains, as promised in the opening pages of this chapter, is to ask whether our limited evidence regarding the earliest history of the text necessitates interpretive adjustments. The answer is: Not many.

Soon after the discovery of the Guodian *Laozi* manuscripts, it was observed that they do not contain the same mordant attacks on Confucian morality. The notorious slogan "Heaven and Earth are not humane" from chapter 5, for example, does not appear in any of the Guodian texts (or "Explaining *Lao*" or "Illuminating *Lao*," for that matter).[50] But they do contain chapters that portray the emergence of Confucian virtues as by-products of devolution from the spontaneous simplicity and authenticity of the Way.[51] The Guodian C version of chapter 18 is almost identical to the corresponding Wang Bi text, discussed above:

故大道廢，焉有仁義；六親不和，焉有孝慈；邦家昏亂，焉有正臣。[52]

Thus, when the Great Way declined, there were humanity and righteousness; when the six cardinal relationships were no longer harmonious, there was filial kindness; when the state and its families were bedimmed and disordered, there were upright ministers.

Guodian A opens with a significantly different version of chapter 19:

絕智棄辨，民利百倍；絕巧棄利，盜賊亡有；絕偽棄詐，民復孝慈。[53]

If we abrogate wisdom and cast aside discrimination, the people will profit
a hundredfold; if we abrogate craftiness and cast aside profit, there will be
no robbers or bandits; if we abrogate artifice and cast aside chicanery, the
people will return to filial kindness.

While it is noticeable that although Guodian A has the blander phrase
"artifice and chicanery" where the Wang Bi recension more provocatively
targets "humanity and righteousness," the former still advocates "abrogat-
ing wisdom," one of the cardinal Confucian virtues. Thus although the
wording of the Guodian manuscripts may not be as challenging, they
certainly evince antipathy toward received wisdom, with all its "discrimination" (*bian* 辨), as misguided rubbish that needs to be cleared away.
Yet the Wang Bi version is more arresting and hence more memorable.
Proposing the elimination of artifice and chicanery would hardly be controversial in any era. Proposing the elimination of humanity and righteousness, especially in the intellectual milieu limned in part 1 of this
book, marks one as an arch iconoclast.

Essentially the same pattern holds for all the distinctive themes of
*Laozi*: they are attested in the Guodian texts, but not as fully, and sometimes in gentler language. Neither the cosmogony of *Laozi* 42 nor the
description of the Way as "the mother of Heaven and Earth" in *Laozi* 52
appears in the Guodian manuscripts, but the theme is still present in the
Guodian A version of *Laozi* 25, which is almost identical (after palaeographical interpretation and transcription) to the Wang Bi recension:

有狀混成，先天地生。脫寥，獨立不改，可以為天下母。未知其名，
字之曰道。吾強為之名曰大。大曰逝，逝曰轉，轉曰返。天大，地
大，道大，王亦大。域中有四大焉，王處一焉。人法地，地法天，
天法道，道法自然。[54]

There was a form undifferentiated and perfect before the birth of Heaven
and Earth. Unapproachable and vast, it stands autonomous and does not
change; it is able to be the mother of Heaven and Earth. I do not know
its name; I style it "the Way." If I were forced, I would make the name

"Great" for it. Great means progressing; progressing means revolving; revolving means returning. Heaven is great; Earth is great; the Way is great; the King is also great. Within the realm, there are four great things, and the King abides in one place among them. People model themselves on Earth; Earth models itself on Heaven; Heaven models itself on the Way; the Way models itself on *ziran*.

Nor do the Guodian manuscripts include chapters 3, 65, and 80, with their ruthless vision of a populace undisturbed by the awareness that life is different in other domains, but their King still dwells in his reserved place, tranquil and immovable. In sum, the Guodian *Laozi* texts present a vision that, although inchoate, is already recognizable as a *Laozi* vision, only more disjointed and less compellingly phrased than the recension we have known for centuries. At the same time, they show why it is unacceptable to read *Laozi* as though it were the work of a single author, whether Lao Dan, Scribe Lao, or any other legendary genius.

# CHAPTER SIX

# *Zhuangzi*

Scarcely anything is known about Zhuang Zhou 莊周, and his name has been shown to be suspiciously meaningful.[1] Whereas, in most previous chapters, one of the necessary tasks of the exposition was to demonstrate the implausibility of a theory of single authorship, it is not necessary to build such a case for *Zhuangzi*, as virtually all serious scholars accept that it comprises layers of diverse origin and date.[2] Some chapters may be as late as the Han dynasty.[3] Since the twentieth century, there have been several attempts to identify the various strata and associate them with particular philosophical camps: syncretists, primitivists, and so on.[4] The details of each scheme vary, but there has been a rough consensus that the "inner chapters" (*neipian* 內篇, *Zhuangzi* 1–7) represent the closest surviving approximation of the work of Zhuang Zhou himself, while the "outer" (*waipian* 外篇, *Zhuangzi* 8–22) and "mixed chapters" (*zapian* 雜篇, *Zhuangzi* 23–33) are a grab bag of pieces by Zhuang Zhou's disciples, epigones, and enthusiasts.

Two strong objections to such reconstructions have been raised in print: first, their many postulated authorial groups might be figments, as they are not satisfactorily attested,[5] and second, statistical analysis reveals that ancient writers did not display a preference for the "inner chapters" when they cited *Zhuangzi*.[6] Rather, they seem to have regarded all sections as equally valid.

There is a third objection: the notion that the "inner chapters" are the most authentic is based on the dubious assumption that Guo Xiang, the redactor of the received text, would have been in a position to make such judgments, even though he lived some six centuries after Zhuang Zhou, and was himself relying on previous editions compiled by unknown hands applying unknown criteria (see p. 10). The most one can say is that the "inner chapters" comprise the material that Guo Xiang considered the philosophical core. They do, to be sure, contain some of the most complex and interesting passages. But to go beyond this is to deny Guo Xiang's role in shaping the text.[7]

Archaeological evidence suggests, furthermore, that earlier readers might not have shared Guo Xiang's taste. In contrast to *Laozi*, which lordlings evidently prized and wished to take with them to the afterworld, *Zhuangzi* was not commonly interred in tombs. (One reason is that *Zhuangzi* is less amenable to a ruler's purposes,[8] as we shall see.) Yet there are three significant finds. The oldest is a single strip from a miscellany unearthed at Guodian, which is very similar to a line in "Prying Open Valises" ("Quqie" 胠篋), one of the "outer chapters."[9] Next in age is a sequence of forty-four bamboo strips from Zhangjiashan 張家山 Tomb No. 336 (ca. 170 BC), which overlaps significantly with "Robber Zhi" ("Dao Zhi" 盜跖), one of the "mixed chapters." Lastly, a tomb at Shuang-gudui 雙古堆, dating to just a few years later, yielded many texts, including several strips that are said to be fragments of *Zhuangzi*—once again, mostly from the "outer" and "mixed chapters."[10] It is striking that the earliest finds represent the sections of *Zhuangzi* that modern studies have considered the *least* authentic.[11]

Accordingly, the discussion below will refer to relevant passages from the "outer" and "mixed chapters" without embarrassment. Indeed, in some cases, our understanding would be impaired without them. Moreover, the inquiry is delimited by a necessary recognition: what we find in *Zhuangzi* are repeatedly revisited philosophical *themes* rather than sustained and internally consistent philosophical *arguments*. With a text that contains material of diverse origin, covering a span of centuries, it would be unjustifiable to presume coherence.[12] While the range of themes is generally stable, we shall see that different passages often explore them in dissimilar ways.

The first theme is the relativity of perspectives, all of which are encompassed by the Way. The text, in Guo Xiang's recension, begins with a story about a very big fish. Or is it a bird?[13]

北冥有魚，其名為鯤。鯤之大，不知其幾千里也。化而為鳥，其名為鵬。鵬之背，不知其幾千里也。怒而飛，其翼若垂天之雲。是鳥也，海運則將徙於南冥。(*Zhuangzi* 1)[14]

In the Northern Darkness there is a fish whose name is Kun. Kun's size is such that no one knows how many thousand *li* [he extends]. He transforms into a bird whose name is Peng. Peng's back is such that no one knows how many thousand *li* [it extends]. When he is incensed, he takes flight, his wings like clouds hanging from Heaven. When the seas move, this bird begins to migrate to the Southern Darkness.

Just as we are being drawn into the story, there is a strange interjection: "The Southern Darkness is the Pool of Heaven" 南冥者, 天池也. How does this article of trivia help us understand the mind-bending nature of Kun and Peng (especially since "the Pool of Heaven" is scarcely less abstruse than "the Southern Darkness")? Perhaps the line is a stray bit of commentary that has been carelessly conflated with the main text, or perhaps it is written *to sound like* a stray bit of commentary, in order to highlight the inanity of all the names and allusions. Where *Laozi* refuses to join in the commonplace of larding one's text with references to historical personages and events, *Zhuangzi* undermines the rhetorical tactic by larding itself with patently absurd ones. No reader, however credulous, would be obtuse enough to believe that there *really* is an unimaginably big fish named Kun that turns itself into an unimaginably big bird named Peng. Be prepared, the tone seems to convey: there is a lot more parody and hilarity to come.

The text soon returns to the matter at hand and clarifies that although perspectives are relative, they can reflect "greater" (*da* 大) or "lesser" (*xiao* 小) wisdom. Too many people make judgments about the world on the basis of narrow experience:[15]

小知不及大知, 小年不及大年。奚以知其然也? 朝菌不知晦朔, 蟪
蛄不知春秋, 此小年也。楚之南有冥靈者, 以五百歲為春, 五百歲
為秋; 上古有大椿者, 以八千歲為春, 八千歲為秋。而彭祖乃今以
久特聞, 眾人匹之, 不亦悲乎! (*Zhuangzi* 1)[16]

Lesser wisdom does not measure up to greater wisdom; a lesser lifespan does not measure up to a greater lifespan. How do we know that this is so? Morning fungi do not know the new moon; *huigu* cicadas do not know the seasons. These are [creatures] of lesser life spans. South of Chu there is the *mingling* tree; it regards five hundred years as spring and five hundred years as autumn.[17] In high antiquity there was a great cedar; it regarded eight thousand years as spring and eight thousand years as autumn. Today, Ancestor Peng (i.e., the Chinese Methuselah) is especially well known for his longevity, and the multitudes try to match him—is it not pitiful?

The multitudes are so ignorant that they think of Ancestor Peng (not the same name as the Peng bird)[18] as a paragon of longevity. If they would only look more broadly, they would discover that his lifespan pales in comparison to that of the *mingling* tree or the "great cedar" of antiquity. They are small-minded and prejudiced, like the little quail who laughs smugly at the Peng bird:

斥鴳笑之曰：「彼且奚適也？我騰躍而上，不過數仞而下，翱翔蓬
蒿之間，此亦飛之至也。而彼且奚適也？」此小大之辯也。故夫知
效一官，行比一鄉，德合一君，而徵一國者，其自視也亦若此矣。
(*Zhuangzi* 1)[19]

A quail laughed at [the Peng bird], saying: "Where is he going? I go up by flitting and hopping and come back down after a few yards. I flutter around in the underbrush; this is indeed the pinnacle of flying! So where is he going?" This is the distinction between lesser and greater. Thus a man whose wisdom is valid for a single office, whose conduct is commensurate [to lead] a single township, whose virtue meets [the demands] of a single lord or enables him to be recruited for service in a single state will have the same kind of self-regard.

It is typical of *Zhuangzi* to begin with flights of fancy and then suddenly relate the action to the mundane discourse of Warring States moral and political philosophy. The Peng and the quail do not represent equally legitimate perspectives: the quail is like "a man whose wisdom is valid for a single office," a drudge with misplaced self-regard. The same pattern is apparent in another line that is chock-full of images:

井蟲不可以語於海者，拘於虛也；夏蟲不可以語於冰者，篤於時
也；曲士不可以語於道者，束於教也。(*Zhuangzi* 17)[20]

One cannot speak about the ocean with a frog in a well because it is confined to its own space; one cannot speak about ice with a summer insect because it is dedicated to its season; one cannot speak about the Way with involuted scholars because they are bound by what they have been taught.

If readers begin by wondering what is meant by "frogs in a well" (*jingwa* 井蠅), the text does not make them wait long for the answer: involuted scholars who are bound by what they have been taught—just the type that we "self-regarding" intellectuals are in danger of becoming.

But in other passages, the theme of the relativity of perspectives has different implications. The contrasts between the quail and the Peng bird, or Ancestor Peng and the great cedar, involve disparities on the same scale: the quail simply does not fly as far as the Peng bird; Ancestor Peng simply does not live as long as the great cedar. When different perspectives cannot be compared on the same scale, however, the judgment is usually that each one is appropriate in its own context, and none is unconditionally superior to any other.

民溼寢則腰疾偏死，鰌然乎哉？木處則惴慄恂懼，猨猴然乎哉？三者孰知正處？民食芻豢，麋鹿食薦，蝍且甘帶，鴟鴉耆鼠，四者孰知正味？猨猵狙以為雌，麋與鹿交，鰌與魚游。毛嬙麗姬，人之所美也；魚見之深入，鳥見之高飛，麋鹿見之決驟。四者孰知天下之正色哉？自我觀之，仁義之端，是非之塗，樊然殽亂，吾惡能知其辯！ (*Zhuangzi* 2)[21]

If people sleep while soaked, they will become paralyzed from the waist down, but is the same true of loaches? If they dwell in trees, they will tremble in fear, but is the same true of apes or monkeys? Which of the three knows the right dwelling place? People eat the meat of herbivores and carnivores; elk and deer eat straw; centipedes find the taste of garter snakes sweet; owls and ravens crave rodents. Which of the four knows the right taste? Apes like to take the female role with *bianju* apes; elk have intercourse with deer; loaches sport with fish. Mao Qiang and [Lady] Ji of Li (d. 651 BC) are what humans consider beautiful, but if a fish were to see them, it would plunge into [the water]; if a bird were to see them, it would fly aloft; if an elk or deer were to see them, it would bolt. Which of the four knows the right sexuality in the world? From my perspective, the beginnings of humanity and righteousness and the paths of right and wrong are bewilderingly confused and disordered. How could I know how to distinguish them?

The phrase "the beginnings of humanity and righteousness" (*renyi zhi duan* 仁義之端) looks like an allusion to, and hence an implicit attack on, the Mencian tradition[22] (see pp. 85–86). Confucians, it seems, are not good at seeing the world from anyone else's point of view.

Most distinctions that we make merely reflect our biases, which the Sage, like a free-swinging pivot, overcomes by recognizing *all* perspectives. Thus he encompasses all perspectives without being limited by any one of them—like the Way itself.

物无非彼, 物无非是。自彼則不見, 自知則知之。故曰彼出於是, 是亦因彼。彼是方生之說也, 雖然, 方生方死, 方死方生; 方可方不可, 不可方可; 因是因非, 因非因是。是以聖人不由, 而照之於天, 亦因是也。是亦彼也, 彼亦是也。彼亦一是非, 此亦一是非。果且有彼是乎哉? 果且无彼是乎哉? 彼是莫得其偶, 謂之道樞。樞始得其環中, 以應无窮。是亦一无窮, 非亦一无窮也。故曰莫若以明。 (*Zhuangzi* 2)[23]

All objects have a "that"; all objects have a "this." You cannot see it from "that," but you can come to know it with wisdom. Thus it is said: "That" emerges from "this," and "this" also accords with "that." This is to say that "that" and "this" are born at the same time. This being the case, we are living and dying at the same time, dying and living at the same time. Things are acceptable and unacceptable at the same time, unacceptable and acceptable at the same time. According with what is right [from one perspective] means according with what is wrong [from another]; according with what is wrong means according with what is right. Therefore, the Sage does not follow [such a course] but sheds light on the matter with Heaven. He indeed accords with "this," but his "this" is also a "that," and his "that" is also a "this." His "that" also unifies right and wrong; his "this" also unifies right and wrong. Consequently, does he really have a "that" and a "this"? Or does he have no "that" or "this"? When "that" and "this" no longer attain their opposites—we call this "The Pivot of the Way." Once a pivot is allowed [to swing] in a circle, it can respond endlessly. Its "right" is a single endlessness; its "wrong" is also a single endlessness. Thus it is said: Nothing compares to using insight.

This passage often bewilders Western readers—I suspect that it may have bewildered some classical Chinese readers as well, as the original phrasing is highly unusual—but it is merely a rational extension of the previous observations about the relativity of perspectives. Whether we call an object "this" or "that" depends on an adventitious criterion: our momentary proximity to it. I may speak of "this table," but if it is further away from you, you will naturally call it "that table." (Moreover, on some other day, located somewhere else, I might refer to the same table as "that table" as well.) The distinction says nothing about the table itself, which is a table regardless of who is looking at it. "Insight" (*ming* 明) seems to refer to a God's-eye perspective that only a Sage can attain: the recognition that the table is *both* "this" and "that."[24]

Sadly, most people make no attempt to attain this kind of "insight"; rather, they speciously discriminate on the basis of their position and frame of reference. The effect is that they literally do not see.

聖人懷之，眾人辯之以相示也。故曰辯也者有不見也。(*Zhuangzi* 2)[25]

The Sage embraces things; the multitudes discriminate and display [these discriminations] before one another. Thus it is said: Among those who discriminate are those who do not see.

The image of the multitude hopelessly entangled by its prejudices invites comparison with modern concepts such as cognitive bias, cognitive illusion, and categorical inflexibility.[26] Mirror imaging is a similar term from modern intelligence analysis: "If I were a Soviet dictator, what would I do?" might seem like a commonsense question to ask when reviewing inconclusive data, but it yields faulty inferences precisely because American intelligence analysts are *not* Soviet dictators: they do not have the same experiences, values, or aspirations. Mirror imaging is projecting one's own biases onto the rest of humanity, and consequently failing to interpret evidence properly.[27]

A holistic vision of all the nooks and crannies of the cosmos, akin to the Sage's "insight," is conveyed in an archetypal parable. Cook Ding[28] is carving beef for his lord, who marvels at the performance and praises Ding's "skill" (*ji* 技), a word that can be interpreted as a backhanded compliment, if not simply a churlish mischaracterization.[29] Then we read:

庖丁釋刀對曰：「臣之所好者道也，進乎技矣。始臣之解牛之時，所見无非牛者。三年之後，未嘗見全牛也。方今之時，臣以神遇而不以目視，官知止而神欲行。依乎天理，批大卻，導大窾，因其固然。技經肯綮之未嘗，而況大軱乎！良庖歲更刀，割也；族庖月更刀，折也。今臣之刀十九年矣，所解數千牛矣，而刀刃若新發於硎。
彼節者有閒，而刀刃者无厚：以无厚入有閒，恢恢乎其於遊刃必有
餘地矣，是以十九年而刀刃若新發於硎。」(*Zhuangzi* 3)[30]

Cook Ding set down his knife and replied: "What I love is the Way, which goes beyond skill. When I first started carving beef, all I could see was the ox. After three years, I would no longer see the whole ox. Now, I encounter it with my spirit and do not look at it with my eyes; my sensory organs and my wisdom have come to a stop, and my spirit proceeds as it wishes. I accord with the natural grain (lit.: matrix provided by Heaven): I strike in the largest fissures and guide [the knife] through the largest recesses. I follow its inherent structure. My skill is such that I never run through any joints, much less large bones! A good cook will change his knife every year because he cuts. An ordinary cook will change his blade every month because he chops. Now my blade is nineteen years old, and it has carved several thousand oxen, but the blade is as sharp as when it was first set to the whetstone. There are spaces within the nodes, and my knife is so sharp that it has no thickness. If you insert something with no thickness into an area with space,[31] then—how roomy!—the knife must have sufficient territory wherever it roams. This is why, after nineteen years, my knife is as sharp as when it was first set to the whetstone."

Ding avoids dulling his cleaver by letting the architectonics of the ox determine his cuts, rather than forcing some preconceived pattern onto it. The interpretations of the passage are understandably varied, but what seems to distinguish this breathtaking cook from an ordinary or even superior cook is his ability to "accord with the natural grain" (*si hu tianli* 依乎天理) and "follow [the ox's] inherent structure" (*yin qi guran* 因其 固然). Only in this manner can he keep from colliding with bones and tendons and thereby damaging his blade. Moreover, this ability is *acquired*: cooks with less experience and insight merely hack away, insensitive to the situation before them.[32]

• • •

The story of Cook Ding is the only example in the "inner chapters" of a topos that is considerably expanded in the "outer chapters": people who have "a special knack," in A. C. Graham's words.[33] These anecdotes do not all address the same philosophical themes. One of them deals with the familiar problem of ineffability:

桓公讀書於堂上。輪扁斷輪於堂下,釋椎鑿而上,問桓公曰:「敢問,公之所讀者何言邪?」

　公曰:「聖人之言也。」

　曰:「聖人在乎?」

　公曰:「已死矣。」

　曰:「然則君之所讀者,古人之糟魄已夫!」

　桓公曰:「寡人讀書,輪人安得議乎! 有說則可,无說則死。」

　輪扁曰:「臣也以臣之事觀之。斷輪,徐則甘而不固,疾則苦而不入。不徐不疾,得之於手而應於心,口不能言,有數存焉於其間。臣不能以喻臣之子,臣之子亦不能受之於臣,是以行年七十而老斷輪。古之人與其不可傳也死矣,然則君之所讀者,古人之糟魄已夫!」
(*Zhuangzi* 13)[34]

Lord Huan was reading a book in the upper part of the hall; Wheelwright Bian was chiseling a wheel in the lower part of the hall. Setting aside his mallet and awl, he ascended and asked Lord Huan: "I venture to ask what words you are reading, milord."

The lord said: "The words of sages."

[Wheelwright Bian] said: "Are the sages present?"

"They are dead."

"Then what you are reading, Sir, is just the dregs and specters of the ancients."

Lord Huan said: "How would a wheelwright be able to give a disquisition on what I am reading? If you can persuade me, then fair enough; if not, you will die."

Wheelwright Bian said: "I, your servant, look at it from my occupation. When I am chiseling a wheel, if I go too slowly, it will be sweet but unsound; if I go too quickly, it will be bitter, and [the spokes] will not fit into [their sockets]. Neither too slowly nor too quickly—I attain this [balance] in my hands and respond [as necessary] in my mind. My mouth cannot put it into words, but there is a knack to it that resides within me. I have not been able to explain it to my son, and my son has not been able to receive it from me. This is why, at the age of seventy, I still chisel wheels, as old as I am. The ancients and [the teachings] of theirs that cannot be transmitted are dead, so what you are reading, my lord, is just the dregs and specters of the ancients."

It is perilous for a book to attack the utility of books. Surely *Zhuangzi* does not mean that we should never read, for then we should never read *Zhuangzi*. (*A fortiori!*) The issue, then, is not reading, but the role of language in communicating ideas.[35] Language is but a tool, not the end in itself—although the continuously innovative language of *Zhuangzi* reminds us that its authors cherished and honed this tool. A passage in the "mixed chapters" puts it more explicitly: once you have used language to convey your meaning, set language aside. Its task is done.

荃 [=筌] 者所以在魚, 得魚而忘荃 [=筌]; 蹄者所以在兔, 得兔而忘蹄; 言者所以在意, 得意而忘言。吾安得忘言之人而與之言哉? (*Zhuangzi* 26)[36]

A trap is a means to catch fish; when you get the fish, you forget about the trap. A snare is a means to catch rabbits; when you get the rabbit, you forget about the snare. Words are a means to catch ideas; when you get the idea, you forget about the words. Where can I get someone who has forgotten about words, and share a word with him?

Other knack stories depict eccentric individuals whose authenticity lies in their readiness to flout norms of behavior:[37]

宋元君將畫圖, 眾史皆至, 受揖而立; 舐筆和墨, 在外者半。有一史後至者, 儃儃然不趨, 受揖不立, 因之舍。公使人視之, 則解衣般礴臝。君曰:「可矣, 是真畫者也。」(*Zhuangzi* 21)[38]

Lord Yuan of Song (r. 531–517 BC) wished to have some drawings made. His multitude of secretaries arrived and stood by after being received and bowing. They licked their brushes and ink; [they were so numerous] that half of them [had to stand] outside [the chamber]. There was one secretary who arrived last; he seemed indecisive and did not rush. After being received and bowing, he did not stand by; he proceeded to his lodging. The lord sent men to observe him and found that he had taken off his clothes and was squatting naked. The lord said: "He will do; this is an authentic draftsman."

All too many artists have endeavored to present themselves as non-conformists like the draftsman from Song.[39] I remember a painter at an outdoor exhibit in Manhattan who worked furiously in bare feet, as though her genius were too great to be confined by shoes.

• • •

"Among those who discriminate are those who do not see" is not the only claim in *Zhuangzi* that poor cognition stunts one's physical powers. Seeing through arbitrary distinctions is not just an intellectual exercise: someone who can overcome them is impervious to extremes of cold or heat. In the following dialogue, the famed recluse Jieyu 接輿 has told a dullard named Jian Wu 肩吾 about a distant being with spectacular abilities. Jian Wu initially dismisses Jieyu's words as preposterous but then confers with his wiser friend Lian Shu 連叔.

曰：「藐姑射之山，有神人居焉，肌膚若冰雪，淖約若處子，不食五穀，吸風飲露。乘雲氣，御飛龍，而遊乎四海之外。其神凝，使物不疵癘而年穀熟。吾以是狂而不信也。」

連叔曰：「然。瞽者无以與乎文章之觀，聾者无以與乎鐘鼓之聲。豈唯形骸有聾盲哉？夫知亦有之。是其言也，猶時女也。之人也，之德也，將旁礡萬物以為一，世蘄乎亂，孰弊弊焉以天下為事！之人也，物莫之傷。大浸稽天而不溺，大旱金石流土山焦而不熱。是其塵垢粃糠，將猶陶鑄堯舜者也，孰肯以物為事！」 (*Zhuangzi* 1)[40]

[Jian Wu] said: "[Jieyu said that] there is a spirit man who dwells on distant Mount Guye. His skin is like ice or snow, and he is as graceful and restrained as a maiden. He does not eat of the Five Cereals; he breathes the wind and drinks dew. He rides on clouds and *qi* (i.e., what we would call air), drives a flying dragon, and wanders beyond the Four Seas. His spirit is congealed, so he can cause creatures not to suffer from epidemics, and he can make a bumper harvest of grain. I thought this was crazy and did not believe it."

Lian Shu said: "It is so. The blind have no means to see shining patterns; the deaf have no means to hear bells and drums. And is it only in the physical body that there is deafness and blindness? They exist in wisdom, too; this applies to you, on account of these words of yours. Such a person [as the spirit that Jie Yu mentioned], with such virtue, takes the whole range of the Myriad Things and makes them one; the age begs for [deliverance from] disorder, but why would he corrupt himself with the affairs of the world? Nothing can harm such a person. A great flood may reach as high as Heaven, yet he would not drown; a great drought may melt metal and stone or scorch the soil and mountains, yet he would not be burned. One could mold a Yao or Shun from his very dust and dregs—why would he be willing to concern himself with ordinary things?"

Compare the fantastic description of the "Ultimate Person" (*zhiren* 至人), who also rides on clouds and *qi* and is unaffected by harrowing natural phenomena:

至人神矣！ 大澤焚而不能熱， 河漢冱而不能寒， 疾雷破山飆風振海而不能驚。 若然者， 乘雲氣， 騎日月， 而遊乎四海之外。 死生无變於己， 而況利害之端乎！ (*Zhuangzi* 2)[41]

The Ultimate Person is godlike. Great marshes might blaze, yet he cannot be burned. The Yellow River and the Han River might freeze, yet he cannot be made cold. Swift lightning might smash mountains; a cyclone might shake the seas; yet he cannot be alarmed. Someone like this rides on clouds and *qi*, mounts the sun and moon, and wanders beyond the Four Seas. Life and death effect no change in him, let alone the measures of profit and loss!

How much of this is to be understood literally? These passages are similar to (and probably inspired) later portrayals of "transcendents" (*xian* 仙), or beings who have learned how to overcome natural decay. Abstaining from the Five Cereals is a common detail.[42] In later hagiographical literature, this attribute is indeed meant literally: abstaining from grain becomes a hallmark of the insouciant immortal. In the *Zhuangzi*, where almost every word has a resonance beyond its literal meaning, abstaining from cereals symbolizes a broader theme: unwillingness to profit from domestication, since that would lead only to *one's own* domestication. Instead, an Ultimate Person seeks purer nourishment in wild and untamed nature. In ancient China—the epitome of agrarian society—refusing to eat cereals would be tantamount to rejecting the entire human economy.[43] To the mind of a peasant, this would be mad self-destruction, but an Ultimate Person, far from being handicapped by forgoing the fruits of civilization, is rendered immune to its corruption. Whereas men like Jian Wu, with their narrow horizons, are as good as blind and deaf, the awesome denizen of Mount Guye owns no worldly things but travels to heights and distances that the multitudes cannot even imagine.[44]

"Discrimination" is repeatedly singled out as a characteristic of people who are bonded to their finite perspectives, to an ingrained understanding of the world that has been distorted by socialization.[45] One who can cast off this stultifying dross is capable of feats that would appear as nothing short of miraculous to the unenlightened. Whether a sensation is apperceived as "hot" or "cold" depends on one's frame of reference; Jieyu's spirit, who takes the whole universe as his frame of reference, is unencumbered by such distinctions. He retains his integrity in the face of drastic stimuli because he refuses to discriminate between phenomena that moribund society regards as polar opposites. But his magical abilities are no less natural than any other human activity: they are accessible to anyone who makes the effort to transcend false dichotomies. What is *unnatural* is our confined and rapacious way of life. One price we pay for husbandry and profiteering is losing the ability to ride on clouds and *qi* and soar unscathed over blazing marshes. If one were to object, like Jian Wu, that this is "crazy" (*kuang* 狂)—nobody can *really* ride on clouds and *qi*—the text's response would be: "How would you know? You've never tried."

Even a drunkard exhibits some of the Ultimate Person's attributes, though in necessarily limited form:

夫醉者之墜車，雖疾不死。骨節與人同而犯害與人異，其神全也，乘亦不知也，墜亦不知也，死生驚懼不入乎其胷中，是故遻物而不慴。彼得全於酒而猶若是，而況得全於天乎？ (*Zhuangzi* 19)[46]

When a drunkard falls out of a carriage, [his injuries] may be dire,[47] but he will not die. His bones and sinews are like those of others, but his [ability] to withstand harm is different because his spirit is intact. He is unaware of whether he is still riding or falling out; the alarm and apprehension of life or death do not enter his breast. Therefore, he meets objects without fear. If one who attains intactness through liquor is like this, how much more [wondrous] are those who attain intactness through Heaven?

The multitudes should be chastened to learn that their state of consciousness is inferior to that of a drunkard who cannot even tell whether he is riding in a carriage or falling out of it.

• • •

Rejecting specious distinctions and accepting all things requires equanimity in the face of death. Clinging to life would betray an inability to recognize that life and death are interdependent. (Recall that "we are living and dying at the same time, dying and living at the same time" 方生方死, 方死方生.) In one of the "outer chapters," the figure of Zhuangzi applies this sober reasoning to the death of his own wife, scandalizing his more traditional friend, Hui Shi:[48]

> 莊子妻死，惠子弔之，莊子則方箕踞鼓盆而歌。
>
> 惠子曰：「與人居，長子老身，死不哭亦足矣，又鼓盆而歌，不亦甚乎！」
>
> 莊子曰：「不然。是其始死也，我獨何能無概然！察其始而本無生，非徒無生也，而本無形，非徒無形也，而本無氣。雜乎芒芴之間，變而有氣，氣變而有形，形變而有生，今又變而之死，是相與為春秋冬夏四時行也。人且偃然寢於巨室，而我噭噭然隨而哭之，自以為不通乎命，故止也。」 (*Zhuangzi* 18)[49]

Master Zhuang's wife died. When Master Hui came to console him, Master Zhuang was sitting with his legs splayed like a winnowing basket (i.e., squatting informally);[50] he was banging on a basin and singing.

Master Hui said: "You lived with her; she raised your children and grew old. Now that she is dead, it is enough that you do not weep for her; but banging on a basin and singing—is this not extreme?"

Master Zhuang said: "It is not so. When she first died, how indeed could I not have been melancholy? But I considered that in the beginning, she was without life; not only was she without life, but she was originally without form; not only was she without form, but she was originally without *qi*. In the midst of mixing with cloud and blur, there was a change, and there was *qi*; the *qi* changed, and there was form; the form changed, and there was life; and now there is another change, and there is death.[51] This is the same as the progression of the four seasons, spring, autumn, summer, winter. Moreover, she sleeps now, reclining in a giant chamber; if I were to have accompanied her, weeping and wailing, I would have considered myself ignorant of destiny. So I stopped."

Mourning is irrational because Zhuangzi's wife's death not only is inevitable but is caused by the same cosmic transformations that originally brought about her very life. To love his wife entails accepting her death as another one of the world's mysterious processes, and our unreflective differentiation between "life" and "death" is shown to be one of those artificial distinctions that the text loves to discredit.[52]

Similar views are expressed in the "inner chapters" as well. Four illustrious (and, needless to say, thoroughly fictitious) gentlemen make a pact: "Whoever knows that death, life, existence, and nonexistence are one body—we will be friends with him" 孰知生死存亡之一體者，吾與之友矣. Soon one of the four, Ziyu 子輿, is racked with a disfiguring disease, and his friend Zisi 子祀 comes to visit him:

子祀曰：「女惡之乎？」

曰：「亡，予何惡！浸假而化予之左臂以為雞，予因以求時夜；浸假而化予之右臂以為彈，予因以求鴞炙；浸假而化予之尻以為輪，以神為馬，予因而乘之，豈更駕哉！且夫得者，時也，失者，順也；安時而處順，哀樂不能入也。此古之所謂縣解也，而不能自解者，物有結之。且夫物不勝天久矣，吾又何惡焉！」(*Zhuangzi* 6)[53]

Zisi said: "Do you detest it?"

[Ziyu] said: "No, how could I detest it? Suppose my left arm were transformed into a rooster; I would comply and keep track of the time of night. Suppose my right arm were transformed into a crossbow; I would comply and look for an owl to roast. Suppose my buttocks were transformed into wheels and my spirit into a horse; I would comply and ride—why would I ever need a car? Moreover, what we obtain, we obtain because it is the right time; what we lose, we lose because of the flow. If we are at peace with our time and dwell in the flow, sorrow and joy cannot enter into us. This is what the ancients called 'unencumbered.' Those who are unable to release themselves are tied down by objects. Moreover, things do not last longer than Heaven. So why should I detest it?"

Suddenly, a third friend, Zilai 子來, falls deathly ill as well, and says:

今之大冶鑄金，金踊躍曰：「我且必為鏌鋣」，大冶必以為不祥之金。
今一犯人之形，而曰：「人耳人耳」，夫造化者必以為不祥之人。今
一以天地為大鑪，以造化為大冶，惡乎往而不可哉！成然寐，蘧然
覺。(*Zhuangzi* 6)[54]

Suppose there were a great smith smelting metal, and the metal leapt up
and said: "I must become a Moye (a legendary sword)." The great smith
would consider it inauspicious metal. Now that I have happened upon a
human form, suppose I were to say, "[Let me remain] human! Human!"
The Instantiator and Transformer (i.e., the Way) would consider me an inauspicious person. Once I comprehend Heaven and Earth as a great fur-
nace, and the Instantiator and Transformer as the great smith, where
could I go that would not be acceptable? In an instant, I shall fall asleep;
with start, I shall awaken.

These passages raise mind-body problems that I have explored elsewhere,[55] and accordingly do not wish to belabor here. (In a nutshell, the
issue is that the text seems to suppose a disembodied mental power
within Ziyu that can continue to function despite massive corporeal
disintegration, and other passages offer mutually contradictory speculations regarding the nature of postmortem existence—recall, for example,
that Zhuangzi's wife "sleeps now, reclining in a giant chamber" 偃然
寢於巨室.) For the purposes of the present discussion, suffice it to say
that the four gentlemen recognize the folly of privileging life over death
when neither can exist without the other. The theme recurs in many
chapters:

麗之姬，艾封人之子也。晉國之始得之也，涕泣沾襟；及其至於王
所，與王同筐床，食芻豢，而後悔其泣也。予惡乎知夫死者不悔其
始之蘄生乎！(*Zhuangzi* 2)[56]

[Lady] Ji of Li was the child of a border guard in Ai. When [the Lord of]
Jin first gained possession of her, she shed tears until she had soaked her
bodice. But once she had come to the king's residence, shared his com-
fortable bed, and eaten grass- and grain-fed [meat], she regretted her
tears. How do we know that the dead do not regret their earlier hankering
after life?[57]

Until we have experienced death, we cannot adjudge it inferior to life, and as long as we are alive, we have not yet experienced death.

As in *Laozi*, the goal is not immortality, but "to fulfill one's Heaven-ordained years and not die prematurely along the way":[58]

知天之所為，知人之所為者，至矣。知天之所為者，天而生也；知人之所為者，以其知之所知以養其知之所不知，終其天年而不中道天者，是知之盛也。(*Zhuangzi* 6)[59]

Those who know what Heaven does and what human beings do have reached the pinnacle. Those who know what Heaven does live in accord with Heaven; those who know what human beings do use what their knowledge knows in order to nourish what their knowledge does not know.[60] They fulfill their Heaven-ordained years and do not die prematurely along the way. This is the flourishing of wisdom.

For the most part, *Zhuangzi* looks askance at the macrobiotic exercises of soi-disant masters:

吹呴呼吸，吐故納新，熊經鳥申，為壽而已矣；此道引之士，養形之人，彭祖壽考者之所好也。(*Zhuangzi* 15)[61]

They blow and breathe, inhale and exhale, expectorate the old and take in the new, do the "bear-climb" and "bird-stretch"; they pursue longevity and nothing more—these are the masters of gymnastics, the nurturers of the body, devotees of the longevity of Ancestor Peng.[62]

• • •

The inability to perceive the world in its multifarious totality, to ride like an immortal on clouds and *qi*, is not the only cost of pursuing tangible goals like profit and promotion. The other cost is our health. Nothing is more dangerous than to be useful, especially in a commercial sense. (Note the contrast with *Laozi*, which refers repeatedly to the usefulness of the Way as one of its most precious qualities.) "Everyone knows the use of usefulness, but no one knows the use of uselessness" 人皆知有用之用，而莫知无用之用也。[63] A tree with valuable timber is the first to be felled; an able-bodied subject is the first to be called on for wearying *corvée*.[64]

Only creatures with no calculable economic value live out their natural lives.[65]

匠石之齊，至於曲轅，見櫟社樹。其大蔽數千牛，絜之百圍，其高臨山十仞而後有枝，其可以為舟者旁十數。觀者如市，匠伯不顧，遂行不輟。

弟子厭觀之，走及匠石，曰：「自吾執斧斤以隨夫子，未嘗見材如此其美也。先生不肯視，行不輟，何邪？」

曰：「已矣，勿言之矣！散木也，以為舟則沈，以為棺槨則速腐，以為器則速毀，以為門戶則液樠，以為柱則蠹。是不材之木也，無所可用，故能若是之壽。」

匠石歸，櫟社見夢曰：「女將惡乎比予哉？若將比予於文木邪？夫柤梨橘柚，果蓏之屬，實熟則剝，剝則辱；大枝折，小枝泄。此以其能苦其生者也，故不終其天年而中道夭，自掊擊於世俗者也。物莫不若是。且予求无所可用久矣，幾死，乃今得之，為予大用。使予也而有用，且得有此大也邪？且也若與予也皆物也，奈何哉其相物也?而幾死之散人，又惡知散木？」

匠石覺而診其夢。弟子曰：「趣取無用，則為社何邪？」

曰：「密！若無言！彼亦直寄焉，以為不知己者詬厲也。不為社者，且幾有翦乎！且也彼其所保與眾異，而以義喻之，不亦遠乎！」

(*Zhuangzi* 4)[66]

Carpenter Shi was going to Qi when he came to Quyuan and saw a cork oak that served as a shrine to the god of soil. It was so large that it would cover several thousand oxen. Measured by tape, it was a hundred spans around. It was so high that it would look down on mountains. Only twenty-five yards up did it have any branches, and there were more than ten of them that could have been made into boats. People gathered to gaze at it as though at a market, but the carpenter did not even turn to look; he kept walking without a halt.

When his disciple had gotten tired of gazing at it, he ran up to Carpenter Shi and said: "For as long as I have wielded my hatchet and followed you, master, I have never seen timber this beautiful. Yet you were unwilling to look at it; you walked away without halting. Why was that?"

[The carpenter] said: "Enough! Do not speak of it! It is unsound wood. If you were to make a boat out of it, it would sink; if you were to make a coffin out of it, it would soon rot; if you were to make a bowl out of it, it would soon break; if you were to make a door out of it, it would ooze sap; if you were to make a pillar out of it, it would be infested with worms. This is a tree with bad timber. It has no use; that is why it has been able to live so long."

When Carpenter Shi had arrived back home, the cork-oak shrine appeared to him in a dream, saying: "What are you comparing me with? Would you compare me with fine-grained trees? The fructiferous kind—cherry-apple, pear, orange, pomelo—are stripped when their fruit ripens, and, stripped, they are abused. Their larger branches are broken, their smaller branches snapped off. These are trees that make their lives bitter through their own abilities; thus they do not live out their Heaven-ordained years but always die halfway down their path. They have let themselves be assailed by the vulgar rabble. All things are like this. I, on the other hand, have been in search of uselessness for a long time; now, near death, I have attained it, and it has been of great use to me. If you were to make me useful, how would I get to be this big? Moreover, you and I are both things; what is the use of our treating each other as things? You, an unsound man nearing death—how can you know unsound wood?"

Carpenter Shi awoke and reported his dream. His disciple said: "If its intention is to secure uselessness, why has it become a shrine?"

"Silence! Do not speak! It has only consigned itself there because it regards those who do not understand it as an affliction. If it did not become a shrine, it would be in jeopardy of being cut down. Moreover, the manner in which it has protected itself is out of the ordinary; if we should explain it by conventional principles, would we not be wide of the mark?"

The words used to describe the cork oak recall *Laozi*'s Sage: "out of the ordinary" (*yu zhong yi* 與眾異), literally, "different from the multitudes." If we can suppose that readers would have known their *Laozi*, we might also observe the irony of Shi's profession: he is a carpenter but, at least before this conversion experience, is woefully unaware of the Great Carpenter, the Way (see p. 118).

Several other passages reprise the theme of the useless trees that grow unimpeded because no one abuses them for their fruit or timber.[67] The very next anecdote speaks of a tree so inimical to domestication that it will give you fever blisters if you try to taste its leaves.[68] The trees are, manifestly, metaphors conveying a particular stance about what qualifies as a good life.[69] For it is not just useless trees that "live out their Heaven-ordained years"; useless people have a knack for it too.

支離疏者，頤隱於臍，肩高於頂，會撮指天，五管在上，兩髀為脅。挫鍼治繲，足以餬口；鼓筴播精，足以食十人。上徵武士，則支離攘臂而遊於其間；上有大役，則支離以有常疾不受功；上與病者粟，則受三鍾與十束薪。夫支離其形者，猶足以養其身，終其天年，又況支離其德者乎！ (*Zhuangzi* 4)[70]

Scattered Apart: his cheeks are hidden in his navel; his shoulder is higher than the crown of his head; his neck and backbone point to the sky; his five organs are on top; his two thighs are at his flank. By wielding a needle and devoting himself to darning, he earns enough to put gruel in his mouth; by banging a flail and threshing grain, he earns enough to feed ten people. When the ruler enlists soldiers, Scattered rolls his sleeves up his arm (a sign of nonchalance) and wanders among them; when the ruler has a great labor project, Scattered does not receive an assignment because of his chronic ailments. When the ruler gives grain to the sick, he receives three bushels and ten bundles of firewood. If those with scattered bodies can still support themselves and fulfill their Heaven-ordained years, how much more [could they do] with scattered virtue!

On first hearing the story of Scattered Apart, most of us might not be eager to emulate him, but the more one ponders the alternatives, the more one doubts that what most people call "happiness" is truly preferable:

今俗之所為與其所樂，吾又未知樂之果樂邪，果不樂邪？吾觀夫俗之所樂，舉羣趣者，誙誙然如將不得已，而皆曰樂者。 (*Zhuangzi* 18)[71]

What the vulgar people of today do and what they consider happiness—I have never been able to tell whether it really is happiness or unhappiness. I have observed what they consider happiness, what they flock toward; they are doggedly determined, as though unable to stop, and they all call this happiness.

These sentiments can been difficult for Americans to digest, because "dogged determination" (*kengkeng* 誙誙) is normally reckoned a *virtue* in our society. (How many self-made billionaires, according to our crypto-Calvinist hypocrisy, attained their wealth and status through "dogged determination"?) But in ancient China, where the standard avenue to success, namely serving a king, was known to be fraught with danger, "dogged determination" in pursuit of royal favor could be seen as willfully hurling oneself toward an early end. (For the concrete example of Han Fei, see p. 201.)

This theme animates many memorable anecdotes in the "outer" and "mixed chapters." In one of them, the figure of Zhuang Zhou brashly declines an offer of service from the King of Chu because he does not want to become a relic:

莊子釣於濮水，楚王使大夫二人往先焉，曰：「願以境內累矣！」

莊子持竿不顧，曰：「吾聞楚有神龜，死已三千歲矣，王巾笥而藏之廟堂之上。此龜者，寧其死為留骨而貴乎？寧其生而曳尾於塗中乎？」

二大夫曰：「寧生而曳尾塗中。」

莊子曰：「往矣！吾將曳尾於塗中。」 (*Zhuangzi* 17)[72]

Master Zhuang was angling by the River Pu. The King of Chu sent two grandees to appear before him, saying: "I wish to trouble you with [the administration] of the territory within my borders."

Master Zhuang held on to his fishing rod; without turning his head, he said to them: "I have heard that there is a spirit tortoise (i.e., an oracle bone) in Chu that has been dead for three thousand years. The King keeps it wrapped in a wicker box and stores it in the inner sanctum of his temple. Would this tortoise prefer to be dead, honored as a relic, or alive, dragging its tail in the mud?"

The two grandees said: "It would prefer to be alive, dragging its tail in the mud."

Master Zhuang said: "Go away! I will drag my tail in the mud."

Another passage likens self-important mandarins to sacrificial hogs:

祝宗人玄端以臨牢筴，說彘曰：「汝奚惡死？吾將三月豢汝，十日戒，三日齊，藉白茅，加汝肩尻乎彫俎之上，則汝為之乎？」為彘謀，曰不如食以糠糟而錯之牢筴之中，自為謀，則苟生有軒冕之尊，死得於腞楯之上、聚僂之中則為之。為彘謀則去之，自為謀則取之，所異彘者何也？ (*Zhuangzi* 19)[73]

The Invocator of the Ancestors, in his black ritual robe, faced the pigpen and cajoled the hogs, saying: "Why should you detest dying? I will batten you for three months, purify myself for ten days, fast for three days, spread white reeds, and place your shoulders and rump on the sacrificial chopping block. Wouldn't you take that?"

Then he strategized in behalf of the hogs, saying: "It would be better to be fed chaff and dregs, and be left alone in the pigpen."

If he were strategizing for himself, then if he could be honored with an official cap and carriage while alive, and be placed in a *julü* (perhaps a kind of fancy sarcophagus) on an authorized platform when he died, he would take it. If he were strategizing in behalf of the hogs, he would reject this, but, for himself, he chose it. How is he different from a hog?

So profound are these convictions that one of the "mixed chapters," "Yielding the Throne" ("Rangwang" 讓王, *Zhuangzi* 28),[74] is devoted to wise men of antiquity who did everything they could to avoid the "the distress of being a ruler" (*wei jun zhi huan* 為君之患). One hapless prince flees to a cave because he knows that the people will choose him as their sovereign, only to be captured and carted back to the palace like a prisoner:

越人三世弒其君，王子搜患之，逃乎丹穴。而越國無君，求王子搜不得，從之丹穴。王子搜不肯出，越人薰之以艾，乘以王輿。王子搜援綏登車，仰天而呼曰：「君乎君乎！獨不可以舍我乎！」王子搜非惡為君也，惡為君之患也。若王子搜者，可謂不以國傷生矣，此固越人之所欲得為君也。(*Zhuangzi* 28)[75]

The people of Yue assassinated three of their rulers in succession. Prince Sou was distressed by this, so he fled to Cinnabar Cave. (Cinnabar is the ore of immortality.) But the state of Yue was without a ruler. They sought out Prince Sou unsuccessfully and followed him to Cinnabar Cave. Prince Sou was unwilling to emerge, so the people of Yue smoked him out with mugwort and placed him in the royal chariot. Prince Sou ascended the wagon, grasping a pennant for support; he looked up to Heaven and exclaimed: "Lord, lord! Could you not have spared me?" It is not that Prince Sou detested being a ruler; he detested the distress of being a ruler. Those who are like Prince Sou can be said not to endanger their lives for the sake of a kingdom. It was for this reason that the people of Yue wanted him to be their ruler.

Other chapters refer to the loss of one's dignity rather than one's health:

宋人有曹商者，為宋王使秦。其往也，得車數乘；王說之，益車百乘。反於宋，見莊子曰：「夫處窮閭阨巷，困窘織屨，槁項黃馘者，商之所短也；一悟萬乘之主而從車百乘者，商之所長也。」
　　莊子曰：「秦王有病召醫，破癰潰痤者得車一乘，舐痔者得車五乘，所治愈下，得車愈多。子豈治其痔邪？何得車之多也？子行矣！」
(*Zhuangzi* 32)[76]

Among the men of Song there was one Cao Shang (the name means "mercenary government employee"), who was sent by the King of Song as an ambassador to Qin. When he set out, he received several chariots; the King [of Qin] was so delighted with him that he added a hundred more.

When he returned to Song, he saw Master Zhuang and said: "I could not readily dwell in a ramshackle lane in a miserable hamlet, weaving my own sandals in embarrassing poverty, with a withered neck, and jaundiced as though missing an ear. But I excel at immediately reaching an understanding with a lord of myriad chariots and having my own retinue of a hundred chariots."

Master Zhuang said: "When the King of Qin has an ailment, he summons a doctor. One who pops his boils or drains his carbuncles receives one chariot; one who licks his hemorrhoids receives five chariots. The lower the location to be cured, the greater the number of chariots. Did you cure his hemorrhoids, sir? How else would you have received so many chariots? Go away!"

This sustained and inimitably entertaining critique of political engagement distinguishes *Zhuangzi* from *Laozi*[77] (and throws into question the analytical value of categories like "Daoist philosophy" and "Lao-Zhuang").[78] Whereas "nonaction" was, for *Laozi*, a technique of governing the world, in *Zhuangzi* it is extolled as the only way to approach the goal of living out one's years in utmost joy.[79] Similarly, *Laozi* used the doctrine of "knowing sufficiency" as a weapon to keep the populace ignorantly satisfied, but *Zhuangzi* emphasizes knowing contentment *for oneself*, and understanding that it is not attained through wealth and tawdry honors.[80] For as long as one's happiness depends on external factors, one is not in control of one's life. Those who aspire to "free and distant wandering" (*xiaoyao you* 逍遙遊), like a Peng bird or an Ultimate Person, cannot be answerable to a social superior.[81]

My favorite anecdote in *Zhuangzi* brings all these themes into clear focus.

> 惠子謂莊子曰:「魏王貽我大瓠之種, 我樹之成而實五石, 以盛水漿, 其堅不能自舉也。剖之以為瓢, 則瓠落無所容。非不呺然大也, 吾為其無用而掊之。」
>
> 莊子曰:「......今子有五石之瓠, 何不慮以為大樽而浮乎江湖, 而憂其瓠落無所容? 則夫子猶有蓬之心也夫!」 (*Zhuangzi* 1)[82]

> Master Hui said to Master Zhuang: "The King of Wei presented me with the seeds of a great calabash. I planted them, and when it was grown, it could hold five pecks, but when I filled it with water or sauce, it was so bulky that I could not lift it. I split it in half to make ladles, but they were so unwieldy as to be impractical. It's not that the calabash wasn't tremendously large, but I considered it useless and smashed it."
>
> Master Zhuang said: ". . . Sir, you had a calabash [that could hold] five pecks. Why didn't you think of using it as a great buoy so that you could float along rivers and lakes instead of fretting because it was so unwieldy as to be impractical? It is as though you have thatch for brains!"

The calabash is a metaphor for the Way:[83] formless, capacious, and beyond the comprehension of anyone whose thinking is limited to practical applications. Master Hui has been given a gift of unimaginable value, but cannot appreciate it because value, in his mind, must be quantifiable. Like Confucians and Mohists,[84] like all the pettifoggers who divide the world into little pieces, Master Hui finally smashes the calabash in impotent frustration. With just a bit more sagacity, he could have used it to escape this dog-eat-dog culture, and be free.

# CHAPTER SEVEN

# *Sunzi*

*Sunzi* or *Sunzi Bingfa* 孫子兵法 (*Master Sun's Methods of War*) is a military treatise attributed to Sun Wu (which means Grandson Warlike), an all too appropriately named general who is said to have transformed the harem of King Helu of Wu 吳王闔廬 (r. 514–496 BC) into a fearsome battalion in order to demonstrate his qualifications.[1] Beyond this patently romanticized story, the only other significant piece of information about Sun Wu is that he had a descendant with another suspiciously appropriate name: Sun Bin (Kneecaps Sun), who lost his legs to penal amputation after being framed by a rival, and supposedly went on to compose a military treatise of his own, known to posterity as *Sun Bin Bingfa* 孫臏兵法. Manuscripts of both *Sun Wu Bingfa* and *Sun Bin Bingfa* were discovered in a tomb at Yinqueshan in 1972.[2] A minority of scholars accept the traditional attribution of *Sunzi* and hence recognize it as one of the oldest philosophical books in Chinese history. On this theory, Chinese philosophy emerged from strategic thinking necessitated by the incessant warfare of the age.[3]

But the vocabulary of the text is not in keeping with the world of 500 BC. One specific anachronism is that *Sunzi* refers to crossbows and triggers, which were not widely used before the late fourth century.[4] (The crossbow figures even more prominently in *Sun Bin's Methods of War*, which is evidently a later work.) More generally, the philosophical lexicon suggests a milieu in which concepts such as Heaven and the Way had already become influential. Although the author or authors of *Sunzi* may have had real combat experience,[5] one of its rhetorical purposes was to carve out a place for military affairs in philosophical discourse.[6]

Consider Samuel B. Griffith's instructively misleading translation—in an otherwise first-rate work—of the "five matters" (*wu shi* 五事) that must be assessed when an army is about to go to battle:

一曰道，二曰天，三曰地，四曰將，五曰法。(*Sunzi* 1)[7]

The first of these factors is moral influence; the second, weather; the third, terrain; the fourth, command; and the fifth, doctrine.[8]

Anyone who does not look at the Chinese original will be astonished to learn that, aside from *jiang* 將 (the commander), *Sunzi's* "factors" are all extremely familiar philosophical keywords: *dao* (the Way), *tian* (Heaven), *di* (Earth), and *fa* (method—a concept to be discussed at greater length in chapter 9, below). *Sunzi* anticipates an audience well versed in classical philosophical literature and argues that "the commander" should be added to everybody's list of technical terms.

To be sure, it is not easy to capture the effect of this phrasing in unmarked English. On the one hand, translating *tian* as nothing more than "weather" fails to convey its connotations for classical Chinese readers;[9] on the other hand, Griffith was right that *Sunzi* does not use *tian* to mean much more than "natural phenomena," including weather.[10] There are no references to Heaven's Mandate, the Son of Heaven, or Heaven as a source of moral principles.[11] The references to *dao, tian, di*, and *fa* have little function other than to whet a philosophical reader's appetite, for *Sunzi's* innovations lie elsewhere.

The text proceeds, in broadly amoral fashion, from the basic recognition that waging war is costly.[12] A clear expression of this premise comes in one of the final chapters, but it is operative throughout:

孫子曰：凡興師十萬，出征千里，百姓之費，公家之奉，日費千金，內外騷動，怠于道路，不得操事者七十萬家。(*Sunzi* 13)[13]

Master Sun said: Whenever an army[14] of one hundred thousand [men] is raised and sent on a campaign of a thousand *li*, the levies on the Hundred Surnames and contribution by the ducal house amounts to a thousand gold pieces per day. There will be turmoil at home and abroad; [people] will be exhausted on the roads; the affairs of seven hundred thousand households will be thrown into disarray.

This appears at the head of a chapter on the cost-effectiveness of spies. In the face of so much economic disruption, it is incumbent on the commander to use every possible means to conclude campaigns swiftly. Moralists may sneer at espionage, but it is not wicked to try to save lives and resources.[15]

Since the purpose of a military campaign is to increase the state's power (in this respect, *Sunzi* is often compared to Clausewitz),[16] a commander must always remember that warfare is a matter of rational self-interest rather than valor or bloodlust.

孫子曰：凡用兵之法：全國為上，破國次之；全軍為上，破軍次之；全旅為上，破旅次之；全卒為上，破卒次之；全伍為上，破伍次之。是故百戰百勝，非善之善者也；不戰而屈人之兵，善之善者也。

故上兵伐謀，其次伐交，其次伐兵，其下攻城。攻城之法，為不得已；修櫓轒輼，具器械，三月而後成；距闉，又三月而後已。將不勝其忿而蟻附之，殺士卒三分之一，而城不拔者，此攻之災也。

故善用兵者，屈人之兵而非戰也，拔人之城而非攻也，毀人之國而非久也。必以全爭於天下，故兵不頓而利可全，此謀攻之法也。
(*Sunzi* 3)[17]

Master Sun said: According to the method of using troops, [capturing] a state intact is always best; destroying it is inferior. [Capturing] its forces intact is best; destroying them is inferior. [Capturing] a battalion intact is best; destroying it is inferior. [Capturing] a company intact is best; destroying it is inferior. [Capturing] a squadron intact is best; destroying it is inferior. For this reason, [one who attains] a hundred victories in a hundred battles is not the most adept of the adept. One who subdues the enemy's troops without a battle is the most adept of the adept.

Thus the best military [strategy] is to attack [the enemy's] strategy; next comes attacking his alliances; next comes attacking his troops; last comes attacking cities. The method of attacking cities is to do so only when there is no alternative. Armored siege vehicles and other machinery take three months to complete; the earthworks take another three months to finish. If the commander cannot overcome his frustration and has [his troops] climb the walls like ants, one in three of his warriors will be killed, and the city will still not be seized. This would be a disastrous attack.

Thus one who is adept at using troops subdues the enemy's troops, but not through battle; he seizes the enemy's cities, but not by attacking; he annihilates the enemy's state, but not through protracted [campaigns]. [One's goal] must be to contend with the rest of the world by [capturing enemy targets] intact; thereby one's troops will not be depleted, but one's gains can be kept intact. This is the method of attacking strategically.

Whereas contemporary literature delighted in the exploits of legendary or semilegendary heroes, *Sunzi* reminds its reader—who is evidently envisioned as a lord or strategist with national interests to consider—that although military glory may inspire encomiasts, it does not necessarily benefit the state. "Protracted campaigns," in particular, are unlikely to yield enough spoils to compensate for draining the state's coffers. Thus the best battlefield strategy is often the one that *avoids* confrontation on the battlefield. Decisive action, especially when attacking cities, is inadvisable unless "there is no alternative" (*de bu yi* 不得已).[18]

It is difficult to assess the originality of this passage because some of the ideas are echoed in other classical texts. *Mozi* also stresses the economic costs of war, with concrete examples,[19] and contains several chapters devoted to techniques of resisting sieges, as mentioned above (p. 61). Similarly, whoever wrote the following line from *Laozi* was evidently familiar with the strategy of avoiding confrontation in order to capture the enemy intact:

善為士者不武；善戰者不怒；善勝敵者不與。 (*Laozi* 68)

One who is adept at using warriors does not fight; one who is adept at battle does not rage; one who is adept at defeating the enemy does not engage him.

It is not possible, with our incomplete knowledge, to determine whether *Sunzi* took the idea from *Laozi*, *Laozi* took the idea from *Sunzi*, or both texts simply reflect the military culture of the time.

But *Sunzi* departs from anything to be found in *Mozi* or *Laozi* when it explains *how* the enemy should be defeated if not by direct assault. The trick is to find victory in the relative advantages afforded by battlefield conditions:

計利以 [=已] 聽，乃為之勢，以佐其外。勢者，因利而制權也。 (*Sunzi* 1)[20]

Once you have heeded my calculations of advantage, create situational power for this purpose, in order to boost [your strength] externally.[21]

"Situational power" refers to controlling the balance by relying on an advantageous [position].

The term translated here as "situational power" is *shi* 勢 (Old Chinese *ŋet-s), which literally means "setting" and is derived from *she* 設 (*ŋet), "to set up."[22] Thus *shi* refers to the "setting" of a battlefield, with its inherent yet transient advantages and disadvantages. The shrewd commander, who knows how to read the "setting," will infer the most advantageous position and strategy, and smash his foe almost as a matter of pure physics. This "external boost" is decisive, moreover, for in most real-world encounters, forces are relatively evenly matched. Victory will usually come from a correct analysis of the situation, not from the strength or courage of one's soldiers. "The *shi* of one who is adept at sending men into battle is like rolling a round boulder down from a mountain a thousand yards high" 故善戰人之勢, 如轉圓石於千仞之山者 (*Sunzi* 5).[23] No special military skill is required to roll a boulder downhill, but the effects are nonetheless devastating. The skill lies in apperceiving and harnessing the boulder's immense potential energy.[24]

Occasionally, a naturally advantageous position may present itself spontaneously (just as, occasionally, one is dealt a dominant hand in a card game), but, more often, a commander will have to earn the advantage through farsighted maneuvers (as one more typically has to play an uncertain hand). Accordingly, much of the book has to do with manipulating the enemy into an inferior position.[25]

故善動敵者, 形之, 敵必從之; 予之, 敵必取之。以利動之, 以卒待之。故善戰者, 求之於勢, 不責於人。(*Sunzi* 5)[26]

Thus one who is adept at battle causes the enemy to adhere to a certain formation. He offers [a minor sacrifice] that the enemy is sure to seize. He uses this [inconsequential] advantage to move [the enemy], then waits with his troops. Thus one who is adept at battle seeks [victory] in situational power; he does not demand it of his men.

The commander must also take care not to be duped in the same manner, never displacing his forces or jeopardizing his supply lines by chasing after some trivial advantage.[27]

Even if the enemy does not fall for such a gambit, it is still possible to weaken his defenses by concealing one's plans. The more possibilities that the enemy must take into account, the more feeble his preparations for each one.[28]

故形人而我無形，則我專而敵分。我專為一，敵分為十，是以十攻
其一也，則我眾而敵寡，能以眾擊寡者，則我之所與戰者，約矣。
吾所與戰之地不可知，不可知，則敵所備者多；敵所備者多，則吾
所與戰者，寡矣。故備前則後寡，備後則前寡；備左則右寡，備右
則左寡。無所不備，則無所不寡。(*Sunzi* 6)[29]

Thus if we induce them to assume a formation while we remain without a formation, we will be concentrated and the enemy divided; if we are concentrated as one, and the enemy divided into ten parts, we will be using ten to attack one. If we can use many to strike few, then those whom we engage in battle will be straitened. The place where we engage in battle cannot be known. Since it cannot be known, the enemy will prepare in many places; if the enemy prepares in many places, those whom we engage in battle will be few. If he prepares to the front, [his troops] in the rear will be few; if he prepares to the rear, those in the front will be few; if he prepares to the left, those on the right will be few; if he prepares to the right, those on the left will be few; if there is no place where he does not prepare, there will be no place where they will not be few.

"Formlessness" (*wuxing* 無形) means avoiding any type of committed formation until the enemy has already disclosed his intentions.[30] It is the enemy who determines how he is to be destroyed: for every situation and for every enemy tactic, a wise commander will know the appropriate response.

故策之而知得失之計，作之而知動靜之理，形之而知死生之地，角
之而知有餘不足之處。故形兵之極，至于無形；無形，則深間不能
窺，智者不能謀。因形而錯勝於眾，眾不能知。人皆知我所以勝之
形，而莫知吾所以制勝之形。故其戰勝不復，而應形於無窮。
(*Sunzi* 6)[31]

Jab him[32] so as to know the calculation of success or failure. Make him act so as to know the pattern of his movement and repose. Make him assume a formation so as to know the terrain of life and death (i.e., where troops will thrive and where they will perish).[33] Probe him so as to know the areas where he has abundance and insufficiency. Thus the ultimate in deploying one's troops in formation is to be without formation. If we are without formation, then those planted deeply among us cannot spy us out, nor can the wise lay plans. We present victory to our host by according with [the enemy's] formation, but they are incapable of understanding. Everyone knows the formation by which we have been victorious, but no one knows the formation by which we have carved out victory.[34] Thus when we are victorious in battle, we do not repeat [our tactics]; we respond to formations inexhaustibly.

*Sunzi* devotes a great deal of space to the theme of scrutinizing the minutest evidence in order to determine the enemy's status, as the enemy commander or his troops will usually be careless enough to give off valuable cues. Only the rare enemy who refrains from exposing himself is difficult to defeat.

眾樹動者，來也；眾草多障者，疑也。鳥起者，伏也；獸駭者，覆也。塵高而銳者，車來也；卑而廣者，徒來也；散而條達者，樵採也；少而往來者，營軍也。辭卑而益備者，進也；辭彊而進驅者，退也。輕車先出，居其側者，陳也。無約而請和者，謀也。奔走而陳兵車者，期也；半進半退者，誘也。杖而立者，飢也；汲而先飲者，渴也；見利而不進者，勞也。鳥集者，虛也；夜呼者，恐也。軍擾者，將不重也；旌旗動者，亂也；吏怒者，倦也。殺馬肉食，軍無懸甀，不返其舍者，窮寇也。諄諄翕翕，徐與人言者，失眾也。數賞者，窘也；數罰者，困也；先暴而後畏其眾者，不精之至也；來委謝者，欲休息也。兵怒而相迎，久而不合，又不相去，必謹察之。(*Sunzi* 9)[35]

If many trees move, he is approaching. If there are many blinds in the grass, he is misleading us. If birds take flight, he is lying in ambush. If beasts are startled, he has poured out [his entire force]. If the dust is high and piercing, his chariots are approaching. If the dust is low and wide, his infantry is approaching. If the dust is scattered and wispy, his firewood-gatherers are working. If the dust is slight and comes and goes, he has encamped his forces. If he speaks humbly but increases his preparations, he will advance. If he speaks with strength and charges forward, he will retreat. If his light chariots emerge first and settle by his flank, he is deploying. If he is not yet pressed but requests peace, he is plotting. If he runs to deploy his troops and chariots, he has set the time [for battle]. If half [his forces] advance and half retreat, he is luring us. If they lean on their weapons, they are hungry. If those who are sent to draw water are the first to drink, they are thirsty. If they see an advantage but do not advance, they are overworked. If birds gather, [his camp] is empty. If they call out at night, they are afraid. If his forces sway, the commander has no gravity. If the flags and pennants move, they are in discord. If the officers are angry, they are exhausted. If they kill their horses and eat the meat, if the troops do not hang up their pots, if they do not return to their lodgings, the invaders are desperate. If they repeatedly gather and speak to each other softly, he has lost [the confidence of] his host. If he frequently rewards them, he is in distress. If he frequently punishes them, he is in difficulty. If he is cruel at first, but then fears his army, he is the epitome of incompetence. If he sends a conciliatory emissary, he wishes to rest. If his soldiers are warlike and face one for a long time without either attacking or leaving, one must certainly investigate this carefully.

Most commentators agree that the commander in the last example is planning a spectacular surprise-attack; for *Sunzi*, this is the most dangerous kind of enemy, because it is not possible to prepare for him. Perhaps this is a commander who is following the very same principles that *Sunzi* propounds.

Having attained victory, "we do not repeat ourselves" (*bu fu* 不復): a successful strategy can never be reused, because never again will precisely the same situation obtain.[36] But this does not mean that the commander will eventually run out of schemes. There may be a limited set of factors to consider on the battlefield, but by combining them creatively, *Sunzi*'s commander can contrive an infinite number of strategies just as musicians can use the five notes of the pentatonic scale to compose an infinite number of songs, artists can use the five colors to paint an infinite number of pictures, and chefs can use the five tastes to cook an infinite number of dishes.

凡戰者，以正合，以奇勝。故善出奇者，無窮如天地，不竭如江河。……聲不過五，五聲之變，不可勝聽也。色不過五，五色之變，不可勝觀也。味不過五，五味之變，不可勝嘗 [=嚐] 也。戰勢不過奇正，奇正之變，不可勝窮也。奇正相生，如循環之無端，孰能窮之？ (*Sunzi* 5)[37]

One may join battle with regular [tactics], but one is victorious with anomalous ones. Thus one who is adept at producing anomalous [tactics] is as inexhaustible as Heaven and Earth, as unceasing as the Yangzi and Yellow Rivers. . . . There are no more than five tones, but when the five tones are alternated, there is no end to the [melodies] that one can hear. There are no more than five colors, but when the five colors are alternated, there is no end to the [images] that one can see. There are no more than five tastes, but when the five tastes are alternated, there is no end to the [flavors] that one can distinguish. In battle, there is only situational advantage derived by regular and anomalous means, but when regular and anomalous means are alternated, [the resulting tactics] are inexhaustible. The anomalous and the regular are mutually generating, like a circle with no endpoints. Who can exhaust them?

The word "anomalousness" (*qi* 奇) has two powerful connotations: as the antonym of "regularity" (*zheng* 正), it refers here to the advantage of surprise that is attained by avoiding predictable formations and attacks,[38] but *qi* is also a standard term for anomalies such as ghosts and shooting stars. *Sunzi*'s commander is as terrifying to an enemy as an omen of woe.

• • •

In phrases like "formlessness" (attested in *Laozi* 41), "mutual generation" (*xiang sheng* 相生, *Laozi* 2), and "the territory of death" (*sidi* 死地, *Laozi* 50—see p.122), classical readers could not have failed to notice resonances with the diction of *Laozi*. Hence it is not surprising that *Sunzi* includes an extended simile comparing troops to water, which, as we have seen (pp. 115–17), is one of *Laozi*'s favorite images.[39]

夫兵形象水，水之形，避高而趨下；兵之形，避實而擊虛。水因地而制流，兵因敵而制勝。故兵無常勢，水無常形。能因敵變化而取勝者，謂之神。故五行無常勝，四時無常位，日有短長，月有死生。(*Sunzi* 6)[40]

A formation of troops is like water. The form of water is such that it avoids high places and rushes downward; a formation of troops avoids well defended places and assaults weakly defended ones. Water carves out its flow by according with the terrain; troops carve out victory by according with the enemy. Thus in war there is no constant situational advantage; water has no constant form. One who can seize victory by changing in accord with the enemy is called divine. None of the Five Phases constantly prevails;[41] none of the four seasons has constant standing. The days grow shorter and longer; the moon dies and is reborn.

Although *Sunzi* and *Laozi* do not espouse identical philosophies[42]—for example, *Sunzi* is interested in victory *on the battlefield*, rather than domination in the political realm, and emphasizes situational advantage rather than the timeless Way[43]—the two texts use distinctive language to signal their affinity.

*Sunzi* leaves no doubt that the commander is subordinate to the ruler (who does best by staying out of the way). In the heat of battle, the commander is authorized to disobey a ruler's instructions if he has reason to believe that he will thereby reap greater benefits,[44] but this does not mean that he is disloyal: "He protects others and brings profit to his ruler; he is a treasure of state" 唯人是保, 而利合於主, 國之寶也 (*Sunzi* 10).[45]

In one important respect, however, *Sunzi*'s commander is similar to *Laozi*'s sage king: both act as though they are the only human being that can think, treating their underlings like mindless infants.

視卒如嬰兒, 故可與之赴深谿; 視卒如愛子, 故可與之俱死。 (*Sunzi* 10)[46]

[The commander] regards his soldiers as infants; thus they will proceed through deep gorges with him. He regards them as beloved children; thus they are prepared to die with him.

In the same vein, the commander keeps his troops "without knowledge" (*wu zhi* 無知, also found in *Laozi* 3—see p. 125). They are like chessmen, with no inkling of how he plans to use them.[47]

將軍之事, 靜以幽, 正以治。能愚士卒之耳目, 使之無知。(*Sunzi* 11)[48]

It is the business of the commander to be silent and obscure, rectified and disciplined, so that he can stultify the ears and eyes of his soldiers and cause them to be without knowledge.

These convictions underlie one of the commander's most important abilities: controlling emotion, both in himself and in his troops. If war is a matter of rational self-interest, the ruler and the commander cannot allow themselves to be goaded into battle:

主不可以怒而興師，將不可以慍而致戰；合於利而動，不合於利而止。怒可以復喜，慍可以復悅，亡國不可以復存，死者不可以復生。故明君慎之，良將警之，此安國全軍之道也。(*Sunzi* 12)[49]

The ruler cannot raise his army out of rage; the commander cannot engage in battle out of indignation. If it is profitable, advance, but if it is not, halt. One who is enraged can be restored to happiness; one who is indignant can be restored to contentment; but an annihilated state cannot be restored to existence; the dead cannot be restored to life. An enlightened ruler is cautious and a fine commander vigilant about the right way to keep the state secure and its forces intact.

The commander cannot function unless he cultivates equanimity:

故將有五危：必死，可殺也；必生，可虜也；忿速，可侮也；廉潔，可辱也；愛民，可煩也。凡此五者，將之過也，用兵之災也。覆軍殺將，必以五危，不可不察也。(*Sunzi* 8)[50]

Thus there are five hazards for a commander: If he is intent on dying, he can be killed; if he is intent on living, he can be captured; if he is short-tempered, he can be provoked; if he is punctilious, he can be shamed; if he is devoted to his people, he can be harassed. These five are faults in a commander and calamities when using troops. When forces are routed and their commander slain, it must be because of one of these five hazards. One cannot fail to study them.

Another aspect of emotional discipline is the commander's obligation to project a demeanor appropriate to each situation, an art that often requires dissimulation.

故能而示之不能，用而示之不用，近而示之遠，遠而示之近。(*Sunzi* 1)[51]

Thus, if you are competent, show that you are incompetent; if you are using [your forces], show that you are not using them; if you are near, show that you are far; if you are far, show that you are near.

When recruiting spies, similarly, the commander is advised to exemplify four unmistakably Confucian-sounding virtues: sagacity, wisdom, humanity, and righteousness.[52] This should not be misinterpreted as a *general* recommendation (for a commander who reliably adheres to Confucian virtues can be victimized as easily as "the punctilious can be shamed"); the point is that the commander must know how to assume the right persona if he hopes to inspire the loyalty of secret agents.

At the same time, the commander must understand that soldiers—both his own and his enemy's—lack any such self-awareness; they are merely containers of *qi* that behave as predictably as clockwork.

是故朝氣銳, 晝氣惰, 暮氣歸。故善用兵者, 避其銳氣, 擊其惰歸, 此治氣者也。 (*Sunzi* 7)[53]

In the morning, their *qi* is keen; during the day it flags; by the evening, it has retrogressed.[54] Thus one who is adept at using troops will avoid [enemies] with keen *qi* but strike those with flagging or retrogressing *qi*. This is mastering *qi*.

The soldiers' *qi* is akin to what we call "fighting spirit," but the key is that they themselves do not control it.[55] It is a natural and hence manipulable aspect of their character, which a competent commander cannot fail to exploit, just as he would try to glean "situational power" from any other feature of the battlefield. One example of not "being devoted to one's people" (*aimin* 愛民) is the cold-blooded observation that placing troops in a desperate position will motivate them to fight to the death.[56]

Gongs, drums, and colorful pennants are effective devices for inciting or diminishing the troops' ardor, as circumstances require.

夫金鼓旌旗者, 所以一人之耳目也; 人既專一, 則勇者不得獨進, 怯者不得獨退。 (*Sunzi* 7)[57]

Gongs, drums, and pennants are the means by which one unifies the ears and eyes of one's men. Once they are unified, it is not only the brave who advance nor only the cowardly who retreat.

*Sunzi* is careful to opine solely on the world of the military, where it is, perhaps, possible to whip foot soldiers into a frenzy while keeping them ignorant of the overarching strategy. But part of the reason why the text was prized by aristocrats of diverse stripes, many of whom would not have dared to bear arms themselves, must be that they were enthralled by the prospect of controlling people like marionettes. The wishful notion of the sovereign as the sole mind governing a sea of witless humanity persisted well into the imperial era.[58] The problem is that people—even ordinary workers and farmers—are not witless. Now and then, they have their own ideas; some of them even become sages, as Xunzi will assert in the next chapter.

PART III

# Two Titans at the
End of an Age

# CHAPTER EIGHT

# *Xunzi*

With Xunzi, we come to a thinker unlike any that we have encountered before. Most apparently to Western readers, Xunzi, unlike the first two great Confucians, has no Latinized name—a direct reflection of the fact that when the Jesuits arrived in China and began to study Confucianism, Xunzi had already been repudiated by Chinese scholasticism as at best an imperfect Confucian, and certainly not a member of the *daotong* 道統 (genealogy of the Way), the term for the orthodox tradition stretching back to the sages.

Xunzi's prestige has, correspondingly, reached extreme highs and lows over the centuries. In his own day, he was revered as "the most senior of the masters" (*zui wei lao shi* 最爲老師)[1] and numbered among his students some of the most influential men in the Chinese world. He was still widely celebrated in the Western Han dynasty, when Dong Zhongshu 董仲舒 (fl. 152–119 BC),[2] one of the leading intellectual figures, is reported to have written a paean to him (now lost).[3] But by Eastern Han times, Mencius—construed throughout Chinese history as Xunzi's nemesis—had eclipsed him in the minds of most literati.[4]

Thus the first three or four centuries after Xunzi's death witnessed a slow but continuous decline in his reputation. Thereafter the pace of this decline quickened. By the Tang dynasty (618–906), even literati who admired Xunzi—such as Han Yu 韓愈 (768–824)[5]—were careful to add that his works contain grave mistakes. In the Song, there were still some voices that praised him, but the opinion with the greatest long-term consequences was that of Zhu Xi 朱熹 (1130–1200), who declared that Xunzi's philosophy resembled those of non-Confucians such as Shen Buhai 申不害 (fl. 354–340 BC) and Shang Yang 商鞅 (d. 338 BC), and that he was indirectly responsible for the notorious disasters of the Qin dynasty (221–210 BC).[6] For the rest of imperial history,[7] Xunzi was rejected by the cultural mainstream; into the twentieth century, he was criticized by intellectuals such as Kang Youwei 康有爲 (1858–1927),[8] Tan Sitong 譚

嗣同 (1865–98),[9] and Liang Qichao 梁啟超 (1873–1929)[10] as the progenitor of the Confucian scriptural legacy, which, in their view, had derailed the original Confucian mission and plunged China into a cycle of authoritarianism and corruption that lasted for more than two thousand years.

Today the tide has turned almost completely. Xunzi is one of the most popular philosophers throughout East Asia[11] and has been the subject of more books published in English over the past two decades than any other Chinese philosopher, vastly outstripping Mencius.[12] From a twenty-first-century perspective, this revival of interest in Xunzi is not hard to explain: his body of work has always been one of the best preserved, and with the commonplace scholastic objection to his philosophy—namely, that he was wrong to say human nature is evil (*xing e* 性惡)—having lost most of its cogency, it is only to be expected that philosophical readers should be attracted to his creative but rigorous arguments. In this sense one could say that Xunzi has finally been restored, more than two millennia after his death, to his erstwhile position as "the most senior of the masters."

Another conspicuous difference: whereas the texts in the first two parts of this book cannot have been written by single individuals, I believe the bulk of *Xunzi* consists of essays by Xunzi himself (see p. 9). Xunzi did not envision himself as a teacher whose sphere was limited to direct contact with his disciples; rather, he was a new breed of thinker, one who aimed, through writing, to influence diverse classes of readers across the land.[13] In Xunzi's book, the synthetic format and presentation of ideas reflect, like the ideas themselves, the revolutionary intellectual developments of the third century BC.

The most crucial difference of all, finally, is that whereas earlier Confucians had made only the barest statements about the nature of the cosmos and did not by any means consider the study of cosmology to be indispensable to moral self-cultivation, Xunzi had a robust theory of the universe and its relation to moral philosophy. Indeed, Xunzi considered morality impossible without an understanding of the patterns of the cosmos. But before we can appreciate this aspect of Xunzi's philosophy, we must visit the intellectual cul-de-sac that sadly dominated most discussions of Xunzi in imperial China: his theory that *xing* is evil.

In practice, Xunzi's claim that *xing* is evil means that following the impulses of one's *xing*, without reflecting on them and moderating them, will lead one to evil acts.[14] It should be emphasized that *e*, the Chinese word translated here as "evil," is not to be understood in the Christian sense of "diabolical" or "antithetical to God." The basic meaning of *e* is "detestable" (its verbal cognate, *wu* 惡, means "to hate"), but in classical Chinese it is the ordinary antonym of *shan* 善, the word used by Mencius for "good." In Xunzi, *e* refers to human nature in its unremediated—and hence obnoxious—state.

Mencius, we remember, had argued that *xing* is good, but this did not mean that people are all necessarily good; rather, it meant that we all have the capacity to become good, but that some people develop this capacity and others do not. Xunzi arrived at a similar point of view, but with diametrically opposed rhetoric:

孟子曰：「人之學者，其性善。」曰：是不然。是不及知人之性，而不察乎人之性、偽之分者也。凡性者，天之就也，不可學，不可事；禮義者，聖人之所生也，人之所學而能，所事而成者也。不可學、不可事而在人者謂之性，可學而能、可事而成之在人者謂之偽。是性、偽之分也。(*Xunzi* 23.1c)[15]

Mencius said: "Since one can learn, one's *xing* is good." This is not so. This [point of view] does not attain to knowledge of human *xing* and does not investigate the distinction between *xing* and artifice. *Xing* is what is spontaneous from Heaven, what cannot be learned, what cannot be acquired. Ritual and morality arise from the sages. People become capable of them through learning; they perfect themselves by acquiring them. What cannot be learned, what cannot be acquired, in human beings is called *xing*. What they can become capable of through learning, and can acquire in order to perfect themselves, is called "artifice." This is the distinction between *xing* and artifice.

孟子曰：「人之性善。」曰：是不然。凡古今天下之所謂善者，正理平治也；所謂惡者，偏險悖亂也。是善惡之分也已。今誠以人之性固正理平治邪？則有惡用聖王，惡用禮義哉！(*Xunzi* 23.3a)[16]

Mencius said: "Human *xing* is good." I say: This is not so. From ancient times until the present, all that has been called "good" in the world is rectitude, principle, peace, and order. What is called "evil" is partiality, malice, rebelliousness, and disorder. This is the distinction between good and evil. Now can one sincerely believe that human *xing* is originally upright, principled, peaceful, and orderly? Then what use for the sage kings, what use for ritual and morality?

The major difference between Mencius and Xunzi is not that they held incompatible theories of human nature, but that they used the term *xing* in fundamentally dissimilar senses. Whereas Mencius used *xing* to refer to the ideal state that an organism can be expected to attain given the right nurturing conditions, Xunzi operated with a more traditional definition: "What is so by birth is called *xing*" 生之所以然者謂之性 (*Xunzi* 22.1b).[17] Since ritual and morality are manifestly not inborn, they cannot be reckoned as *xing*; rather, in Xunzi's parlance, they are *wei* 偽, "artifice."[18] Thus *xing* refers to the basic faculties, capacities, and desires that we have from birth, "artifice" to all the traits that we acquire through our own conscious actions. And if we achieve any goodness, it must be because of our artifice:

人之性惡，其善者偽也。今人之性，生而有好利焉，順是，故爭奪
生而辭讓亡焉；生而有疾惡焉，順是，故殘賊生而忠信亡焉；生而
有耳目之欲，有好聲色焉，順是，故淫亂生而禮義文理亡焉。然則
從人之性，順人之情，必出於爭奪，合於犯分亂理，而歸於暴。故
必將有師法之化，禮義之道，然後出於辭讓，合於文理，而歸於治。
用此觀之，然則人之性惡明矣，其善者偽也。(*Xunzi* 23.1a)[19]

Human *xing* is evil; what is good is artifice. Now human *xing* is as follows. At birth there is fondness for profit in it. Following this, contention and robbery arise, and deference and courtesy are destroyed. At birth there is envy and hatred in it. Following this, violence and banditry arise, and loyalty and trust are destroyed. At birth there are the desires of the ear and eye: there is fondness for sound and color in them. Following this, perversion and disorder arise, and ritual, morality, refinement, and principles are destroyed. Thus obeying one's *xing* and following one's emotions must result in contention and robbery. This is in accordance with the violation of [social] division and disruption in the natural order, and return to turmoil. Thus there must be the transformation [brought about by] the methods of a teacher and the Way of ritual and morality; then the result will be deference and courtesy, in accordance with refinement and principles, and return to order. Seen by these [considerations], human *xing* is clearly evil; what is good is artifice.

At the same time, since everyone is born with the same *xing*—we all have the same sense organs, and, as we shall see, the same mental faculties—it stands to reason that the path to moral perfection is open to anyone. And thus Xunzi repeats Mencius's assertion that even a beggar in the street can become a sage, as long as he is willing to put forth the effort:

故聖人者，人之所積而致矣。曰：「聖可積而致，然而皆不可積，何也？」曰：可以而不可使也。故小人可以為君子而不肯為君子，君子可以為小人而不肯為小人。小人、君子者，未嘗不可以相為也，然而不相為者，可以而不可使也。故塗之人可以為禹。(*Xunzi* 23.5b)[20]

A sage is a person who has attained [sagehood] by accumulating [learning]. It was asked: Sagehood can be achieved by accumulating [learning], but why is it that not all of us do this? I answered: We can, but we cannot be forced. Thus a petty man could become a noble man but is not willing to do so. A noble man could become a petty man but is not willing to do so. It is not the case that a petty man or a noble man could never become the other. The [reason why] the one does not become the other is not that he cannot, but that he cannot be forced. This is how a person in the street can become Yu.

Not much of Xunzi's essay on *xing*, it should be emphasized, can be said to refute Mencius's position. The two thinkers arrived, in fact, at remarkably similar points of view. Both would have agreed that people can perfect themselves and that such an achievement requires great exertion and self-motivation. And both would have agreed that without lifelong practice of self-cultivation, people are evil. These similarities have led some commentators to suggest that Xunzi's objections "are not quite to the point."[21] What prompted Xunzi to dissent from Mencius's characterization of *xing* as good if his own theory was to be so difficult to distinguish from the one that he criticized?

The question is crucial, for as long as Xunzi's philosophy is reduced to the tenet that *xing* is evil, one cannot appreciate how he went beyond his predecessors, and how readers of later centuries, who seemed not to peruse much of the text beyond *Xunzi* 23, were able to dismiss him all too easily. While it is impossible for us today to be sure of Xunzi's argumentative motivations, my sense is that Xunzi wished to highlight his conviction that the proper models for moral behavior lie outside the self, which is fundamentally opposed to a Mencian notion of Four Beginnings lodged within the human heart. Whereas Mencians have always emphasized looking inward for moral direction—sometimes complicated by their acknowledgment that the heart can be corrupted—self-cultivation in the Xunzian style is inconceivable without looking *outward*.

Xunzi held that for most ordinary people, the best guide is the set of rituals handed down by the sages. ("Ritual and morality arise from the sages," we remember.) And what are these rituals? Western scholarship has lavished attention on Xunzian statements about ritual that would seem to invite a comparison with modern contractarianism, but the inadequacy of this line of analysis will soon become clear. In the most famous of these passages, Xunzi attributes, in a manner reminiscent of Hobbes or Rousseau, the genesis of the rituals to the sages' recognition that unbridled competition produces an unsustainable situation for all, as in the opening of "Discourse on Ritual" ("Lilun" 禮論):

> 禮起於何也？曰：人生而有欲，欲而不得，則不能無求；求而無度量分界，則不能不爭；爭則亂，亂則窮。先王惡其亂也，故制禮義以分之，以養人之欲，給人之求，使欲必不窮乎物，物必不屈於欲，兩者相持而長，是禮之所起也。(*Xunzi* 19.1a)[22]

Whence did rituals arise? I say: People are born with desires; if we desire [something] and do not obtain it, we cannot but seek it. If, in seeking, we have no measures or limits, then there cannot but be contention. Contention makes disorder, and disorder privation. The Former Kings hated such disorder and established ritual and morality in order to divide [the people into classes], in order to nourish people's desires and grant what they seek. They brought it about that desires need not be deprived of objects, that objects need not be depleted by desires; the two support each other and grow. This is where rituals arise from.

Similar statements are found in other chapters:

夫貴為天子，富有天下，是人情之所同欲也。然則從人之欲則執不能容，物不能贍也。故先王案為之制禮義以分之。(*Xunzi* 4.12)[23]

To be honored as the Son of Heaven and richly to possess the world—this is the common desire of humans [by virtue of their] disposition. But if people follow their desires, boundaries cannot contain them, and objects cannot satisfy them. Thus the Former Kings restrained them and established for them ritual and morality in order to divide them [into classes].

To judge from such pronouncements, "ritual" might seem like no more than a shorthand name for the nexus of regulations that allow humankind to enjoy nature's bounty harmoniously.[24] With rituals in place, "desires need not be deprived of objects, that objects need not be depleted by desires." Replace "rituals" with "contracts" (or the like), and Xunzi would seem to emerge as a shining contractarian. We all have desires, and were we to go about satisfying them in a lawless world, the result would only be unrequited desire. The prospect of such chaos is resolved through ritual: with the establishment of a few ground rules, we can fulfill our desires, at least to a level of self-sufficiency, without being unduly impeded by others in our midst.

But there is more to Xunzi's theory of ritual than this. The necessary rituals, in his view, must institute ranks and distinctions in society, for without them harmony cannot be achieved (*Xunzi* 9.3). All people have their place, like hairs in a fur collar (*Xunzi* 1.11). Social organization—which, for Xunzi, always means social stratification—is the method by which human beings, despite their paltry physical gifts, are able to dominate all other forms of life:

水火有氣而無生，草木有生而無知，禽獸有知而無義，人有氣、有生、有知，亦且有義，故最為天下貴也。力不若牛，走不若馬，而牛馬為用，何也？曰：人能群，彼不能群也。人何以能群？曰：分。分何以能行？曰：義。故義以分則和。(*Xunzi* 9.16a)[25]

Water and fire have *qi* but no life; grasses and trees have life but no awareness; birds and beasts have awareness but no morality. Human beings have breath and life and awareness, and they have morality in addition. Thus they are the most noble [beings] in the world. They do not have the strength of an ox, nor do they run like a horse, but oxen and horses are used by them. Why is this? I say: People can form societies; [animals] cannot form societies. How can people form societies? Through division [of labor]. How can division proceed? I say: morality. Thus division with morality brings about harmony.

The reference at the end to morality suggests two reasons why a contractarian reading of Xunzi fails to capture all the nuances of his theory. First, Xunzi elsewhere explicitly denies that an arbitrarily chosen set of rituals would be effective. Rather, the rituals of the sage kings are legitimate because they accord with human nature; by implication, any competing ritual code would necessarily fail:

人之所以為人者，何已也？曰：以其有辨也。飢而欲食，寒而欲煖，勞而欲息，好利而惡害，是人之所生而有也，是無待而然者也，是禹、桀之所同也。然則人之所以為人者，非特以二足而無毛也，以其有辨也。今夫狌狌形笑 [=狀]²⁶，亦二足而無毛也，然而君子啜其羹，食其胾。故人之所以為人者，非特以其二足而無毛也，以其有辨也。夫禽獸有父子而無父子之親，有牝牡而無男女之別，故人道莫不有辨。辨莫大於分，分莫大於禮，禮莫大於聖王。(*Xunzi* 5.4)²⁷

What is it that makes humans human? I say: their making of distinctions. Desiring food when hungry, desiring warmth when cold, desiring respite when toiling, liking profit and disliking harm—these [characteristics] are all possessed by people from birth. They are what is immediately so. In this respect, [the sage] Yu and [the tyrant] Jie were identical. This being the case, what makes humans human is not specifically that they have two feet and no pelt (or plumage—i.e., that humans are featherless bipeds). It is their making of distinctions. Now the *xingxing* (a legendary ape with no hair) resembles us and also has two feet and no pelt. But the noble man sips his soup and eats his food cooked. Thus what makes humans human is not specifically that they have two feet and no pelt. It is their making of distinctions. Birds and beasts have fathers and sons, but no intimacy between fathers and sons. They have males and females, but no separation between man and woman. Thus the Way of Humans is nothing other than to make distinctions. There are no greater distinctions than social distinctions. There are no greater social distinctions than the rituals. There are no greater rituals than those of the Sage Kings.

Xunzi's argument here brings us to territory that Mencius never broached. He claims that human beings, unlike any other species of animal, make certain distinctions and live by them—male is distinguished from female, old from young, and so on—and it is altogether natural that we do so. That is the Way. The rituals of the sage kings identify the natural order and augment it by confirming the distinctions that we are bound to make by nature. The sage kings apprehended this order, and their rituals embody it. Modern contractarians do not, as a rule, postulate that workable social rules must have this kind of cosmological underpinning.

The second reason why Xunzi cannot be adequately understood as a contractarian is that rituals, in his conception, not only facilitate social cohesion but also foster psychological development.[28] Indeed, if they did not, they would be mere instruments of expedience, not rituals. These dimensions become clear when Xunzi begins to discuss specific rituals and their purposes:

> 故事生不忠厚、不敬文謂之野，送死不忠厚、不敬文謂之瘠。君子賤野而羞瘠，故天子棺槨七重，諸侯五重，大夫三重，士再重。然後皆有衣衾多少厚薄之數，皆有翣菨文章之等以敬飾之，使生死終始若一，一足以為人願，是先王之道，忠臣孝子之極也。(*Xunzi* 19.4a–b)[29]

Thus, serving the living without loyal generosity or reverent formality is called uncivil; sending off the dead without loyal generosity or reverent formality is called miserly. The noble man condemns incivility and is ashamed of miserliness; thus the inner and outer coffins consist of seven layers for the Son of Heaven, five layers for a feudal lord, three layers for a grandee, and two layers for a man-of-service. Thereafter, in order to revere and adorn them, there are, for each [rank], protocols regarding the quantity and richness of [mortuary] robes and foodstuffs, and grades for the [corresponding] flabellum and décor. This causes life and death, ending and beginning, to be [treated] as one, and people's yearnings to be satiated. This is the Way of the Former Kings, the ridgepole of the loyal minister and filial son.

We observe sumptuary regulations, in other words, in order to learn how to avoid incivility and miserliness. Later in the same chapter, Xunzi discusses the purpose of the mandatory three-year mourning period for deceased rulers and parents (which, in practice, lasted only until the twenty-fifth month—that is, the first month of the third year) and explains that, here too, the rituals have a moral purpose: they help us conduct ourselves properly by providing suitable forms for us to express emotions that are so deep as to be potentially debilitating.

創巨者其日久，痛甚者其愈遲，三年之喪，稱情而立文，所以為至痛極也；齊衰、苴杖、居廬、食粥、席薪、枕塊，所以為至痛飾也。三年之喪，二十五月而畢，哀痛未盡，思慕未忘，然而禮以是斷之者，豈不以送死有已，復生有節也哉！......

　將由夫愚陋淫邪之人與？則彼朝死而夕忘之，然而縱之，則是曾鳥獸之不若也，彼安能相與羣居而無亂乎？將由夫脩飾之君子與？則三年之喪，二十五月而畢，若駟之過隙，然而遂之，則是無窮也。故先王聖人安為之立中制節，一使足以成文理，則舍之矣。(*Xunzi* 19.9a and 9c)[30]

When a wound is colossal, its duration is long; when pain is profound, the recovery is slow. The three-year mourning period is a form established with reference to emotions; it is the means by which one conveys the acme of one's pain. The untrimmed sackcloth garment, the [hatband and waistband] of the female nettle plant, the staff,[31] the hut where one dwells, the gruel that one eats, the brushwood that one uses as a mat and clod of earth that one uses as a pillow—by these means, one conveys the acme of one's pain. The three-year mourning period ends with the twenty-fifth month; one's pain of grief is not yet exhausted, nor have pining and longing yet departed from one's heart, but the rituals discontinue [the mourning period] here because there is an endpoint to sending off the dead and a period [after which] one must return to the living. . . .

Shall we follow those foolish, rude, licentious, and perverse people who forget by the evening those who have died in the morning? If we were to allow this, we would not even be the equals of birds and beasts. How could we dwell without disorder in the same society as such people? Or shall we follow cultivated and refined gentlemen, for whom the three-year mourning period, ending with the twenty-fifth month, passes as swiftly as a team of four horses [glimpsed through] a crack in a wall? If we were to go along with them, [the mourning period] would be interminable. Thus the Former Kings and Sages accordingly determined the [right] period by establishing the midpoint. Once [mourning] has become sufficient to attain a due form and pattern, it is set aside.

Xunzi's discussion of the village wine-drinking ceremony (*xiang* 鄉), similarly, reviews the rite in extenso, showing how each element bespeaks an underlying moral principle. The fact that the host fetches the guest of honor himself, but expects the other guests to arrive on their own, underscores the distinctions that need to be drawn between noble and base. And the detail that each participant toasts the next, serially and according to their ages, demonstrates that one can align society according to seniority without excluding anyone. (Everyone eventually drinks; some just have to wait longer than others.) When the guest of honor retires, the host bows and escorts him out, and the formal occasion comes to an end: this is to make it known that one can feast at leisure without becoming disorderly. The clear implication is that by taking part in the rite, we can gradually comprehend the moral principles that the sages wished us to embody (*Xunzi* 20.5).

Xunzi's rituals have such an important role to play in our emotional and moral development that he spends an entire chapter limning what are essentially rituals of artistic expression. The term he uses is "music" (*yue* 樂), which is not identical to ritual, but Xunzi's conception of their origin and purpose is so similar that one can scarcely speak of one without the other. Thus "ritual and music" (*liyue* 禮樂) are to be understood as two aspects of human artifice: "ritual" refers to forms that affect social cohesion, "music" to those involving the orderly expression of human emotions. The crucial point is that the sages created both.

> 夫樂者，樂也，人情之所必不免也，故人不能無樂。樂則必發於聲音，形於動靜，而人之道，聲音、動靜、性術之變盡是矣。故人不能不樂，樂則不能無形，形而不為道，則不能無亂。先王惡其亂也，故制雅、頌之聲以道之，使其聲足以樂而不流，使其文足以辨而不諰，使其曲直、繁省、廉肉、節奏足以感動人之善心，使夫邪汙之氣無由得接焉。(*Xunzi* 20.1)[32]

Music is joy; it is what human emotions cannot avoid. Thus humans cannot be without music. If we are joyous, then we must express [our joy] in sounds and tones and give form to it in movement and quietude. And the Way of Humanity is fulfilled in sounds and tones, in movement and quietude, and in the changes in the progression of the *xing*.[33] Thus humans cannot be without joy, and joy cannot be without form, but if that form is not [in line with] the Way, then there cannot but be disorder. The Former Kings hated this disorder; thus they instituted the sounds of the Odes and Hymns in order to make them accord with the Way. They brought it about that their sounds were sufficient [to give form] to joy but were not dissipated; they brought it about that their patterned [compositions] were sufficient to make distinctions but were not timorous;[34] they brought it about that the directness, complexity, richness, and rhythm were sufficient to move people's good minds; they brought it about that heterodox and impure *qi* would have no opportunity to attach itself.

Like all Confucians, Xunzi accepts that human beings have certain irrepressible impulses, which are not objectionable in themselves. The problem is that unreflective outbursts driven solely by our emotional responses may cause harm, and thus we are enjoined to be mindful of our impulses, rather than to extinguish them.[35] To aid us in this process, the sages left behind appropriate musical forms that we can use to channel our need to express ourselves. That is to say, everyone feels a need to sing or dance at some point, and it would be folly to suppress these urges, but the danger is that we might begin to sing disruptive songs such as "Let's Plant in the Autumn and Harvest in the Spring,"[36] whose influence could be harmful to an agrarian society. In order to keep us from spontaneously intoning such destructive songs, the sages gave us wholesome songs to sing instead—such as, to continue the example, the "Let's Plant in the Spring and Harvest in the Autumn" song. What Xunzi meant by this corpus of songs is the canonical collection of Odes that all Confucians seem to have regarded as an unrivaled repository of edifying literature.

Xunzi's immediate purpose in this section was to counter the Mohist view that music is wasteful. We remember from Mencius's discussion with King Xuan of Qi that the ruler's lavish musical productions provoked resentment among the populace (because they were prevented from enjoying them), and Mohists expanded on what must have been widespread popular outrage to argue against such performances. Xunzi countered that by focusing exclusively on the material costs, Mo Di and his followers failed to recognize the psychological utility of music as an instrument of moral suasion.[37]

夫聲樂之入人也深，其化人也速，故先王謹為之文。樂中平則民和而不流，樂肅莊則民齊而不亂。民和齊則兵勁城固，敵國不敢嬰也。如是，則百姓莫不安其處，樂其鄉，以至足其上矣。然後名聲於是白，光輝於是大，四海之民莫不願得以為師。是王者之始也。樂姚冶以險，則民流僈鄙賤矣。流僈則亂，鄙賤則爭。亂爭則兵弱城犯，敵國危之。如是，則百姓不安其處，不樂其鄉，不足其上矣。故禮樂廢而邪音起者，危削侮辱之本也。故先王貴禮樂而賤邪音。其在序官也，曰：「修憲命，審誅賞 [=詩章][38]，禁淫聲，以時順修，使夷俗邪音不敢亂雅，太師之事也。」 (*Xunzi* 20.2)[39]

Sounds and music enter people deeply; they transform people quickly. Thus the Former Kings were careful to make [music] patterned. When music is centered and balanced, the people are harmonious and not dissipated. When music is stern and grave, the people are uniform and not disorderly. When the people are harmonious and uniform, the army is firm and the citadels impregnable; enemy states dare not invade. When this is the case, then the Hundred Surnames, without exception, are secure in their dwellings; all are joyous in the neighborhoods and fully satisfied with their superiors. Only then will the name and repute [of the ruler of such a state] be shining and his glory great; within the Four Seas, none among the people will be unwilling to accept him as their teacher. This is the beginning of true kingship. When music is overwrought and seduces us to malice, the people are dissipated, indolent, crude, and base. Dissipation and indolence lead to disorder, crudity and baseness to contention. When there is disorder and contention, the army is soft and the citadels plundered; enemies will threaten [such a state]. When this is the case, the Hundred Surnames are not secure in their dwellings; they are not joyous in their neighborhoods or satisfied with their superiors. Thus when rituals and music lapse, and heterodox tones arise, this is the root of territorial encroachment, humiliation, and disgrace. Thus the Former Kings took ritual and music to be noble and heterodox tones to be base. This [principle] appears in *Procedures of the Officials*:[40] "The affairs of the Grand Music-Master are: to cultivate the edicts and commands; to investigate poetic stanzas; to proscribe licentious sounds—so that [the people] act in

accord with the seasons, and barbarous customs and heterodox tones dare
not bring disorder on the 'Elegantiae.' "[41]

Thus ritual-and-music is, for Xunzi as for Confucius, a mode of moral
self-cultivation, but his underlying cosmology is radically different. Confucius had nothing to say about the origin of the rituals; they were but a
cultural given, which one is required to attune and adjust, with sincere
moral consciousness, as circumstances demand. And this practice, in
Confucius's view, trains us in the discipline of moral reasoning that is
necessary to lead a respectable life. For Xunzi too, practicing the rituals
propels our moral development, but not because we are supposed to alter
them to suit varying conditions; rather, the rituals are the practicable
code that the Sages, who penetrated the fundamental patterns of the
cosmos, left behind for the benefit of their less talented posterity:

水行者表深，表不明則陷；治民者表道，表不明則亂。禮者，表也。
非禮，昏世也。昏世，大亂也。故道無不明，外內異表，隱顯有常，
民陷乃去。(*Xunzi* 17.11)[42]

Those who have forded a river mark the deep spots; if the markers are not
clear, one will stumble. Those who have brought order to the people mark
the Way; if the markers are not clear, there will be disorder. The rituals
are the markers; to oppose the rituals is to blind the world; to blind the
world is a great disorder. Thus if nothing is left unclear about the Way,
if there are different markers for the outer and inner, and a constancy
pertaining to the hidden and the manifest, then the people will stumble
no more.

What Xunzi meant by this "constancy" is the Way. Confucius and
Mencius had used this term, but never with any necessary cosmological
connotations; for earlier Confucians, *dao* simply referred to "the right
path." Xunzi, who lived after such texts as *Laozi* had gained currency,
turned the Confucian Way into something more complex.

天行有常，不為堯存，不為桀亡。應之以治則吉，應之以亂則凶。
彊本而節用，則天不能貧，養備而動時，則天不能病；脩道而不貳，
則天不能禍。故水旱不能使之飢，寒暑不能使之疾，祅怪不能使
之凶。本荒而用侈，則天不能使之富；養略而動罕，則天不能使
之全；倍道而妄行，則天不能使之吉。故水旱未至而飢，寒暑未薄

而疾，袄怪未至而凶。受時與治世同，而殃禍與治世異，不可以怨
天，其道然也。(*Xunzi* 17.1)[43]

There is a constancy to Heaven's processes. It is not preserved by Yao, and
it does not perish because of Jie. To respond to it with the right order is
auspicious; to respond to it with disorder is inauspicious. If you strengthen
the base and spend in moderation, Heaven cannot impoverish you. If the
nourishment [of the people] is achieved and your movements are in accordance with the seasons, Heaven cannot cause you to be ill. If you cultivate the Way and are not of two [minds], Heaven cannot ruin you. Thus
floods and drought cannot bring about famine; cold and heat cannot bring
about disease; portents and wonders cannot bring about inauspiciousness.
But if the base is neglected and expenditures are extravagant, Heaven
cannot enrich you. If the nourishment [of the people] is desultory and
your movements are irregular, Heaven cannot cause you to be hale. If you
turn your back on the Way and act thoughtlessly, Heaven cannot bring
about auspiciousness. Thus there will be famine even without floods or
drought, disease even without cold or heat, inauspiciousness even without
portents and wonders. The seasons will be received just as in an orderly
age, but your calamities and ruination will be unlike [the bounty of] an
orderly age. You cannot complain to Heaven, for its Way is such.[44]

Heaven's processes (*tianxing* 天行) do not change from one epoch to
the next;[45] thus one must learn how to respond to them with "the right
order" (*zhi* 治), whereafter it would be either ignorant or hypocritical to
blame Heaven for one's misfortune. When a ruler governs a state well,
there are bound to be good results; when a ruler governs a state badly,
there are bound to be bad results. Disasters can have no long-term consequences because a well-governed state will prosper even in the face of
disasters, and a poorly governed state will be vanquished even if it avoids
disasters altogether. (Xunzi's opinion of foreseeable natural disasters such
as hurricanes would undoubtedly have been that they strike *all* states, but
a well-governed state will be prepared for such an event, whereas a poorly
governed state will be in no position to respond to it.) Consequently,
Heaven plays a sure but indirect role in determining our fortune or misfortune. Heaven never intercedes directly in human affairs, but human
affairs are certain to succeed or fail according to a timeless pattern that
Heaven determined before human beings existed.

治亂天邪？曰：日月、星辰、瑞曆，是禹、桀之所同也，禹以治，
桀以亂，治亂非天也。時邪？曰：繁啟蕃長於春夏，畜積收藏於秋
冬，是禹、桀之所同也，禹以治，桀以亂，治亂非時也。(*Xunzi* 17.4)[46]

Are order and disorder due to Heaven? I say: The revolutions of the sun,
moon, and stars, and the cyclical calendar—these were the same under Yu
and Jie. Since Yu brought about order and Jie disorder, order and disorder
are not in Heaven. Or the seasons? I say: Luxuriantly, [vegetation] begins
to bloom and grow in spring and summer; crops are harvested and stored
in autumn and winter. This, too, was the same under Yu and Jie. Since Yu
brought about order and Jie disorder, order and disorder are not in the
seasons.

If we attempt to conduct ourselves or our society in a manner that is
incompatible with "the constancy," we will suffer—and have only ourselves to blame.

天不為人之惡寒也輟冬，地不為人之惡遼遠也輟廣，君子不為小人
之匈匈也輟行。天有常道矣，地有常數矣，君子有常體矣。(*Xunzi* 17.5)[47]

Heaven does not stop winter because people dislike cold; Earth does not
stop its expansiveness because people dislike great distances; the noble
man does not stop his right conduct because petty men rant and rave.
Heaven has a constant Way; Earth has its constant dimensions; the noble
man has a constant bearing.

Next, Xunzi makes a crucial distinction between knowing Heaven and
knowing its Way. The former is impossible, and therefore a waste of time
to attempt, but the latter is open to all who try. To cite a modern parallel,
it is not difficult to understand *how* the force of gravity works by carefully
observing its effects in the phenomenal world, but to understand *why*
gravity works is a different matter altogether. Xunzi would say that one
should constrain one's inquiries to learning how gravity works, and then
think about how to apply this irresistible force of nature to improve the
lives of humankind. His attitude was not scientific in our sense.[48]

故明於天人之分，則可謂至人矣。不為而成，不求而得，夫是之謂
天職。如是者，雖深，其人不加慮焉；雖大，不加能焉；雖精，不

加察焉；夫是之謂不與天爭職。……所志於天者，已其見象之可以期者矣；所志於地者，已其見宜之可以息者矣：所志於四時者，已其見數之可以事者矣；所志於陰陽者，已其見和之可以治者矣。(*Xunzi* 17.2a–3b)[49]

Thus one who is enlightened about the distinction between Heaven and man can be called an Ultimate Person.[50] What is completed without any action, what is attained without being sought—this is called the agency of Heaven. Therefore, however profound they may be, such people do not add their reasoning to it; however great they may be, they do not add their abilities to it; however perceptive they may be, they do not add their investigations to it. This is what is called not competing with the agency of Heaven. . . . Their aspiration with respect to Heaven is no more than to observe the phenomena that can be taken as regular periods (e.g., the progression of the seasons or stars). Their aspiration with respect to Earth is no more than to observe the matters that yield [crops]. Their aspiration with respect to the four seasons is no more than to observe the data that can be made to serve [humanity]. Their aspiration with respect to *yin* and *yang* is no more than to observe their harmonious [interactions] that can bring about order.

In a moment of poetic exuberance, Xunzi concludes with a fusillade of rhymed couplets:

大天而思之，孰與物畜而制之？
從天而頌之，孰與制天命而用之？
望時而待之，孰與應時而使之？
因物而多之，孰與騁能而化之？
思物而物之，孰與理物而勿失之也？
願於物之所以生，孰與有物之所以成？ (*Xunzi* 17.10)[51]

To extol Heaven and long for it—how does that compare to
    domesticating its creatures and controlling them?
To follow Heaven and sing paeans to it—how does that compare to
    administering Heaven's Mandate and making use of it?
To gaze at the seasons and await them—how does that compare to
    responding to the seasons and employing them?

To accord with things and let them reproduce [at their own pace]—how
  does that compare to unleashing one's ability and transforming them?
To long for things and regard them as [external] things—how does that
  compare to arranging things in patterns and never losing them?
To yearn for whatever gives birth to things—how does that compare to
  possessing what brings them to completion?

For Xunzi, then, rituals are not merely received practices, nor convenient social institutions; they are practicable forms in which the sages
aimed to encapsulate the fundamental patterns of the universe. No
human being, not even a sage, can know Heaven, but we can know Heav-
en's Way, which is the surest path to a flourishing and blessed life. Because
human beings have limited knowledge and abilities, it is difficult for us
to attain this deep understanding, and therefore the sages handed down
the rituals to help us follow in their footsteps.

There is a radically different understanding of Xunzi than the one
advanced here; Kurtis Hagen,[52] the most articulate exponent of this other
view, contends that Xunzi's Way is not an unchanging cosmological reality to which we must conform, but something constructed by human
beings. There is one ambiguous passage that might be taken as support
for Hagen's interpretation:

道者，非天之道，非地之道，人之所以道也，君子之所道也。
(*Xunzi* 8.3)[53]

The Way is not the Way of Heaven, nor the Way of Earth; it is what people
regard as the Way, what the noble man is guided by.

This seems to say, despite all the material in *Xunzi* 17 about appre-
hending the constancy of Heaven and then applying it profitably to daily
life, that we are supposed to disregard the Way of Heaven, and create our
own Way instead. The basic problem is that the surviving text of *Xunzi*
is vague enough to permit various interpretations, but the repeated references to the importance of observing and appropriately "responding"
(*ying* 應) to the seasons suggest that natural patterns are indeed to be
taken as normative.

Yang Liang 楊倞 (fl. AD 818), the author of the oldest extant commentary to the *Xunzi*, evidently recognized this problem and tried to
soften the impact of *Xunzi* 8.3 by making it fit with the rest of the text:

重說先王之道非陰陽、山川、怪異之事，是人所行之道。

This emphasizes that the Way of the Former Kings was not a matter of *yin* and *yang*, or mountains and rivers, or omens and prodigies, but the Way that people practice.

Yang Liang's opinion is surely not decisive; he was but an interpreter of Xunzi, not Xunzi himself, and his glosses are not always regarded as the most compelling today. But in this case I think he was right that Xunzi meant to say no more than that the Way is to be found not in prodigies and other freakish occurrences, but in the "constancies" that people can put into practice. Indeed, the very notion that the Way of Heaven, the Way of Earth, and the Way of human beings are distinct entities would contradict a point that Xunzi makes more than once: there is only one Way.

天下無二道，聖人無兩心。(*Xunzi* 21.1)[54]

There are no two Ways in the world, and the Sage is never of two minds.

This single and holistic Way, moreover, serves as the enduring standard for all times because all ramified truths of the universe are unified within it:

曰：精於道者也，精於物者也。精於物者以物物，精於道者兼物物。故君子壹於道而以贊稽物。壹於道則正，以贊稽物則察，以正志行察論，則萬物官矣。(*Xunzi* 21.6b)[55]

It is said: There are those who have refined their skill at the Way, and those who have refined their skill at things. Those who have refined their skill at things treat each separate thing as a separate thing; those who have refined their skill at the Way treat each separate thing as part of an all-inclusive thing. Thus the noble man derives unity from the Way and uses it as an aid in canvassing things. Since he derives unity from the Way, he is rectified; since he uses it as an aid in canvassing things, he is perspicacious; and since he advances perspicacious theories with a rectified will, he is the officer of all the myriad things.

道者，古今之正權也，離道而內自擇，則不知禍福之所託。
(*Xunzi* 22.6b)[56]

The Way is the correct scale for past and present; if one departs from the Way and chooses on the basis of one's own innards, then one does not know whence ruination and fortune are sent.

What we need to understand, then, is the Way *as it pertains to human beings*. Unusual celestial phenomena such as shooting stars must, theoretically, be explainable by a comprehensive formulation of the Way—there can be no violations of the Way in the natural world—but this is exactly why we do not aim for a comprehensive formulation of the Way.[57] We can safely ignore shooting stars as irrelevant to human beings because they do not provide replicable patterns for use in moral and social development. Responding to the seasons with timely planting and harvesting is, once again, a more productive model.

In accordance with his notion of the Way as the observable "constancies" that can be profitably applied to human conduct, Xunzi argued strongly against the old idea that weird occurrences on earth can be rationalized as monitory signs from Heaven.

星隊、木鳴，國人皆恐。曰：是何也？曰：無何也，是天地之變，陰陽之化，物之罕至者也，怪之可也，而畏之非也。夫日月之有蝕，風雨之不時，怪星之黨見，是無世而不常有之。上明而政平，則是雖並世起，無傷也；上闇而政險，則是雖無一至者，無益也。(*Xunzi* 17.7)[58]

When stars shoot down and trees squall, the denizens of the city are all terrified. They say, "What is this?" I say, "It is nothing." These are the shifts in Heaven and Earth, transformations of *yin* and *yang*, material anomalies. It is acceptable to wonder at them, but it is not acceptable to fear them. No generation has been without eclipses of the sun and moon, untimely winds and rains, or the appearance of wondrous stars. If the ruler is enlightened and the government peaceful, then even if such things arise all together, they cannot cause any harm. If the ruler is benighted and the government precarious, then even if none of these things should happen, [their absence] will still confer no benefit.

What is crucial is not how loudly the trees may have squalled this year, but how people have behaved. Xunzi goes on to expound his theory of "human portents" (*renyao* 人祅), a term that would have seemed as counterintuitive in Xunzi's language as it does in ours. "Human portents" are the many shortsighted and immoral acts through which human beings bring on their own destruction.[59]

物之已至者，人祅則可畏也。楛耕傷稼，耘耨失薉，政險失民，田薉稼惡，糴貴民飢，道路有死人，夫是之謂人祅。政令不明，舉錯不時，本事不理，夫是之謂人祅。禮儀不修，內外無別，男女淫亂，則父子相疑，上下乖離，寇難竝至，夫是之謂人祅。祅是生於亂，三者錯，無安國。(*Xunzi* 17.7)[60]

Among material [anomalies] that may occur, it is human portents that are to be feared: poor plowing that harms the harvest, hoeing and weeding out of season, governmental malice that causes the loss of the people. When agriculture is untimely and the harvest bad, the price of grain is high and the people starve. In the roads and streets there are dead people. These are called human portents. When governmental commands are unenlightened, *corvée* miscalculated or untimely, fundamental affairs chaotic—these are called human portents. When ritual and morality are not cultivated, when internal and external are not separated, when male and female are licentious and disorderly, when father and son are suspicious of each other, when superior and inferior are obstinate and estranged; when crime and hardship occur together—these are called human portents. Portents are born of disorder; when these three types [of human portents][61] obtain, there is no peace in the country.

Heaven has no part in such wrongdoing. Now and then strange things may happen in the skies, but they have happened at all moments in history, and they have never been sufficient to destroy a prudent and moral society, whereas an imprudent and immoral society will fail even if it is spared an eclipse. Good acts have good consequences; bad acts have bad consequences; and only fools (and hypocrites) wait for Heaven to intercede.

Xunzi even extends this theory of "human portents" to contend that religious ceremonies have no numinous effect; we carry them out merely for their inherent beauty and the social cohesion that they promote. In this connection, he has been compared to Durkheim.[62]

雩而雨，何也？曰：無何也，猶不雩而雨也。日月食而救之，天旱而雩，卜筮然後決大事，非以為得求也，以文之也。故君子以為文，而百姓以為神。以為文則吉，以為神則凶也。(*Xunzi* 17.8)[63]

If the sacrifice for rain [is performed], and it rains, what of it? I say: It is nothing. Even if there had been no sacrifice, it would have rained. When the sun and moon are eclipsed, we rescue them [by performing the proper rites]; when Heaven sends drought we perform the sacrifice for rain; we decide great matters only after divining with turtle and milfoil. This is not in order to obtain what we seek, but in order to embellish [such occasions]. Thus the noble man takes [these ceremonies] to be embellishment, but the populace takes them to be spiritual. To take them as embellishment is auspicious; to take them as spiritual is inauspicious.

• • •

Xunzi's idea of man-made rituals based on immutable cosmic norms, which is distinctive among classical Confucians, can be used to test some of the more questionable chapters in the *Xunzi*, such as "Discussion of Warfare" ("Yibing" 議兵, *Xunzi* 15), which is presented as a debate between Xun Kuang and a certain Lord Linwu 臨武君 before King Xiaocheng of Zhao 趙孝成王 (r. 265–245 BC).[64] Scholars have long recognized that "Discussion of Warfare" could not have been written by Xun Kuang himself, because it consistently refers to Xunzi as Sun Qingzi 孫卿子, "Master Chamberlain Sun," a title that he would not have used.[65] Moreover, the use of the posthumous name of King Xiaocheng of Zhao implies that *Xunzi* 15 was, at the very least, edited after 245 BC. (It is uncertain whether Xunzi himself was still alive at this time.)[66] And there is no reason why the date of the text could not be even later than that.[67]

"Discussion of Warfare" squares extremely well with Xunzi's undisputed writings, however—so well, in fact, that the author, whoever he was, must have been intimately familiar with Xunzi's philosophy, and applied it cogently to the question of warfare. Similarly, while it is uncertain whether the debate between Xun Kuang and Lord Linwu really took place—or, if it did, whether the chapter faithfully reproduces the participants' arguments—it is still plausible that we are dealing with a close approximation of what Xun Kuang once said in a live debate on warfare. To be sure, the figure of "Master Chamberlain Sun" assumes an oratorical tone in "Discussion of Warfare" unlike that of his expository works, but a difference in register is only to be expected in material that was not originally composed in essay form.

The debate begins with some pronouncements by Lord Linwu on surprise tactics and timely mobilizations:

觀敵之變動，後之發，先之至，此用兵之要術也。(*Xunzi* 15.1a)[68]

Observe the enemy's movements; "set out after him but arrive before him." This is the essential technique in using troops.

"Set out after him but arrive before him" is an unmistakable allusion to *Sunzi*.[69] Xunzi responds by denying the long-term value of clever battlefield maneuvers: the basis of all military action lies not in skillful generalship, but in unifying the populace. By practicing humanity and morality, Xunzi argues, a sage ruler can undermine the power of an aggressor:

且夫暴國之君，將誰與至哉？彼其所與至者，必其民也，而其民之親我歡若父母，其好我芬若椒蘭；彼反顧其上，則若灼黥，若仇讐。(*Xunzi* 15.1b)[70]

Moreover, whom would the ruler of a cruel state send [to the battlefield]? Those whom he would send must be his own people. But his people would feel intimate toward us; they would be as complaisant as if we were their father and mother. They would be as attracted to us as to the pepper and orchid (i.e., sweet-smelling plants). But when they look back at their ruler, then he will seem like a brand or a tattoo, like a sworn enemy.

In other words, even with brilliant strategies, a ruler cannot rely on his army if his people do not serve him gladly; and conversely, a benevolent ruler—one who deserves the name "King"—can always be sure of victory, because the soldiers of his enemy will simply desert their commander. Xunzi continues:

故王者之兵不試。湯、武之誅桀、紂也，拱挹指麾而強暴之國莫不趨使，誅桀、紂若誅獨夫。(*Xunzi* 15.1d)[71]

Thus the troops of a true king are never tested. When Tang and Wu punished Jie and Zhòu, they bowed with their hands folded and gave the signal with their finger, whereupon not one of the mighty and cruel states failed to rush to their service and execute Jie and Zhòu as though they were executing a forsaken man.

As he has related it so far, Xunzi's view of warfare is not original. The idea that a sage can evoke unquestioning devotion, even in his enemies, is commonplace in Confucian discussions of warfare. Mencius, as we saw (pp. 103–4), also argued that a beneficent ruler will always defeat his opponents in battle, because in winning over the people, he secures for himself the most effective weapon of all. What is unique in Xunzi's "Discussion of Warfare," however, is his emphasis on ritual as the key to a well-ordered state. To be sure, earlier writings had also discussed the idea of ritual as the foundation of statecraft; the *Zuo Commentary*, in particular, is famous for its scenes in which a ruler who is about to attack his neighbor publicly justifies his aggression on the grounds that he is merely "punishing" his enemy's intolerable violations of ritual.[72] But Xunzi raises the significance of ritual to a new level: in his view, the ruler's ability to govern his state in accordance with ritual is the sole criterion that will determine success or failure on the battlefield.

君賢者其國治，君不能者其國亂；隆禮貴義者其國治，簡禮賤義者其國亂。(*Xunzi* 15.1c)[73]

If the ruler is worthy, his state will be ordered; if the ruler is incompetent, his state will be chaotic. If he exalts ritual and esteems morality, his state will be ordered; if he is lax about rituals and debases morality, his state will be disordered.

Having established the principle that "exalting ritual" is the true path to order and strength, Xunzi proceeds to expatiate on the concept of ritual in characteristic language.

禮者，治辨之極也，強固之本也，威行之道也，功名之總也。王公由之，所以得天下也；不由，所以隕社稷也。故堅甲利兵不足以為勝，高城深池不足以為固，嚴令繁刑不足以為威，由其道則行，不由其道則廢。(*Xunzi* 15.4)[74]

Ritual is the ridgepole of order and discrimination; it is the foundation of a strength and security, the Way of awesome practice, the chief precondition for a successful reputation. When kings and dukes follow [the rituals], that is how they obtain the world; when they do not follow [the rituals], that is how they damage their own altars of soil and grain. Thus firm armor and keen weapons are not enough to bring about victory; lofty fortifications and deep moats are not enough to bring about security; strict commands and manifold punishments are not enough to instill awe. If one follows the Way, then one will progress; if one does not follow the Way, then one will perish.

One will notice that the rituals are repeatedly associated with the Way in these passages; at times, the two terms appear to be used interchangeably, as though "exalting the rituals" were essentially the same thing as "following the Way." The figure of Master Chamberlain Xun in "Discussion of Warfare" evidently views military combat as one of the many fields of analysis that can be engaged profitably with the fundamental and all-encompassing model of the Way manifested through ritual practice. The chapter is not really about warfare at all.

• • •

So too Xunzi's famous essay on language, "Rectifying Names" ("Zhengming" 正名): while it includes some impressive insights into the nature of verbal communication,[75] the primary concern of the chapter is morality, not linguistics.[76] The thrust of the essay is easily missed because a few of Xunzi's comments sound as though they came out of a twentieth-century pragmatics textbook:

名無固宜，約之以命。約定俗成謂之宜，異於約則謂之不宜。名無固實，約之以命實，約定俗成謂之實名。名有固善，徑易而不拂，謂之善名。(*Xunzi* 22.2g)[77]

Names have no inherent appropriateness. We designate them [by some word] in order to name them. If it is fixed by convention and implemented by custom, then it is called appropriate. If [the name that people use] is different from what has been agreed on, then it is called inappropriate.

As much as this may remind one of Saussure, Xunzi was not interested in the same questions as modern linguists. In "Rectifying Names," Xunzi also discusses sophistic paradoxes that were rampant in his day (the most famous being "A white horse is not a horse"—see p. 16), dividing them into three typological categories. His conclusion discloses that his main purpose is not a proper taxonomy of falsidical paradoxes, but an assertion of the moral purpose of language: "All heretical theories and aberrant sayings depart from the correct Way and are presumptuously crafted according to these three categories of delusion" 凡邪說辟言之離正道而擅作者, 無不類於三惑者矣 (*Xunzi* 22.3d).[78] The paradoxes of the sophists cannot be used as a basis for moral governance and thus would be objectionable even if they were not false; they are "disputes with no use" 辯而無用 (*Xunzi* 6.6).[79] The only legitimate purpose of language, like that of government itself, is to serve as the king's tool in propagating moral excellence.

> 故王者之制名, 名定而實辨, 道行而志通, 則慎率民而一焉。故析辭擅作名以亂正名, 使民疑惑, 人多辨訟, 則謂之大姦, 其罪猶為符節、度量之罪也。 ......其民莫敢託為奇辭以亂正名, 故壹於道法而謹於循令矣。如是, 則其跡長矣。跡長功成, 治之極也, 是謹於守名約之功也。(*Xunzi* 22.1c)[80]

When a true king determines names, if names are fixed and realities distinguished, if the Way is practiced and his intentions communicated, then he may carefully lead the people and unify them by this means. Thus splitting phrases and presumptuously creating [new] names in order to bring disorder on rectified names causes the people to be doubtful and confused. When there are many disputes and indictments among people, this is called "great sedition"; this crime is as [serious as] crimes pertaining to [the falsification of] contracts and measures. . . . When one's people dare not circulate odd phrases to bring disorder on rectified names, they will be unified by the Way and its methods and will be careful to obey [the King's] orders. In such a case, his traces will be long-lasting. To have long-lasting traces and to achieve merit is the acme of establishing order. This is what is achieved by carefully defending the convention of names.

The task of determining names and then enforcing their use belongs to the King alone, not to any lord and certainly not to the people. "A true king" (*wangzhe* 王者, literally "one who is a king"), in Confucian language, refers not to the person who happens to be sitting on the throne, but someone who has lived up to the moral requirements of that office and duly rules the world by his charismatic example. Accordingly, a phrase like "leading and unifying the people" (*shuai min er yi yan* 率民而一焉) refers not to expedient rulership, but to implementing the Confucian project of morally transforming the world. Language is useful in that enterprise because without it the people cannot even understand the ruler's wishes, let alone carry them out.

Just as the rituals need to be based on the foundation of the Way, the ruler's names, though they can be arbitrary as designations, must correspond to reality. You can make up the word for "reality," but you cannot make up reality.

然則何緣而以同異？曰：緣天官。凡同類、同情者，其天官之意物也同，故比方之疑似而通，是所以共其約名以相期也。形體、色、理以目異，聲音清濁、調竽、奇聲以耳異，甘、苦、鹹、淡、辛、酸、奇味以口異，香、臭、芬、鬱、腥、臊、洒、酸 [=漏、庮]⁸¹、奇臭以鼻異，疾、養 [=癢]⁸²、凔、熱、滑、鈹、輕、重以形體異，說、故、喜、怒、哀、樂、愛、惡、欲以心異。(22.2c–d)⁸³

What does one rely on to [determine] same and different? I say: One relies on the Heaven-endowed organs. The senses of all members of the same species with the same essence perceive things in the same manner. Thus we associate things that appear similar upon comparison; in this manner we provide designated names for them in order to define them with respect to each other. Shape, body, color, and pattern are distinguished by the eyes. Sound, tone, treble, bass, mode, harmony—diverse sounds are distinguished by the ears. Sweet, bitter, salty, bland, pungent, sour—diverse tastes are distinguished by the mouth. Fragrant, foul, ambrosial, odorous, rank, fetid, putrid, acrid—diverse smells are distinguished by the nose. Painful, itchy, cold, hot, smooth, sharp, light, and heavy are differentiated by the body. Statements, reasons, happiness, resentment, grief, joy, love, hate, and desire are distinguished by the heart-mind.

The notion that we rely on our senses to perceive the world around us represents a substantial claim on Xunzi's part, because other philosophers had already suggested that reality is not straightforwardly discerned; on the contrary, one's partial perspective on reality necessarily informs one's perception of it (recall *Zhuangzi*, p. 135). For Xunzi, however, reality is reality, regardless of how we perceive it. Once again, some scholars question whether Xunzi is such a strong realist,⁸⁴ but I find any alternative, "constructivist" interpretation of Xunzi difficult to reconcile with his repeated assertions that language must conform to reality and the Way.

名也者，所以期累實也。辭也者，兼異實之名以論一意也。辨說也
者，不異實名以喻動靜之道也。期命也者，辨說之用也。辨說也者，
心之象道也。心也者，道之工宰也。道也者，治之經理也。心合於
道，說合於心，辭合於說。(*Xunzi* 22.3f)[85]

Names are that by which one defines different real objects.[86] Phrases are
that by which one combines the names of different real objects in order
to expound a single idea. Polemical statements are that by which one
analogizes about the movements of the Way without causing names to
diverge from reality. Definitions and names are what polemical persua-
sions use [as their basis]. Polemical statements are what the heart-mind
uses to depict the Way. The heart-mind is the master craftsman of the Way.
The Way is the canonical pattern of order. One's heart-mind should accord
with the Way, one's statements with one's heart-mind, one's phrases with
one's statements.

With the heart-mind, we come at last to the keystone of Xunzi's philosophy, the one piece that links together all the others. The Chinese
word, *xin* 心, meaning "heart," is the same that Mencius had used, but
Xunzi attributes such strong and varied mental processes to this organ
that one has to construe it as not only the heart but also the mind.

First, the heart-mind is the organ that we use to discover the Way.
Xunzi's discussion of Heaven presented his argument that moral self-
cultivation is a matter of correctly perceiving and then applying the Way,
but it did not explain how we perceive the Way in the first place. Elsewhere, he addresses the question explicitly:

人何以知道？曰：心。心何以知？曰：虛壹而靜。心未嘗不藏也，
然而有所謂虛；心未嘗不滿也，然而有所謂一；心未嘗不動也，然
而有所謂靜。人生而有知，知而有志。志也者，藏也，然而有所謂
虛，不以所已藏害所將受謂之虛。心生而有知，知而有異，異也者，
同時兼知之。同時兼知之，兩也，然而有所謂一，不以夫一害此一
謂之壹。心，臥則夢，偷則自行，使之則謀。故心未嘗不動也，然
而有所謂靜，不以夢劇亂知謂之靜。(*Xunzi* 21.5d)[87]

How does one know the Way? I say: the heart-mind. How does the heart-
mind know? I say: emptiness, unity, and tranquility. The heart-mind never
stops storing, but it has something called "emptiness." The heart-mind
never stops being filled, but it has something called "unity." The heart-

mind never stops moving, but it has something called "tranquility." From birth humans have awareness; with awareness come thoughts; thoughts are stored. But [the heart-mind] has something called "emptiness": it does not take what is stored to harm what is to be received; this is called "emptiness." From birth the heart-mind has awareness; with awareness comes differentiation; different things are known at the same time. Knowing different things at the same time is duality. But [the heart-mind] has something called "unity": it does not take one thing to harm another; this is called "unity." The heart-mind dreams when it sleeps; it moves spontaneously when it relaxes; it plans when it is employed. Thus the heart-mind never stops moving, but it has something called "tranquility": it does not take dreams and fancies to bring disorder on knowledge; this is called "tranquility."

"Emptiness," "unity," and "tranquility" are three nurturable faculties that we all possess from birth, but do not all employ to the same degree. (The title of chapter 21, "Resolving Blindness," refers to the self-destructive acts that people undertake because they fail to employ their heart-minds correctly.) Xunzi patently borrowed these three terms from earlier discourse, particularly *Zhuangzi*, though he used them very differently.[88] "Emptiness" refers to the heart-mind's ability to store a seemingly unlimited amount of information; we do not have to erase one datum in order to make room for another. "Unity" refers to the heart-mind's ability to synthesize diverse data into meaningful paradigms. And "tranquility" refers to the heart-mind's ability to distinguish fantasy from rational thinking. ("Not taking dreams and fancies to bring disorder on knowledge" may be an oblique allusion to the famous episode at the end of *Zhuangzi* 2, where Zhuang Zhou is said not to be able to tell whether he is Zhuang Zhou or a butterfly in his dream.)[89] Armed with these powers, we can infer the patterns of the Way by taking in, and then pondering, the data transmitted to the heart-mind by the senses.

Second, the heart-mind is the chief among the organs. It is the only organ that can command the others; indeed, it is the only organ with any self-consciousness.

心者，形之君也，而神明之主也，出令而無所受令。自禁也，自使也，自奪也，自取也，自行也，自止也。故口可劫而使墨 [=默][90]

云，形可劫而使詘申，心不可劫而使易意，是之則受，非之則辭。(*Xunzi* 21.6a)[91]

The mind is the lord of the body and the master of "godlike insight."[92] It issues commands but does not receive commands. It prohibits on its own; it employs on its own; it considers on its own; it takes on its own; it acts on its own; it ceases on its own. Thus the mouth can be forced to be silent or to speak; the body can be forced to contract or expand; the mind cannot be forced to change its intention. If it accepts [something, the mind] receives it; if it rejects [something, the mind] forgoes it.

Third, because the heart-mind can control both itself and all other organs of the body, it is the font of "artifice," or the deliberate actions that begin to transform the morally deficient *xing*:

心慮而能為之動謂之偽。慮積焉、能習焉而後成謂之偽。(*Xunzi* 22.1b)[93]

When the heart-mind reasons and the other faculties put it into action—this is called "artifice." When reasoning is accumulated in this manner and the other faculties practice it, so that [morality] is brought to completion—this is called "artifice."

And most explicitly:

人之所欲，生甚矣，人之所惡，死甚矣，然而人有從生成死者，非不欲生而欲死也，不可以生而可以死也。故欲過之而動不及，心止之也。心之所可中理，則欲雖多，奚傷於治！欲不及而動過之，心使之也。心之所可失理，則欲雖寡，奚止於亂！故治亂在於心之所可，亡於情之所欲。(*Xunzi* 22.5a)[94]

People's desire for life is deep; their hatred of death is deep. Yet when people discard life and cause their own death, this is not because they do not desire life or because they desire death. Rather, this is because it is not [morally] acceptable for them to live; it is acceptable for them only to die. Thus when one's desires are excessive but one's actions do not reach [the same degree], it is because the heart-mind brings them to a halt. If the heart-mind has accepted correct patterns, then even if one's desires are manifold, how would they harm order? And when one's desires do not reach [the level of excess], but one's actions are excessive, it is because the heart-mind causes one [to act in this manner]. If the mind has accepted invalid patterns, then even if one's desires are few, how would one refrain from disorder? Thus order and disorder lie with whatever the heart-mind will accept, and not with the desires or the emotions.

The human instinct of self-preservation must be the starkest example of *xing*, yet the heart-mind is capable of overriding even this impulse by "halting" (*zhi* 止) it if it clashes with the correct "patterns" (*li* 理).[95] We have the necessary faculties to recognize immorality when we see it, and if we permit ourselves to tread an immoral path, we cannot blame our emotions or desires but must accept that our heart-mind has failed to exert the requisite discipline. We know that we could have done better. Indeed, when we speak of "we," we are speaking of our heart-mind.[96] For the heart-mind is the crucible where these teeming moral deliberations take place.

Thus Xunzi ends, like all Confucians, with individual responsibility. Mencius would have called this "living up to our destiny"; for Xunzi, with his more ramified cosmology, it is more accurately stated as the heart-mind's obligation to process the principles of the Way and then command the rest of the body to conform. Because we are not sages, we are advised to follow the rituals in order to attain this degree of understanding, but, fundamentally, the path to morality is open to anyone who sees and thinks.[97]

Xunzi's conception of the heart-mind also figures in a distinctive congruence that he postulates between a kingdom and a human being. A kingdom possesses an initial set of features—it may be large or small, rich or poor, hilly or flat—but these are immaterial to its ultimate success or failure, for any territory, however small, provides enough of a base for a sage to conquer the world. Thus it is the management of the state, and not its natural resources, that determine whether it will become the domain of a king or be conquered by its neighbors. This management, furthermore, comprises two elements: a proper method, namely the rituals of the sage kings; and a decisive agent, namely the lord, who chooses either to adopt the rituals or unwisely discard them.

In much the same way, human beings are made up of two parts: their *xing*, or detestable initial condition, and *wei*, their conscious conduct. They may reform themselves, or they may remain detestable: the outcome depends entirely on their conduct. The management of the self, just like the management of the state, comprises two elements: a proper method, which is, once again, the rituals of the sage kings; and a decisive agent, which chooses either to adopt the rituals or unwisely discard them. This agent, the analogue of the lord of a state, is the heart-mind.[98] As in the Broadway song, "It's not where you start; it's where you finish."[99]

# CHAPTER NINE

# *Han Feizi*

Like every other text addressed in this book, *Han Feizi* has to be distinguished from its author, Han Fei, a prolific philosopher who was executed on trumped-up charges in 233 BC. But this time, there is a new reason. Although Han Fei is probably responsible for the lion's share of the extant *Han Feizi*, this does not permit readers to identify the philosophy of Han Fei himself with the philosophy (or philosophies) advanced in the *Han Feizi*, as though these were necessarily the same thing. When we read the works of philosophers, whether Eastern or Western, we generally assume, without much fuss, that the authors meant what they said. Recent trends in hermeneutics have led some critics to assail this as naive,[1] but we still tend to assume that Hobbes endorsed what he wrote in *Leviathan*, Zhu Xi endorsed what he wrote in his *Collected Commentaries on the Four Books, by Chapter and Verse* (*Sishu zhangju jizhu* 四書章句集注), and so on. The case of Han Fei and the *Han Feizi* is more complex because Han Fei was slippery. What Han Fei said varied with his expected audience, a point that scholarship has not always accounted for. Most of his chapters are addressed to kings; at least one, "The Difficulties of Persuasion" ("Shuinan" 說難), is addressed to ministers; and for many chapters we can only guess at the intended audience.

As with so many other figures from this period, almost all our information about the life of Han Fei comes from his biography in *Records of the Historian*,[2] whose credibility is bolstered by the fact that it names several chapter titles found in the received *Han Feizi* before quoting "The Difficulties of Persuasion" in toto. Clearly Sima Qian read at least some part of what we now call the *Han Feizi*. Fortunately, the details of Han Fei's life are not crucial to interpreting the *Han Feizi*, and the major pieces of information in Sima Qian's biography, namely that Han Fei was descended from the ruling house of Hán 韓 and that he was talked into suicide after being entrapped by Li Si 李斯 (who was himself executed in 208 BC), are probably not far from the truth. As an adult, he abandoned Hán and sought his fortune as a minister in Qin, the mighty western state that would soon annex Hán before unifying all China under the famed First Emperor (r. 221–210 BC). It is in Qin that he must have written the essays that have secured his name for all time, and it is in Qin that he succumbed to the skullduggery of court politics, which he described so memorably in his works.

• • •

To understand the attitude of the *Han Feizi*, and the issues in which the text does and does not take an interest, one might imagine a counselor speaking before a newly crowned king. "You are the king!" he says. "Congratulations—everyone wants to kill you now. Listen to me, and you might survive."[3] All his lovers and sycophants, it turns out, only wish the ruler dead, because they all stand to profit from his demise.

> 人主之患在於信人，信人則制於人。人臣之於其君，非有骨肉之親
> 也，縛於勢而不得不事也。故為人臣者，窺覘其君心也無須臾之休，
> 而人主怠傲處其上，此世所以有劫君弒主也。為人主而大信其子，
> 則姦臣得乘於子以成其私，故李兌傅趙王而餓主父。為人主而大信
> 其妻，則姦臣得乘於妻以成其私，故優施傅麗姬，殺申生而立奚齊。
> 夫以妻之近與子之親而猶不可信，則其餘無可信者矣。
> 　且萬乘之主，千乘之君，后妃、夫人、適子為太子者，或有欲其
> 君之蚤死者。何以知其然？夫妻者，非有骨肉之恩也，愛則親，不
> 愛則疏。語曰：「其母好者其子抱。」然則其為之反也，其母惡者其
> 子釋。丈夫年五十而好色未解也，婦人年三十而美色衰矣。以衰美
> 之婦人事好色之丈夫，則身死見疏賤，而子疑不為後，此后妃、夫
> 人之所以冀其君之死者也。唯母為后而子為主，則令無不行，禁無
> 不止，男女之樂不減於先君，而擅萬乘不疑，此鴆毒扼昧之所以用
> 也。故桃左春秋曰：「人主之疾死者不能處半。」人主弗知則亂多資，
> 故曰利君死者眾則人主危。(*Han Feizi* 17)[4]

A ruler's troubles come from trusting others; if he trusts others, he will be controlled by them. A minister does not have a relationship of flesh and bone with his lord; he cannot avoid serving only because he is bound by [the ruler's] power. Thus ministers spy on their lord's heart without even a moment's respite, while the ruler dwells above them, indolent and haughty.

This is why, over the generations, lords have been bullied and rulers assassinated. If a ruler puts great trust in his son, treacherous ministers will be able to take advantage of the son and fulfill their private interests. Thus [the minister] Li Dui mentored the King of Zhao (i.e., Huiwen 惠文, r. 299–266 BC) and starved the Ruler's Father (i.e., King Wuling 武靈, r. 325–299, who had abdicated in favor of his son).[5] If a ruler puts too much trust in his wife, treacherous ministers will be able to take advantage of the wife and fulfill their private interests. Thus Jester Shi mentored [Lady] Ji of Li, killed [Crown Prince] Shensheng (d. 656 BC) and installed [her son] Xiqi (665–651 BC).[6] If someone as intimate as one's wife and as close as one's son cannot be trusted, then none among the rest can be trusted either.

Whether one is the ruler of a state of ten thousand chariots or the lord of a state of a thousand, among one's consort, ladies, and the son chosen to be the Crown Prince, there are those who desire the early death of their lord. How do I know this to be so? Between husband and wife, there is not the kindness of a relationship of flesh and bone. If he loves her, she is intimate with him; if he does not love her, she is estranged. There is a saying: "If the mother is favored, her son will be embraced." If this is the case, the inverse is: If the mother is disliked, her son will be disowned. The lust of a man of fifty has not yet dissipated, whereas the beauty and allure of a woman of thirty have faded. If a woman whose beauty has faded serves a man who still lusts, she will be estranged and disesteemed until her death; her son will be viewed with suspicion and will not succeed to the throne. This is why consorts and ladies hope for their lord's death.

But if the mother becomes a dowager and her son becomes the ruler, then all her commands will be carried out, all her prohibitions observed. Her sexual pleasure will be no less than with her former lord, and she may arrogate to herself power over the ten thousand chariots without suspicion. Such is the use of poison, strangling, and knifing. Thus is it said in the *Springs and Autumns of Tao Zuo*: "Less than half of all rulers die of illness." If the ruler of men is unaware of this, disorders will be manifold and unrestrained. Thus it is said: If those who benefit from a lord's death are many, the ruler will be imperiled.

Although Han Fei emphasized that none of the ruler's associates can be trusted, most of what appears in the *Han Feizi* deals with the ruler's relations with his ministers. Evidently, they were regarded as the party most likely, in practice, to cause him harm, because they were indispensable: by Han Fei's time, states were already so large and complex that a ruler could not hope to oversee the administration personally.[7] But relying on ministers is dangerous, because they act in their own interest, not that of their employer and certainly not that of the kingdom they represent.

外使諸侯，內耗其國，伺其危嶮之陂，以恐其主曰：「交非我不親，怨非我不解」，而主乃信之，以國聽之，卑主之名以顯其身，毀國之厚以利其家，臣不謂智。(*Han Feizi* 6)[8]

Abroad, they act as ambassadors to the other lords; within the state, they only waste [its resources]. They wait for the precipice of a crisis and terrify their ruler, saying: "If you do not establish your relations through me, [your allies] will not be intimate with you; if you do not address [your enemies'] resentment through me, it cannot be defused." The ruler then trusts them and listens to them in matters of state. They debase the name of the ruler in order to make themselves prominent; they destroy the riches of the state for the profit of their own families. I, your servant, would not call them wise.

In Han Fei's technical language, the problem is that lords do not distinguish between *gong* 公 and *si* 私. *Si* is the easier of the two terms to translate: it means "private," especially in the senses of "private interest" or "judgments reached by private and hence arbitrary criteria." Ministers who make proposals always do so out of *si*, in expectation of some private benefit. *Gong* is derived from the old word meaning "patriarch" or "duke,"[9] and by Han Fei's time it had come to refer more broadly to the interests of the ruler. In modern writing, *gong* is often translated as "public," but this is misleading, as there was nothing like our concept of "the public interest" in ancient China. (Thus a phrase like *gongyong che* 公用 車 means "vehicle for public use" in modern Chinese, but would have meant "vehicle for the [exclusive] use of the Duke" in the classical language.) Sometimes *gong* is interpreted as something like "the general interests of the state as opposed to the private interests of its ministers,"[10] but I would be cautious about this too, because the interests of a particular ruler—even long-term, prudential interests—are not necessarily identical to those of the abstract state.[11]

Han Fei defined *gong* straightforwardly as "that which opposes *si*":

古者蒼頡之作書也，自環者謂之私，背私謂之公，公私之相背也，乃蒼頡固以知之矣。(*Han Feizi* 49)[12]

In ancient times, when Cangjie invented writing, he called acting in one's own interest *si*; what opposes *si*, he called *gong*. So Cangjie certainly knew already that *gong* and *si* oppose each other.

What a ruler needs, then, are instruments of *gong* that will thwart his minions' aspirations of *si*.

黃帝有言曰：「上下一日百戰。下匿其私，用試其上；上操度量，以割其下。」故度量之立，主之寶也；黨與之具，臣之寶也。臣之所以不弒其君者，黨與不具也。故上失扶寸，下得尋常。(*Han Feizi* 8)[13]

The Yellow Thearch had a saying: "Superiors and inferiors fight a hundred battles a day. Inferiors conceal their private interests, which they use to test their superiors; superiors wield gauges and measures, with which they divide their inferiors." Thus the establishment of gauges and measures is the ruler's treasure; the formation of cliques is the ministers' treasure. The [only] reason why ministers do not assassinate their lords is that they have not formed cliques. Thus if superiors lose an inch, inferiors gain a yard.

Rulers are not defenseless against the depredations of their ministers; to counter their inferiors' crafty profit seeking, lords can "wield gauges and measures" (*cao duliang* 操度量). Han Fei had much to say about these instruments, which are better known by the name of *fa* 法 (literally "methods" or "standards"). Elsewhere, I have defined *fa* as "an impersonal administrative technique of determining rewards and punishments in accordance with a subject's true merit."[14] Armed with this crushing weapon, a ruler can keep his underlings docile and productive, but he must always remember that they wish for nothing more fervently than to throw off the yoke of *fa*. A ruler who fails to recognize this is soon disabused:

若是，則群臣廢法而行私，重 [私]¹⁵ 輕公矣。數至能人之門，不壹至
主之廷；百慮私家之便，不壹圖主之國。屬數雖多，非所以尊君也；
百官雖具，非所以任國也。然則主有人主之名，而實托於群臣之家
也。故臣曰：亡國之廷無人焉。廷無人者，非朝廷之衰也。家務相
益，不務厚國；大臣務相尊，而不務尊君；小臣奉祿養交，不以官為
事。此其所以然者，由主之不上斷於法，而信下為之也。故明主使法
擇人，不自舉也；使法量功，不自度也。能者不可弊，敗者不可飾，
譽者不能進，非者弗能退，則君臣之間明辨而易治，故主讎法則可也。
(*Han Feizi* 6)¹⁶

In this case, the thronging ministers will ignore *fa* and implement their
private interests, which will be weighty for them while they make light of
the lord's interests. They will come in multitudes to the gates of men of
consequence, but not one will come to the ruler's court; they will deliberate a hundred times for the convenience of their own families but will not
make a single plan for the ruler's state. Although the number of such men
attached [to the ruler's administration] may be great, it is not because
they esteem their lord; although all administrative offices may be filled, it
is not because they take responsibility for the state. Thus the ruler will
have the title of "ruler," but in reality he will be dependent on the families
of the thronging ministers.

Thus I, your servant, say: "There are no men in the court of a doomed
state." When [I say] "there are no men in the court," it is not that the
court itself is dwindling. I mean that [powerful] families feel obliged to
benefit one another, not to enrich the state. Great ministers feel obliged
to esteem one another, not to esteem the lord. Lesser ministers accept
their salaries and tend to their connections; they do not act in accordance with [the requirements of] their office. The reason why this is the
case is that the ruler has made his decisions not by means of *fa*, but by
trusting his inferiors. Thus the enlightened ruler uses *fa* to choose his
men; he does not select them himself. He uses *fa* to measure their merit;
he does not gauge it himself. Those who are capable cannot be demeaned;
those who fail cannot prettify themselves. Those who are praised [base-
lessly] cannot advance; those who are criticized [slanderously] cannot
be made to retire. Thus the distinctions between lord and subject will be
clear, and order will be easily attained. But this will be possible only if the
ruler adopts *fa*.

Simply put, *fa* refers to laws and policies inimical to private interests.[17]

主用術則大臣不得擅斷，近習不敢賣重；官行法則浮萌趨於耕農，而游士危於戰陳。則法術者乃群臣士民之所禍也。(*Han Feizi* 13)[18]

If the lord makes use of such techniques, the great ministers will not be able to make decisions on their own authority; those who are familiar [with the ruler] will not dare to peddle influence. If the administration carries out *fa*, vagabond commoners will have to rush to their tilling and knights-errant will have to brave danger at the battlefront. Thus the techniques of *fa* are a disaster for thronging ministers and men-of-service.

But how does *fa* work in practice? The first answer is that a ruler must harness people's self-serving nature by rewarding and punishing them as their behavior warrants. Rewards and punishments are called "the two handles" (*erbing* 二柄), which the ruler must always keep firmly within his grasp. It would be a mistake, according to the *Han Feizi*, to try to reform people's visceral likes and dislikes; rather, the very impulses that lead them to profit at the king's expense can be turned against them with devastating effect. The root of the solution is provided by the problem itself: as long as the ruler's rewards and punishments are ineluctable, his subordinates will exert themselves so as to secure the rewards and avoid the punishments. Indeed, it is precisely those ministers who claim to be guided by principles beyond reward and punishment—in other words, the allegedly selfless and high-minded ones extolled by *other* schools of thought—who arouse suspicion. For if a ruler cannot control a minister with rewards and punishments, he cannot control that minister by any means at all.[19]

For this reason, one of Han Fei's most important counsels is that a ruler must never allow a functionary to reward or punish on his own authority. That would amount to transferring all real power to a future usurper.

夫虎之所以能服狗者，爪牙也，使虎釋其爪牙而使狗用之，則虎反服於狗矣。人主者，以刑德制臣者也，今君人者釋其刑德而使臣用之，則君反制於臣矣。故田常上請爵祿而行之群臣，下大斗斛而施於百姓，此簡公失德而田常用之也，故簡公見弒。子罕謂宋君曰：「夫慶賞賜予者，民之所喜也，君自行之；殺戮刑罰者，民之所惡

也，臣請當之。」於是宋君失刑而子罕用之，故宋君見劫。田常徒用
德而簡公弒，子罕徒用刑而宋君劫。故今世為人臣者兼刑德而用之，
則是世主之危甚於簡公、宋君也。故劫殺擁蔽之主，非失刑德而使
臣用之而不危亡者，則未嘗有也。(Han Feizi 7)[20]

The tiger dominates the dog because of his claws and fangs. If one were to make the tiger relinquish his claws and fangs, and allow the dog to use them, the tiger would be dominated by the dog. The ruler uses punishments and rewards to control his ministers, but if the lord were to relinquish his punishments and rewards, and allow his ministers to apply them, the lord would be controlled by the ministers.

Thus Tian Chang requested titles and stipends of his sovereign, which he distributed among the thronging ministers; in dealing with the lower classes, he used large measures [to dole out grain] and spread it among the Hundred Surnames. In this manner, Lord Jian (of Qi, r. 484–481 BC) lost control of rewards, and Tian Chang applied them; thus Lord Jian was assassinated.[21]

Zihan (i.e., Dai Xi 戴喜, d. 329 BC) said to Lord [Huan II] of Song (r. 372–356 BC): "Now rewards and gifts are what the people like, so you, Lord, distribute them yourself; executions and penalties are what the people dislike, so I, your servant, request to administer these." Thereupon the Lord of Song lost control of punishments, and Zihan applied them; thus the Lord of Song was bullied.[22]

Tian Chang applied only rewards (i.e., without control over punishments), and Lord Jian was assassinated; Zihan applied only punishments, and the Lord of Song was bullied. Thus if ministers in today's age apply *both* punishments *and* rewards, rulers of the age will be in even greater danger than Lord Jian and the Lord of Song. Thus when rulers are bullied, assassinated, obstructed, or demeaned, if they lose control of punishments and rewards, and allow ministers to apply these, they will unfailingly be endangered or even perish.

Being so crucial to a ruler's self-preservation, rewards and punishments must be brought to bear precisely as they are earned; a ruler must never let his personal preferences affect his terrible dispensation of the two handles.

是故明君之行賞也，曖乎如時雨，百姓利其澤；其行罰也，畏乎如
雷霆，神聖不能解也。故明君無偷賞，無赦罰。賞偷則功臣墮其業，

赦罰則姦臣易為非。是故誠有功則雖疏賤必賞，誠有過則雖近愛必
誅。近愛必誅，則疏賤者不怠，而近愛者不驕也。(*Han Feizi* 5)[23]

Thus, in bestowing rewards, an enlightened lord is bountiful like a seasonable rain; the Hundred Surnames benefit from his fecundity. In carrying
out punishments, he is dreadful like a thunderclap; even spirits and sages
cannot absolve themselves. Thus the enlightened lord does not reward
recklessly or remit punishments. If he rewards recklessly, meritorious
ministers will let their enterprises slide. If he remits punishments, treacherous ministers will find it easy to do wrong. For this reason, those whose
accomplishments are real must be rewarded, even if they are lowly and
base; those whose transgressions are real must be punished, even if they
are close and beloved. Then the lowly and base will not become insolent
nor the close and beloved haughty.

Rewards and punishments must be dispensed without regard for rank
or reputation:

今若以譽進能，則臣離上而下比周；若以黨舉官，則民務交而不求
用於法。故官之失能者其國亂。以譽為賞，以毀為罰也，則好賞惡
罰之人，釋公行，行私術，比周以相為也。(*Han Feizi* 6)[24]

If they are promoted to powerful positions on the basis of their reputation,
ministers will abandon their [ruler] above and associate with those below;
if recruitment to office is handled by cliques, then the people will feel
obliged to foster relationships and will not seek employment by means of
*fa*. Thus the administration will lose all men of ability, and the state will
be in turmoil. If they are rewarded on the basis of their reputation and
punished on the basis of calumny, then people—who like rewards and
dislike punishments—will absolve themselves of the lord's business and
carry out their private operations instead, forging associations to promote
one another.

法不阿貴，繩不撓曲。法之所加，智者弗能辭，勇者弗敢爭。刑過
不避大臣，賞善不遺匹夫。(*Han Feizi* 6)[25]

*Fa* does not curry favor with the noble born, [just as] the plumb line does
not yield to curves. What is assigned by *fa* the wise cannot decline and the
brave dare not challenge. In applying the law to transgressions, one does

not pardon great ministers; in rewarding good conduct, one does not pass over commoners.

It stands to reason that by not currying favor with the noble born or passing over deserving commoners, an administration guided by *fa* would disappoint anyone expecting traditional privileges based on social status. The text uses the familiar example of Lord Shang 商君 (i.e., Gongsun Yang 公孫鞅), whose radical reforms alienated bigwigs unaccustomed to submitting to the same protocols as mere husbandmen. As soon as they got the chance, Lord Shang's enemies had him rent asunder by chariots, but this does not mean that his policies were wrong—for the ruler and his state benefited mightily from them.[26]

Han Fei recognized that *fa* will not only outrage the aristocracy, but will inevitably come into conflict with popular morals as well. By doing what they have been taught to believe is righteous and honorable, people will inevitably subvert the interests of the ruler. One chapter takes up the example of vengeance killings, which are known to have been a nuisance for early administrators.[27]

> 今兄弟被侵必攻者廉也，知友被辱隨仇者貞也。廉貞之行成，而君上之法犯矣。人主尊貞廉之行，而忘犯禁之罪，故民程於勇而吏不能勝也。(*Han Feizi* 49)[28]

Nowadays, those who make sure to attack anyone who impugns their brothers are considered honorable; those who join against an enemy when their friends are insulted are considered faithful. When such honorable and faithful acts are brought to fruition, the *fa* of the lord above is violated. The ruler might esteem such honorable and faithful acts, and forget about the crime of violating his prohibitions, and thus the people compete in feats of bravery, and officials cannot prevail over them.

Filial piety is another widely respected virtue that is singled out for its destructiveness. Later in the same chapter, Han Fei refers to Upright Gong, the figure known from *Analects* 13.18 (see p. 51):

> 楚之有直躬，其父竊羊而謁之吏。令尹曰：「殺之。」以為直於君而曲於父，報而罪之。以是觀之，夫君之直臣，父之暴子也。魯人從君戰，三戰三北 [=背]。仲尼問其故。對曰：「吾有老父，身死莫之養也。」仲尼以為孝，舉而上之。以是觀之，夫父之孝子，君之背臣

也。故令尹誅而楚姦不上聞，仲尼賞而魯民易降北 [=背]。上下之
利若是其異也，而人主兼舉匹夫之行，而求致社稷之福，必不幾矣。
(*Han Feizi* 49)[29]

In Chu there was Upright Gong; his father stole a sheep, and [Gong] reported this to an official. The Prime Minister said: "Let [Gong] be killed";
he considered [Gong] upright to his lord but crooked to his father, and
[the Prime Minister] convicted him in requital. Seen from this perspective, a lord's upright subject is a father's cruel son.

There was a man of Lu who followed his lord into battle; three times
he went into battle and three times he fled. When Confucius asked him
the reason, he replied; "I have an aged father; if I die, there will be no one
to take care of him." Confucius, considering this filial, recruited and promoted him. Seen from this perspective, a father's filial son is a lord's ren-
egade subject.

Thus the Prime Minister executed [Gong], and in Chu treachery was
never communicated to any superiors; Confucius rewarded [the man of
Lu], and the people of Lu thought nothing of surrendering or fleeing [in
battle]. What is beneficial to superiors and inferiors being so dissimilar, if
a ruler sanctions the actions of commoners, and at the same time seeks
good fortune for his altars of Soil and Grain, he surely will not come close.

Once again taking aim at Confucians, Han Fei argued that winning
the hearts of the people is a doomed strategy because they cannot even
recognize what is best for them:

今不知治者必曰：「得民之心。」欲得民之心而可以為治，則是伊尹、
管仲無所用也，將聽民而已矣。民智之不可用，猶嬰兒之心也。夫
嬰兒不剔首則腹痛，不副[30]痤則寖益，剔首、副痤必一人抱之，慈
母治之，然猶啼呼不止，嬰兒子不知犯其所小苦致其所大利也。
(*Han Feizi* 50)[31]

Now those who do not know about governing always say: "Win the hearts
of the people!" If you could govern just by desiring to win the hearts of
the people, [the legendary counselors] Yi Yin and Guan Zhong would be
of no use; you would need to do no more than listen to the people. But the
people's wisdom is useless because it is like the mind of an infant. If you
do not shave an infant's head, its belly will hurt;[32] if you do not lance its
boil, the pus will increase. In order to shave its head or lance its boil, one

person must hold it down while the kind mother cures it, but it whoops and hollers unceasingly, for the infant does not know the great benefits brought about by this small discomfort.

The ruler oversees four great enterprises: colonization of new land, penal law, taxation, and military service; all four contribute to order and security, "but the people do not know enough to rejoice in them" 民不知悅 也. Instead of worrying about his popularity, the ruler should listen to advisers like Yi Yin and Guan Zhong (that is to say, like Han Fei himself), and carry out his impersonal administration with ironclad resolve.

This is not to say that the ruler can simply trample on the common folk as he wishes. If he abuses them to the point of desperation, they will turn to powerful ministers for succor. Thus he must maintain a minimum standard of well-being in the realm, lest the people appeal to potential demagogues for deliverance:

徭役多則民苦, 民苦則權勢起, 權勢起則復除重, 復除重則貴人富。 苦民以富, 貴人起勢, 以藉人臣, 非天下長利也。 故曰徭役少則民 安, 民安則下無重權, 下無重權則權勢滅, 權勢滅則德在上矣。 (*Han Feizi* 17)[33]

If there is too much mandatory labor, the people will become embittered; if the people are embittered, the power [of local officials] will rise; if the power [of local officials] rises, those who can exempt [the people from service] will become influential; if those who can exempt [the people from service] are influential, such magnates will become wealthy. To embitter the people by enriching magnates, to let the power [of local officials] arise by [allowing desperate people] to rely on ministers—this is not very beneficial to the world. Thus it is said: If mandatory labor is lessened, the people will be secure; if the people are secure, there will be no men of influence and power below; if there are no men of influence and power below, the power [of local officials] will be extinguished; if the power [of local officials] is extinguished, all rewards will remain the province of the sovereign.

Notice that the argument is framed according to the *ruler's* interests, not those of the people; the welfare of the people is relevant only to the extent that their misery, if channeled by opportunists, can jeopardize the ruler's authority.

• • •

But how can a ruler, surrounded as he is by ministers intent on hood-winking him at every turn, be sure that he is correctly apportioning rewards and punishments as they are earned? How can he know who deserves to be rewarded and who to be punished? To address this problem, Han Fei advocated another technique of *fa*: "performance and title" (*xing-ming* 刑/形名, sometimes translated as "forms and names"). Instead of imposing some preconceived vision of bureaucratic organization, a ruler simply responds as each minister makes his talents and aspirations apparent.

有言者自為名，有事者自為形，形名參同，君乃無事焉，歸之其情。
(*Han Feizi* 5)[34]

One who speaks spontaneously produces a "title"; one who acts spontaneously produces a "performance." When "performance and title" match identically, then everything returns to its essence without any action on the part of the ruler.

故羣臣陳其言，君以其言授其事，事以責其功。功當其事，事當其言則賞；功不當其事，事不當其言則誅。明君之道，臣不陳言而不當。(*Han Feizi* 5)[35]

Thus the thronging ministers utter their words; the lord hands down their duties according to their words and assesses their accomplishments according to their duties. If their accomplishments match their duties and their duties match their words, they are rewarded. If their accomplishments do not match their duties or their duties do not match their words, they are punished. According to the way of the enlightened lord, ministers do not utter words that they cannot match.

The best way to select a deputy for some task is not to seek out the minister whose particular talents one judges to be most appropriate, for then the scheming ministers at court will dissimulate so as to appear most appropriate for the positions that they covet for their own self-interested reasons. (Cruder manuals of statecraft proposed scrutinizing each administrator's abilities,[36] but that would be the work of a statistician, not a prince.) Rather, the best method is simply to wait until one enterprising minister offers to do the task. This then becomes the minister's "title." After the appointed term, the ruler compares the minister's "performance" to his "title" and rewards or punishes accordingly.[37] Restated in modern terms, this means that if a certain bridge needs to be repaired, one does *not* pick the minister who seems to know the most about repairing bridges; rather, one waits until some minister comes forward with a proposal to do it at a certain cost and within a certain time frame. Once again, the key is to turn the ministers' selfishness against them. As in a standard "call for bids" today, in which competing businesses submit carefully calculated proposals for a contract with a local government or agency, Han Fei assumed that ministers will naturally promise as much as they can in order to win the "title," but will be wary of promising too much, lest they be held responsible for any deficit.

One important difference is that a call for bids today will usually specify the task to be completed, whereas Han Fei advised rulers to leave the very definition of the task to the competing ministers. Han Fei does not seem to have anticipated the objection that by waiting for ministers to come forward with their own proposals, the government effectively lets them set the agenda, and certain types of problems might be systematically neglected. For example, it is hard to imagine how modern problems like overfishing or global warming could be solved by this method because self-interested ministers could not readily anticipate profit in those areas (though we must not pretend that we have solved such problems ourselves). One modern criticism of pharmaceutical companies, similarly, is that they focus on developing medicines that will be profitable, not necessarily the ones most needed across the globe.[38]

Another difference between *xingming* and our "calls for bids": whereas no contractor today would expect to be penalized for finishing a project *under* budget, Han Fei wrote that a minister who ends up delivering more than he promised should be punished as surely as if he had underperformed. Ministers must live up to their "title"—no more and no less.

故羣臣其言大而功小者則罰，非罰小功也，罰功不當名也；羣臣其言小而功大者亦罰，非不說 [=悅] 於大功也，以為不當名也害甚於有大功，故罰。昔者韓昭侯醉而寢，典冠者見君之寒也，故加衣於君之上，覺寢而說 [=悅]，問左右曰：「誰加衣者？」左右對曰：「典冠。」君因兼罪典衣與典冠。其罪典衣，以為失其事也；其罪典冠，以為越其職也。非不惡寒也，以為侵官之害甚於寒。故明主之畜臣，臣不得越官而有功，不得陳言而不當。越官則死，不當則罪，守業其官所言者貞也，則羣臣不得朋黨相為矣。(*Han Feizi* 7)[39]

Thus if the thronging ministers make great statements, but their achievement is small, they are punished, not because one punishes small achievements, but because one punishes achievements that do not match their "title." If the thronging ministers make small statements, but their achievement is great, they are punished too, not because one is displeased by great achievements, but because not matching the "title" is considered more damaging than [not] having great achievements.

In the past, Marquis Zhao of Han (r. 362–333 BC) once got drunk and fell asleep; the Supervisor of the Hat saw that his lord was cold and put a robe over him. When [the marquis] awoke from his sleep, he was pleased and asked his attendants: "Who put this robe on me?"

The attendants replied: "The Supervisor of the Hat." The lord accordingly convicted both the Supervisor of the Robe and the Supervisor of the Hat. He convicted the Supervisor of the Robe of dereliction of duty and convicted the Supervisor of the Hat of overstepping his office—not because [the Marquis] did not dislike being cold, but because he considered the overextension of offices more damaging than cold. Thus the enlightened ruler domesticates his ministers as follows: ministers cannot attain merit by overstepping their offices or failing to match the words they put forth. If they overstep their offices, they are to die; if they fail to match [their words], they are to be convicted. If they keep to their offices and remain faithful to their words, the thronging ministers will be unable to form cliques and act on one another's behalf.

Implementing *xingming* requires that the ruler be the *last*, not the first, to speak. In ancient times, this was probably not the habit of most rulers. Thus the *Han Feizi* frequently reminds its lordly reader, in language manifestly borrowed from *Laozi*, that he ought not to reveal his inner thoughts, or even to try to outwit his underlings by dissembling (for dissembling too can be detected); instead, he should present a blank poker face to the outside world, leaving his enemies without any toehold whatsoever.[40]

聽言之道, 溶若甚醉。唇乎齒乎, 吾不為始乎; 齒乎唇乎, 愈惛惛
乎。彼自離之, 吾因以知之。是非輻湊, 上不與構。虛靜無為, 道
之情也; 參伍比物, 事之形也。(*Han Feizi* 8)[41]

The Way of Listening is to be giddy as though soused. "Lips! Teeth! May
I not be the first [to speak]! Teeth! Lips! Be dumber and dumber. Let others deploy themselves, and accordingly I shall know them." Right and
wrong whirl around him like spokes on a wheel, but the sovereign does
not complot. Emptiness, stillness, nonaction—these are the characteristics
of the Way. By checking and comparing how it accords with reality, [one
ascertains] the "performance" of an enterprise.

Like every other aspect of *fa*, moreover, *xingming* must be maintained
even when the ruler is with his bedfellows, entourage, or kin:

明君之於內也, 娛其色而不行其謁, 不使私請。其於左右也, 使其
身必責其言, 不使益辭。其於父兄大臣也, 聽其言也必使以罰任於
後, 不令妄舉。(*Han Feizi* 9)[42]

When dealing with the women in his harem, an enlightened lord amuses
himself with their sex but does not carry out their petitions or grant them
any personal requests. When dealing with his attendants, he must hold
them responsible for what they say as he employs them; he does not allow
them to speak extravagantly. When dealing with his father, elder brother,
and great ministers, he listens to what they say but must use penalties to
hold them accountable for the consequences; he does not let them act
recklessly.

Unable to share his innermost thoughts and feelings with anyone around
him, or to love or hate or be motivated by any emotion at all, a ruler is
the loneliest of men. We are even told that he ought to sleep alone, lest
he reveal his plans as he mutters in his dreams.[43]

All these harsh measures are necessary because people are fickle and
self-interested (or, more precisely, fickle *because* self-interested), and *fa*
is the only way to guarantee their obedience. Other political philosophies,
such as Confucianism, might seem more agreeable because they appeal
to virtue and principle, but the problem, for Han Fei, is that one can wait
eons before finding people who are motivated by virtue and principle. A

political philosophy that relies on a sage ruler is effective only when the ruler is a sage. And that does not happen very often.

世之治者不絕於中。吾所以為言勢者，中也。(*Han Feizi* 40)[44]

The rulers of this age do not exceed mediocrity. When I speak of power, it is with reference to the mediocre.

Several passages in "The Five Vermin" repeat this theme:

宋人有耕田者，田中有株，兔走，觸株折頸而死，因釋其耒而守株，冀復得兔，兔不可復得，而身為宋國笑。今欲以先王之政，治當世之民，皆守株之類也。(*Han Feizi* 49)[45]

Among the men of Song there was one who tilled his fields; in his fields there was a stump. A rabbit ran by, crashed headfirst against the stump, broke its neck, and died. Thereupon [the man] set aside his plow and kept watch by the stump, hoping to get another rabbit, but no other rabbit was to be gotten, and he became the laughingstock of Song. Now those who wish to use the governance of the Former Kings to bring order to the people of our time are all of the same type as the stump watcher.

今學者之說人主也，不乘必勝之勢，而務行仁義則可以王，是求人主之必及仲尼，而以世之凡民皆如列徒，此必不得之數也。(*Han Feizi* 49)[46]

Learned men today persuade a ruler not to take advantage of his invincible power, but to make it his duty to carry out benevolence and righteousness, and thereby become a "king." This is like demanding that a ruler measure up to Confucius, and that all the people of our age be like his disciples. This is a strategy that cannot be successful.

今貞信之士不盈於十，而境內之官以百數，必任貞信之士，則人不足官，人不足官則治者寡而亂者眾矣。故明主之道，一法而不求智，固術而不慕信，故法不敗，而群官無姦詐矣。(*Han Feizi* 49)[47]

Today there are no more than ten faithful and trustworthy men-of-service, but the offices in the realm number in the hundreds. If one must assign them to faithful and trustworthy men-of-service, there would not be enough men for the offices, and if there are not enough men for the offices, the orderly will be few and the disorderly will be many. Thus the Way of the enlightened ruler is to unify the *fa* instead of seeking out the wise, to consolidate his techniques instead of admiring the trustworthy. Thus *fa* will not fail, and among the thronging ministers there will be no treachery or machination.

• • •

Judged by the texts presented so far, Han Fei would rank as an outstanding writer, but a somewhat derivative thinker. Readers of the *Han Feizi* are immediately struck that they are in the presence of one of the most distinctive voices in all Chinese literature.[48] "Thus, in bestowing rewards, an enlightened lord is bountiful like a seasonable rain; the Hundred Surnames benefit from his fecundity. In carrying out punishments, he is dreadful like a thunderclap; even spirits and sages cannot absolve themselves"—few philosophers writing in any language have been able to muster such rhetorical power. Not surprisingly, the *Han Feizi* is the source of a large number of so-called set phrases (*chengyu* 成語) in Modern Chinese.[49] But none of the ideas that we have seen to this point would have been considered original in the third century BC. *Xingming* is borrowed, with hardly any innovation, from philosophers working a century earlier, especially Shen Buhai,[50] and the foundational understanding of *fa* as an impersonal administrative technique is anticipated by another fourth-century thinker, Shen Dao 慎到 (b. ca. 360 BC), who wrote in a surviving fragment:

> 君人者，舍法而以身治，則誅賞從君心出矣，然則受賞者雖當，望
> 多無窮；受罰者雖當，望輕無已。君舍法而以心裁輕重，則是同功
> 殊賞，同罪殊罰也；怨之所由生也。是以分馬者之用策，分田之用
> 鈎也，非以鈎策為過人智也；所以去私塞怨也。故曰：大君任法而
> 弗躬為，則事斷於法矣。法之所加，各以其分蒙其賞罰，而無望於
> 君也。是以怨不生而上下和矣。[51]

If the lord of men abandons *fa* and governs with his own person, then penalties and rewards, seizures and grants, will all emerge from the lord's mind. If this is the case, then those who receive rewards, even if these are commensurate, will ceaselessly expect more; those who receive punishment, even if these are commensurate, will endlessly expect more lenient treatment. If the lord of men abandons *fa* and decides between lenient and harsh treatment on the basis of his own mind, then people will be rewarded differently for the same merit and punished differently for the same fault. Resentment arises from this. Thus the reason why those who apportion horses use *ce* lots, and those who apportion fields use *gou* lots, is not that they take *ce* and *gou* lots to be superior to human wisdom, but that one may eliminate private interest and stop resentment by these means.[52] Thus it is said: "When the great lord relies on *fa* and does not act personally, affairs are judged in accordance with *fa*." The benefit of *fa* is that each person meets his reward or punishment according to his due, and there are no further expectations of the lord. Thus resentment does not arise, and superiors and inferiors are in harmony.

No learned appeals to historical example, and fewer arresting similes, but philosophically this exposition of *fa* is no different from anything in the *Han Feizi*.[53]

The material that remains to be considered, however, complicates the picture. As stated at the outset, Han Fei's positions varied with his audience, and so far all we have discussed are essays addressed to rulers. In one extraordinary chapter, "The Difficulties of Persuasion" ("Shuinan" 說難), Han Fei turned his attention to ministers.[54] And here we find him unabashedly encouraging them to maximize their interests by taking advantage of their sovereign's frailties. I do not know of any other document like it.

譽異人與同行者，規異事與同計者。有與同汙者，則必以大飾其無傷也；有與同敗者，則必以明飾其無失也。彼自多其力，則毋以其難概之也；自勇其斷，則無以其謫怒之；自智其計，則毋以其敗窮之。大意無所拂悟，辭言無所繫縻，然後極騁智辯焉。此道所得親近不疑而得盡辭也。(*Han Feizi* 12)[55]

Eulogize other people who act in the same manner [as the ruler]; take as a model those affairs of others that are similar to his plans. If there is someone as vile as he, you must use [that person's] greatness to prettify him, as though he were harmless. If there is someone who has had the same failures as he, you must use [that person's] brilliance to prettify him, as though there were no real loss. If he considers his own strengths manifold, do not cause him to regret his [past] difficulties. If he considers his decisions brave, do not anger him by reprimanding him. If he considers his plans wise, do not diminish him [by citing] his failures. Only if there is nothing contrary in your general import and nothing stringent in your speech will your wisdom and rhetoric gallop forward to the ultimate. This is the way of attaining both intimacy without suspicion and effectual speech.

Such advice, however, is limited to this one chapter; elsewhere, ministers who try to gauge the king's mind in order to further their careers are called "treacherous" (*jian* 姦):

凡姦臣皆欲順人主之心以取信幸之勢者也。是以主有所善，臣從而譽之；主有所憎，臣因而毀之。(*Han Feizi* 14)[56]

Treacherous ministers all want to accord with the ruler's mind in order to attain a position of trust and favor. Therefore, if the ruler likes something, the ministers will duly praise it; if the ruler hates something, the ministers will accordingly disparage it.

"The Difficulties of Persuasion" also broaches topics in epistemology and the philosophy of language that are not discussed to any comparable extent in the work of Han Fei's predecessors. Consider the following instructive anecdote:

昔者鄭武公欲伐胡，故先以其女妻胡君以娛其意。因問於羣臣：「吾欲用兵，誰可伐者？」大夫關其思對曰：「胡可伐。」武公怒而戮之，曰：「胡，兄弟之國也，子言伐之何也？」胡君聞之，以鄭為親己，遂不備鄭，鄭人襲胡，取之。宋有富人，天雨，牆壞。其子曰：「不築，必將有盜。」其鄰人之父亦云。暮而果大亡其財。其家甚智其子，而疑鄰人之父。此二人說者皆當矣，厚者為戮，薄者見疑，則非知之難也，處知則難也。(*Han Feizi* 12)[57]

In the past, Lord Wu of Zheng (r. 770–744 BC) wished to attack Hu, so the first thing he did was to marry his daughter to the Lord of Hu in order to make amusement his [sole] intention. Then [Lord Wu] asked his thronging ministers: "I wish to make use of my troops; whom would it be acceptable to attack?"

The grandee Guan Qisi replied: "It is acceptable to attack Hu."

Lord Wu was enraged and executed him, saying: "Hu is a brother state. How could you say to attack it?" When the Lord of Hu heard of this, he assumed that Zheng would treat him as a relative, so he did not prepare for [an incursion from] Zheng. The men of Zheng invaded Hu and seized it.[58]

In Song there was a rich man whose walls were damaged by exposure to rain. His son said: "If you do not rebuild them, there will surely be thieves." His neighbor's father said the same thing. One night, as expected, there was a great loss to his wealth. His family considered his son very wise but suspected their neighbor's father.[59]

What these two men [namely, Guan Qisi and the neighbor's father] said fit the facts, and yet in the more extreme case one was executed, and in the less extreme case one was suspected [of burglary]. This is because it is not difficult to know, but it is difficult to place one's knowledge.[60]

To take the second example first: the rich man's son and his neighbor's father say the same thing, but the implications of their utterances are fundamentally divergent. In the case of the son, the family naturally assumes that the boy has his father's financial interests in mind and lauds him for his ability to anticipate disaster. But in the case of the neighbor's father, the same assumption is no longer natural; indeed, the very opposite is plausible. To use the terminology of contemporary philosophy of language: the two statements, though lexically identical, have radically different implicature.[61] The same sentence does not mean the same thing when spoken by two different people with two different ostensible intentions. It is the situation, more than the words themselves, that determines the significance of any statement;[62] or, to formulate the same principle in different words: there is no such thing as a statement with universally valid implications.

Writers who cast Han Fei as a protototalitarian[63] might be tempted to associate his oratorical prestidigitation with what Hannah Arendt called "the totalitarian contempt for facts and reality."[64] But "The Difficulties of Persuasion" does not lay out anything like a totalitarian ideology; on the contrary, Han Fei's vision of government is that of a crude despot who is subverted at every turn by knaves and inveiglers. He was authoritarian rather than totalitarian.[65]

• • •

"The Difficulties of Persuasion" bears on the vexed question of the authenticity of the *Han Feizi*. It is remarkable that a minister who follows Han Fei's prescriptions in one chapter would be condemned as a traitor in another. Scholars sometimes cite such contradictions as evidence that the *Han Feizi* could not have been written by one man.[66] As I have written elsewhere,[67] the weakness of this theory is that it does not take into account the underlying similarities: the basic issue in all these contexts is the natural and inevitable antagonism between the ruler and his ministers. Han Fei's avowed opinion simply changes with his audience. Now he may excoriate duplicitous ministers; now he may explain how to gull a king.[68] It is impossible to say which is the "real" Han Fei, because in neither authorial mode does Han Fei disclose his personal views. And for this reason, most scholars today are disinclined to accept such contradictions as decisive evidence that one or another chapter could not have been written by Han Fei.[69]

But certain other internal contradictions are more difficult to resolve. For example, at the end of a passage enumerating the familiar benefits of instituting *fa* (the text can be repetitive on this point), Han Fei added what might appear to be an innocuous ornament:

刑重則不敢以貴易賤，法審則上尊而不侵。上尊而不侵則主強，而守要，故先王貴之而傳之。人主釋法用私，則上下不別矣。(*Han Feizi* 6)[70]

If the law is harsh, the noble will not dare to disparage the base. If *fa* is made known, the sovereign will be esteemed and not impugned; if the sovereign is esteemed and not impugned, the ruler will be strong and will hold firm to the essentials. Thus the Former Kings valued [*fa*] and transmitted it. If the ruler relinquishes *fa* and uses his private judgment, superior and inferior will not be distinguished.

Here we are told not only that *fa* is effective, but that the Former Kings "valued and transmitted it" (*gui zhi er chuan zhi* 貴之而傳之). In a rhetorical context in which appeals to the past were commonplace (see p. 19), the additional reference to the Former Kings is not trivial. But it clashes with the more typical expressions of disdain for anyone guided by the example of the ancients. In most other chapters, *Han Feizi* ridicules those who would attempt to solve today's problems by yesterday's means.[71]

不知治者，必曰：「無變古，毋易常。」變與不變，聖人不聽，正治而已。(*Han Feizi* 18)[72]

Those who know nothing of rulership always say: "Do not change old ways; do not alter what has endured." Sages do not pay attention to whether there should be change or no change; they do no more than rule correctly.

然則今有美堯、舜、湯、武、禹之道於當今之世者，必為新聖笑矣。是以聖人不期脩古，不法常可，論世之事，因為之備。(*Han Feizi* 49)[73]

Those who would praise the ways of Yao, Shun, Yu, Tang, and Wu for today's age must be ridiculed by the new sages. Thus sages do not expect to cultivate the past and do not take any enduring postulates as their *fa*. They sort through the affairs of the age and institute expedients accordingly.

Are we supposed to concern ourselves with the deeds of the former sages or not? For most chapters, the answer would be "not," but there are a few other passages where the Former Kings are invoked as a positive example[74] or the reader is warned against altering precedents.[75] We do not have enough information about the original context of the various chapters to explain such discrepancies with any certitude. The chapters expressing indifference toward the Former Kings may have been written for a ruler who dismissed them as intellectual relics (perhaps the King of Qin?), the others for a ruler who was not prepared to abandon tradition entirely (perhaps the King of Hán?). There is no way to know.

On the level of cosmology, there are even more puzzling contradictions. Most of the text is intelligible without specific cosmological commitments: we do not need to know much about how the universe operates because we know how *people* operate, and that is all that matters in politics. One of the peculiarities of Sima Qian's biography, however, is that he goes out of his way to state that Han Fei favored a particular cosmological theory:

喜刑名法術之學，而其歸本於黃老。[76]

He enjoyed the study of "performance and title" and methods and techniques [of governance], but he came home to his roots in Huang-Lao.

Huang-Lao is a philosophy named for Huang and Lao, that is, the Yellow Thearch (*Huangdi* 黃帝).[77] As it has been analyzed from the Mawangdui manuscripts,[78] Huang-Lao exemplifies what R. P. Peerenboom has aptly called "foundational naturalism":

> First, as a *naturalism*, humans are conceived as part of the cosmic natural order understood as an organic or holistic system or ecosystem. In the language of Huang-Lao, dao as the cosmic natural order embraces both the way of humans (*ren dao* 人道) as well as that of nonhuman nature (*tian dao* 天道). Second, Huang-Lao privileges the cosmic natural order: the natural order has normative priority. It is taken to be the highest value or realm of highest value. Third, and correlate to the second, the human-social order must be consistent and compatible with the cosmic natural order rather than nature and the natural order being subservient to the whims and needs of humans.
>
> Huang-Lao advances a *foundational* naturalism in that the cosmic natural order serves as the basis, the foundation, for construction of human order.[79]

Did Han Fei agree that "the cosmic natural order serves as the basis, the foundation, for construction of human order"? Some passages on *dao* in the extant *Han Feizi* do seem to bear out this notion:

> 道者，萬物之始，是非之紀也。是以明君守始以知萬物之源，治紀以知善敗之端。故虛靜以待令，令名自命也，令事自定也。虛則知實之情，靜則知動者正。有言者自為名，有事者自為形，形名參同，君乃無事焉，歸之其情。(*Han Feizi* 5)[80]

The Way is the origin of the Myriad Things, the skein of right and wrong. Therefore, the enlightened lord holds to the origin in order to know the source of the Myriad Things and masters the skein in order to know the endpoints of gain and loss. Thus, in emptiness and tranquility, he awaits commandment—the commandment for titles to assign themselves and for duties to determine themselves. Since he is empty, he knows the es-

sence of objects; since he is tranquil, he knows what is correct for everything that moves. One who speaks spontaneously produces a "title"; one
who acts spontaneously produces a "performance." When "performance
and title" match identically, then everything returns to its essence without
any action on the part of the ruler.

This appears to contradict the statement, encountered above, that
sages "do not take any enduring postulates as their *fa*" (*bufa changke* 不
法常可). If anything qualifies as an "enduring postulate," it is the Way
itself, "the skein of right and wrong." *Chang* and a synonymous term, *heng*
恆, were frequently deployed in connection with the *dao* in contempo-
raneous literature,[81] and thus the phrase *changke* would immediately
make any reader think of the Way. Time and again, the *Han Feizi* has
insisted that the patterns of the past are not in themselves relevant to the
world today, because circumstances necessarily change, but now we seem
to read that there are certain eternally valid principles after all.

I can propose several possible explanations of this conundrum, in
increasing order of probability:

1. The simplest explanation—though not, in my view, a likely one—would
   be that passages affirming the primacy of the Way were written by someone else. It may be significant that the two chapters displaying the most
   pointed use of *dao* rhetoric, namely "The Way of the Ruler" ("Zhudao" 主
   道,[82] *Han Feizi* 5) and "Brandishing Authority" ("Yangquan" 揚權, *Han
   Feizi* 8), are not included in the brief list of Han Fei's writings given by
   Sima Qian.[83] The problem with this hypothesis is that even if Sima Qian
   did not ascribe "The Way of the Ruler" and "Brandishing Authority" to
   Han Fei, he got the idea that Han Fei was a devotee of Huang-Lao from
   *somewhere*—presumably from portions of Han Fei's work that he did not
   cite specifically.

2. Han Fei may have changed his mind over the course of his life, and died
   too soon to edit out the inconsistencies in the papers that he left behind. (It is important to remember that the *Han Feizi* did not exist as
   such in his own day; it was put together after his death, by an unknown
   editor or editors, out of the many essays attributed to him.) One can
   only speculate, on this theory, whether he began his career as a nihilist
   and gradually came to accept "foundational naturalism," or whether he

began with a conventional acceptance of the Way as the great irresistible natural force, and eventually discarded it as unverifiable or irrelevant in practice.[84]

3. Bearing in mind Han Fei's counsels in "The Difficulties of Persuasion,"
perhaps we need to accept that Han Fei was unafraid to contradict himself as occasions demanded. Before a king with a cultivated appreciation
of *Laozi* and related texts, Han Fei duly spoke with what might be called
"*Laozi* diction"; before a king with no such philosophical concerns, Han
Fei focused on ministers and their cajolery, leaving out all the metaphysics. We are frustrated when he appears incoherent because coherence is
our concern, and not his.

4. Lastly, references to the ineffable Way tend to be followed quickly and
conspicuously by concrete administrative recommendations.[85] The major
purpose of using "*Laozi* diction" seems to be to show how that scripture
helps one become a better ruler by teaching one to imitate the empty and
inscrutable Way. For example, immediately after the opening paragraph
of "The Way of the Ruler," we read:

故曰：君無見其所欲，君見其所欲，臣自將雕琢；君無見其意，君
見其意，臣將自表異。故曰：去好去惡，臣乃見素，去舊去智，臣
乃自備。(Han Feizi 5)[86]

Thus it is said: The lord ought not to make his desires apparent. If the lord's
desires are apparent, the ministers will carve and polish themselves [to his
liking]. The lord ought not to make his intentions apparent. If the lord's
intentions are apparent, the ministers will display themselves falsely. Thus
it is said: Eliminate likes; eliminate dislikes. Then the ministers will appear
plainly. Eliminate tradition; eliminate wisdom. Then the ministers will
prepare themselves.

This is once again the philosophy of the poker face and could be defended with or without any particular cosmology. The reason why the
lord ought to conceal his desires is not that the Way decrees such-and-
such, but that his ministers will cannibalize him if given half the chance.
The reference to the Way is useful solely because the Way was commonly
understood, in the intellectual world after *Laozi*, as privileging no single
characteristic over any other. If the lord can impersonate the Way, and
reveal no tendencies of his own, he is sure to triumph over his adversaries.

And it follows that courtiers and common folk should never be permitted to imitate the Way themselves (whereas Xunzi would have said that the Way is open to anybody). The Way has been reduced to something like a magic cloak for the sovereign.

A similar pattern is found in "Brandishing Authority." The relevant passage begins with distinctive "*Laozi* diction":

> 用一之道，以名為首。名正物定，名倚物徙。故聖人執一以靜，使名自命，令事自定。

The Way of Using Unity is to place titles at the forefront. If titles are rectified, things are fixed; if titles are askew, things deviate. Thus the Sage holds to unity in stillness; he causes titles to assign themselves and duties to determine themselves.

But then it immediately moves to the theme of letting ministers initiate the process of *xingming* by making their own proposals, and then unfailingly rewarding or punishing them as their "performance" demands:

> 不見其采，下故素正。因而任之，使自事之。因而予之，彼將自舉之。正與處之，使皆自定之。上以名舉之。不知其名，復脩其形。形名參同，用其所生。二者誠信，下乃貢情。(*Han Feizi* 8)[87]

He does not let his colors be seen; thus inferiors align themselves straightforwardly. He delegates tasks by according with [their proposals], causing them to make their own duties. He grants [rewards] according to their [merit], so that they promote themselves. He sets the benchmark and abides by it, causing all things to settle themselves. The sovereign promotes according to the "titles"; if he does not know the "title," he traces their "performance." The extent to which "performance and title" match like two halves of a tally is what generates [reward or punishment]. If the two are perfect and reliable, inferiors will present their true nature.

Han Fei's approach to the *Laozi* is reminiscent of other early commentaries in that he tried to show how the language of the original could be illuminating for *his* purposes, not to offer what we would uphold, by academic criteria, as a faithful interpretation. The *Laozi* refers to "names" (*ming* 名)? Oh, that refers to the "titles" that ministers propose for themselves. The *Laozi* says the *dao* is "empty" (*xu* 虛) and "still" (*jing* 靜)? These are the characteristics that a ruler would do well to embody if he does not want to be exploited. What the original authors of the *Laozi* may have meant by their work is not nearly as important as what you can gain from it.

Perhaps the point of all the references to the Way is that change is only to be expected on superficial levels, but the most fundamental processes of the universe are inalterable. However, unlike other texts that advance such a view,[88] *Han Feizi* never clarifies the matter along these lines. The fact that the text is content to leave the matter unresolved is revealing in itself. We do not know what Han Fei believed, and we cannot ever know, because Han Fei did not deign to tell us. His concerns lay elsewhere. Throughout the *Han Feizi*, what we read are statements not about truth, but about how truths can be profitably applied. He did not declare whether he thought human beings can improve themselves, to take a parochial Confucian concern; what matters is that most never will, and a crafty ruler can apply this knowledge with awesome results. "It is not difficult to know; what is difficult is to place one's knowledge."

# Appendix

## WHAT IS *QI* 氣 AND WHY WAS IT A GOOD IDEA?

### WHAT IS *QI*?

The prolific Chinese word *qi* 氣 has so many interrelated but distinct senses[1] that any student of Chinese philosophy will want to unravel them so as to understand the history of the concept. Clarity about the etymology[2] of the word will doubtless also reduce the notorious range of vague and perplexing translations, such "stuff," "fluid," "pneuma," "ether," "energy" (sometimes "material energy"), and "vital force." One accomplished translator has even employed "psychophysical stuff"[3]—a valiant attempt to capture all the salient connotations of *qi* in a single phrase, but outlandish nonetheless.

*Qi* has two general sets of meanings:[4] on the one side, "breath," "vapor," and "air"; on the other, "matter," "material," "the physical substance of the world," and hence also "the substance of the human body," "the physical basis of one's energy," and even "fighting spirit." But which came first, and how did these diverse senses emerge? For such questions, evidence from historical linguistics is indispensable.

The system of Old Chinese reconstruction recently published by William H. Baxter and Laurent Sagart, which includes a series of uvular initials,[5] sheds great light on the question. They reconstruct *qi* 气/氣 as *C.qʰəp-s (where *C- represents an indeterminate consonant), which shows a manifest connection with *xi* 吸, *qʰəp, "to breathe." *Qi*, *C.qʰəp-s, simply reflects an unknown prefix.[6] (Before the reconstruction of uvulars, the connection between *qi* and *xi* was not readily discernible.)[7] Little doubt can remain that the basic meaning of *qi* is "breath," and all the other senses are derived from it. This insight would scarcely have been possible before the twenty-first century; most previous work, which has focused on the shape of the graph (*zixing* 字形) rather than the sound of the word,[8] has been methodologically fallacious.

Once the link between *qi* and *xi* is established, it seems obvious that *xi* 翕/噏/歙, "to suck in," belongs to the same family. All three forms are recognizable as *qʰəp in the Baxter and Sagart system. This is no minor point, because *xi* 翕 is frequently associated with *qi* 氣 in medical literature, as in the following text from Mawangdui:

幾已，內脊毋動，翕氣，抑下之，靜身須之，曰待贏。[9]

When you are nearly finished, do not move the inner spine; suck in the *qi* and push it down; keep your torso still while you wait for it; this is called "attending to gain."

This manuscript, which was given the title *Discussion of the Highest Dao under Heaven* (*Tianxia zhidao tan* 天下至道談) by its modern editors, relates methods of macrobiotic self-cultivation by means of sexual intercourse.[10] In this particular context, *xi* does not refer to inhalation; the reference is to "sucking in" the *qi* that a woman emits at the moment of orgasm. The phrase "sucking in the *qi*" 翕氣 is *qʰəp C.qʰəp-s in Old Chinese; the assonance would have been unmistakable.[11]

In the Confucian *Analects*, the older sense of "breath" is solidly attested, as in the following:

出辭氣，斯遠鄙倍矣。(*Analects* 8.4)[12]

May he avoid boorishness and turpitude in the words that he utters with his breath.

攝齊升堂，鞠躬如也，屏氣似不息者。(*Analects* 10.4)[13]

He would gather up his skirt while ascending to the hall, as though bending his body; he would hold in his breath and seem not to be respiring.

In the same text, however, *qi* also comes to refer to the substance of the body more generally:

肉雖多，不使勝食氣。(*Analects* 10.8)[14]

Even when meat was plentiful, he did not let himself exceed what would feed his *qi*.

Likewise, *Mozi* and *Springs and Autumns of Master Yan* use *qi* in a manner that must mean more than simply "breath":

其為食也，足以增氣充虛，彊體適腹而已矣。(*Mozi* 6)[15]

[Under the Sages,] one would eat no more than what was sufficient to augment the *qi*, fill the emptiness, fortify the limbs, and satiate the belly.

氣鬱而疾，志意不通，則仲由、卜商侍。(*Yanzi chunqiu* 3)[16]

When [Confucius's] *qi* grew stagnant and he fell ill with his aspirations unrealized, Zhong You and Bu Shang (b. 507 BC) served him.

Such conceptions of *qi* are evident across a range of texts with multiple philosophical perspectives. Two of the most famous examples are from *Guanzi* and *Zhuangzi*:

氣者，身之充也。(*Guanzi* 37)[17]

*Qi* is what fills the body.

人之生，氣之聚也，聚則為生，散則為死。(*Zhuangzi* 22)[18]

The birth of a human being is an agglomeration of *qi*. While it agglomerates, there is life; when it disperses, there is death.

Lastly, *qi* can also refer to a person's temperament, demeanor, or mood, as in the following examples:

居移氣，養移體。(*Mencius* 7A.36)[19]

One's dwelling affects one's temperament [just as] nourishment affects one's body.

孝子之有深愛者，必有和氣。[20]

A filial son who has deep love [for his parents] must have a harmonious temperament.

百姓無怨氣。[21]

The common people are not inclined to complain.

One of the most interesting texts relating a person's temper to the state of his or her *qi* is an undatable passage from *Luxuriant Dew of the Springs and Autumns* (*Chunqiu fanlu* 春秋繁露):

公孫之《養氣》曰：裏藏泰實則氣不通，泰虛則氣不足，熱勝則氣 □，寒勝則氣□，泰勞則氣不入，泰佚則氣宛至，怒則氣高，喜則 氣散，憂則氣狂，懼則氣懾。凡此十者，氣之害也，而皆生於不中 和。(*Chunqiu fanlu* 77)[22]

*Nourishing qi* by Gongsun [Nizi 尼子?] says: "When the internal store-houses (i.e., organs) are too full, the *qi* does not circulate; when they are too empty, the *qi* is insufficient. When heat dominates, the *qi* [lacuna]; when cold dominates, the *qi*. . . . When one is overworked, the *qi* does not enter; when one is too idle, the *qi* arrives, but circuitously. When one is enraged, the *qi* rises; when one is happy, the *qi* is dispersed; when one is worried, the *qi* is crazed; when one is afraid, the *qi* is terrified. These ten [disorders] are impairments of *qi*, and they all arise from not being centered and harmonious."

This passage is noteworthy for several reasons. First, it is the first text we have examined that attempts to coordinate the diverse senses of *qi* within a larger paradigm. Speakers of the language must have noticed, just as we can plainly see today, that *qi* can bear many senses—breath, the substance of the body, one's demeanor or temper, and so on—and would naturally have been motivated to construct a schema to account for all of them. Relating diverse observable types of distemper to variations in the state of one's *qi* was one of the leading strategies of medical theory.

Second, the passage provides a tantalizing glimpse of the intellectual history of Confucianism and its responses to such questions. It appears today in *Luxuriant Dew of the Springs and Autumns*, which is attributed to Dong Zhongshu, but modern scholarship has questioned how much of that text Dong himself could have written.[23] Thus the quote is virtually impossible to date.[24] Moreover, regardless of who is responsible for preserving it in *Luxuriant Dew*, it is attributed specifically to *Gongsun zhi Yangqi* 公孫之《養氣》, a phrase with multiple defensible interpretations. Many, but not all, scholars take *Yangqi* as the title of a text (*Nourishing qi*), and this seems most likely, inasmuch as it is followed by the verb *yue* 曰 (says), commonly placed after names of people and texts. *Yangqi* could, however, refer more generally to a practice or tradition of nurturing one's *qi*.

And who is Gongsun? Some commentators identify him as Gongsun Nizi, a philosopher of uncertain date whose works are listed in the Han imperial catalogue as comprising twenty-eight chapters.[25] All are lost today,[26] but if this is an accurate quote, it permits the inference that Gongsun Nizi advocated seeking equanimity by controlling one's *qi*. Moreover, because of the emphasis on the mental state that he calls "centered and harmonious" (or "equilibrium and harmony," *zhonghe* 中和), he might have been associated with the tradition that produced the famous text *Application of Equilibrium* (*Zhongyong*), which uses the same distinctive phrase.[27]

To return to our running biography of the concept of *qi*: from the conviction that *qi* is the material substance of the body, it was a small step to identifying *qi* as the substance of the entire material world.[28] In the same way that *qi* circulates in the body,[29] it was thought to progress through cycles in the cosmos as well:

精氣一上一下，圜周複雜，無所稽留，故曰天道圜。[30]

The essential *qi* rises and falls, cycling in convolutions, never halting. Thus it is said that the Way of Heaven is cyclical.

In discussions of both the body and the cosmos, *qi* was often divided into complementary aspects, most notably *yin* and *yang* and the Five Phases 五行 (or Five Powers 五德) of Metal 金, Wood 木, Water 水, Fire 火, and Earth 土. References to *yin* and *yang* are usually references to *qi*; references to the Five Phases are always references to *qi*. Recent decades have seen many convincing studies of these aspects,[31] which therefore do not require a detailed treatment here, but I should emphasize one point as groundwork for the rest of the discussion: theorists organized the Five Phases of *qi* into different sequences. The two most common were the sequences of "mutual generation" (*xiangsheng* 相生) and "mutual conquest" (*xiangke* 相克):[32] in the former, one phase eventually produces another; in the latter, one phase eventually overpowers another. Crucially, these processes always followed the same sequence.

Mutual generation: Earth → Metal → Water → Wood → Fire
Mutual conquest: Earth ← Water ← Fire ← Metal ← Wood

The rationale for these relationships is sometimes unclear (and disputed), but some of them—for example, the principle that water conquers fire—are intuitively comprehensible. The significance of such sequences is that they permitted the conceptualization of eternal cycles: matter moves apace through each of its Five Phases, recommencing the sequence at the completion of each cycle. Sometimes a single cycle was thought to take one year, with each emerging phase of *qi* representing a new season.[33] Other cycles, such as a dynastic cycle to be considered below, were thought to take many years, perhaps even centuries. Thus it was by no means problematic to imagine different cycles with different rhythms operating all at the same time. These cycles were then used to explain observed phenomena—with uneven records of success.[34]

## WHY WAS IT A GOOD IDEA?

*Qi* was regarded as a useful concept in early China for three major reasons.

(1) The first is congruent with a general intellectual rebellion, commencing around the beginning of the Warring States period, against the hegemony of ghosts and spirits in Bronze Age thinking. The new role of *qi* is especially clear in the conception of disease. From the beginning of the written record, disease was construed as a consequence of influence by ghosts or spirits,[35] as in the following typical oracle-bone inscriptions:

貞：王疾身，維妣己害？[36]

Divined: The King is sick to his body; is Ancestress Ji harming [him]?

壬寅卜，般貞：王尤 [or 疣?]，維父乙害？[37]

Prognostication on *renyin* day. Ke divined: The King is unwell [or perhaps "has a wart"]; is Father Yi harming [him]?

Disease was one of the most urgent topics of Shang oracle-bone divination because it was construed as a manifestation of some spirit's discontent (see p. 31). Because the scope of oracle-bone inscriptions is so narrow, we cannot eliminate the possibility that there were other, unrecorded, conceptions of disease in other contexts. For the royal family, however, visitation by irate spirits seems to have been the only explanation that was entertained.

The conception of disease as a consequence of possession by malign spirits is amply attested in transmitted texts as well.[38] Here is a tale from the *Zuo Commentary*, at least a millennium later than the Shang dynasty:[39]

公疾病，求醫于秦，秦伯使醫緩為之。未至，公夢疾為二豎子，曰：彼良醫也，懼傷我，焉逃之？

其一曰：居肓之上，膏之下，若我何？

醫至，曰：疾不可為也，在肓之上，膏之下。攻之不可，達之不及，藥不至焉，不可為也。

公曰：良醫也。厚為之禮而歸之。[40]

Lord [Jing of Jin 晉景公, r. 599–581 BC] fell ill and requested a doctor from Qin. Lord [Huan 桓] of Qin (r. 603–577 BC) sent Doctor Huan to treat him. Before he arrived, the Lord [of Jin] had dreamt that his illness was two boys, [one of whom] said: "He is a good doctor; I fear that he will harm us. How shall we avoid him?"

The other said: "If we lodge above the diaphragm and beneath the fat below the heart; what can he do to us?"

When the doctor arrived, he said: "The illness cannot be treated; it is above the diaphragm and beneath the fat below the heart. It cannot be attacked; it cannot be reached [sc. by acupuncture]; and medicine will not arrive there. Thus [the disease] cannot be treated."

The Lord [of Jin] said: "You are a good doctor." He did generous ceremonies for him and sent him home.

The two boys are often understood by commentators as the ghosts of Zhao Tong 趙同 and Zhao Kuo 趙括, whom Lord Jing had put to death in 583. This interpretation dispels any mystery surrounding the cause of Lord Jing's illness—perhaps he even deserved it—but at the heavy metaphysical cost of postulating conscious and vengeful ghosts.

*Qi* permitted a reconceptualization of disease as a symptom of material depletion or imbalance.[41] A very different passage from the *Zuo Commentary* provides a good example:

天有六氣。降生五味，發為五色，徵為五聲，淫生六疾。六氣
曰: 陰、陽、風、雨、晦、明也。分為四時，序為五節；過則為菑，
陰淫寒疾，陽淫熱疾，風淫末疾，雨淫腹疾，晦淫惑疾，明淫
心疾。[42]

There are six kinds of *qi* under Heaven. When they are born [in plants and
animals, they produce] the Five Flavors; they emerge as the Five Colors;
they are discerned as the Five Tones; when they overflow, they produce
the Six Ailments. The six kinds of *qi* are *yin*, *yang*, wind, rain, darkness,
and light. Their division forms the Four Seasons, their order the Five Measures.[43] But in excess they cause calamities. An overflow of *yin* causes cold
ailments; an overflow of *yang* causes hot ailments; an overflow of wind
causes ailments in the extremities; an overflow of rain causes ailments in
the abdomen; an overflow of darkness causes ailments of delusion; an
overflow of light causes ailments in the heart.

This scheme is different from the system of the Five Phases mentioned
above (and older than the fullest expositions of Five Phases thought,
which appear in the Han dynasty and later), but in dividing protean *qi*
into six different kinds, which must be kept in proper balance, its orientation is similar. Perceptible physical ailments supervene on an excess of
one or another kind of *qi*.[44]

Another *qi*-based theory of disease focused on one's total store of it,
rather than the balance among different kinds. For example, according
to this passage from *Inner Canon of the Yellow Thearch* (*Huangdi neijing*
黃帝內經), people ignorantly drive themselves to an early death by depleting their *qi* through self-abuse:

以酒為漿，以妄為常。醉以入房，以欲竭其精，以耗散其真。不知持
滿，不時御神，務快其心，逆於生樂，起居無節，故半百而衰也。[45]

[People of today] take liquor as their beverage, and debauchery is their
norm. They enter the bedroom drunk; they expend their vital essence (i.e.,
their refined *qi*) in desire and wastefully disperse their original substance.
They do not know how to maintain plenitude or control their spirit as
befits the moment; they are devoted to quickening their hearts and are
opposed to life-affirming pleasures. They are immoderate in their activity
and repose and thus decline at half a century.[46]

A different section of the same text explains that such a depleted body (called *xu* 虛, "emptied") will succumb to disease when it encounters pathogenic *qi*:

歧伯曰：「風雨寒熱不得虛，邪不能獨傷人。卒然逢疾風暴雨而不病者，蓋無虛，故邪不能獨傷人。此必因虛邪之風，與其身形，兩虛相得，乃客其形。」[47]

Qibo[48] said: "If wind, rain, cold, or heat do not gain access to a depleted [body], such pathogens alone cannot harm a person. If one suddenly meets a serious wind or vicious rainstorm and does not become sick, it is because there was no depletion. Thus a pathogen alone cannot harm a person. It must be that when a depleting and pathogenic wind engages a [depleted] body, the two depletions potentiate each other and invade the body.[49]

The term that I have translated (perhaps too freely) as "pathogen" is *xie* 邪, literally "deviance." Here it surely refers to *xieqi* 邪氣, "deviant *qi*," that is, the kind of *qi* that causes disease.[50] Such *qi* circulates throughout the world in the form of wind,[51] rain, cold, and heat, but it does not harm anyone who is healthy. Only someone whose store of healthy *qi* has been depleted beforehand will be unable to prevent pathogenic *qi* from invading (*ke* 客, lit. "to be a guest"—a term borrowed from military literature)[52] his or her body. The same, or nearly the same, viewpoint must have informed the judgment, found today in Sima Qian's biography of Chunyu Yi 淳于意 (fl. 180–154 BC),[53] that a certain patient's "illness was obtained by encountering great wind *qi* after frequently drinking liquor" 病得之數飲酒以見大風氣.[54]

The intellectual revolution wrought by the concept of *qi* ultimately led to the denial, on materialistic grounds, of the very possibility of ghosts. Far from accepting that ghosts cause disease, now some writers openly questioned whether ghosts could even exist. Wang Chong is the clearest such voice:

人之所以生者，精氣也，死而精氣滅，能為精氣者，血脈也，人死血脈竭，竭而精氣滅，滅而形體朽，朽而成灰土，何用為鬼？[55]

That by which people are alive is their vital *qi*. When they die, their vital *qi* is extinguished. That which can produce vital *qi* are the blood vessels.

> When people die, their blood vessels dry out; when [the blood vessels] are dried out, the vital *qi* is extinguished; when [the vital *qi*] is extinguished, the body decays; when [the body] decays, it becomes ash and dust. By what means would it become a ghost?

This passage is frequently quoted as representative because it is so plain-spoken,[56] but plenty of Chinese people continued to believe in ghosts and spirits long after Wang Chong—down to the present day, in fact.

Thus an important caveat is necessary: the newer worldview based on *qi* did not utterly and immediately displace the older explanation of disease as a consequence of spirit possession.[57] As the above examples from the *Zuo Commentary* show, both conceptions coexisted for centuries. Another case in point is the term *zhu* 注, "infusion" or "possession" (as in *guizhu* 鬼注, "demonic possession"). Doctors committed to theories of *qi* classified such pestilential forces as pathogenic *qi* but proceeded to cure it by means of rituals that were borrowed from the realm of exorcism.[58] Similarly, the power asserted by Daoist priests to exorcise the demons that caused illness was one of their primary means of eliciting reverence from the laity.[59] They had no trouble accommodating the idea that demons consisted of *qi*.[60]

The Mawangdui manuscript *Prescriptions for Fifty-Two Diseases* (*Wushier bing fang* 五十二病方) furnishes another instructive pair of examples. At one juncture, we are told that wind *qi* can exacerbate wounds, along with advice for counteracting the effect:

諸傷，風入傷，傷癰痛⋯⋯下膏勿絕，以驅寒氣。[61]

> Various wounds become abscessed and painful when wind enters them. . . . Continually push lard down [into the wound] so as to expel the cold *qi*.

But the same text also contains numerous exorcistic imprecations, such as the following, which is intended for use against illnesses caused by a spirit called Lizard (*yuan* 蚖):

湮汲一 [杯] 入奚蠡中，左承之，北嚮，嚮人禹步三，問其名，即曰：某某年□今□。飲半 [杯]，曰：病□□已，徐去徐已。即覆。[62]

> Draw one cup of stagnant water into a *jili* gourd. Hold it with the left hand and face north. Face [the afflicted] person and do the Pace of Yu[63] three

times. Ask his or her name, then say: "Such-and-such a year [lacuna] now [lacuna]" Drink half the glass, and say: "Illness [lacuna] desist! Gently depart; gently desist." Then turn [the cup] over.

Once again, the conceptions of illness as a consequence of spirit possession and as a consequence of disorder in one's *qi* appear in the very same text.

(2) To turn now from medicine to politics: the second noteworthy application of the concept of *qi* involved dynastic succession. From the Western Zhou 西周 (1045–771 BC) onward, the leading theory of political legitimacy was that of Heaven's Mandate (*tianming*).[64] "The Many Officers" ("Duoshi" 多士), transmitted as a chapter of the received *Exalted Documents* (*Shangshu* 尚書), is one of the clearest extant statements of the theory:

我有周佑命，將天明威，致王罰，敕殷命終于帝。肆爾多士！非我小國敢弋殷命。惟天不畀允罔固亂，弼我，我其敢求位？惟帝不畀，惟我下民秉為，惟天明畏。[65]

We, possessors of Zhou, assisted in the Mandate; led by Heaven's brilliant authority, we brought about the King [of Yin's] punishment, setting the Mandate of Yin aright and [thereby] fulfilling [the will of] the Deity. Thus, you many officers, it was not that our small kingdom dared to take aim at the Mandate of Yin; it was that Heaven, not cooperating with those who are deceitful, prevaricatory, ignorant, and disorderly, supported us. Would we dare seek this status [ourselves]? It was that the Deity would not cooperate [with you]. What our lowly people uphold and act on is the brilliant dreadfulness of Heaven.

The idea is that "Heaven," an irresistible ethical force, chooses a virtuous individual on earth as its vicegerent and installs him and his descendants to rule on earth as the so-called Son of Heaven (*tianzi* 天子).[66] If, however, the Son of Heaven fails in his obligation to rule with virtue, Heaven will choose another champion to overthrow him. This was the reasoning that the lords of Zhou put forward when explaining their astonishing success to the defeated Shang officers: the last King of Shang was evil; he mistreated his subjects; and Heaven appointed the Zhou to punish him and take his place. The avowed intention of the Zhou was not brute conquest, but beneficent and Heaven-ordained rule.

When, several centuries later, the great western state of Qin was about to usher in a new political order by uniting the warring kingdoms of the Chinese subcontinent, it made scant appeal to Heaven's Mandate,[67] perhaps because it could not realistically present itself as a model of virtue and beneficence. *Qi* once again proved useful. The ideological architects of the Qin dynasty proposed an account of dynastic succession that was based on the "mutual conquest" cycle of the Five Phases and thus fundamentally distinct from the theory of Heaven's Mandate:

凡帝王者之將興也，天必先見祥乎下民。

黃帝之時，天先見大螾大螻，黃帝曰：土氣勝，土氣勝，故其色尚黃，其事則土。

及禹之時，天先見草木秋冬不殺，禹曰：木氣勝，木氣勝，故其色尚青，其事則木。

及湯之時，天先見金刃生於水，湯曰：金氣勝，金氣勝，故其色尚白，其事則金。

及文王之時，天先見火，赤烏銜丹書集於周社，文王曰：火氣勝，火氣勝，故其色尚赤，其事則火。

代火者必將水，天且先見水氣勝，水氣勝，故其色尚黑，其事則水。水氣至而不知，數備，將徙于土。[68]

Whenever an emperor or king is about to flourish, Heaven must first cause an omen to appear to the people below.

At the time of the Yellow Thearch, Heaven first caused great earthworms and mole crickets to appear. The Yellow Thearch said: "Earth *qi* prevails." Since Earth *qi* prevailed, he exalted yellow as his color and modeled his activities after Earth.

When it came to the time of Yu, Heaven first caused grasses and trees to appear throughout autumn and winter without dying. Yu said: "Wood *qi* prevails." Since Wood *qi* prevailed, he exalted green as his color and modeled his activities after Wood.

When it came to the time of Tang, Heaven first caused metal blades to appear growing in the water. Tang said: "Metal *qi* prevails." Since Metal *qi* prevailed, he exalted white as his color and modeled his activities after Metal.

When it came to the time of King Wen, Heaven first caused fire to appear, and red rooks with cinnabar writings in their beaks to gather at the altars of Zhou. King Wen said: "Fire *qi* prevails." Since Fire *qi* prevailed, he exalted red as his color and modeled his activities after Fire.

What will replace Fire is surely Water. Heaven will first make it apparent that Water *qi* prevails; and since Water *qi* will prevail, [the new ruler]
will exalt black as his color and model his activities after Water. Water *qi*
will reach its limit, and then, without our knowing it, the sequence will
come full circle and shift back to Earth.

The significance of the system becomes clear when one recalls that
Qin chose to associate itself with Water[69] (hence all the flapping black
pennants in modern cinematic representations of the Qin army). The rise
of Qin is portrayed as neither good nor bad, but simply a matter of material necessity. To be sure, foretelling the dominion of Qin on the strength
of the Five Phases came with the acknowledgment that it would eventually have to be replaced by a new Earth power.[70] But presumably that day
was thought to lie comfortably in the future.

(3) In the third and final development to be discussed here, certain
traditions promised extraordinary power by learning how to control *qi*—
both in oneself and in others. The oldest extant example is probably "The
Internal Enterprise" ("Neiye" 內業), now transmitted as a chapter in
*Guanzi*:

凡物之精, 此則為生下生五穀, 上為列星。流於天地之間, 謂之鬼
神, 藏於胸中, 謂之聖人。[71]

The vital essence of all creatures—it is this that endows them with life.
Below, it gives birth to the five grains; above, it creates the arrayed stars.
When it flows between Heaven and Earth, it is called "ghostly" and "spirit-
like." Those who store it within their breasts are called "sages."

Ghosts and spirits are conceptualized as *jing* 精 (glossed in the text
itself as refined *qi* and translated above as "vital essence") flowing between
Heaven and Earth, and "sages" are understood here as practitioners who
have perfected the art of storing *qi* within their breast. The text
continues:

能正能靜, 然後能定。定心在中, 耳目聰明, 四枝堅固, 可以為精
舍。精也者, 氣之精者也。[72]

Only after one is able to be rectified and tranquil is one able to be settled. With a settled mind within, the ears and eyes will be keen of hearing and keen of sight; the four limbs will be firm and solid, and [one's

body] can be a lodge for vital essence. Vital essence is the refined essence of *qi*.

If *qi* is indeed the substance of the body, it stands to reason that cultivating and refining one's *qi* will strengthen one's mind, limbs, and powers of perception.[73] Although "The Internal Enterprise" gives few concrete prescriptions, it may have been taught by masters who would add unwritten physical and meditative exercises,[74] such as are known from later materials.[75]

Among the most pretentious of these masters was Zou Yan 鄒衍 (305?–240? BC), whose works do not survive,[76] but are described by Sima Qian:

深觀陰陽消息而作怪迂之變，《終始》、《大聖》之篇十餘萬言。其語閎大不經，必先驗小物，推而大之，至於無垠。先序今以上至黃帝，學者所共術，并世盛衰，因載其禨祥度制，推而遠之，至天地未生，窈冥不可考而原也。[77]

He carefully observed the growth and decay of *yin* and *yang* and wrote about freakish and enigmatic changes in essays such as *Ends and Beginnings* and *The Great Sage*, comprising more than one hundred thousand words. His statements were grandiose and extraordinary. He was sure to start by examining small things, then enlarge his [insight] by extending it until he reached infinity. He started by ordering contemporary affairs, reaching backward [in time] to the Yellow Thearch, who furnished all scholars with their techniques. He [explained] the flourishing and decline of adjacent generations and on this basis recorded a system of omens, which he extended far back to the time before Heaven and Earth had been born, to the abyssal darkness that cannot be studied or traced.

By offering rulers the prospect of understanding the significance of historical events great and small, literally without limit (*wuyin* 無垠), Zou Yan made himself one of the most sought-after counselors in Warring States China. The only difficulty, as we shall see, was putting his teachings into practice.

Some traditions went so far as to assert that one can control people's emotions if one knows how to control their *qi*. The underlying theory in the following passage, from *The Master of Huainan* (*Huainanzi* 淮南子)

is one of *qi*, as manifested in the phenomenon of sympathetic resonance. Musical tones were understood as *qi* as well:[78] stimulating one type of *qi* on a string elicits a sympathetic response in the corresponding *qi* all around.[79]

夫榮啟期一彈，而孔子三日樂，感於和；鄒忌一徽，而威王終夕悲，感於憂。動諸琴瑟，形諸音聲，而能使人為之哀樂。[80]

When Rong Qiqi plucked [his instrument] once, Confucius was joyous for three days; he was stimulated by harmony. When Zou Ji (d. 319 BC) strummed once wildly, King Wei [of Qi, r. 357–320 BC] was sorrowful all night; he was stimulated by melancholy.[81] If one moves them with the *qin* and *se* zithers, and forms them with tones and sounds, one can make the people grieve or be joyous.

The terrifying consequence of this worldview was that the ruler can force the people to feel any emotion he wishes—provided that he knows the technique of manipulating their *qi*.[82]

## LIMITATIONS

This study would be incomplete without considering the limitations of theories based on *qi*.

Most apparently, domination by means of *qi*, though undoubtedly attractive to men of great ambition, proved difficult to achieve. Sima Qian recounts the clamor that initially surrounded Zou Yan, but that soon gave way to disappointment, in a memorable line:

王公大人初見其術，懼然顧化，其後不能行之。[83]

When kings and dukes and great men first beheld [Zou Yan's] technique, they were stunned and became devotees, but later they were unable to put it into practice.

The weakness of most grandiloquent theories of *qi* was that they did not withstand even the most rudimentary empirical tests.[84] Partly this is because *qi* was routinely divided into complementary aspects, but never constituent elements. With no room for molecules, ions, and so on in the framework, the theory of *qi* was incapable of explaining chemical reactions. This is not a criticism of China per se; science in the West was no better equipped before Lavoisier.[85] But as an attempt to account for properties of matter, it is nevertheless an obsolete paradigm.[86]

The lack of a more effective theory to explain physical phenomena led to the habit of postulating gradations of *qi*, such as "pure" (*qing* 清) and varying degrees of "turbid" (*zhuo* 濁), without any exposition of the *cause* of such divergences.[87] Thus Wang Chong, who subscribed to the distinction between *qing* and *zhuo*, attributed disasters to the operations of *qi* rather than supposed censure (*qian'gao* 譴告)[88] from a conative Heaven, but without specifying the mechanisms by which disasters do and do not occur.

夫天無為，故不言。災變時至，氣自為之。夫天地不能為，亦不能知也。腹中有寒，腹中疾痛，人不使也，氣自為之。[89]

Heaven does not act; thus it does not speak. Disasters and disturbances occur from time to time; *qi* spontaneously produces them. Heaven and Earth cannot act and, moreover, cannot be sentient. When there is cold in the belly, the belly will ache. People do not cause this; *qi* spontaneously produces it.

In response to the popular notion that Heaven sends down disasters as admonition or censure, Wang Chong argued that Heaven is inanimate and hence incapable of action. Physical phenomena such as catastrophes and bellyaches must be caused by *qi*.[90] Superficially, this materialist view may seem more modern, but without an account of how and why *qi* sometimes produces bellyaches—but usually does not—its scientific value is nil.[91] As long as one can always declare, in the aftermath of a disaster, "Oh, that was turbid *qi*," and conversely, when things seem to be going well, "The *qi* must be clear today!" one is not really presenting a theory at all.[92] The consequence of such casuistry, then, was to turn *qi* into a nontheory that was unfalsifiable in a Popperian sense.[93] As Wolfgang Pauli would have said, it was "not even wrong."[94]

In the end, the idea of *qi* survived where it was useful and was inevitably discarded where it was not. In areas such as Chinese medicine, art,[95] and *fengshui* 風水,[96] *qi* remains a versatile concept to this day.

# Notes

## INTRODUCTION. WHAT ARE WE READING?

1. This was the outstanding insight of Xu Fuguan, *Zhongguo renxinglun shi*, 15–56. The unnamed master of "Record of Signs" ("Biaoji" 表記) recognizes the trend: whereas "the men of Yin (i.e., Shang) honored spirits and led its people to serve them" 殷人尊神, 率民以事神, "the men of Zhou honor ritual and esteem philanthropy" 周人尊禮尚施 (*Liji zhengyi* 44.1642a). Cf. Perkins, *Heaven and Earth Are Not Humane*, 16.

2. For this topic, the best study in English remains Lewis, *Sanctioned Violence in Early China*.

3. The name "Warring States" appears to have first been used by Jia Yi in *Xinshu jiaozhu* 1.14 ("Guo Qin lun xia" 過秦論下).

4. This is still the approach in Sterckx, *Chinese Thought*.

5. The oldest reference I can find is Lu Shiyi, *Lu Futing Sibian lu jiyao*, 1.9a.

6. Goldin, "Persistent Misconceptions about Chinese 'Legalism.'"

7. The relevant scholarly literature is too large to be cited in extenso here. The classic study remains Zhu Ziqing, *Shi yan zhi bian*. Many key sources are assembled in Owen, *Readings in Chinese Literary Thought*, 19–56. See also Xu Zhengying, *Xian-Tang wenxue yu wenxue sixiang kaolun*, 261–75; and Chow Tse-tsung, "Early History of the Chinese Word *shih* (Poetry)," 155ff.

8. *Shiji* 65.2161–62.

9. See, e.g., Fleming, "On Translation of Taoist Philosophical Texts."

10. For a recent study, see Hunter, "Did Mencius Know the *Analects*?"

11. See esp. Ke Mading, "*Shiji* li de 'zuozhe' gainian"; and Kern, "'Masters' in the *Shiji*"; also Hanmo Zhang, *Authorship and Text-Making in Early China*, 249; Wai-yee Li, "Concepts of Authorship," 373–74; Beecroft, *Authorship and Cultural Identity in Early Greece and China*, 56; and Vankeerberghen, "Texts and Authors in the *Shiji*."

12. *Shiji* 130.3300. Compare the close parallel in the famous letter to Ren An 任安 (d. 91 BC?), *Hanshu* 62.2735, which adds: "Those like Zuoqiu Ming, who did not have [the use of] his eyes, or Master Sun, whose feet were cut off, could never be employed; they retired to write books in which they exposed their outrage, yearning to reveal themselves in the legacy of their insubstantial literature" 及如左丘明無目, 孫子斷足, 終不可用, 退論書策以舒其憤, 思垂空文以自見.

13. All translations in this book are my own unless otherwise indicated. I have not provided dates for Qu Yuan and Zuoqiu Ming because that would be guesswork.

14. This topic is likewise too large to document in a single note, but standard treatments include Klein, *Reading Sima Qian from Han to Song*, 26–76; Hanmo Zhang, *Authorship and Text-Making in Early China*, 241–305; Lü Shihao, *Cong Shiji dao Hanshu*, 24–46 and 151–201; Zhang Dake, *Shiji yanjiu*, 38–66; and Hardy, *Worlds of Bronze and Bamboo*, esp. 40–41.

15. *Shiji* 97.2699; and *Hanshu* 43.2113.

16. Cf. Taniguchi, "Fu ni jijo o tsukeru koto."

17. E.g., Nylan, *Yang Xiong and the Pleasures of Reading and Classical Learning in China*, 48–61; and Wang Qing, *Yang Xiong pingzhuan*, 281–96.

18. E.g., McLeod, *Philosophical Thought of Wang Chong*, 28ff.; Zufferey, *Wang Chong*, 385–88; and Zhong Zhaopeng and Zhou Guidian, *Huan Tan Wang Chong pingzhuan*, 119–82.

19. E.g., Schwermann, "Composite Authorship in Western Zhou Bronze Inscriptions," esp. 30–37; Richter, *Embodied Text*, esp. 65–72; Fischer, "Authentication Studies (辨偽學) Methodology and the Polymorphous Text Paradigm"; Li Ling, *Jianbo gushu yu xueshu yuanliu*, 209–16; Harbsmeier, "Authorial Presence in Some Pre-Buddhist Chinese Texts"; and Nivison, "Classical Philosophical Writings," 745–47.

20. Cf. Nylan, *Chinese Pleasure Book*, 274ff.; and Hanmo Zhang, *Authorship and Text-Making in Early China*, 12–13. Boltz, "Composite Nature of Early Chinese Texts," proposes "building blocks" consisting of just twenty-two or twenty-four graphs (i.e., the length of a single bamboo strip). But there can be little doubt that some irreducible units are longer than that. For some examples, see Gentz, "Defining Boundaries and Relations of Textual Units."

21. For example, the *Zuoce* Ban *yan* 作冊般甗 and *Zuoce* Ban *yuan* 作冊般黿 inscriptions indicate that late Shang scribes were tasked with producing texts on bamboo, but these were probably brief and occasional; see Zhu Fenghan, "Zuoce Ban yuan tanxi." Appointment ceremonies recorded in Zhou bronze inscriptions also imply that texts were written on bamboo first; see, e.g., Kern, "Performance of Writing in Western Zhou China," 150 (see also Kern's survey of references to writing in early received sources, 122–27). The closest reference to a book that I have found is *Mozi jiaozhu* 12.47.673 ("Guiyi" 貴義): Mozi "carried many books in his trunk" 關中載書甚多. Cf. *Baopuzi waipian jiaojian*, 127 ("Xuxue" 勖學): "Mo Di was a great worthy; his carriage was filled with written texts" 墨翟大賢，載文盈車.

22. For the example of Wu Zixu 伍子胥 (d. 484 BC), see, e.g., Hardy, *Worlds of Bronze and Bamboo*, 143; also Joseph Roe Allen, "Introductory Study of Narrative Structure in the *Shiji*," 47ff.; Jäger, "Die Biographie des Wu Tzu-hsü"; and two studies by David Johnson: "Wu Tzu-hsü *pien-wen* and Its Sources" and "Epic and History in Early China."

23. Consider Lord Mu of Qin 秦穆公 (r. 659–621 BC): in the Battle of Han 韓 (645 BC), he is portrayed as a paragon of virtue and forbearance, who wisely heeds his advisers; eighteen years later, in the Battle of Yao 殽, he plans a greedy and unsound campaign of conquest despite the pointed remonstrances of his ministers (Goldin, "Hermeneutics of Emmentaler"). See *Chunqiu Zuozhuan zhu*, 1:351–66 (Xi 僖 15 = 645 BC), for the Battle of Han; and 1:489–91 (Xi 32 = 628 BC) and 497–501 (Xi 33 = 627 BC), for the Battle of Yao.

24. Kern and Meyer, "Introduction," in *Origins of Chinese Political Philosophy*, 6n20, have revived an important insight by Jiang Shanguo (*Shangshu zongshu*, 133): the relevant question is not when a text was composed, but when it was redacted.

25. See the convenient volume Yu Jiaxi, *Yu Jiaxi shuo wenxianxue*, which includes his best-known study, *Gushu tongli* 古書通例 (159–267).

26. In English, the fullest treatment of the Guodian manuscripts is Cook, *Bamboo Texts of Guodian*. For my view of their significance, see Goldin, *After Confucius*, 36–57.

27. Cf. Li Rui, *Zhanguo Qin Han shiqi de xuepai wenti yanjiu*, 195–240; and Gu Shikao, "Yi Zhanguo zhushu chongdu *Gushu tongli*."

28. Some editions of the text do not even bother to include it. Classical prefaces are usually omitted from modern translations as well, and presses ought to insist that translators include them in the front matter.

29. Deng Junjie, *Liu Xiang jiaoshu kaolun*, is a recent study of Liu Xiang's methods. See also the concise discussion in Bumbacher, "Reconstructing the *Zhuang zi*," 643–50; as well as Lü Shaoyu, *Zhongguo muluxue shi gao*, 6–34; and Yao Mingda, *Zhongguo muluxue shi*, 39–60. These are not superseded by Lee Hur-Li, *Intellectual Activism in Knowledge Organization*, 37–58.

30. For the term *taishi shu* 太史書 in this context, see, e.g., Meng Wentong, *Zhongguo zhexue sixiang tanyuan*, 60.

31. I am unaware of any explanation of the arithmetic. One would expect that removing 638 episodes from an original total of 838 should yield 200 episodes, not 215. Cf. Cook, "Changing Role of the Minister in the Warring States," 186n6.

32. For the difficult phrase *jin po lüe jian* 謹頗略楲, I follow Cheng Shuijin and Feng Yiming, "*Liezi* kaobian shuping yu *Liezi* weishu xinzheng," 46.

33. *Yanzi chunqiu jishi*, 22.

34. This is a formulaic closing (*Yanzi chunqiu jishi*, 25n28).

35. Cf. Cook, "Changing Role of the Minister in the Warring States," 187; Liu Wenbin, Yanzi chunqiu *yanjiu shi*, 3ff.; Zheng Liangshu, *Zhuzi zhuzuo niandai kao*, 22–36; and Chen Ruigeng, *Yanzi chunqiu kaobian*, 127–77. Incidentally, this preface shows that Liu did not use the word *pian* consistently: at first, it refers to the bamboo bundles that he found in various collections, but then it refers to the chapters that he created by reorganizing the material.

36. Liu Xiang does not clarify the term *fuchong*, but since *Springs and Autumns of Master Yan* often contains different versions of what seems to be the same basic story, these "duplicates" would seem to be verbatim (or nearly verbatim) copies of the same piece of text. This is only an inference, however. Cf. Van der Loon, "On the Transmission of the *Kuan-tzŭ*," 363.

37. Sun Xingyan 孫星衍 (1753–1818) observed that some of these were graphic, others aural (*Yanzi chunqiu jishi*, 23n7).

38. Notoriously, these discrepancies led Liu Zongyuan 柳宗元 (773–819) to classify Master Yan as a Mohist (apparently forgetting that Master Yan antedated Mo Di by about a century); see Cao Minggang, *Liu Zongyuan quanji*, 4.33–34 ("Bian *Yanzi chunqiu*" 辯晏子春秋). Master Yan's supposed philosophical affiliation remained a red herring into the twentieth century. Cf. Milburn, *Spring and Autumn Annals of Master Yan*, 46–54; Liu Wenbin, Yanzi chunqiu *yanjiu shi*, 30–36; and Andrew Meyer, "'Altars of the Soil and Grain Are Closer than Kin,'" 62.

39. These two features are trenchantly discussed in Stumpfeldt, "Ein Diener vieler Herren." See also Milburn, *Spring and Autumn Annals of Master Yan*, 9–10; and Zheng Liangshu, *Zhuzi zhuzuo niandai kao*, 49ff.

40. Holzer, *Yen-tzu und das Yen-tzu ch'un-ch'iu*, 15.

41. Thus I disagree with Andrew Meyer's characterization of *Yanzi chunqiu* as "a patronage text of the Qi state" ("'Altars of the Soil and Grain Are Closer Than Kin,'" 62). Perhaps that is valid for one of Liu Xiang's many sources, but not for all of them.

42. The best survey is now Milburn, *Spring and Autumn Annals of Master Yan*, 13–42.

43. Cf. Timpanaro, *Genesis of Lachmann's Method*, esp. 115–18; also Most, "What Is a Critical Edition?"

44. Shaughnessy openly adopts a Lachmannian approach in "Of Trees, a Son, and Kingship," 603–4, but it was already implicit in his *Rewriting Early Chinese Texts*, where differences among extant editions are repeatedly explained as a consequence of someone's "misreading" or "rewriting" (e.g., 43: "the difference between the two versions certainly seems to show one editor consciously rewriting the text"—where "the text" cannot mean anything other than a postulated *codex archetypus*). Nevertheless, in his conclusion (*Rewriting Early Chinese Texts*, 258), Shaughnessy goes on to disavow the concept of an urtext.

45. The most notable recent exponents of an accretion theory are Brooks and Brooks, e.g., *Original Analects*; see also their extension of their method to the entire classical corpus in *Emergence of China*. For the weaknesses of their suppositions, see Hunter, *Confucius beyond the* Analects, 231–44; and Schaberg, "'Sell It! Sell It!,'" esp. 131–39. In China, the model is called "the theory of accumulated layers" (*cenglei shuo* 層累說) and is associated primarily with Gu Jiegang 顧頡剛 (1893–1980), e.g., *Autobiography of a Chinese Historian*, 96ff.

46. Chen Shike 陳士珂 (fl. 1818) identified parallels for 307 of the text's 320 sections. Cf. Goldin, *Rituals of the Way*, 135n53. Van Ess, "Einige Anmerkungen zur Biographie des Konfuzius im *Shih-chi* und vergleichbaren Stellen im *K'ung-tzu chia-yü*," compares the biography of Confucius in *Shiji* with its parallels in *Kongzi jiayu*, concluding that the latter postdated the former.

47. Translated and discussed in Kramers, *K'ung tzŭ chia yü*, 91–100.

48. Precisely this misconception is reflected in Yang Zhaoming and Song Lilin's introduction to *Kongzi jiayu tongjie*, 1–40.

49. For example, his preface to *Guanzi* 管子 suggests that he thought it consisted of works by Guan Zhong (d. 645 BC), a position no longer seriously held by most modern scholars. Cf. Van der Loon, "On the Transmission of the *Kuan-tzŭ*," 360ff.

50. Scholars disagree over Xunzi's dates. Knoblock, *Xunzi*, 1:3–35, argues for ca. 310–ca. 210 BC.

51. Cf. Goldin, "Xunzi and Early Han Philosophy."

52. Cf. Cook, "Changing Role of the Minister in the Warring States," 187n8; more generally, Sato, *Confucian Quest for Order*, 27–36. Martin Kern (private communication) has pointed out a problem with this reasoning: Liu Xiang reported a very high number of duplicates in his preface to *Guanzi* as well.

53. Cf. Denecke, *Dynamics of Masters Literature*, 180.

54. See, generally, Knoblock, *Xunzi*, 1:105–28.

55. Thus when we read in *Shiji* 74.2348 that Xunzi edited his works before he died, whatever text he produced cannot be the same as our *Xunzi* today. Machle, *Nature and Heaven in the* Xunzi, 57–58, points out that the chapter titles are unreliable as well.

56. Knoblock, *Xunzi*, 3:237.

57. The fullest study in English remains Knechtges, "Riddles as Poetry."

58. Cf. Kern, "Style and Poetic Diction in the *Xunzi*," 2ff.; and Hutton, *Xunzi*, xviii–xxiii. Kern, it should be noted, doubts my view that the bulk of the text derives from Xun Kuang, emphasizing stylistic differences among the various chapters, whereas I would chalk these up to the dissimilar demands of each occasion and audience.

59. The leading studies of the authenticity of *Han Feizi* remain Zheng Liangshu, *Han Fei zhi zhushu ji sixiang*; and Lundahl, *Han Fei Zi*.

60. Even in antiquity, however, Guo Xiang was accused of having plagiarized large

portions from Xiang Xiu 向秀 (ca. AD 227–72), one of the so-called Seven Worthies of the Bamboo Grove 竹林七賢. See the well-annotated discussions in Kohn, *Zhuangzi*, 93–94; and Tang Yijie, *Guo Xiang yu Wei Jin xuanxue*, 127–48. Ziporyn, *Penumbra Unbound*, 25–26, also explains why the charge is unfair and simplistic.

61. Cf. Bumbacher, "Reconstructing the *Zhuang zi*," 636–50. More recently, Bumbacher, "Ge Hong's *Zhuang zi*," discusses some possible glimpses of the text before Guo Xiang.

62. Zhao Qi's commentary is less frequently studied as a work in its own right than Guo Xiang's, but see Tang Minggui, "Zhao Qi *Mengzi zhangju* de quanshi tese"; and Fuehrer, "*Mencius* for Han Readers."

63. The relevant literature is much too large to cite in a single note, but Robinet, *Les commentaires du Tao Tö King jusqu'au VIIᵉ siècle*, is still a useful guide. See also Yang Yi, *Laozi huanyuan*, 191–98.

64. For some examples, see Cook, *Bamboo Texts of Guodian*, 1:199–216; and Boltz, "Why So Many *Laozi*-s?"

65. For the example of Du Yu's 杜預 (AD 222–84) commentary on *Zuozhuan*, see Tashima, "Fragments Speak."

66. See the translation and study in Bokenkamp, *Early Daoist Scriptures*, 29–142; another thorough study is Ōfuchi, *Shoki no Dōkyō*, 247–308. See also Eskildsen, *Daoism, Meditation, and the Wonders of Serenity*, 62–74; Puett, "Forming Spirits for the Way"; and Kobayashi, *Rikuchō Dōkyō shi kenkyū*, 296–327. *Xiang'er* looks like a good example of what Eco called "overinterpretation" in *Interpretation and Overinterpretation*, esp. 52ff.

67. Cf. Kern, "Methodological Reflections on the Analysis of Textual Variants and the Modes of Manuscript Production in Early China," 164–65; more generally, Pian Yuqian, *Jianbo wenxian gangyao*, 171–201.

68. For similar observations in connection with the *Analects*, see Makeham, *Transmitters and Creators*, 9–20; and Ivanhoe, "Whose Confucius? Which *Analects*?"

69. See, e.g., Sternberg, *Poetics of Biblical Narrative*, 7–23.

70. For an overview of the evolution of this text, see Brockington, *Sanskrit Epics*, 130–58.

71. Cf. Williams, *Mahāyāna Buddhism*, 29–33.

72. For the illuminating example of *Les contes d'Hoffmann*, which has been published (and performed) in many versions since the death of Jacques Offenbach (1819–80), see Giroud and Kaye, *Real Tales of Hoffmann*, esp. 135–42. Compare Beardsley, *Aesthetics*, 22: "It is not even agreed which of the widely different versions of Bruckner's *C Minor Symphony* (*No. 8*) he wanted performed: the 1887 original, the 1890 version, the 1892 version—or some compromise like that reflected in the Hass version of 1935."

73. I have been criticized, incidentally, *both* for endorsing historicist interpretation *and* for objecting to it. For the former, see Carmichael, "*Daode jing* as American Scripture," 175; for the latter, Bhattacharya, "What the Cārvākas Originally Meant," 529–30. Bhattacharya has understood me better (though he disagrees with me too); essentially, my view is that historicism turns texts into fossils if it disregards their reinterpretation and reconfiguration in later contexts.

74. I take this phrase from Dworkin, *Law's Empire*, e.g., 47; as Georgia Warnke notes in *Justice and Interpretation*, 159, it is an inherently pluralistic standard.

75. Cf. Coutinho, *Zhuangzi and Early Chinese Philosophy*, 34ff.

## CHAPTER ONE. NONDEDUCTIVE ARGUMENTATION
## AND THE ART OF CHINESE PHILOSOPHY

1. The academic debate over the legitimacy of Chinese philosophy has occasioned numerous recent publications. For representative overviews, see Perkins, *Heaven and Earth Are Not Humane*, 4–5; Denecke, *Dynamics of Masters Literature*, esp. 11–18; Defoort, "Is There Such a Thing as Chinese Philosophy?"; Defoort, "Is 'Chinese Philosophy' a Proper Name?"; and Lin Tongqi et al., "Chinese Philosophy," esp. 746ff.

2. For an example of this sort of complaint, see Munro, *Concept of Man in Early China*, ix; see also the response in Van Norden, "What Should Western Philosophy Learn from Chinese Philosophy?," 230. Also Hartwell, "Historical Analogism, Public Policy, and Social Science in Eleventh- and Twelfth-Century China," 722ff. In earlier generations, the typical complaint was that "the Chinese mind" was incapable of higher logic; e.g., Forke, "Chinese Sophists," 5. One can only suppose that such opinions were influenced by the ignorant and chauvinistic representation of China by G.W.F. Hegel (1770–1831), for which see, e.g., Griffioen, "Hegel on Chinese Religion."

3. Hu Shih, *Development of the Logical Method in Ancient China*, 6. For a survey of modern Chinese ideas about the presence or absence of logic in classical sources, see Kurtz, *Discovery of Chinese Logic*, esp. 277–337.

4. Trans. A. J. Jenkinson in Barnes, *Complete Works of Aristotle*, 1:40. Nisbett's declaration that "Aristotle had testable propositions about the world while the Chinese did not" (*Geography of Thought*, 134) is a flagrant overstatement. Consider that scientists have criticized Aristotle precisely for advancing hypotheses that are not testable (e.g., Moore, *Science as a Way of Knowing*, 41).

5. More precisely: "Although Aristotle was aware that there are several kinds of valid argument which cannot be reduced to syllogistic form, he did not, so far as we know, succeed in giving a formal analysis of any of them" (Kneale and Kneale, *Development of Logic*, 99).

6. Cf. Barnes, "Aristotle," 120–21.

7. See, e.g., Quine, *Methods of Logic*, 102–8.

8. E.g., Modrak, *Aristotle*, 128–28.

9. Cf. Nylan, "Lots of Pleasure but Little Happiness," 212; Coutinho, *Zhuangzi and Early Chinese Philosophy*, 19; more generally, Zhang Wenxiu, "Zhongguo zhexue zhong de zhengming wenti."

10. *Lunyu jishi* 10.337.

11. Compare the many Latin variations on the theme of "second thoughts are wiser," e.g., *Posteriores enim cogitationes, ut aiunt, sapientiores solent esse* (Shackleton Bailey, *Philippics 7–14*, 190), in the formulation of Cicero (106–43 BC).

12. *Lunyu jishi* 18.623.

13. Other traditions alluded to the same properties of evergreens; one of the legendary sages of the Daoist tradition, for example, is Master Red Pine (Chisongzi 赤松子, see p. 75).

14. For further reflections on metaphor in Chinese philosophy, see Slingerland, "Metaphor and Meaning in Early China."

15. Cf. Lightbody and Berman, "Metaphoric Fallacy to a Deductive Inference."

16. This is by no means an exhaustive list; for example, for my thoughts on paronomasia, see Goldin, *After Confucius*, 14ff. Bodde observed some of these types of reasoning in his *China's First Unifier*, 223–32.

17. Because such paradoxes and their various proposed "solutions" seem straightforwardly reducible to logic problems familiar from Western philosophy, they have received inordinate attention over the last few decades, as Pines bemoans (*Envisioning Eternal Empire*, 225n18). Even a representative bibliography would be impossible in the space of one note. Incidentally, I do not mean the same thing as riddles, which are explored as a technique of remonstrance in Wai-yee Li, "Riddles, Concealment, and Rhetoric in Early China." See also Patt-Shamir, "To Live a Riddle."

18. In previous work (e.g., *Rituals of the Way*, 83ff.), I translated *bianzhe* as "dialecticians," but I now think this is misleading.

19. I borrow this terminology from Quine, *Ways of Paradox and Other Essays*, 1–18.

20. *Zhuangzi jishi* 10B.33.1103 ("Tianxia" 天下).

21. Cf. Solomon, *On the School of Names in Ancient China*, 36–37. For other interpretations, see Harbsmeier, *Language and Logic in Traditional China*, 296–97; Graham, *Disputers of the Tao*, 79–80; and Reding, *Les fondements philosophiques de la rhétorique*, 369–72.

22. *Xunzi jijie* 2.3.38 ("Bugou" 不苟); also *Zhuangzi jishi* 10B.33.1105 ("Tianxia").

23. *Zhuangzi jishi* 10B.33.1106 ("Tianxia").

24. The explanation in Reding, *Les fondements philosophiques de la rhétorique*, 439, is that "Sheep" might be the dog's proper name.

25. Cf. Goldin, *Rituals of the Way*, 91. I believe the point was first made by Mou Zongsan, *Mingjia yu Xunzi*, 3ff.

26. E.g., Lawrence H. Powers, "Equivocation."

27. *Zhuangzi jishi* 10B.33.1106 ("Tianxia"); see Reding, *Les fondements philosophiques de la rhétorique*, 440–41.

28. *Gongsun Longzi xingming fawei* 2.24 ("Baima lun" 白馬論). The likeliest interpretation of this paradox, from a historical point of view, is Harbsmeier, "Mass Noun Hypothesis and the Part-Whole Analysis of the White Horse Dialogue." Note that *Han Feizi xin jiaozhu* 11.32.674 ("Wai chushuo zuo shang" 外儲說左上) attributes it to an obscure figure named Ni Shui 兒說 (the Boy Persuader). For a discussion of the implications, see Goldin, *Rituals of the Way*, 138n3.

29. The scholarship on this one line is too massive to cite in a single note, but the most plausible treatment, to my mind, is Harbsmeier, *Language and Logic in Traditional China*, 298–321.

30. *Mozi jiaozhu* 11.45.630 ("Xiaoqu" 小取); also Graham, *Later Mohist Logic, Ethics and Science*, 492 (NO 18), though his translation of *ji* as "bramble" reflects a different understanding of the statement.

31. Thus Sun Yirang 孫詒讓 (1848–1908) in *Mozi jiaozhu* 11.45.639n64. Fung, "Logical Perspective on the Parallelism in Later Moism," 348, dismisses it simply as an "invalid argument."

32. Cf. De Reu, "Right Words Seem Wrong," esp. 286–89; and Van Norden, "Method in the Madness of the *Laozi*," 197; more generally, Graham, *Disputers of the Tao*, 231–34.

33. "Defamiliarization" is one of several proposed translations of the Russian word *ostranenie*, which was coined by Shklovsky in *Theory of Prose*, esp. 6ff. In his "Translator's Introduction" (*Theory of Prose*, xviii–xix), Benjamin Sher argues for "enstrangement" (*sic*), a jarring neologism like *ostranenie* itself. In brief, defamiliarization refers to any artistic device that serves to problematize concepts, patterns, or prejudices obscured by mainstream discourse.

34. For recent surveys, see Lloyd, *Analogical Investigations*, esp. 43–57; Reding,

*Comparative Essays in Early Greek and Chinese Rational Thinking*, 31–48; and Volkov, "Analogical Reasoning in Ancient China."

35. Cf. MacCormack, *Spirit of Traditional Chinese Law*, 166–74; and Bodde and Morris, *Law in Imperial China*, 517–30.

36. See, e.g., Pauline Yu, *Reading of Imagery in the Chinese Poetic Tradition*, 57–67; also Kao, "Comparative Literature and the Ideology of Metaphor, East and West," 102ff.; Ming Dong Gu, "*Fu-bi-xing*"; and François Cheng, "*Bi* 比 et *xing* 興."

37. *Mengzi zhengyi* 23.783.

38. On this concept, see Ivanhoe, "McDowell, Wang Yangming, and Mengzi's Contributions to Understanding Moral Perception," 285ff.; and Hutton, "Moral Connoisseurship in Mengzi."

39. "The Many People" ("Zhengmin" 烝民, Mao 260), a poem in the *Odes*, states this principle as clearly as any philosophical text: "Heaven engendered the many people; there are creatures; there are patterns" 天生烝民, 有物有則. Natural patterns are normative because they derive from Heaven. Cf. Pauline Yu, *Reading of Imagery in the Chinese Poetic Tradition*, 37–43: Chinese poetry tends to rely on the notion that natural correspondences are real and discovered, rather than metaphorical and invented.

40. Perhaps the sternest voice has been that of Waley, *Three Ways of Thought in Ancient China*, 194.

41. Cf. David B. Wong, "Reasons and Analogical Reasoning in Mengzi"; and Lau, *Mencius*, 362–90.

42. *Shangshu jiaoshi yilun*, 3:1098.

43. See, more generally, Goldin, *Culture of Sex in Ancient China*, 48ff.

44. *Baihu tong shuzheng* 10.452 ("Jiaqu" 嫁娶).

45. For some other thoughts on the weaknesses of analogical reasoning in Chinese thought, see Lo, "From Analogy to Proof."

46. Bentham, *Bentham's Handbook of Political Fallacies*, 43–53.

47. See Goldin, "Appeals to History in Early Chinese Philosophy and Rhetoric."

48. The best discussion is now Pines, "From Historical Evolution to the End of History"; see also Graham, *Disputers of the Tao*, 270–73.

49. *Han Feizi xin jiaozhu* 19.49.1085 ("Wudu" 五蠹).

50. *Xinshu jiaozhu* 1.17 ("Guo Qin xia" 過秦下).

51. *Zhanguo ce zhushi* 18.613 ("Zhang Mengtan ji gu Zhao zong" 張孟談既固趙宗).

52. For this and other appeals to history, literature, and apophthegms in *Zhanguo ce*, see Goldin, *After Confucius*, 82–83.

53. *Lunyu jishi* 14.482.

54. On the *Analects*, see Olberding, *Moral Exemplars in the* Analects. The phrase "being cautious when alone" (*shen qi du* 慎其獨 or sometimes just *shen du*) is found in many texts, the oldest of which is probably *Wuxing* 五行 (Cook, *Bamboo Texts of Guodian*, 1:496). When one is alone, one is bereft of helpful models.

55. In two recent publications, Matthias L. Richter has argued that such moral judgments derive from the bureaucratic practice of succinctly noting an official's strengths and weaknesses. See his "Roots of Ru 儒 Ethics in *shi* 士 Status Anxiety"; and his *Guan ren*.

56. *Han Feizi xin jiaozhu* 19.49.1085 ("Wudu").

57. *Han Feizi xin jiaozhu* 3.10.228–29. The three ministers are Shudiao 豎刁, Ducal Son Kaifang of Wei 衛公子開方, and Yiya 易牙, who go on, in this account, to imprison

Lord Qi until he starves to death. Cf. *Guanzi jiaozhu* 11.32.608–9 ("Xiaocheng" 小稱); and *Lüshi chunqiu xin jiaoshi* 16.978–80 ("Zhijie" 知接).

58. *Han Feizi xin jiaozhu* 15.36.849–52. Ducal Son Kaifang of Wei does not appear in this passage.

59. Cf. Goldin, "Introduction," in *Dao Companion to the Philosophy of Han Fei*, 2ff.

60. E.g., the subtitle of Victor H. Mair's translation, *Wandering on the Way: Early Taoist Tales and Parables of Chuang Tzu*.

61. "Anecdote" comes close to *zhanggu* 掌故, the locus classicus of which is *Shiji*, e.g., 128.3224. The standard Chinese translation of "parable" is now *yuyan* 寓言, which is borrowed from a chapter in *Zhuangzi* (*Zhuangzi jishi* 9A.27.947–64), where it has a much broader meaning. The term *diangu* 典故 denotes any kind of literary allusion and overlaps with "anecdote" too. But none of these terms was used consistently in any kind of premodern Chinese genre theory. See further Jack W. Chen, "Introduction," in Chen and Schaberg, *Idle Talk*, 4; and Schaberg, "Chinese History and Philosophy," 394ff.

62. *Zhuangzi jishi* 3C.7.309 ("Ying diwang" 應帝王).

63. On these names, see, e.g., Ye Shuxian, *Zhuangzi de wenhua jiexi*, 128–32. Blob (*hundun* 渾沌) must be related to "dumpling" (*huntun* 餛飩, better known in English by the Cantonese pronunciation "wonton"), so called because of its shapelessness. Chin, *Savage Exchange*, 40–48, discusses the similar use of fictitious personages in early Chinese economic treatises; see also Goldin, *After Confucius*, 6–13.

64. Cf. Goldin, "Why Daoism Is Not Environmentalism," 80. For other interpretations, see, e.g., Chen Zhibin, "Lun Zhuangzi zhexue de benyu"; Girardot, *Myth and Meaning in Early Taoism*, 81–98; Kaltenmark, *Lao Tzu and Taoism*, 101; Needham, *Science and Civilisation in China*, 2:112ff.; Waley, *Three Ways of Thought in Ancient China*, 66ff.; Granet, *La pensée chinoise*, 320–21; and Granet, *Danses et légendes de la Chine ancienne*, 544.

65. The most extensive discussion known to me is Harbsmeier, *Language and Logic in Traditional China*, 278–86. Cikoski, "On Standards of Analogic Reasoning in the Late Chou," 325, proposes a passage from *Lüshi chunqiu* as an example of "the syllogism form," but I fail to see how it qualifies as a syllogism; cf. Chmielewski, "Concerning the Problem of Analogic Reasoning in Ancient China," 67n4. Some syllogisms from the Mohist Canons are discussed in Zhan Jianfeng, *Mojia de xingshi luoji*, 110–18.

66. *Mozi jiaozhu* 4.16.172 (Jian'ai xia" 兼愛下).

67. This sentence is no less repetitive in the original Chinese.

68. Cf. Goldin, "Appeals to History in Chinese Philosophy and Rhetoric," 88–89. My understanding of this passage differs slightly from that of Pines, "Disputers of Abdication," 289ff. Cf. also Luo Genze, *Zhuzi kaosuo*, 72ff.

69. Following the commentary of Yu Yue 俞樾 (1821–1907).

70. *Xunzi jijie* 12.18.331–32 ("Zhenglun" 正論). Since there is no universally recognized citation system for passages in *Xunzi*, I shall use the section numbers in Knoblock, *Xunzi*. My translations, however, will often diverge from those of Knoblock substantially.

71. *Zhanguo ce zhushi* 4.148 ("Qin Xuan taihou ai Wei Choufu" 秦宣太后愛魏醜夫).

72. This name appears to mean "the Grotesque Man from Wei."

73. *Chunqiu Zuozhuan zhu*, 3:1106 (Xiang 襄 25 = 548 BC).

74. Cf. Saussy, *Great Walls of Discourse and Other Adventures in Cultural China*, 35–74.

75. For similar attitudes toward the canonical *Odes*, see Goldin, *After Confucius*, 26–35.

76. *Lunyu jishi* 13.448. Compare *Analects* 1.15, where Confucius applauds his disciple Zigong: "I told you about what comes first, and you knew what comes after" 告諸 往而知來者 (*Lunyu jishi* 2.56).

77. Cf. Mattice, *Metaphor and Metaphilosophy*, 91–100.

## CHAPTER TWO. THE *ANALECTS* OF CONFUCIUS

1. Cf. Liu Yuan, *Shang Zhou jizuli yanjiu*, 237–65; Von Glahn, *Sinister Way*, 19ff.; Keightley, *Ancestral Landscape*, 102–3; Itō, "Religion and Society," in Itō and Takashima, *Studies in Early Chinese Civilization*, 1:38–49; and Tsung-tung Chang, *Der Kult der Shang-Dynastie im Spiegel der Orakelinschriften*, 34–62.

2. See esp. Kern, "Kongzi as Author in the Han"; also Nylan and Wilson, *Lives of Confucius*, 74–87.

3. See the annotated discussion in Goldin, "Some Shang Antecedents of Later Chinese Ideology and Culture," 121–23.

4. Cf. Sor-hoon Tan, "Three Corners for One."

5. *Lunyu jishi* 23.787.

6. Cf. Harbsmeier, "On the Nature of Early Confucian Classical Chinese Discourse on Ethical Norms," 521–26. In Chinese, this is often called Confucius's method of "[teaching] each [student] according to his capacity" (*ge yin qi cai* 各因其材). The locus classicus, I believe, is the comment by Cheng Yi 程頤 (1033–1107) on *Analects* 2.7–8 (Cheng Yi is quoted in Zhu Xi, *Sishu zhangju jizhu*, 56).

7. Cf. Vogelsang, "Beyond Confucius," 55–56. Compare Confucius's objection to a legal code inscribed on an iron cauldron, as recorded in *Chunqiu Zuozhuan zhu*, 4:1504 (Zhao 昭 29 = 513 BC): writing down the law eliminates the possibility of discretion (Schaberg, *Patterned Past*, 294ff.). In the West, the foremost expression of such fears is *Phaedrus*, 275d–e. Cf. Kern, "Speaking of Poetry," 179–80.

8. See *Hanshu* 30.1717.

9. The best overview is now Hunter, *Confucius beyond the* Analects; also Hanmo Zhang, *Authorship and Text-Making in Early China*, 103–11.

10. Cf. Pines, "Lexical Changes in Zhangguo Texts," e.g., 697; I present further evidence in "Confucius and His Disciples in the *Lunyu*."

11. For example, I do not agree with Tsuda, *Rongo to Kōshi no shisō*, who argued that the text is riddled with internal contradictions and therefore cannot be used to reconstruct Confucius's philosophy.

12. See, e.g., Lau, *Confucius*, 265–75.

13. Despite Makeham, "Between Chen and Cai"; see my review of Roger T. Ames, *Wandering at Ease in the Zhuangzi*, 475–76. See also Littlejohn, "Kongzi in the *Zhuangzi*."

14. Useful treatments of Confucius's life include Csikszentmihalyi, "Confucius"; Lévi, *Confucius*; Roetz, *Konfuzius*; Kaizuka, *Confucius*; Creel, *Confucius and the Chinese Way*, esp. 25–172; and Wilhelm, *Confucius and Confucianism*, 3–95.

15. The classic statement of this problem is Gu Jiegang, "Chunqiu shi de Kongzi he Handai de Kongzi."

16. For an overview of the problems and some ingenious, if speculative, suggestions, see Eno, "Background of the Kong Family of Lu and the Origins of Ruism."

17. *Lunyu jishi* 14.501.

18. Cf. *Zhongyong* 13: "The Way is not distant from human beings. If people practice the Way so as to make it distant from human beings, they cannot be practicing the Way" 道不遠人。人之為道而遠人，不可以為道 (Zhu Xi, *Sishu zhangju jizhu*, 23). Tu Wei-ming has emphasized the notion of the Confucian "fiduciary community" in several publications, most notably *Centrality and Commonality*, 39–66.

19. *Lunyu jishi* 12.406.

20. *Zhongyong*, 16 (Zhu Xi, *Sishu zhangju jizhu*, 25), also emphasizes the power of the spirits and the importance of remembering them in the midst of ritual performance.

21. *Lunyu jishi* 22.760.

22. *Lunyu jishi* 35.1227.

23. Though it is commonly misread as Shen, the correct pronunciation of this name is Can. See the commentary in (*Shiji*) *Shiki kaichū kōshō* 67.32.

24. *Lunyu jishi* 8.257–67. As this may be the most important line in the whole book, the commentary is, understandably, extensive.

25. The secondary literature is enormous. A representative list since the 1990s alone: Nivison, *Ways of Confucianism*, 59–76; Sin Yee Chan, "Disputes on the One Thread of *Chung-Shu*"; Van Norden, "Unweaving the 'One Thread' of *Analects* 4:15"; Bo Mou, "Re-examination of the Structure and Content of Confucius' Version of the Golden Rule"; and Ivanhoe, "'Golden Rule' in the *Analects*."

26. *Lunyu jishi* 31.1055.

27. *Lunyu jishi* 32.1106.

28. The similarity to the Golden Rule (e.g., Matthew 7:12) is one of the features of Confucianism that inspired early Jesuits such as Matteo Ricci (1552–1610). Cf. Rule, *K'ung-tzu or Confucius?*, 10–69; more generally, Mungello, *Curious Land*.

29. Cf. Nussbaum, "Golden Rule Arguments," esp. 6: "The Chinese forms [of the Golden Rule] do not say, 'Treat another as you would have that other treat you,' but 'Treat another as you would have anyone else related to you as you are related to that other treat you.'"

30. Zhu Xi, *Sishu zhangju jizhu*, 23.

31. Cf. Goldin, "Theme of the Primacy of the Situation in Classical Chinese Philosophy and Rhetoric," 1–2.

32. Alan Gewirth has considered these problems in "Golden Rule Rationalized" and *Reason and Morality*.

33. Perhaps I was unduly influenced by passages such as *Mencius* 6A.7, e.g., "Thus all things that are of the same species are alike; why would one doubt this only of human beings?" 故凡同類者，舉相似也，何獨至於人而疑之. Contrast *Mencius* 6B.6, which recognizes that different ways of pursuing *ren* 仁 can all be legitimate.

34. Lau, *Confucius*, 33.

35. See the fuller defense in Goldin, "When *zhong* 忠 Does Not Mean 'Loyalty,'" esp. 168–70.

36. *Lunyu jishi* 1.18. According to Seneca the Younger (d. AD 65), Quintus Sextius (fl. ca. 50 BC) would ask himself similar questions every night at bedtime; see *De ira*, 3.36.

37. The best study is now Behr, "Der gegenwärtige Forschungsstand zur Etymologie von *rén* 仁 im Überblick." On paronomasia in the *Analects* generally, see Ames, "Paronomasia."

38. *Lunyu jishi* 12.408.

39. *Lunyu jishi* 12.427–30.

40. *Lunyu jishi* 9.316.

41. *Lunyu jishi* 24.817–24.

42. This is a rhetorical question intended to convey that the practice of humanity surely emerges from the self, and does not depend on others.

43. For example, Fingarette, *Confucius—the Secular as Sacred*, 9ff., discusses the convention of shaking hands as an example of *li* (which would make Confucius something like a tacit contractarian), but this is inadequate from a Confucian point of view because shaking hands is not in and of itself conducive to moral self-cultivation. Even tyrants know how to shake hands in a socially acceptable manner. As we shall see in chapter 8 (p. 176), the question of whether the rites can be arbitrarily constructed and still retain their effectiveness became an important one in Chinese philosophy, and the Confucian view was always the same: *li* can only be conventions that facilitate social interaction *while also* inducing its performers to improve themselves morally. Social cohesion is not a sufficient goal per se.

44. *Lunyu jishi* 3.68.

45. *Lunyu jishi* 17.571–73.

46. Compare *Analects* 3.16: "When the Master entered the Great Temple, he asked about everything. Someone said: 'Who says this son of a man from Zou knows ritual? When he entered the Great Temple, he asked about everything.' Confucius heard about it and said: 'This is ritual'" 子入大廟，每事問。或曰：「孰謂鄹人之子知禮乎？入大廟，每事問。」子聞之曰：「是禮也。」 (*Lunyu jishi* 6.183–84).

47. *Lunyu jishi* 5.157–60.

48. The first two lines (though not the third line) are found in Mao 57, a poem in the *Odes*.

49. Cf. Goldin, *After Confucius*, 19–35.

50. Of the many recent interpretations of *li*, mine is probably closest to Ames, "Observing Ritual 'Propriety' (*li* 禮) as Focusing the 'Familiar' in the Affairs of the Day"; and Kwong-loi Shun, "*Rén* 仁 and *lǐ* 禮 in the *Analects*." See also Lai, "*Li* in the *Analects*."

51. *Lunyu jishi* 25.864.

52. See further Schwartz, *World of Thought in Ancient China*, 103.

53. *Lunyu jishi* 26.901.

54. *Lunyu jishi* 25.864.

55. *Lunyu jishi* 25.866.

56. *Lunyu jishi* 18.604–6.

57. *Lunyu jishi* 25.855–57.

58. Compare *Analects* 14.23, on the right way to serve a ruler: "Oppose him without deceiving him" 勿欺也，而犯之 (*Lunyu jishi* 29.1002).

59. Compare *Mencius* 1B.8, where the slaughter of the tyrants Jie and Zhòu is sanctioned on the grounds that they were not true kings.

60. I do not consider here the very different argument for rectifying names in *Analects*, 13.3, since there are long-standing doubts about its authenticity. For the reasons, see Waley, *Analects of Confucius*, 21–22 and 172n1; and Creel, *Confucius and the Chinese Way*, 321n13. For an insightful interpretation by a scholar who takes it straight, see Loy, "*Analects* 13.3 and the Doctrine of 'Correcting Names.'"

61. Other philosophers, such as those interested in logic, would go on to use non-

moral criteria to determine appropriate names. The best study remains Graham, *Later Mohist Logic, Ethics and Science*, esp. 25–72, but for an important methodological criticism of this book, see Geaney, "Critique of A. C. Graham's Reconstruction of the 'Neo-Mohist Canons.'"

62. Cf. Pines, "Confucius' Elitism," 165–72; also Cho-yun Hsu, *Ancient China in Transition*, 158ff., and Gassmann, "Die Bezeichnung *jun-zi*."

63. For my views, see Goldin, *Confucianism*, 115–20; and Goldin, *Culture of Sex in Ancient China*, 55ff. See also Clark and Wang, "Confucian Defense of Gender Equity."

64. *Lunyu jishi* 7.247. Compare *Mencius* 2A.2: "Confucius was one who took office when it was acceptable, retired when it was acceptable, remained long [in office] when it was acceptable, and [withdrew] quickly when it was acceptable" 可以仕則仕，可以止則止，可以久則久，可以速則速，孔子也 (*Mengzi zhengyi* 6.215—also the similarly worded 5B.1, *Mengzi zhengyi* 20.672); and *Zhongyong* 14: "The noble man acts as befits his station" 君子素其位而行 (Zhu Xi, *Sishu zhangju jizhu*, 24), which is, of course constantly changing.

65. *Lunyu jishi* 27.922–26.

66. The name can also be taken to mean "Self-Righteous." See Goldin, *After Confucius*, 8.

67. *Lunyu jishi* 8.270.

68. *Lunyu jishi* 1.27.

69. *Lunyu jishi* 1.1–9. Compare *Analects* 13.5: "If one recites the three hundred *Odes* but fails to apply them to government; if one is incapable of rendering one's own replies when on missions within the four quarters; then although [one's learning] may be abundant, what indeed has one done with it?" 誦詩三百，授之以政，不達；使於四方，不能專對；雖多，亦奚以為？ (*Lunyu jishi* 26.900).

70. *Lunyu jishi* 18.601.

71. See, e.g., Hardy, *Worlds of Bronze and Bamboo*, 199–200.

72. E.g., *Analects* 1.16: "The Master said: 'I am not vexed that others do not know me; I am vexed that I do not know others'" 子曰：「不患人之不己知，患不知人也」. See, generally, Henry, "Motif of Recognition in Early China," 19ff.

73. Cf. Kwong-loi Shun, "*Le* in the *Analects*."

74. Cf. Hattori, "Confucius' Conviction of His Heavenly Mission."

75. *Lunyu jishi* 17.576–79.

## CHAPTER THREE. *MOZI*

1. Qian Mu, *Xian-Qin zhuzi xinian*, §32. Fang Shouchu, *Moxue yuanliu*, 3–7, disagreed and held that Mo is simply a surname.

2. E.g., Tan Jiajian, *Mozi yanjiu*, 2.

3. *Huainanzi jishi* 21.1459 ("Yaolüe" 要略). Cf. Yang Yi, *Mozi huanyuan*, 12–18; and Qin Yanshi, *Mozi kaolun*, 1–16.

4. Cf. Nylan, "Kongzi and Mozi," 5–11.

5. For a careful study, see Zheng Jiewen, *Zhongguo Moxue tongshi*, 1:75–111; also Qin Yanshi, *Mozi kaolun*, 144–63.

6. Compare, for example, *Analects*, 1.5: "moderate expenditure and love others" 節用而愛人 (*Lunyu jishi* 1.21).

7. Zhu Xi, *Sishu zhangju jizhu*, 3–4. Compare *Mencius* 4A.4–5.

8. *Mengzi zhengyi* 17.598.

9. For a thoughtful criticism along these lines, see Hammer, "Confucian Thought and China's Moral Crisis." Parks, "Rabelais of Naples," observes a similar and conspicuously non-Christian disparity in the treatment of kin and nonkin in the fairy tales of Giambattista Basile (1575–1632).

10. Incidentally, the focus in this chapter on Confucius and his disciples suggests that the term *ru*, at least in this context, is to be understood in the old-fashioned sense of "Confucians," and not, as has recently been suggested, in the less committal sense of "classicists." See Harbsmeier, "Birth of Confucianism from Competition with Organized Mohism," 13–19; for a general overview of the controversy, see Zufferey, *To the Origins of Confucianism*.

11. Thus Watson, *Mozi*, 138n9.

12. See the details in Goldin, "Appeals to History in Early Chinese Philosophy and Rhetoric," 85.

13. Cf. Sun Zhuocai, *Moxue gaiyao*, 121–22.

14. Cf. Kurtz, *Discovery of Chinese Logic*, 287ff.

15. For other suggestions, see, e.g., Zhang Xifeng, "Lun Moxue shuailuo de yuanyin." Another common explanation is that Mohism was effectively subsumed within Confucian ethics (e.g., Gentz, "Mohist Traces in the Early *Chunqiu fanlu* Chapters"; Nylan, "Kongzi and Mozi," 12–19; and Fukui, "Zen Kan ni okeru Bokuka no saisei"). Tong Shuye, *Tong Shuye shiji kaozheng lunji*, 1:320–28, argued that Dong Zhongshu was influenced by Mohism through Xunzi and Li Si. The case makes little sense to me.

16. The ten core doctrines are listed in *Mozi jiaozhu* 13.49.721–22 ("Luwen" 魯問), but with slightly different names for "Tianzhi" and "Minggui," namely "Revering Heaven" ("Zuntian" 尊天) and "Serving Ghosts" ("Shigui" 事鬼), respectively. Cf. Graham, *Divisions in Early Mohism Reflected in the Core Chapters of Mo-tzu*, 1.

17. For representative opinions, see Defoort and Standaert, Mozi *as an Evolving Text*, 9–29; Yang Yi, *Mozi huanyuan*, 53–62; Yoshinaga, *Sengoku shisōshi kenkyū*, 74–78; Qin Yanshi, *Mozi kaolun*, 164–77; Maeder, "Some Observations on the Composition of the 'Core Chapters' of the *Mozi*"; Watanabe, *Kodai Chūgoku shisō no kenkyū*, 471–525; and Luo Genze, *Zhuzi kaosuo*, 175–82. Generally, I shall cite freely from the *shang* 上, *zhong* 中, and *xia* 下 versions (with the exception of "Jian'ai shang," "Feigong shang," and "Jieyong shang," since I am persuaded by Graham, *Divisions in Early Mohism Reflected in the Core Chapters of Mo-tzu*, 3–4, that these are later digests, not original chapters in their own right).

18. Alfred Forke may have been the first in the West to point this out. See his *Mê Ti des Sozialethikers und seiner Schüler philosophische Werke*, 5–11; and his *Geschichte der alten chinesischen Philosophie*, 372.

19. See esp. Graham, *Later Mohist Logic, Ethics and Science*, 65ff.; also Zhang Youlin and Zhang Xiyu, "*Mozi* zhongyao banben de chuancheng guanxi kaolüe," 152.

20. On this question, Sivin, *Medicine, Philosophy and Religion in Ancient China*, chap. 4, is still helpful.

21. Although concordances reveal several dozen uses of the term *dao* in the extant *Mozi*, these usually take the form of "the *dao* of So-and-so," i.e., So-and-so's mode of living, as in *Mozi jiaozhu* 6.25.258 ("Jiezang xia" 節葬下): "My forebears were those who transmitted the Way of Yao, Shun, Yu, Tang, Wen, and Wu" 吾上祖述堯舜禹湯文武之道者也. (This happens to be an important passage because it represents an acknowledg-

ment by Mohists that they recognize the same sages as the Confucians, despite their opposition to Confucianism on almost all philosophical points.) Hansen, *Daoist Theory of Chinese Thought*, 106, sums up Mohist usage well: "*Dao* could be bad, crooked, wasteful or, like Confucius' *dao*, simply wrong. Mozi wanted a new and more beneficial *dao*[way] to guide that training process."

22. See, e.g., Campany, *To Live as Long as Heaven and Earth*, 329–30 and 508–10; Fukunaga, *Dōkyō shisōshi kenkyū*, 198–202; and Durrant, "Taoist Apotheosis of Mo Ti."

23. For some representative views of the religious dimensions of Mohism, see Emmerich, "Religiöse Einstellungen der Mohisten"; Lowe, *Mo Tzu's Religious Blueprint for a Chinese Utopia*; Cai Renhou, *Mojia zhexue*, 95–97; Mote, *Intellectual Foundations of China*, 87–88; Fang Shouchu, *Moxue yuanliu*, 97–107; Mei, *Motse*, 145–63; Hu Shi, *Zhongguo zhexueshi dagang*, 126–33; and Liang Qichao, *Mozi xue'an*, 45–60. In a strange inquiry grounded in philological analysis (to the exclusion of any other method), Chow Tse-tsung, "New Theory on the Origins of Mohism," concludes that the Mohists descended from a prehistoric tribe of fertility worshippers. This does not do much to elucidate Mohist philosophy, even if it is true. Marxist-inspired Chinese scholarship tends to avoid the subject; for example, Ren Jiyu, *Zhongguo zhexueshi*, 1:124–26, criticizes Mozi's religious views as well intentioned but socially counterproductive.

24. On Mozi's utilitarianism, see, e.g., Graham, *Disputers of the Tao*, 39–45; and Hansen, *Daoist Theory of Chinese Thought*, 108–24. One of the few general surveys of utilitarianism to include a section on *Mozi* is Scarre, *Utilitarianism*, 27–33.

25. *Mozi jiaozhu* 4.16.172 ("Jian'ai xia"). This passage was discussed more briefly on p. 23.

26. Bentham, *Introduction to the Principles of Morals and Legislation*, 12–13 (i.e., chapter 1, §§3 and 9–10). The manner of reasoning is so similar that one might even ask whether Bentham was, knowingly or unknowingly, inspired by Mohism, the influence of Chinese sources on eighteenth-century European philosophy being generally underappreciated. Ralph, "Mo Ti and the English Utilitarians," 59, notices that the "religious flavor" of Mohism is incompatible with the philosophy of the English utilitarians.

27. The most famous example is *Lüshi chunqiu xin jiaoshi* 19.1266 ("Shangde" 上德). Cf. Kanaya, *Kanaya Osamu Chūgoku shisō ronshū*, 1:312–11 and 404.

28. For studies, see Qin Yanshi, *Gudai fangyu junshi yu Mojia heping zhuyi*; Yates, "Early Poliorcetics"; and Watanabe, *Kodai Chūgoku shisō no kenkyū*, 451–70.

29. DeWoskin, *Song for One or Two*, 31, notes that Mohists were repelled by the opulence of performances for aristocrats, not necessarily music in itself, as in *Mozi jiaozhu* 8.32.374 ("Feiyue shang"): "If musical instruments redounded to the benefit of the people in the same way [as boats and carts], I would not dare to object to them" 然則樂器反中民之利亦若此，即我弗敢非也.

30. Mohists evidently did not consider that money spent on luxuries might be recycled back into the general economy when musicians and undertakers find themselves in need of food and housing, as Xunzi pointed out in *Xunzi jijie* 13.19.349 ("Lilun" 禮論). The passage is lucidly interpreted in Lien-sheng Yang, *Studies in Chinese Institutional History*, 65.

31. *Mozi jiaozhu* 2.9.75 ("Shangxian zhong"); and *Mozi jiaozhu* 2.10.95 ("Shangxian xia").

32. *Mozi jiaozhu* 2.9.74 ("Shangxian zhong").

33. *Mozi jiaozhu* 2.9.75 ("Shangxian zhong").

34. *Mozi jiaozhu* 2.8.66 ("Shangxian shang"); and *Mozi jiaozhu* 2.9.75 ("Shangxian zhong").

35. E.g., *Analects* 11.8 and 19; *Mencius* 6A.16 and 7A.3.

36. *Mozi jiaozhu* 7.26.288 ("Tianzhi shang").

37. There is apparently some missing text here; the clause in brackets represents my best guess. Commentators suggest various possibilities, but they are all conjectural.

38. *Mozi jiaozhu* 7.27.296 ("Tianzhi zhong").

39. Righteousness is defined as "[bringing about] benefit" 義，利也 in *Mozi jiaozhu* 10A.40.461 ("Jing shang" 經上); Graham, *Later Mohist Logic, Ethics and Science*, A 8. Cf. Yang Junguang, *Mojing yanjiu*, 96–109; also Wang Yu'an, "Mozi 'guiyi' xinxi," 48–50.

40. Cf. Yoshinaga, *Sengoku shisōshi kenkyū*, 207; and Cai Renhou, *Mojia zhexue*, 68–73.

41. Following the commentary of Wu Yujiang, *Mozi jiaozhu* 7.27.304n20. See also Zhou Fumei, *Mozi jiajiezi jizheng*, 112.

42. *Mozi jiaozhu* 7.27.297–98 ("Tianzhi zhong").

43. Cf. *Mozi jiaozhu* 7.27.300 ("Tianzhi zhong").

44. Cf. Cai Renhou, *Mojia zhexue*, 66–67, who finds that complying with Heaven's dictates must be conceptually anterior to impartial love. Also Qianfan Zhang, "Human Dignity in Classical Chinese Philosophy," 249–50: "A person wants to be good not for the sake of the good itself, but apparently for the hope to reap benefits from acting in accordance with the will of heaven."

45. *Mozi jiaozhu* 7.26.290 ("Tianzhi shang").

46. *Mozi jiaozhu* 7.26.288 ("Tianzhi shang").

47. *Mozi jiaozhu* 3.11.107 ("Shangtong shang"). In *Mozi jiaozhu* 3.13.136 ("Shang-tong xia"), it is less clear who appointed the Son of Heaven; the implication is that it was "those in the world who wished to unite the [standards of] righteousness in the world" 欲同一天下之義, i.e., human beings, not Heaven. Heaven only ratified their choice ex post facto. Cf. Schwartz, *World of Thought in Ancient China*, 143–44.

48. *Mozi jiaozhu* 3.11.107–8 ("Shangtong shang"). The text goes on to demand that inferiors "restrain and remonstrate with" (*guijian* 規諫) superiors who commit trans-gressions, but it is evident from the context that this refers to superiors who have strayed from their own principles; despite Brindley, "Human Agency and the Ideal of *shang tong* (Upward Conformity) in Early Mohist Writings," 417–20, the claim is decidedly not that inferiors should use their own notions of righteousness to criticize their superiors. Creel, *Chinese Thought from Confucius to Mao Tse-tung*, 58ff., expressed some American misgivings about this arrangement.

49. *Mozi jiaozhu* 7.28.312–13. ("Tianzhi xia"). Cf. *Mozi jiaozhu* 7.26.288 ("Tianzhi shang"). *Zheng* 正 and *zheng* 政 are freely interchanged in these passages.

50. Cai Renhou, *Mojia zhexue*, 21–22, is incisive on this point.

51. *Mozi jiaozhu* 3.11.108–9 ("Shangtong shang"). Cf. *Mozi jiaozhu* 3.12.116 ("Shang-tong zhong").

52. Cf. esp. Puett, *To Become a God*, 101–4; also Qianfan Zhang, "Human Dignity in Classical Chinese Philosophy," 242–44; and Kanaya, *Kanaya Osamu Chūgoku shisō ronshū*, 1:251–58.

53. Cf. Fraser, *Philosophy of the* Mòz ĭ , 117–27.

54. On the theological utilitarians, see, generally, Quinton, *Utilitarian Ethics*, 23–26. John Stuart Mill (1806–73) also wrote: "if men believe, as most profess to do, in the

goodness of God, those who think that conduciveness to the general happiness is the essence, or even only the criterion, of good, must necessarily believe that it is also that which God approves." See his *Utilitarianism*, in *Collected Works of John Stuart Mill*, vol. 10, *Essays on Ethics, Religion and Society*, 228.

55. I do not mean the same thing as Metzger's "epistemological optimism," for which see his "Some Ancient Roots of Ancient Chinese Thought," esp. 76–89.

56. E.g., *Mozi jiaozhu* 2.9.76 ("Shangxian zhong"); *Mozi jiaozhu* 7.26.289 ("Tianzhi shang"); *Mozi jiaozhu* 7.27.300 ("Tianzhi zhong"); *Mozi jiaozhu* 7.28.314 ("Tianzhi xia").

57. Ning Chen, "Problem of Theodicy in Ancient China," 59–60. See also Schwartz, *World of Thought in Ancient China*, 140; and Forke, *Geschichte der alten chinesischen Philosophie*, 379–80.

58. They are called *sanfa* in *Mozi jiaozhu* 9.36.406 ("Feiming zhong") and 9.37.415–16 ("Feiming xia"); the term *sanbiao* is used in *Mozi jiaozhu* 9.35.394 ("Feiming shang").

59. On this issue, I agree with McLeod, *Theories of Truth in Chinese Philosophy*, 59–75. Philosophers (e.g., Loy, "Justification and Debate," 455) sometimes object to characterizing the doctrine of the Three Standards as a theory of truth because it does not attempt to specify the nature of truth. For other general studies of the Three Gnomons, see, e.g., Fraser, *Philosophy of the Mòzǐ*, 62–69; Van Norden, *Virtue Ethics and Consequentialism in Early Chinese Philosophy*, 151–61; Hu Zizong et al., *Mozi sixiang yanjiu*, 253–57; Graham, *Disputers of the Tao*, 36–39; Cai Renhou, *Mojia zhexue*, 58–62; Yang Rongguo, *Zhongguo gudai sixiangshi*, 150–55; Mei, *Motse*, 61–84; and Hu Shih, *Development of the Logical Method in Ancient China*, 72–82.

60. Following the commentary of Wang Niansun 王念孫 (1744–1832), *Mozi jiaozhu* 9.35.398n10.

61. *Mozi jiaozhu* 9.35.394 ("Feiming shang").

62. The wordy phrases "verifying the root," "verifying the origin," and "verifying the utility" are required in English to reflect the fact that *ben* 本, *yuan* 原, and *yong* 用 are verbs.

63. E.g., *Mozi jiaozhu* 9.35.395–96. ("Feiming shang"). This contention is being independently supported, incidentally, by modern neuroscience; see, e.g., Shariff and Vohs, "World without Free Will."

64. Following the commentary of Sun Yirang. On the phrase *dangruo* 當若 in *Mozi*, see Graham, *Divisions in Early Mohism Reflected in the Core Chapters of Mo-tzu*, 3 and 11.

65. Following the commentary of Bi Yuan 畢沅 (1730–97).

66. The phrase *ruo yiwei buran* 若以爲不然 before *shiyi* 是以 is excrescent, according to Wang Niansun, and is omitted here.

67. Following the commentary of Wu Yujiang. Zhou Fumei, *Mozi jiajiezi jizheng*, 125, reads this as *dui* 譈 (to despise) instead.

68. Most commentators hold that the twenty-one characters at this point in the text are excrescent, and consequently they are omitted here (despite Wu Yujiang's opinion in *Mozi jiaozhu* 8.31.364n176).

69. *Mozi jiaozhu* 8.31.336 ("Minggui xia"). Because of its textual problems and unusual diction, this is one of the most difficult passages in the core chapters of the *Mozi*, though the general import is clear.

70. Cf. Graham, *Disputers of the Tao*, 47; and Fang Shouchu, *Moxue yuanliu*, 97.

71. Brashier, *Ancestral Memory in Early China*, 41ff., points out that other texts, including some from the Confucian tradition, also refer to the utility of making people believe in ghosts and spirits. Compare the observation of Ferdinand-Olivier Petitpierre (1722–90), quoted in Voltaire's *Dictionnaire Philosophique*: "Mon ami, je ne crois pas plus l'enfer éternel que vous; mais il est bon que votre servante, votre tailleur et même votre procureur le croient" (178) (My friend, I do not believe in eternal Hell any more than you do, but it is good that your servant, your tailor, and even your lawyer believe in it).

72. Cf. Benjamin Wong and Loy, "War and Ghosts in Mozi's Political Philosophy," 350. However, I disagree with their presentist argument that *Mozi* does not really attempt to prove the existence of ghosts. Wong and Loy attempt to renovate the Mohist arguments to suit modern philosophical tastes, but the only reason why they are reluctant to accept the straightforward wording of the text is that it seems irredeemably absurd today. Cf. Van Norden, *Virtue Ethics and Consequentialism in Early Chinese Philosophy*, 178–79. Gibas, "Mozi and the Ghosts," argues that Mozi is agnostic about the existence of ghosts; the real issue is *ming* (translated above as "percipience"), which a sage can exemplify.

73. *Mozi jiaozhu* 12.48.692 ("Gongmeng" 公孟), records an episode in which Die Bi 跌鼻 (otherwise unknown, and whose name can be construed to mean "tripping over one's nose") visits Mozi when he is sick, and asks: "Teacher, you are a sage, so what is the reason why you are sick? Is it that there is some part of your teaching that is not good, teacher? Or is it that the ghosts and spirits are not percipient and aware?" 今先生聖人也，何故有疾？意者，先生之言有不善乎？鬼神不明知乎. The figure of Mozi circumvents this challenge by responding that because disease can have more than one cause—in other words, Die Bi is wrong to assume that Mozi's illness came from ghosts. Xu Keqian, *Xian-Qin sixiang wenhua lunzha*, 240–41, argues on the basis of this and other passages that Mohists harbored doubts about their theory of Heaven. See also Ding Sixin, "Lun *Mozi* 'Moyu' Mojia houxue zhi guishenguan." Surprisingly, Sterckx, "*Mozi* 31," does not discuss Die Bi. Sterckx's thesis is that references to ghosts across the whole of *Mozi* suggest "a more polyphonic Mohist view of the spirit world" (139), i.e., uncertainty about the supposed percipience of ghosts.

74. These are found in two clusters in "Minggui xia": *Mozi jiaozhu* 8.31.331–33 (corresponding to *yuan*, the practice of ordinary people in history) and 333–36 (corresponding to *ben*, the practice of the sages).

75. *Mozi jiaozhu* 7.28.314–15 ("Tianzhi xia").

76. Cf. Sun Zhuocai, *Moxue gaiyao*, 123ff. and 167–72. Ting-mien Lee, "Mozi as a Daoist Sage?," notes an instance in the *Mozi* itself where the presentation of an anecdote suggests that Daoist virtues were already being attributed to him.

77. On *Shenxian zhuan* generally, see Campany, *To Live as Long as Heaven and Earth*, 1–117; Bumbacher, "On the *Shenxian zhuan*"; and Benjamin Penny, "Text and Authorship of *Shen xian zhuan*."

78. *Shenxian zhuan jiaoshi* 4.124.

79. This is a reference to physiognomy (*xiang* 相), the belief that people's destinies are manifest in their physical bodies.

80. For details, see Goldin, "Why *Mozi* Is Included in the Daoist Canon," 86–87.

81. On the Sage Lord, see, e.g., Bokenkamp, *Early Daoist Scriptures*, 281–82.

82. *Shangqing housheng daojun lieji*, 7b. See Bokenkamp, *Early Daoist Scriptures*, 352n.

83. *Laozi Xiang'er zhu jiaojian*, 25.

84. Bokenkamp, *Early Daoist Scriptures*, 54.

85. Once again, see the details in Goldin, "Why *Mozi* Is Included in the Daoist Canon," 88ff.

86. For other comparisons between Mohism and religious Daoism, see, e.g., Zheng Jiewen, *Zhongguo Moxue tongshi*, 1:216–25; Fukunaga, *Dōkyō shisōshi kenkyū*, 177–205; Wang Ming, *Daojia he Daojiao sixiang yanjiu*, 99–107; and Qing Xitai, *Zhongguo Daojiao sixiangshi gang*, 1:129ff.

87. Cf. Kirkland, "Hermeneutics and Pedagogy," 150: "When Westerners encountered the religious and intellectual traditions of Asia, they went about making sense of those traditions by comparing and contrasting what they saw in them with what they 'knew' from their own tradition"; also Said, *Orientalism*, 58–59.

## CHAPTER FOUR. *MENCIUS*

1. *Shiji* 74.2343.

2. Cf. Deng Ruiquan and Wang Guanying, *Zhongguo weishu zongkao*, 216–17.

3. Lau, *Mencius*, 332–40, surveys the surviving references.

4. *Mengzi zhengyi* 15.520–22.

5. On *quan*, see Goldin, "Theme of the Primacy of the Situation in Classical Chinese Philosophy and Rhetoric," esp. 19ff.; Vankeerberghen, "Choosing Balance"; and Zhang Duansui, *Xi-Han Gongyangxue yanjiu*, 91–158.

6. For a general study, see Weingarten, "Chunyu Kun."

7. *Mengzi zhengyi* 6.199–208.

8. The original is confusing here and may be garbled. Presumably Mencius means that one must make it one's constant duty to nourish one's "flood-like *qi*."

9. Cf. A. Chan, "Matter of Taste," though I think he misses the allusion to contemporary theories of physical self-cultivation. See, e.g., Puett, *To Become a God*, 134; also Rainey, "Mencius and His Vast, Overflowing *qi* (*haoran zhi qi*)."

10. *Mengzi zhengyi* 13.456–58.

11. See my review of Graham, *Chuang-tzu*, and Roth, *A Companion to Angus C. Graham's Chuang-tzu*, 204ff.; also Defoort, "Unfounded and Unfollowed," 166–69; and Andreini, *Il pensiero di Yang Zhu*, 11–18. Western-trained philosophers sometimes depict Yang Zhu as a Chinese egoist and turn him into a more influential figure than he really was. For informative responses, see Villaver, "Does *guiji* Mean Egoism?"; and Brindley, *Individualism in Early China*, 70–76.

12. *Mengzi zhengyi* 11.402–7.

13. The first substantial study of Mencius's exchange with Yi Zhi was Nivison, *Ways of Confucianism*, 133–48. See also Van Norden, *Virtue Ethics and Consequentialism in Early Chinese Philosophy*, 305ff.; and Kwong-loi Shun, *Mencius and Early Chinese Thought*, 127–35.

14. Cf. Munro, *Chinese Ethics for the New Century*, esp. 49–52.

15. American philosophers (presumably influenced by the parable of the farmer of Song in 2A.2) sometimes translate *siduan* as "Four Sprouts," but *duan* means "begin-

ning, cusp, incipient point." I am not aware of any instance in Chinese literature where it means "sprout."

16. For Confucius and Mencius, I have translated *xin* 心 as "heart," bearing in mind Bloom's observation that the associations of the word "were visceral rather than cerebral" ("On the Matter of the Mind," 300). For Xunzi, however, we shall see that "heart" no longer captures all the dimensions of *xin*.

17. Fear of falling into a well is attested in other early sources, e.g., *Analects*, 6.24; *Mozi jiaozhu* 1.5.35 ("Qihuan" 七患); and the aforementioned *Mencius* 3A.5.

18. *Mengzi zhengyi* 7.232–34.

19. Or perhaps "cannot abide the sound [of the wailing infant]."

20. *Mengzi zhengyi* 3.80–83.

21. *Mengzi zhengyi* 3.85.

22. *Mengzi zhengyi* 7.235.

23. Compare *Analects* 7.23: "Heaven engendered virtue in me" 天生德於予 (*Lunyu jishi* 14.484).

24. Compare *Mencius* 4B.19: "That by which people are different from birds and beasts is slight. Common people abandon it; the noble man preserves it" 人之所以異於禽於獸者幾希，庶民去之，君子存之 (*Mengzi zhengyi* 16.567); and 4B.28: "That by which the noble man is different from other people is his preservation of his heart" 君子所以異於人者，以其存心也 (*Mengzi zhengyi* 17.595).

25. A modern analogue of Mencius's "brigand" might be "psychopath." Cf. Gray, "Psychopathy and Will to Power," 198: "Remorselessness and lack of shame arise in people who either have not developed the capacity to relate to others' suffering or have become hardened. In either case it is impossible for them to relate to the pain that they have caused or to feel shame for the things they have done. Both of these capacities require the ability to relate to the suffering of others or to feel the reality of deserved consequences. Psychopaths can do neither."

26. Cf. Van Norden, *Virtue Ethics and Consequentialism in Early Chinese Philosophy*, 234–46; also Ivanhoe, "Confucian Self Cultivation and Mengzi's Notion of Extension."

27. *Mengzi zhengyi* 26.897–900. Compare *Mencius* 7B.31.

28. Graham, *Studies in Chinese Philosophy and Philosophical Literature*, 7–66; see also his *Disputers of the Tao*, 117–32.

29. The fullest discussion is Van Norden, *Virtue Ethics and Consequentialism in Early Chinese Philosophy*, 225ff. and 278–301; see also Kwong-loi Shun, *Mencius and Early Chinese Thought*, 210–22.

30. *Mengzi zhengyi* 22.737–42.

31. Nivison, *Ways of Confucianism*, 150–52, struggled with it too.

32. Cf. Goldin, *After Confucius*, 38.

33. Compare Burke, *What Is Cultural History?*, 101: "founders succeed precisely because they signify many things to many people. When the followers try to interpret the founder's message, the latent contradictions become manifest."

34. This point has been most forcefully articulated by Ames, e.g., "Mencian Conception of *Ren xing* 人性"; see also Bloom, "Mencian Arguments on Human Nature (*jen-hsing*)." Ames is most persuasive when he stays close to Mencius; he errs, in my opinion, when he begins to argue as though Mencius's conception of *xing* were valid for all Confucians, as in his "What Ever Happened to 'Wisdom'?"

35. *Mengzi zhengyi* 23.775–78.

36. Literally, "by the days' nights," but clearly the nighttime, when the lumberjacks are not assailing the mountain, is intended here.

37. The Chinese word is *cai* 才, which is essentially the same as the word used to refer to the "timber" (*cai* 材) on Ox Mountain.

38. Compare *Mencius* 7B.21: "A footpath in the mountains, if it is used steadfastly, will become a road, but if it is not used for a while, it will be blocked by weeds. Now weeds are blocking your heart" 山徑之蹊間，介然用之而成路，為間不用，則茅塞之矣。今茅塞子之心矣 (*Mengzi zhengyi* 28.982). This line has been made famous in modern times by allusions by Lu Xun 魯迅 (1881–1936) and Barack Obama; see (respectively) Lu Xun, *Nahan*, 94; and Ho, *Transition Study of Postsocialist China*, 223n1.

39. *Mengzi zhengyi* 23.792–95.

40. *Mengzi zhengyi* 26.877–82.

41. Oscar Wilde (1854–1900), *The Importance of Being Earnest*, in *Complete Works of Oscar Wilde*, 330.

42. Thus I do not fully agree with the accounts in Kwong-loi Shun, *Mencius and Early Chinese Thought*, 77–83, and Ning Chen, "Concept of Fate in *Mencius*."

43. Cf. also *Mencius* 1A.2.

44. *Mengzi zhengyi* 4.137–40.

45. Mao 250; the received text is slightly different.

46. Mao 237.

47. Cf. Nylan, *Chinese Pleasure Book*, 143ff.

48. Cf. Cua, *Human Nature, Ritual, and History*, 354–68.

49. *Mengzi zhengyi* 2.35–44.

50. That is to say, the regicides already possess one-tenth of their state's total number of chariots.

51. Wang Chong complained that Mencius rashly took *li* to mean "profit pertaining to goods and wealth" 貨財之利, but it could also refer to "the profit of security and good fortune" 安吉之利 (*Lunheng jiaoshi* 10.30.450 ["Ci Meng" 刺孟]), in other words, "profit" of a less materialistic kind. He went on to criticize Mencius for not asking King Hui to clarify. Cf. Defoort, "Profit That Does Not Profit," 170–71.

52. Neo-Confucians such as Cheng Yi and Zhu Xi, commenting on this passage, observed that humanity and righteousness are profitable in their own right (Zhu Xi, *Sishu zhangju jizhu*, 235). Cf. Defoort, "Profit That Does Not Profit," 168.

53. See also *Mencius* 4A.8.

54. *Mengzi zhengyi* 24.825–26.

55. *Mengzi zhengyi* 3.93–94. Cf. *Mencius* 1A.3, 1A.5, 6A.7, and 7A.22–23. Some non-Confucian texts also recognized that keeping the people well fed is necessary to inspire morality, e.g., *Guanzi jiaozhu* 1.1.2 ("Mumin" 牧民): "If the granaries are full, they will know ritual and moderation" 倉廩實則知禮節, which was frequently quoted in ancient literature. Compare Mac's line in Brecht's *Dreigroschenoper*: "Erst kommt das Fressen, dann kommt die Moral" (69) (roughly, "First comes fodder, then comes morality").

56. E.g., Chun-chieh Huang, *Mencian Hermeneutics*, 249. For objections, see, e.g., Li Cunshan, "Dui Zhongguo wenhua minben sixiang de zai renshi"; Goldin, "Hsiao Kung-chuan on Mencian Populism"; and Tiwald, "Right of Rebellion in the *Mengzi*?"

57. *Mengzi zhengyi* 19.643.

58. *Mengzi zhengyi* 19.644.

59. *Mengzi zhengyi* 19.646–47.

60. *Mengzi zhengyi* 19.649.

61. *Mengzi zhengyi* 9.311.

62. Cf. Pines, "Disputers of Abdication," 275ff.

63. Cf. Graham, *Disputers of the Tao*, 113.

64. *Mengzi zhengyi* 7.221–22.

65. Mao 244.

66. *Mengzi zhengyi* 8.253–54. Many other passages advance the same general claim, e.g., *Mencius* 1A.5–7, 1B.10–11, 2A.5, and 3B.5.

67. *Mengzi zhengyi* 5.160–62.

## CHAPTER FIVE. *LAOZI*

1. For the Wang Bi recension of *Laozi*, I rely on Lou Yulie, *Wang Bi ji jiaoshi*, 1:1–193. Specialists must bear in mind that "the Wang Bi recension" is something of a fiction because it has been transmitted in multiple editions, which often conflict with Wang Bi's own commentary. Hence we may never know precisely which edition or editions Wang Bi used. See the discussion in Wagner, *Chinese Reading of the* Daodejing, 3–31 (followed by an attempt to reconstruct Wang Bi's text).

2. For a lucid overview, see Cook, *Bamboo Texts of Guodian*, 1:195–223; also Yin Zhenhuan, *Chongshi Laozi yu* Laozi, 27–38.

3. The number 81 recurs throughout Granet's magisterial study of numbers in Chinese philosophy (*La pensée chinoise*, 127–248).

4. Other Chinese texts were also organized in numerologically significant ways; for example, Schaberg, "Speaking of Documents," 350–51, observes that the New Script version of the *Canon of Documents* (*Jinwen Shangshu* 今文尚書) contains the same number of chapters as there were astronomical "lodges" (*xiu* 宿) in the sky (twenty-eight).

5. For two recent studies, see Queen, "*Han Feizi* and the Old Master"; and Kim, "Other *Laozi* Parallels in the *Hanfeizi*." Kim's conclusion is that "Jie Lao" and "Yu Lao" cannot derive from the same author; Queen accepts this possibility but notes that they might also have been written by Han Fei at different stages of his life. I do not see any way to settle the question with the available evidence.

6. Graham, *Studies in Chinese Philosophy and Philosophical Literature*, 111–24.

7. See, e.g., Graziosi, *Inventing Homer*, 16ff.; and Nagy, "Hesiod and the Ancient Biographical Traditions."

8. *Guoyu jijie* 17.502–5 ("Lingwang nüe, Bai gongzi Zhang Zhou jian" 靈王虐, 白公子張驟諫). According to the commentary of Wei Zhao 韋昭 (AD 204–73), the scribe's courtesy name was Lao Ziwei 老子亹. In his otherwise thorough study, Graham, *Studies in Chinese Philosophy and Philosophical Literature*, did not consider this reference. Previous scholars have considered the possibility that Lao is a surname, but not, as far as I am aware, in connection with Scribe Lao: e.g., Zhang Songhui, *Laozi yanjiu*, 21–26; Gao Heng, *Chongding Laozi zhenggu*, 157ff.; and Ma Xulun, *Laozi jiaogu*, 57.

9. *Shiji* 63.2139.

10. Cf. Bokenkamp, *Early Daoist Scriptures*, 39. On the apotheosis of Laozi generally, see Seidel, *La divinisation de Lao tseu dans le taoïsme des Han*; more recently, Zhang Songhui, *Laozi yanjiu*, 1–8; and Kohn, "Lao-tzu Myth."

11. Schwartz, *World of Thought in Ancient China*, 62ff., interprets Confucius's "Way" as the equivalent of a "good system," but the word "system" sounds a false note, inasmuch as Confucius cannot be plausibly categorized as a systematic philosopher.

12. Cf. Wang Zhongjiang, *Daojia xueshuo de guannianshi yanjiu*, 80–86; Xu Keqian, *Zhuangzi zhexue xintan*, 38–45; and Eno, "Cook Ding's Dao and the Limits of Philosophy," 145n10. Texts that do not use *dao* in this sense still occasionally appeal to cosmic regularities, e.g., *Mencius* 4B.26: "Despite the height of Heaven and the distance of stars and constellations, if you seek out the right premises, you can calculate solstices from a thousand years ago while sitting [at your workplace]" 天之高也, 星辰之遠也, 苟求其故, 千歲之日至, 可坐而致也 (*Mengzi zhengyi* 17.588). Compare *Laozi* 47: "One may know the world without going out through the doorway; one may see the Way of Heaven without peering through the window" 不出戶, 知天下, 不窺牖, 見天道. If one grasps the underlying principles, one does not even have to witness phenomena in order to understand them.

13. For more on *de*, see, e.g., Ivanhoe, "Concept of *de* ('Virtue') in the *Laozi.*" *Laozi* 38, is reminiscent of *The Methods of Guo Yan* (*Guo Yan zhi fa* 郭偃之法), as quoted in *Shangjun shu zhuizhi* 1.1.2 ("Gengfa" 更法): "One who discourses on supreme virtue does not harmonize with the vulgar" 論至德者不和於俗. Too little is known about this tradition, however, to be sure of any substantive connections. On Guo Yan, see Pines, *Book of Lord Shang*, 268n7.

14. The very phrase *da zhangfu* might have been lifted from Mencian discourse, as it appears in *Mencius* 3B.2. The more general term *daren* 大人 (great person) is widely attested and would merit a specialized study.

15. Cf. Schipper, "Chiens de paille et tigres en papier," 91.

16. Cf. Qian Zhongshu, *Guanzhui bian*, 2:403–10; and Zhang Longxi, "Qian Zhongshu on Philosophical and Mystical Paradoxes in the *Laozi*," 103. Also Graham, *Disputers of the Tao*, 219–23.

17. This was voiced even in antiquity: see, for example, the Mohist attempt at reductio ad absurdum in Graham, *Later Mohist Logic, Ethics and Science*, 452 (B 77). For other examples, see Zhang Songhui, *Laozi yanjiu*, 168–69.

18. Compare also *Laozi* 16: "One should bring about extreme emptiness" 致虛極.

19. For the variants *zhong* 盅 (cup) and *chong* 沖 (to infuse), see *Boshu Laozi jiaozhu*, 42. The two words are probably cognate: a cup 盅 (Old Chinese *truŋ) is what one pours 沖 (*N-truŋ) water into. (All reconstructed Old Chinese forms in this book are based on the system in Baxter and Sagart, *Old Chinese*.)

20. Compare *Laozi* 40: "The Way moves by being contrary and is useful by being weak" 反者, 道之動; 弱者, 道之用.

21. For a general survey of the image of water in Chinese philosophy, see Allan, *Way of Water and Sprouts of Virtue*; also, Allan, "Great One, Water, and the *Laozi.*"

22. Cf. Puett, *To Become a God*, 165–67. Compare also *Laozi* 17: "In highest antiquity, inferiors knew only that there was [a ruler]" 太上, 下知有之; that is to say, it never even occurred to them that they should love, praise, fear, or hate him. Two editions read *xia bu zhi you zhi* 下不知有之, taking the point even further: "inferiors did not even know that there was [a ruler]." See the variants and discussion in *Boshu Laozi jiaozhu*, 305.

23. Compare *Laozi* 2: "Therefore, the Sage dwells in affairs of nonaction and practices the unspoken teaching" 是以聖人處無為之事, 行不言之教.

24. Cf. Wang Zhongjiang, *Daojia xueshuo de guannianshi yanjiu*, 151–70.

25. *Taran* is not a real word and is not found in any standard dictionary. It happens to be attested in *Taixuan jizhu* 7.187 ("Xuanchi" 玄攡), but in that context *ta* is probably

to be construed as *tuo* 佗/駝, "to bear on one's back": "Earth, bearing [all things], shows people the bright [spirits]" 夫地他 [=佗] 然示人明也.

26. Compare *Laozi* 25: "People model themselves on Earth; Earth models itself on Heaven; Heaven models itself on the Way; the Way models itself on *ziran*"人法地，地法天，天法道，道法自然.

27. Compare Montaigne, *Les essais*, 1088: "Laissons faire un peu à nature: elle entend mieux ses affaires que nous" (3.xiii; roughly: "Let us allow nature a little [freedom] to act; it understands its affairs better than we do."

28. This passage is particularly effective in Chinese (and difficult to capture in English) because of its repeated use of *wei* in slightly different senses (to perform, to act, to do).

29. Compare *Laozi* 34: "To the end, he does not do great things himself; thus he is able to achieve his great things" 以其終不自為大，故能成其大.

30. Several editions read *yu* 浴 (to bathe) in place of *gu* 谷 (valley), not that this would make the text any easier to comprehend (*Boshu Laozi jiaozhu*, 248).

31. See the sampling in *Boshu Laozi jiaozhu*, 30.

32. For a brief survey of other interpretations of "the One," see Robinet, "Diverse Interpretations of the *Laozi*," 137–38.

33. Reading "the Two" as *yin* and *yang* accords with the elaboration on *Laozi* 42 in *Huainanzi jishi* 3.244 ("Tianwen" 天文).

34. Compare *Laozi* 25, discussed below.

35. Compare *Laozi* 4: "It appears to have preexisted the Deity" 象帝之先.

36. Although it can be hazardous to rely on later Daoist practices when trying to interpret *Laozi*, it is worth observing that the purpose of the notorious sexual cultivation rites of the Celestial Masters (*tianshi* 天師) was "the ritual reconstruction of the cosmos" by effectuating a return to the primordial moment when *qi* was undifferentiated and unified. See Raz, *Emergence of Daoism*, 186–202.

37. The Wang Bi edition reads *wu ci* 無雌 (to be without the female), but *wei ci* 為雌 (to act the part of the female) is prolifically attested in other editions (*Boshu Laozi jiaozhu*, 267) and makes more sense.

38. Cf. Moeller, *Philosophy of the* Daodejing, 21–32.

39. *Zui* 朘, "immature penis," is widely attested in place of *quan* 全, "integrity, wholeness" (*Boshu Laozi jiaozhu*, 93). Either reading would fit philosophically.

40. See, generally, Penny, "Immortality and Transcendence"; and Needham, *Science and Civilisation in China*, 2:71–127.

41. On this point, Ellen Marie Chen, "Is There a Doctrine of Physical Immortality in the *Tao Te Ching*?," is still unsurpassed. See also Wang Zhongjiang, *Daojia xueshuo de guannianshi yanjiu*, 210ff.

42. See, e.g., Harper, "Bellows Analogy in *Laozi* V and Warring States Macrobiotic Hygiene."

43. On this concept, see, e.g., Lo, "From a Dual Soul to a Unitary Soul."

44. Several of the earliest strips were collected in Momand, *Keeping Up with the Joneses*; it ran regularly from 1913 to 1938. For modern discussions of happiness from the perspective of social comparison theory, see, e.g., Yamada and Takahashi, "Happiness Is a Matter of Social Comparison"; and Boyce et al., "Money and Happiness." We are happiest when we are happier than someone else.

45. Consider the testimony of a soldier who fled North Korea, reported in Iaccino,

"Kim Young-Il Fled North Korea as a Young Soldier": "I had never seen bananas or clementines. . . . We always thought it was normal to have our freedoms restricted. It is only when my family and I came to South Korea that we finally had means of comparison. We didn't realise how unhappy we were until we came here." Or in Szabłowski's bizarre and fascinating *Dancing Bears*, which compares the struggles of bears rescued from abusive captivity to those of postcommunist citizens adapting to the new order, a keeper says: "For twenty or thirty years they were used to having somebody do the thinking for them, providing them with an occupation, telling them what they had to do, what they were going to eat and where to sleep. It wasn't the ideal life for a bear, but it was the only one they knew" (87).

46. The classic study of anti-intellectualism in Chinese political thought is Yu Yingshi, *Lishi yu sixiang*, 1–75; for his treatment of *Laozi*, see 10ff.

47. Many classical political texts share the conviction that the people should be kept poor and weak, e.g., *Shangjun shu zhuizhi* 1.4.27 and 5.20.121 ("Quqiang" 去彊 and "Ruomin" 弱民, respectively). The difference is that *Shangjun shu* does not recommend subtlety such as "nonaction" in implementing such policies.

48. Cf. Pines, *Envisioning Eternal Empire*, 36–38. Michael, *Pristine Dao*, 40–50, distinguishes between the Sage and the King, but this interpretation does not readily account for passages such as *Laozi* 25.

49. Cf. Goldin, *After Confucius*, 129ff. Two examples of what I mean by "whitewashing" the political dimensions are Chen Guying, *Daojia de renwen jingshen*; and Moeller, *Philosophy of the* Daodejing (e.g., 55–75), both of which ignore the most problematic passages, especially *Laozi* 65. Similarly, some libertarian theorists claim to be inspired by *Laozi*, but only by palliating the extensive role envisioned for government: e.g., Boaz, *Libertarian Reader*, 207; and Rothbard, *Austrian Perspective on the History of Economic Thought*, 1:23–27. The phrase *laissez-faire* is sometimes said to derive from *wuwei* (e.g., Clarke, *Oriental Enlightenment*, 50).

50. Guodian A contains an unrelated passage in the received chapter 5 (Cook, *Bamboo Texts of Guodian*, 1:261–62). "Jie Lao," for its part, makes a sustained attempt to reconcile Confucian virtues with the philosophy of *Laozi* (cf. Queen, "*Han Feizi* and the Old Master," 212–13).

51. Despite Kirkland, *Taoism*, 59: "the Guodian texts show *no* signs of anti-Confucianism" (emphasis in original).

52. Cook, *Bamboo Texts of Guodian*, 1:311–12.

53. Cook, *Bamboo Texts of Guodian*, 1:225–26; for other possible interpretations of the final two graphs, see 1:227n13.

54. Cook, *Bamboo Texts of Guodian*, 1:256–60.

## CHAPTER SIX. *ZHUANGZI*

1. Ye Shuxian, *Zhuangzi de wenhua jiexi*, 83–93.

2. There is, nevertheless, a tendency in some work to begin with this recognition, and refer circumspectly to "the *Zhuangzi*" (i.e., the text), but then soon enough forget the distinction, and start speaking of "Zhuangzi" (the philosopher). See my review of Eske Møllgaard, *Introduction to Daoist Thought*, 178.

3. For the example of *Zhuangzi* 30, see Sanft, "Evaluating Swords"; and Graziani, "Of Words and Swords."

4. Four standard studies: Guan Feng, *Zhuangzi neipian yijie he pipan*, 319–58; Graham, *Studies in Chinese Philosophy and Philosophical Literature*, 283–321; Roth, "Who Compiled the *Chuang Tzu*?"; and Liu Xiaogan, *Classifying the Zhuangzi Chapters*. Less frequently cited accounts include Liu Rongxian, *Zhuangzi waizapian yanjiu*; and Cui Dahua, *Zhuangxue yanjiu*, 52–103. In addition, Littlejohn, "Kongzi in the *Zhuangzi*," attempts to distinguish textual strata on the basis of differing representations of Confucius (positive, negative, neutral, etc.). While his observations about Confucius's varying roles in *Zhuangzi* are cogent, it does not follow that each distinct mode is attributable to a different author or source.

5. Mansvelt Beck, "'Ik' zei de gek, 'I' Mencius, 'I' Laozi, 'Zhuang Zhou' Zhuangzi." One wishes that the redoubtable Mansvelt Beck had chosen a less gnomic title.

6. Klein, "Reading the *Zhuangzi* Anthology," esp. 20–21; and Klein, "Were There 'Inner Chapters' in the Warring States?"

7. Cf. Wang Shumin, *Zhuangzi guankui*, 20; and Xiong Tieji et al., *Zhongguo Zhuangxue shi*, 25.

8. This is Sima Qian's assessment in *Shiji* 63.2144; cf. Billeter, *Études sur Tchouang-tseu*, 67.

9. Li Xueqin, "Looking at the 'Qu qie' Chapter," begins with the questionable assumption that "Quqie" must have antedated the Guodian corpus, then infers, on the basis of the date, that it is either "Zhuangzi's own writing [or] the work of an immediate disciple" (341). My view of the textual history is precisely the opposite: the author or redactor of "Quqie" used a line that was part of the general discourse; its presence in a Guodian manuscript hardly proves that "Quqie" existed at the time.

10. Hu Pingsheng, "Fuyang Shuanggudui Hanjian *Zhuangzi*," 189–96. Note that many of these are too short to be categorized with any certitude. The most lucid discussion of the Zhangjiashan and Fuyang *Zhuangzi* is Bumbacher, "Reconstructing the *Zhuang zi*," 630–36, who concludes that they both belong to the same textual tradition as the received *Zhuangzi*, and pleas for their full publication. See also Klein, "Were There 'Inner Chapters' in the Warring States?," 349–51. Final assessments of these two sets must be deferred until they are published in their entirety; decades after their discovery, the scholarly world is still waiting. Shaughnessy, *Unearthing the Changes*, 190–92, explains that, in the case of the Fuyang manuscripts, the delay is at least partly explained by the painstaking work of preparation and conservation.

11. Cf. Klein, "Reading the *Zhuangzi* Anthology," 21; and Klein, "Were There 'Inner Chapters' in the Warring States?," 355.

12. Philosophers may discern that I am not hewing to the so-called principle of charity, memorably stated by Quine in *Word and Object*, 59: "one's interlocutor's silliness, beyond a certain point, is less likely than bad translation" (i.e., interpretation). In the case of *Zhuangzi*, I do not believe that we have "an interlocutor"; we have several. Generally speaking (I aim to flesh out my thoughts in a future publication), the principle of charity is often historiographically naive.

13. On the possible mythic sources of the fish-bird, see Yang Yi, *Zhuangzi huanyuan*, 24–27; and Ye Shuxian, *Zhuangzi de wenhua jiexi*, 103–18.

14. *Zhuangzi jishi* 1A.1.2 ("Xiaoyao you" 逍遙遊). Occasionally I find that the punctuation could be more reader friendly, but this remains a rock-solid variorum edition.

15. Compare *Zhuangzi jishi* 6B.17.601 ("Qiushui" 秋水): "This is like using a tube to peek at Heaven, using an awl to plumb the Earth" 是直用管闚天，用錐指地也. These

themes underlie the recent characterization of *Zhuangzi*'s relativism as "therapeutic" rather than radical: e.g., Ivanhoe, "Was Zhuangzi a Relativist?," 200: "These passages . . . are better read as a form of therapy, designed to curb our terrible tendency toward self-aggrandizement."

16. *Zhuangzi jishi* 1A.1.11 ("Xiaoyao you").

17. This may be an allusion to the Confucian theory that a sage appears once every five hundred years (e.g., *Mencius* 2B.13 and 7B.38; *Shiji* 130.3296), for which see Klein, *Reading Sima Qian from Han to Song*, 80–81; and Van Ess, "Die Idee des Zyklus von fünfhundert Jahren bei *Mengzi*, Sima Qian und einigen anderen Denkern der Han."

18. Although they are, coincidentally, homophones in Modern Mandarin, they would not have been confused in Old Chinese: 鵬 (*bˤəŋ) vs. 彭 (*C.bˤraŋ). Wang Li, *Tongyuan zidian*, 318, suggested that the name of the bird is related to *feng* 風/鳳, "wind" and "phoenix," respectively (*prəm and *prəm-s), but this is not certain.

19. *Zhuangzi jishi* 1A.1.14–16 ("Xiaoyao you").

20. *Zhuangzi jishi* 6B.17.563 ("Qiushui").

21. *Zhuangzi jishi* 1B.2.93 ("Qiwu lun" 齊物論).

22. Cf. Ting-mien Lee, "'Benevolence-Righteousness' as Strategic Terminology,'" 30.

23. *Zhuangzi jishi* 1B.2.66 ("Qiwu lun").

24. Cf. Yang Guorong, *Zhuangzi de sixiang shijie*, 79–80. For a comparison of such passages with the philosophy of W. V. Quine, see Bo Mou, "Quine's Naturalized Epistemology and Zhuangzi's Daoist Naturalism." I recall proposing similar comparisons to Quine himself (ca. 1994). He did not seem enthusiastic.

25. *Zhuangzi jishi* 1B.2.83 ("Qiwu lun").

26. For one seminal publication, see Kahneman and Tversky, "On the Reality of Cognitive Illusions." The only work I know that draws a comparison between such psychological concepts and *Zhuangzi* is Slingerland, *Trying Not to Try*, 139.

27. Cf. Heuer, *Psychology of Intelligence Analysis*, 70–71.

28. The term *paoding* 庖丁 probably just means "kitchen lackey" but is conventionally translated as Cook Ding.

29. *Ji* is identical, phonologically, to *ji* 伎 (*gre?), "actor," and *ji* 妓, "prostitute." The basic meaning of all these words is "perform(er)."

30. *Zhuangzi jishi* 2A.3.119 ("Yangsheng zhu" 養生主).

31. This phrase is reminiscent of *Laozi* 43: "a thing with no substantiality enters [even where there is] no space" 無有入無間 (see p. 117, above).

32. For four recent interpretations of this passage, see Sellmann, "Butcher Ding"; Fox, "Reflex and Reflectivity," 211ff.; Cook, "Zhuang Zi and His Carving of the Confucian Ox"; and Eno, "Cook Ding's Dao and the Limits of Philosophy."

33. Graham, *Chuang-tzǔ*, 135; more recently, Lai and Chiu, eds., *Skill and Mastery*.

34. *Zhuangzi jishi* 5B.13.490–91 ("Tiandao" 天道).

35. Cf. Raphals, "Wheelwright Bian," 136–37.

36. *Zhuangzi jishi* 9A.26.944 ("Waiwu" 外物). Cf. Yang Yi, *Zhuangzi huanyuan*, 162–64; and Yang Guorong, *Zhuangzi de sixiang shijie*, 146–47. For more radical interpretations, see De Reu, "Ragbag of Odds and Ends?," 247ff.; and Moeller, *Daoism Explained*, 55–62.

37. Chinese critics (e.g., Yang Yi, *Zhuangzi huanyuan*, 50) frequently refer to such eccentricity as *fangwai* 方外 (outside the norm). Cf. Peterson, "Squares and Circles," 50–57. Moeller, "Naked Scribe," 256, calls it "skill of dissociation from social roles"

(also "*zhen*uine skill," after the Chinese word *zhen* 真—though the pun works only in Mandarin).

38. *Zhuangzi jishi* 7B.21.719 ("Tian Zifang" 田子方).

39. For *Zhuangzi*'s influence on Six Dynasties literati, see, e.g., Zhang Songhui, *Zhuangzi yanjiu*, 299–330; Xiong Tieji et al., *Zhongguo Zhuangxue shi*, 122–71; and Balazs, *Chinese Civilization and Bureaucracy*, 234ff.

40. *Zhuangzi jishi* 1A.1.28–31 ("Xiaoyao you").

41. *Zhuangzi jishi* 1B.2.96 ("Qiwu lun").

42. See esp. Campany, *Making Transcendents*, 62–87; also Arthur, *Early Daoist Dietary Practices*, 49–53; Eskildsen, *Asceticism in Early Taoist Thought*, 43–44; and Lévi, "L'abstinence des céréales chez les taoïstes."

43. Compare *Mozi jiaozhu* 1.5.35 ("Qihuan"): "The Five Cereals are what the people rely on" 凡五穀者，民之所仰也.

44. Similar arguments, though with different metaphysical foundations, are found in *Weimojie suoshuo jing* (i.e., *The Holy Teaching of Vimalakīrti*), translated by Kumārajīva 鳩摩羅什 (344–413): armed with their comprehension of "nonduality" (*buer* 不二), buddhas and bodhisattvas are capable of a litany of miracles. These resemblances surely contributed to the *Zhuangzi*'s resurgence in the post-Han era. Cf. Zürcher, *Buddhist Conquest of China*, 1:132. For *Zhuangzi*'s influence on Kumārajīva's student Sengzhao 僧肇 (384–414), see Zhang Songhui, *Zhuangzi yanjiu*, 273–79; Xiong Tieji et al., *Zhongguo Zhuangxue shi*, 205ff.; Chen Shaoming, *"Qiwulun" jiqi yingxiang*, 122–36; and Cui Dahua, *Zhuangxue yanjiu*, 494–537. The parallels were evident to premodern literati as well; consider Feng Mengzhen, *Kuaixuetang ji*, 1.10a: "Is the text of *Zhuangzi*, with Guo's commentary, not a forerunner of the Buddhist dharma?" 莊文郭注其佛法之先驅耶 ("*Zhuangzi* Guo zhu xu" 莊子郭注序).

45. See, above all, Berling, "Self and Whole in Chuang Tzu"; also Møllgaard, *Introduction to Daoist Thought*, 15–20.

46. *Zhuangzi jishi* 7A.19.636 ("Dasheng" 達生).

47. *Sui ji* 雖疾 could also mean "although [the carriage] is moving quickly."

48. On this figure, see, e.g., Wang Shumin, *Zhuangzi guankui*, 33–48; and Raphals, "On Hui Shi."

49. *Zhuangzi jishi* 6B.18.614–15 ("Zhile" 至樂).

50. A *ji* 箕 is a winnowing basket with a trim around three sides and an open mouth on the fourth; thus it looks vaguely like a pair of splayed legs. *Ji* also refers to a constellation of four stars (in modern Sagittarius) that are arrayed like such a basket (Sun Xiaochun and Kistemaker, *Chinese Sky during the Han*, 158). Here it could refer to either the basket or the constellation.

51. Compare *Zhuangzi jishi* 7B.22.733 ("Zhi bei you" 知北遊): "The birth of a human being is the accumulation of *qi*. When it accumulates, there is life; when it dissipates, there is death. Since death and life are in league with each other, what should I be distressed about?" 人之生，氣之聚也；聚則為生，散則為死。若死生為徒，吾又何患！

52. The interpretations of this passage are, understandably, diverse; see, e.g., Yang Guorong, *Zhuangzi de sixiang shijie*, 231–32; Xu Keqian, *Zhuangzi zhexue xintan*, 187ff.; Ames, "Death as Transformation in Classical Daoism," esp. 64–70; Bauer, "Das Stirnrunzeln des Totenkopfes," 259; Graham, *Disputers of the Tao*, 202–4; and Kimura, *Chūgoku tetsugaku no tankyū*, 352ff.

53. *Zhuangzi jishi* 3A.6.260–61 ("Da zongshi" 大宗師).

54. *Zhuangzi jishi* 3A.6.262.

55. Goldin, "Mind-Body Problem in the *Zhuangzi*?," 227ff.; more broadly, Goldin, "Consciousness of the Dead as a Philosophical Problem in Ancient China." Zilai's statement, "In an instant, I shall fall asleep; with start, I shall awaken," seems to hint at the possibility of reincarnation. Regardless of what is meant by this "awakening," who is "I"?

56. *Zhuangzi jishi* 1A.2.103 ("Qiwu lun").

57. Compare *Zhuangzi jishi* 6B.18.617–19 ("Zhile"), where a skull says to Zhuang Zhou in a dream: "How could I abandon the joys of a south-facing king and return to the toils of life among humans?" 吾安能棄南面王樂而復為人閒之勞乎.

58. Cf. Raphals, "Human and Animal in Early China and Greece," 131–33.

59. *Zhuangzi jishi* 3A.6.224 ("Da zongshi").

60. This sentence seems wordy in Chinese too.

61. *Zhuangzi jishi* 6A.15.535 ("Keyi" 刻意).

62. The "bear-climb" 熊經 appears in *Daoyin tu* 導引圖, an illustrated codex of gymnastic positions from Mawangdui, as well as *Yinshu* 引書, a similar manuscript from Zhangjiashan 張家山. See *Mawangdui Hanmu boshu*, 4:95 (with a photograph of the damaged scroll at 52, where *xiongjing* appears at the bottom right); and *Zhangjiashan Hanmu zhujian*, 292. Moreover, the phrase *chuixu huxi* 吹呴呼吸 (blow and breathe, inhale and exhale), taken by most translators of *Zhuangzi* as derisive, must be a technical term, as it appears in *Yinshu* as well (*Zhangjiashan Hanmu zhujian*, 298). On *daoyin* (guiding and pulling) generally, see Despeux, "La gymnastique *daoyin* 導引 dans la Chine ancienne"; Engelhardt, "*Daoyin tu* und *Yinshu*"; Harper, *Early Chinese Medical Literature*, 132ff.; and Gao Dalun, *Zhangjiashan Hanmu Yinshu yanjiu*.

63. *Zhuangzi jishi* 2B.4.186 ("Renjian shi" 人間世).

64. *Mozi jiaozhu* 1.1.2 ("Qinshi" 親士, by all appearances a late chapter), appears to borrow this idea: "If there are five awls, one will be the sharpest, and the sharpest is surely the first to be worn down. If there are five blades, one will be the keenest, and the keenest is surely the first to be blunted. Therefore, the sweetest well soon runs dry; the loftiest tree is soon felled; the numinous tortoise is soon broiled; the divine snake is soon destroyed" 今有五錐, 此其銛, 銛者必先挫。有五刀, 此其錯, 錯者必先靡。是以甘井近竭, 招木近伐, 靈龜近灼, 神蛇近暴. (The "numinous tortoise" almost certainly refers to an oracle bone, as in the tale of fishing by the River Pu, below; commentators opine that the "divine snake" was also used in divination rites.)

65. See Major, "Efficacy of Uselessness." One important passage warns against fetishizing uselessness: *Zhuangzi jishi* 7A.20.667–68 ("Shanmu" 山木), where a goose is selected for dinner precisely because it *cannot* cackle. (Cackling geese served as a premodern burglar alarm.) When a disciple asks Zhuang Zhou how he can reconcile this with his exhortation to be useless, the answer is to know when to be useful and when not: "ascend the Way and its Power and float along, without praise, without criticism, at one moment a dragon, at another a snake, fully transforming with the times, and never willing to act in a single way" 乘道德而浮遊則不然, 无譽无訾, 一龍一蛇, 與時俱化, 而无肯專為. This, I think, is similar to what Ziporyn means by his analogy of the wild card, i.e., learning how to be successful under any possible set of rules ("How Many Are the Ten Thousand Things and I?," 58ff.).

66. *Zhuangzi jishi* 2B.4.170–74 ("Renjian shi"). The following line from Wohlleben, *Das geheime Leben der Bäume*, 7, reminds me of this story: "Krumme, knorrige Bäume,

die ich damals noch als minderwertig einordnete, riefen bei Wanderern Begeisterung hervor" (Crooked, gnarled trees, which, at the time, I still classified as inferior, elicited amazement from hikers).

67. Cf. Svarverud, "Usefulness of Uselessness."

68. *Zhuangzi jishi* 2B.4.176 ("Renjian shi").

69. For a discussion of whether the concept of "metaphor" is appropriate, see Allinson, "How Metaphor Functions in the *Zhuangzi*."

70. *Zhuangzi jishi* 2B.4.180 ("Renjian shi").

71. *Zhuangzi jishi* 6B.18.611 ("Zhile").

72. *Zhuangzi jishi* 6B.17.603–4 ("Qiushui").

73. *Zhuangzi jishi* 7A.19.648 ("Dasheng").

74. "Rangwang" is commonly interpreted as espousing Yangist philosophy (e.g., Liu Rongxian, *Zhuangzi waizapian yanjiu*, 172–77), but it is more plausibly read as a pastiche. The implied positions of the various pieces vary considerably; all they have in common is the theme of "yielding the throne." See my review of Graham, *Chuang-tzŭ*, and Roth, *A Companion to Angus C. Graham's* Chuang-tzu, 207ff.; also Pines, "Disputers of Abdication," 284.

75. *Zhuangzi jishi* 9B.28.968 ("Rangwang").

76. *Zhuangzi jishi* 10A.32.1049–50 ("Lie Yukou" 列禦寇).

77. Cf. Wang Zhongjiang, *Daoism Excavated*, 22.

78. My view is similar to that of Kirkland, *Taoism*, 1–19.

79. *Zhuangzi jishi* 6B.18.612 ("Zhile").

80. Compare *Zhuangzi jishi* 9A.26.924 ("Waiwu"): a local lord proposes to lend Zhuang Zhou far more money than he needs; Zhuang Zhou responds, through a parable, that this would only lead to his death.

81. Thus even Liezi 列子, who could ride the wind, did not perfect the art of "wandering" because he "still had to rely on something" 猶有所待者也 (*Zhuangzi jishi* 1A.1.17 ["Xiaoyao you"]). Cf. Wang Bo, *Zhuangzi zhexue*, 227–28; Wang Shumin, *Zhuangzi guankui*, 181–83; and Puett, *To Become a God*, 124; more generally, Moeller, "Rambling without Destination." Compare also *Zhuangzi jishi* 8B.24.834 ("Xu Wugui" 徐无鬼): those who are unhappy are "confined by external objects" 囿於物者, i.e., they depend on others for their happiness.

82. *Zhuangzi jishi* 1A.1.36–37 ("Xiaoyao you").

83. Cf. Ye Shuxian, *Zhuangzi de wenhua jiexi*, 269–76.

84. Cf. Xu Keqian, *Zhuangzi zhexue xintan*, 15–23 (also 146–71 for various conceptions of freedom in *Zhuangzi*).

## CHAPTER SEVEN. *SUNZI*

1. The best study of Sun Wu's name and biography is still Petersen, "What's in a Name?" The surname Sun, probably shortened from Wangsun 王孫 or Gongsun 公孫, suggests that he descended from an aristocratic family (if he was a real person). For contrasting Chinese interpretations, see, e.g., Yang Shanqun, *Sunzi pingzhuan*, 71–119 (who reads the sources essentially at face value); and Li Ling, *Sunzi shisan pian zonghe yanjiu*, 351–58 (who is skeptical).

2. Both are included in *Yinqueshan Hanmu zhujian*, vol. 1. *Sun Bin Bingfa* was

known from bibliographies but had long since been lost. The Yinqueshan version of *Sun Wu Bingfa*, moreover, differs substantially from the received text. Cf. Li Ling, *Sunzi shisan pian zonghe yanjiu*, 133–72. Many themes in *Sunzi* are expanded in *Sun Bin Bingfa* and other classical military texts, but the scope of this book precludes a detailed exposition of these sources.

3. Two influential proponents are He Bingdi and his student Mark Edward Lewis. See He Bingdi, *He Bingdi sixiang zhidushi lun*, 185–251; and Lewis, *Sanctioned Violence in Early China*, 98 and 285n5. See also Li Guisheng, *Zhuzi wenhua yu xian-Qin bingjia*, 72–91; and Chun-shu Chang, *Rise of the Chinese Empire*, 1:412n38.

4. Cf. Pines, "Lexical Changes in Zhanguo Texts," 703. For the early history of the crossbow in China, see, e.g., Selby, *Chinese Archery*, 153–78. Other lexical anachronisms are discussed in Griffith, *Sun Tzu*, 6–11; to this can be added *zhong* 忠, which always means "loyalty" in *Sunzi*, but did not bear this sense in the earliest philosophical literature (Goldin, "When *zhong* 忠 Does Not Mean 'Loyalty'").

5. Thus Sawyer, *Seven Military Classics of Ancient China*, 150.

6. Cf. Andrew Meyer, "Reading 'Sunzi' as a Master."

7. *Shiyi jia zhu Sunzi jiaoli* A.2–3 ("Ji" 計).

8. Griffith, *Sun Tzu*, 63.

9. For *dao*, at any rate, Griffith soon recognized the inadequacy of "moral influence" and eventually just transliterated it (e.g., *Sun Tzu*, 88).

10. Some examples: "*Tian* consists of *yin* and *yang*, heat and cold, and initiatives appropriate to the season" 天者, 陰陽, 寒暑, 時制也 (A.4 ["Ji"]); "All terrain with canyon streams, natural craters, natural enclosures, natural entanglements, natural pitfalls, or natural fissures must be abandoned forthwith. Do not go near it" 凡地, 有絕澗、天井、天牢、天羅、天陷、天隙, 必亟去之, 勿近也 (B.190–91 ["Xingjun" 行軍]); and "The proper season [for attack by fire] is when the weather is dry" 時者, 天之燥也 (C.279 ["Huogong" 火攻]). Often, *tian* is paired with *di* to refer to the natural world or the natural conditions of the battlefield.

11. One term that is amply attested is *tianxia* 天下, "all under Heaven," "the world."

12. Marxist interpretations present this as evidence of *Sunzi*'s "materialism": e.g., Xie Wenchao, *Xian-Qin bingshu yanjiu*, 139–40; more generally, Yang Shanqun, *Sunzi pingzhuan*, 183–89.

13. *Shiyi jia zhu Sunzi jiaoli* C.289 ("Yongjian" 用間). Cf. A.29–30 ("Zuozhan" 作戰), where the cost of maintaining an army of a thousand quadrigas and one hundred thousand men is estimated at a thousand pieces of gold per day; and *Shiyi jia zhu Sunzi jiaoli* A.34–35, which emphasizes secondary disruptions such as price dislocation.

14. There are several interchangeable words for "army" in *Sunzi*. In this chapter, I translate *shi* 師 as "army," *jun* 軍 as "forces," *zhong* 眾 as "host," and *bing* 兵 as "troops." Occasionally, terms warrant more specificity (for example, *lü* 旅, "battalion," is contrasted with *wu* 伍, "squadron").

15. Cf. Sawyer with Sawyer, *Tao of Spycraft*, 126ff. The financial burden of warfare prompts certain other rational responses: try to feed your troops with your enemy's stores instead of your own (*Sunzi* A.36 ["Zuozhan"]), and always make use of captured *matériel* (*Sunzi* A.38–39).

16. There are important differences, however; see, e.g., Barry Allen, *Vanishing into Things*, 129–39; Meyer and Wilson, "*Sunzi Bingfa* as History and Theory," 114ff.; and Jullien, *Propensity of Things*, 34–38.

17. *Shiyi jia zhu Sunzi jiaoli* A.44–45 ("Mougong" 謀攻).

18. Cf. *Shiyi jia zhu Sunzi jiaoli* A.30 ("Zuozhan"): "If you attack cities, your strength will wane" 攻城則力屈.

19. E.g., *Mozi jiaozhu* 5.18.199 ("Feigong zhong" 非攻中).

20. *Shiyi jia zhu Sunzi jiaoli* A.11–12 ("Ji").

21. The phrase *yi zuo qi wai* 以佐其外 is obscure; my interpretation follows the thrust of the traditional commentaries in *Shiyi jia zhu Sunzi jiaoli* A.11–12.

22. Baxter and Sagart, *Old Chinese*, 29–30; see also Schuessler, *ABC Etymological Dictionary of Old Chinese*, 570–71. For further discussions of *shi* in *Sunzi*, see *Art of War: The Denma Translation*, 70–76; Jullien, *Propensity of Things*, 25–34; and Ames, *Art of Rulership*, 66–72.

23. *Shiyi jia zhu Sunzi jiaoli* B.99 ("Shi" 勢).

24. A notion similar to what we would call potential energy is evident in a line earlier in the same chapter: "His *shi* is like that of a cocked crossbow; his timing is like the release of a trigger" 勢如彍弩，節如發機 (*Shiyi jia zhu Sunzi jiaoli* B.91). (This line is also significant for its reference to the crossbow; cf. above.)

25. Cf. Rand, *Military Thought in Early China*, 44–53.

26. *Shiyi jia zhu Sunzi jiaoli* B.96–98. Cf. B.175 ("Jiubian" 九變): "Belabor the territorial lords with errands and make them scramble [by dangling an inconsequential] advantage" 役諸侯者以業，趨諸侯者以利.

27. E.g., *Shiyi jia zhu Sunzi jiaoli* B.137–40 ("Junzheng" 軍爭).

28. Cf. Rand, *Military Thought in Early China*, 39–40. This must be at least in part the inspiration behind Ullman et al., *Shock and Awe* (e.g., 100–103), a phrase that was popularized during the invasion of Iraq in 2003. Ullman et al. refer to *Sunzi* as many as twenty times. The Denma Translation Group (*Art of War: The Denma Translation*, 121–22) have demonstrated the indebtedness of *Warfighting*, another influential Department of Defense manual, to *Sunzi*.

29. *Shiyi jia zhu Sunzi jiaoli* B.116–17 ("Xushi" 虛實).

30. Thus I question Martin J. Powers's translation of *wuxing* as "randomness" (*Pattern and Person*, 256–59). *Wuxing* is not random when it is practiced strategically.

31. *Shiyi jia zhu Sunzi jiaoli* B.120–23.

32. *Ce zhi* 策之 could also mean "make him formulate a strategy."

33. "Terrain of death" (*sidi* 死地) is defined in *Shiyi jia zhu Sunzi jiaoli* C.239 ("Jiudi" 九地): "Where [troops] may survive by fighting desperately, but will perish otherwise, is terrain of death" 疾戰則存，不疾戰則亡者，為死地. "Terrain of life" is not otherwise attested in the book.

34. Cf. *Shiyi jia zhu Sunzi jiaoli* A.74 ("Xing" 形): "Thus the victory of one who is adept at battle does not provide a reputation for wisdom or merit for bravery" 故善戰者之勝也，無智名，無勇功. According to the commentator Du Mu 杜牧 (803–53?), such victories are secured before the battle even takes place, but ordinary soldiers do not understand this and thus have no reason to attribute wisdom or bravery to the commander.

35. *Shiyi jia zhu Sunzi jiaoli* B.193–202 ("Xingjun").

36. Cf. Ren Jiyu, *Zhongguo zhexueshi*, 1:142.

37. *Shiyi jia zhu Sunzi jiaoli* B.87–90 ("Shi").

38. Cf. *Shiyi jia zhu Sunzi jiaoli* A.12 ("Ji"): "Warfare is the practice of deceit" 兵者,

詭道也. Sawyer with Sawyer, *Tao of Deception*, 61–66, defends the renderings "orthodox" and "unorthodox" for *zheng* and *qi*, with a discussion of other suggestions.

39. Cf. Lévi, *Les sept traités de la guerre*, 39–41. Allan, *Way of Water and Sprouts of Virtue*, does not consider any passages from *Sunzi*.

40. *Shiyi jia zhu Sunzi jiaoli* B.124–26 ("Xushi").

41. Winter, "Suggestions for a Re-interpretation of the Concept of *wu xing* in the *Sungzi bingfa*," e.g., 156, understands *wuxing* 五行 here as "Five Planets." I disagree with Winter that the more straightforward interpretation of *wuxing* as the "Five Phases" does not fit the context. Note the similar passage in *Yuejue shu jiaoshi* 4.5.112 ("Jini neijing" 計倪內經): "Metal, Wood, Water, Fire, and Earth overcome one another in turn; one new moon makes a month after the previous one; no [single power] dominates permanently" 金木水火土更 [相] 勝, 月朔更建, 莫主其常.

42. Cf. Andrew Meyer, "Reading 'Sunzi' as a Master," 20ff.

43. There is a scholarly tendency to overstate the significance of *dao* in *Sunzi*; e.g., Mair, *Art of War*, 47; *Art of War: The Denma Translation*, 76–81; and Yang Shanqun, *Sunzi pingzhuan*, 224–28. The two basic meanings of *dao* in *Sunzi* are merely "road" and "practice, method, way of doing something." Rarely is it observed that, in the latter sense, *dao* is not necessarily good: e.g., *Shiyi jia zhu Sunzi jiaoli* C.225 ("Dixing" 地形): "These six are all practices of defeat" 凡此六者, 敗之道也.

44. E.g., *Shiyi jia zhu Sunzi jiaoli* C.226 ("Dixing"): "Thus if doing battle will certainly result in victory, yet the ruler says, 'Do not do battle,' it is acceptable to do battle anyway; if doing battle will not result in victory, yet the ruler says, 'You must do battle,' it is acceptable not to do battle" 故戰道必勝, 主曰無戰, 必戰可也; 戰道不勝, 主曰必戰, 無戰可也; also A.57–59 ("Mougong"). Cf. *Mencius* 1B.9, which asserts that a ruler's subordinates sometimes have more expertise in their particular field than he does.

45. *Shiyi jia zhu Sunzi jiaoli* C.227 ("Dixing").

46. *Shiyi jia zhu Sunzi jiaoli* C.227 ("Dixing").

47. Cf. Lewis, *Sanctioned Violence in Early China*, 104–14.

48. *Shiyi jia zhu Sunzi jiaoli* C.252–53 ("Jiudi").

49. *Shiyi jia zhu Sunzi jiaoli* C.283–84 ("Huogong").

50. *Shiyi jia zhu Sunzi jiaoli* B.176–78 ("Jiubian").

51. *Shiyi jia zhu Sunzi jiaoli* A.12–13 ("Ji").

52. *Shiyi jia zhu Sunzi jiaoli* C.297 ("Yongjian").

53. *Shiyi jia zhu Sunzi jiaoli* B.149–50 ("Junzheng").

54. Some commentators interpret *gui* 歸 as indicating that, at the end of the day, the troops think of nothing but "returning home."

55. Cf. Lewis, *Sanctioned Violence in Early China*, 222–31; and Sawyer with Sawyer, *Tao of Spycraft*, 457–63.

56. *Shiyi jia zhu Sunzi jiaoli* C.261–63 ("Jiudi"). Concluding the observation with a jingly rhymed couplet may seem callous too: "Only after the host has stumbled into harm (*N-kˤat-s) can it produce victory out of defeat (*N-pˤrat-s)" 夫眾陷於害, 然後能為勝敗.

57. *Shiyi jia zhu Sunzi jiaoli* B.146 ("Junzheng").

58. For a study of this attitude in *Huainanzi* (which I dubbed "autistic"), see Goldin, *After Confucius*, 90–111.

## CHAPTER EIGHT. *XUNZI*

1. The source of this oft-repeated phrase is *Shiji* 74.2348.

2. For an overview of the problems surrounding Dong Zhongshu's dates, see Fukui, *Kandai Jukyō no shiteki kenkyū*, 387–404.

3. This is stated in the preface by Liu Xiang, conveniently included in *Xunzi jijie*, 558.

4. On the rise of Mencianism in this period, see Ommerborn, "Einflüsse des Menzius und seiner Theorie der Politik der Menschlichkeit (*renzheng*) in der Zeit vom 3. Jh. bis zum Ende der Tang-Zeit."

5. Han Yu, *Han Changli wenji jiaozhu*, 1.20–21 ("Du Xun" 讀荀), translated in Hartman, *Han Yü and the T'ang Search for Unity*, 181–82.

6. Zhu Xi's fullest exposition of his distaste for Xunzi appears in *Chuci houyu* 1.1a–2a (preface to "Chengxiang" 成相). See also Li Jingde, *Zhuzi yulei* 137.3255. It is, of course, possible that Song Neo-Confucians were deeply indebted to Xunzi even as they excoriated him. See esp. Dai Junren, *Meiyuan lunxue ji*, 411–20; and Dai Junren, *Meiyuan lunxue xuji*, 272–301; also Wyatt, *Recluse of Loyang*, 83–84 and 177.

7. For the important exception of Ling Tingkan 凌廷堪 (1755–1809), see Kai-wing Chow, *Rise of Confucian Ritualism in Late Imperial China*, 191–97.

8. See Hsiao, *Modern China and a New World*, 46–47 and 79.

9. Tan laid out his objections to Xunzi in §§ 29 and 30 of his *Renxue* 仁學; see the bilingual edition by Chan Sin-wai, *Exposition of Benevolence*, 146–52 (English) and 270–72 (Chinese). Cf. also Carsun Chang, *Development of Neo-Confucian Thought*, 2:423–24.

10. See Hao Chang, *Liang Ch'i-ch'ao and Intellectual Transition in China*, 74ff.; Carsun Chang, *Development of Neo-Confucian Thought*, 2:425; and Levenson, *Liang Ch'i-ch'ao and the Mind of Modern China*, 35.

11. Louie, *Inheriting Tradition*, 165–78, shows that the rehabilitation of Xunzi (along ideological lines) was already well underway during the first two decades of the People's Republic.

12. Just since 2000: Kline and Ivanhoe, *Virtue, Nature, and Moral Agency in the Xunzi*; Sato, *Confucian Quest for Order*; Cua, *Human Nature, Ritual, and History*; Janghee Lee, *Xunzi and Early Chinese Naturalism*; Hagen, *Philosophy of Xunz*; Stalnaker, *Overcoming Our Evil*; Hutton, *Xunzi*; Kline and Tiwald, *Ritual and Religion in the Xunzi*; Hutton, *Dao Companion to the Philosophy of Xunzi*; Siufu Tang, *Self-Realization through Confucian Learning*.

13. Cf. Lewis, *Writing and Authority in Early China*, 62–63.

14. For a lucid overview, see Hutton, "Does Xunzi Have a Consistent Theory of Human Nature?"; also Siufu Tang, *Self-Realization through Confucian Learning*, 51; and Goldin, *Rituals of the Way*, 6ff.

15. *Xunzi jijie* 17.23.435–36 ("Xing'e").

16. *Xunzi jijie* 17.23.439.

17. *Xunzi jijie* 16.22.412 ("Zhengming" 正名). Cf. *Xunzi* 22.5b: "*Xing* is what is wrought by Heaven" 性者，天之就也 (*Xunzi jijie* 16.22.428), i.e., not by human beings.

18. Note that this word often has a pejorative connotation in Classical Chinese ("forged" or "feigned"). Xunzi's usage must have surprised ancient readers.

19. *Xunzi jijie* 17.23.434–35 ("Xing'e").

20. *Xunzi jijie* 17.23.443. Cf. *Xunzi* 8.11.

21. Graham, *Disputers of the Tao*, 250. See also Kwong-loi Shun, *Mencius and Early Chinese Thought*, 222–31.

22. *Xunzi jijie* 13.19.346 ("Lilun").

23. *Xunzi jijie* 2.4.70 ("Rongru" 榮辱).

24. For examples of this view, see Perkins, *Heaven and Earth Are Not Humane*, 189–97; and Ebrey, *Confucianism and Family Rituals in Imperial China*, 26ff.

25. *Xunzi jijie* 5.9.164 ("Wangzhi" 王制).

26. Following the commentary of Yu Yue.

27. *Xunzi jijie* 3.5.78–79 ("Feixiang" 非相). Compare *Xunzi* 10.3a and 19.1c.

28. Cf. Yearley, "Xunzi," 92–101; and Ivanhoe, "Happy Symmetry."

29. *Xunzi jijie* 13.19.359–60 ("Lilun").

30. *Xunzi jijie* 13.19.372 and 373.

31. These accouterments coincide with the prescriptions in *Vestments of Mourning* (*Sangfu* 喪服), an ancient document currently found in the canonical collection called *Ceremonies and Rites* (*Yili* 儀禮), and I supply the explanatory phrase "hatband and waistband" on the basis of that text. Other commentarial explanations of *ju zhang* 苴杖 ("female nettle plant and staff") strike me as less convincing.

32. *Xunzi jijie* 14.20.379–80 ("Yuelun" 樂論).

33. This statement is difficult to construe, and there is a conspicuous lack of commentary about it. *Shu* 術 commonly means "technique"; perhaps Xunzi means to say that music ("sounds and tones, movement and quietude") is a technique for improving the *xing* and thus fulfilling the Way of Humanity. This would be in line with his general views. But as *shu* can also mean "to proceed" (it is interchangeable with *shu* 述), I render it here as "progression."

34. The meaning of *xi* 諰 is unclear here.

35. Compare *Xunzi* 22.5a: "All those who say that order depends on eliminating desires have no means of guiding desires, and thus are distressed that they have any desires at all. All those who say that order depends on reducing desires have no means of moderating desires, and thus are distressed that their desires are so many" 凡語治而待去欲者，無以道欲而困於有欲者也。凡語治而待寡欲者，無以節欲而困於多欲者也 (*Xunzi jijie* 16.22.426 ["Zhengming"]).

36. Xunzi himself does not provide any examples of disruptive or wholesome compositions. I infer a title like "Let's Plant in the Autumn and Harvest in the Spring" from the claim that good music should make the people "act in accord with the seasons" 以時順修 (below).

37. Cf. Cook, "Xun Zi on Ritual and Music," 21ff.; and Graham, *Disputers of the Tao*, 259ff.

38. Following the commentaries of Wang Xianqian 王先謙 (1842–1917) and Wang Yinzhi.

39. *Xunzi jijie* 14.20.380–81 ("Yuelun").

40. *Procedures of the Officials* sounds like the title of an authoritative text of some kind. These lines also appear in *Xunzi jijie* 5.9.167–68 ("Wangzhi").

41. By "Elegantiae" (*ya* 雅) Xunzi may mean either the section of the canonical *Odes* by that name, or the "elegant" music sanctioned by the Sages—or both, since these alternatives amount to essentially the same thing.

42. *Xunzi jijie* 11.17.318–19 ("Tianlun" 天論).

43. *Xunzi jijie* 11.17.306–8 ("Tianlun").

44. Or conceivably "for the way [that you have chosen] is such" (*qi dao ran* 其道然).

45. For this reason, *tian* in *Xunzi* is sometimes construed as akin to natural law and accordingly translated as "nature" or "Nature" (see the evenhanded discussion in David B. Wong, "Xunzi's Metaethics," 142–47), but I prefer "Heaven" in order to retain the rhetorical overtones of archaic religion and politics, which postulated a notion of divine-right monarchy by Heaven's Mandate.

46. *Xunzi jijie* 11.17.311 ("Tianlun").

47. *Xunzi jijie* 11.17.311 ("Tianlun").

48. Cf. Fraser, "Language and Logic in the *Xunzi*," 297–300; and Kanaya, *Kanaya Osamu Chūgoku shisō ronshū*, 2:117–18.

49. *Xunzi jijie* 11.17.308 and 310–11 ("Tianlun").

50. Xunzi appears to borrow this term from *Zhuangzi* (see p. 140).

51. *Xunzi jijie* 11.17.317 ("Tianlun").

52. Hagen, *Philosophy of Xunzi*, 17–40. See also Siufu Tang, *Self-Realization through Confucian Learning*, 59 and 114–21; and Janghee Lee, *Xunzi and Early Chinese Naturalism*, 71ff.

53. *Xunzi jijie* 4.8.122 ("Ruxiao" 儒效).

54. *Xunzi jijie* 15.21.386 ("Jiebi" 解蔽).

55. *Xunzi jijie* 15.21.399–400. For notes on this difficult passage, see Goldin, "Theme of the Primacy of the Situation in Classical Chinese Philosophy and Rhetoric," 25n72. Compare *Xunzi* 5.5: "In antiquity and the present day, there is but one measure. Categories do not diverge; however much time has passed, the patterns are the same" 古今一度也。類不悖，雖久同理 (*Xunzi jijie* 3.5.82 ["Feixiang"]).

56. *Xunzi jijie* 16.22.430 ("Zhengming").

57. Cf. Hutton, "Ethics in the *Xunzi*," 81–83.

58. *Xunzi jijie* 11.17.313 ("Tianlun").

59. Xunzi's idea of "human portents" is adumbrated in *Mencius* 2A.4 and 4A.8, which attribute the same line to *Taijia* 太甲: "When Heaven makes calamities, one can still avoid them, but who makes his own calamities cannot survive" 天作孽，猶可違；自作孽，不可活 (*Mengzi zhengyi* 7.225 and 14.500). The received *Canon of Documents* includes a chapter entitled "Taijia," and this passage is included in it, but the chapter is considered spurious.

60. *Xunzi jijie* 11.17.314 ("Tianlun").

61. I.e.: (1) lack of separation between internal and external, male and female; (2) friction between father and son, superior and inferior; and (3) crime and hardship.

62. E.g., Radcliffe-Brown, *Structure and Function in Primitive Society*, 157ff.; and Campany, "Xunzi and Durkheim as Theorists of Ritual Practice." For objections, see Robson, "Ritual and Tradition in Xunzi and Dōgen," 140; and Goldin, *Rituals of the Way*, 64–65.

63. *Xunzi jijie* 11.17.316 ("Tianlun").

64. For inquiries into Xunzi's military thought, see, e.g., Meyer and Wilson, "*Sunzi Bingfa* as History and Theory," 106ff.; Lewis, *Sanctioned Violence in Early China*, 66–67 and 130–31; and Oliver, *Communication and Culture in Ancient India and China*, 205ff. Lloyd and Sivin, *Way and the Word*, 66, write that the supposed debate is really "a form of entertainment for courtiers," a judgment influenced by the structure of the chapter (but no other evidence).

65. This point evidently escaped Needham and Gawlikowski, "Chinese Literature on the Art of War," 65, who referred to this chapter as Xunzi's own account of the debate.

66. Scholars disagree over Xunzi's dates. Knoblock, *Xunzi*, 1:1–35, argues for ca. 310–ca. 210 BC.

67. The surname Sun (i.e., instead of Xun) may have been used to avoid the taboo-name of Emperor Xuan of the Han 漢宣帝 (r. 76–48 BC), who changed his personal name to Xun 詢 in 64 BC. This suggestion is disputed—but if it is true, the consequence would have to be that someone (perhaps Liu Xiang) had a hand in editing the "Yibing" chapter after 64 BC. See Knoblock, *Xunzi*, 1:233–39.

68. *Xunzi jijie* 10.15.266 ("Yibing").

69. Knoblock, *Xunzi*, 2:331n4. Compare, generally, Raphals, "*Sunzi* versus *Xunzi*," 215ff.

70. *Xunzi jijie* 10.15.269 ("Yibing").

71. *Xunzi jijie* 10.15.275.

72. Cf. Wai-yee Li, *Readability of the Past in Early Chinese Historiography*, 272–73; and Schaberg, *Patterned Past*, 251.

73. *Xunzi jijie* 10.15.270.

74. *Xunzi jijie* 10.15.281.

75. Cf. William S-Y. Wang, "Language in China," 186ff.

76. Cf. Fraser, "Language and Logic in the *Xunzi*," 293–96.

77. *Xunzi jijie* 16.22.420 ("Zhengming").

78. *Xunzi jijie* 16.22.422 ("Zhengming").

79. *Xunzi jijie* 3.6.94 ("Fei shi'er zi" 非十二子).

80. *Xunzi jijie* 16.22.414 ("Zhengming").

81. Following the commentary of Wang Niansun.

82. Following the commentary of Yang Liang.

83. *Xunzi jijie* 16.22.415–16 ("Zhengming").

84. E.g., Hagen, *Philosophy of Xunzi*, 59–84.

85. *Xunzi jijie* 16.22.423 ("Zhengming").

86. On the technical term *shi* 實, see Graham, *Later Mohist Logic, Ethics and Science*, 196–99.

87. *Xunzi jijie* 15.21.395–96 ("Jiebi").

88. Cf. Aaron Stalnaker, "Aspects of Xunzi's Engagement with Early Daoism"; Goldin, *Rituals of the Way*, 22ff.; and Yearley, "Hsün Tzu on the Mind."

89. *Zhuangzi jishi* 1B.2.112 ("Qiwu lun").

90. Following the commentary of Hao Yixing 郝懿行 (1757–1825).

91. *Xunzi jijie* 15.21.397–98 ("Jiebi").

92. For recent overviews of this term, see Small, "Daoist Exploration of *shenming*"; and Szabó, "Term *shenming*."

93. *Xunzi jijie* 16.22.412 ("Zhengming").

94. *Xunzi jijie* 16.22.428.

95. Though they are homophones in Modern Mandarin, *li* 理 (Old Chinese *mə. rəʔ), "pattern," and *li* 禮 (*rˤijʔ), "ritual," had different Old Chinese vowels and are un-related. Speakers of later forms of Chinese sometimes tried to connect them, however; e.g., Wang Shouren, *Wang Yangming quanji*, 7.271 (*Liji zuanyan xu* 禮記纂言序): *Li* is *li* 禮也者，理也.

96. For thoughts on whether this constitutes a mind-body problem, see Goldin, "Mind-Body Problem in the *Zhuangzi*?," 235–36.

97. Cf. *Xunzi* 8.11 and 23.5b.

98. Cf. Goldin, *Rituals of the Way*, 16–17. For similar analogies (the heart-mind is to the person as the lord is to the state) in *Guanzi*, see *Guanzi jiaozhu* 11.31.583 ("Junchen xia" 君臣下), 13.36.759 ("Xinshu shang" 心術上), and 17.52.988 ("Qichen qizhu" 七臣七主). Also two general studies: Raphals, "Body and Mind in Early China and Greece," 148–51; and Wang Jianwen, "Guojun yiti," 251ff.

99. Fields et al., *Seesaw*, 54.

## CHAPTER NINE. *HAN FEIZI*

1. E.g., Keane, "More Theses on the Philosophy of History."

2. *Shiji* 63.2146–55.

3. Compare Shakespeare's "Uneasy lies the head that wears a crown" (*Henry IV, Part II*, 3.1.31).

4. *Han Feizi xin jiaozhu* 5.17.321–22 ("Beinei" 備內").

5. See *Shiji* 43.1813–15.

6. See *Guoyu jijie* 8.275–81 ("Fan zi Jisang" 反自稷桑).

7. E.g., *Han Feizi xin jiaozhu* 2.6.107 ("Youdu" 有度).

8. *Han Feizi xin jiaozhu* 2.6.100.

9. See Goldin, *After Confucius*, 185n6.

10. E.g., Van Norden, "Han Fei and Confucianism."

11. Nor do I think the usage of *gong* in *Lüshi chunqiu* (e.g., *Lüshi chunqiu xin jiaoshi* 1.44–46 ["Guigong" 貴公]), to which the *Han Feizi* is often compared, is identical. In *Lüshi chunqiu*, which envisions a single ruler governing a united and uncontested empire, the interests of the sovereign and those of all humanity begin to converge. *Han Feizi* still conceives of the ruler as but one competitor among many.

12. *Han Feizi xin jiaozhu* 19.49.1105 ("Wudu" 五蠹). For the clever (but palaeographically incorrect) graphic interpretation underlying Han Fei's argument, see Goldin, *After Confucius*, 59.

13. *Han Feizi xin jiaozhu* 2.8.170 ("Yangquan" 揚權).

14. Goldin, "Persistent Misconceptions about Chinese 'Legalism,'" 92. The Mohist Canons explain *fa* as instruments, including "such three things as ideas, compasses, and circles" 意、規、員三也 (*Mozi jiaozhu* 10A.40/42.470), that help determine whether something conforms to a standard (Graham, *Later Mohist Logic, Ethics and Science*, 316–17, A 70). An object is round, for example, if it conforms to a circle. Compare *Mozi jiaozhu* 1.4.28–30 ("Fayi" 法儀), which discusses *fa* as models, inspired by those used by craftsmen, that can be used to bring order to the world.

15. Following the commentary of Chen Qiyou, *Han Feizi xin jiaozhu* 2.6.96n17.

16. *Han Feizi xin jiaozhu* 2.6.91–92 ("Youdu").

17. I borrow this phrase from Watson, *Han Feizi*, 82.

18. *Han Feizi xin jiaozhu* 4.13.273 ("Heshi" 和氏).

19. Cf. Galvany, "Beyond the Rule of Rules," 94ff. Other early texts on statecraft echo this theme, e.g., *Shenzi* (Thompson, *Shen tzu Fragments*, §§29–32), and the Mawangdui text *Cheng* 稱 (Wei Qipeng, *Mawangdui Hanmu boshu* Huangdi shu *jianzheng*, 202). When the loyal farmer Bu Shi 卜式 (fl. 124–110 BC) offered half his wealth to the gov-

ernment as a contribution toward defense expenditures, declining all honorary compensation, the realist chancellor, Gongsun Hong 公孫弘 (d. 121 BC), objected: "This is contrary to human instinct. Such anomalous subjects cannot [assist] in governance, and bring disorder upon *fa*" 此非人情。不軌之臣，不可以為化而亂法 (*Shiji* 30.1432; *Hanshu* 58.2625).

20. *Han Feizi xin jiaozhu* 2.7.120–21 ("Erbing"). Compare *Han Feizi xin jiaozhu* 2.9.190 ("Bajian" 八姦): "With respect to dispensing rewards, unlocking discretionary funds, or opening the heaping granaries, all things that benefit the populace must emerge from the lord. Do not allow ministers to privatize rewards" 其於德施也，縱禁財，發墳倉，利於民者，必出於君，不使人臣私其德.

21. See *Shiji* 32.1512.

22. Zihan went on to usurp the throne and rule as Lord Ticheng 剔成. Cf. Yang Kuan, *Zhanguo shiliao biannian jizheng*, 310–13. This is not the same Zihan from Song who lived two centuries earlier (and with whom he is often confused).

23. *Han Feizi xin jiaozhu* 2.5.81 ("Zhudao" 主道).

24. *Han Feizi xin jiaozhu* 2.6.91 ("Youdu").

25. *Han Feizi xin jiaozhu* 2.6.111.

26. *Han Feizi xin jiaozhu* 4.13.275 ("Heshi").

27. See, e.g., Lewis, *Sanctioned Violence in Early China*, 80–94; Dalby, "Revenge and the Law in Traditional China"; Ch'ü, *Law and Society in Traditional China*, 78–87; and Lien-sheng Yang, "Concept of *pao* as a Basis for Social Relations in China."

28. *Han Feizi xin jiaozhu* 19.49.1102 ("Wudu"). Cf. *Han Feizi xin jiaozhu* 18.48.1082 ("Bajing" 八經): "Under the *dao* of an enlightened ruler, ministers are unable to achieve glory by practicing righteousness" 明主之道，臣不得以行義成榮.

29. *Han Feizi xin jiaozhu* 19.49.1104–5 ("Wudu").

30. Following the commentary of Wang Xianshen 王先慎 (1859–1922).

31. *Han Feizi xin jiaozhu* 19.50.1147 ("Xianxue" 顯學).

32. The basis of this belief is unknown; some commentators suspect that the text is garbled here.

33. *Han Feizi xin jiaozhu* 5.17.323 ("Beinei").

34. *Han Feizi xin jiaozhu* 1.5.66 ("Zhudao").

35. *Han Feizi xin jiaozhu* 1.5.81.

36. E.g., *Shangjun shu zhuizhi* 2.6.50 ("Suandi" 算地): "Make [administrative] appointments by sorting their work and elevating the meritorious" 論勞舉功以任之.

37. The statement in *Zhuangzi jishi* 1A.1.17 ("Xiaoyao you") that "the Sage has no name/title" 聖人无名 might be an allusion to this discourse. The Sage does not permit himself to be charged with any particular task. The Nameless One (*wuming ren* 無/无名人), a hermit who appears in *Zhuangzi jishi* 3B.7.292–94 ("Ying diwang"), and refuses to answer questions about statecraft, might be just such a person.

38. E.g., Angell, *Truth about Drug Companies*.

39. *Han Feizi xin jiaozhu* 2.7.126 ("Erbing"). By contrast, *Han Feizi* 18 refers solely to ministers whose budgets exceed their bad-faith estimates, e.g., *Han Feizi xin jiaozhu* 5.18.330 ("Nanmian" 南面): "When they come before you, they speak of small [expenses], but once they have retired, the outlays turn out to be great" 其進言少，其退費多.

40. Much of the same logic applies to the game of poker (e.g., Caro, *Caro's Book of Poker Tells*). Similarly, in chess, some players at the highest level have adopted a style "to

have no evident plan," in response to the ability of strong computers to analyze and then demolish specific strategies (Max, "Prince's Gambit").

41. *Han Feizi xin jiaozhu* 2.8.156 ("Yangquan").

42. *Han Feizi xin jiaozhu* 2.9.190 ("Bajian").

43. *Han Feizi xin jiaozhu* 13.34.782–83 ("Wai chushuo you shang" 外儲說右上).

44. *Han Feizi xin jiaozhu* 17.40.945 ("Nanshi" 難勢).

45. *Han Feizi xin jiaozhu* 19.49.1085 ("Wudu").

46. *Han Feizi xin jiaozhu* 19.49.1097.

47. *Han Feizi xin jiaozhu* 19.49.1109. Cf. *Han Feizi xin jiaozhu* 19.50.1141–42 ("Xianxue"): "If we were to rely on others to do good in our behalf, within the borders there are not ten [such people]" 恃人之為吾善也，境內不什數.

48. Cf. Yang Yi, *Han Feizi huanyuan*, 75–84.

49. Li Linhao and Chen Sufang, "Shixi yuan zi *Han Feizi* de chengyu."

50. See Creel, *Shen Pu-hai.*

51. Thompson, Shen tzu *Fragments*, §§61–65.

52. The *Shenzi* fragments allude to lotteries for horses and fields elsewhere too (Thompson, Shen tzu *Fragments*, §24). Little is known about the practice.

53. Cf. Harris, Shenzi Fragments, 46–56.

54. Hunter, "Difficulty with 'The Difficulties of Persuasion,'" 184–85, notes that *Xunzi* 5.7–8 (*Xunzi jijie* 3.5.84–85 ["Feixiang"]) contains a section discussing "the general difficulties of persuasion" (*fan shui zhi nan* 凡說之難). Perhaps this was Han Fei's model. See also *Xunzi jijie* 19.27.516 ("Dalüe" 大略): "A gentleman finds persuasion difficult" 君子難說.

55. *Han Feizi xin jiaozhu* 4.12.261 ("Shuinan"). Just before this, the text says: "If [the ruler] has a desire to show off his wisdom and ability, present him with different proposals of the same general type, so as to leave him a wide swath; this will make him support proposals tending toward our side—but pretend that you are unaware, so that he exercises his own wisdom" 有欲矜以智能，則為之舉異事之同類者，多為之地，使之資說於我，而佯不知也，以資其智. Cf. *Han Feizi xin jiaozhu* 18.48.1075 ("Bajing"): "[Ministers] offer a multitude of suggestions in order to effectuate their wisdom; they cause the ruler to choose one among them, and thereby escape conviction" 眾諫以效智故，使君自取一以避罪. Inducing the ruler to make a predictable decision by presenting him with a crafty array of pseudo-options is reminiscent of the so-called magician's choice, or equivoque (see, e.g., Goldstein, *Verbal Control*).

56. *Han Feizi xin jiaozhu* 4.14.278 ("Jian jie shi chen" 姦劫弒臣).

57. *Han Feizi xin jiaozhu* 4.12.266–67 ("Shuinan").

58. There is one other ancient source for this affair, namely *Zhushu jinian* B.12b, which states that "Zheng put to death its grandee Guan Qisi" 鄭殺其大夫關其思 in 763 BC (without explanation).

59. A similar version of the tale of the wise son appears in *Han Feizi xin jiaozhu* 8.23.520 ("Shuilin xia" 說林下).

60. The final comment calls to mind the statement by René Descartes (1596–1650) in *Discours de la méthode*: "Car ce n'est pas assez d'avoir l'esprit bon, mais le principal est de l'appliquer bien" ("For it is not enough to have a good mind; what is crucial is to apply it well"; *Œuvres de Descartes*, 1:122). Cf. *Mencius* 2A.1: "The people of Qi have a saying: 'Even if you have wisdom and cleverness, it is better to take advantage of situations'" 齊人有言曰：「雖有智慧，不如乘勢」(*Mengzi zhengyi* 6.183).

61. The term "implicature" was coined by Grice (*Studies in the Way of Words*, 24). See also Levinson, *Pragmatics*, 127ff.; and Gazdar, *Pragmatics*, 49–50.

62. Schaberg, "Command and the Content of Tradition," 32, notes provocatively that concerns related to implicature may have influenced Chinese writing as early as the oracle-bone inscriptions, which routinely included "narrative material" that "provides a setting and a cast of characters for the ritual of divination." Schaberg adds: "The words of the divinatory charge are intelligible and valid only when they are framed by a knowledge of the conditions of their utterance."

63. Notably Fu, *China's Legalists*.

64. Arendt, *Origins of Totalitarianism*, 397. Cf. also 461: "Before mass leaders seize the power to fit reality to their lies, their propaganda is marked by its extreme contempt for facts as such, for in their opinion fact depends entirely on the power of man who can fabricate it."

65. Here I follow the definitions of "totalitarianism" and "authoritarianism" in Huntington, *Third Wave*, 12.

66. E.g., Rong, *Han Feizi kaozheng*, 31a–33a.

67. Goldin, *After Confucius*, 62.

68. If "The Difficulties of Persuasion" had been addressed to the sovereign, it might have looked somewhat like "Critiquing Speech" ("Nanyan" 難言, *Han Feizi xin jiaozhu* 1.3.47–59): this chapter tries to help the king understand the hazards facing his courtiers, which prevent them from speaking too openly. Cf. Hunter, "Difficulty with 'The Difficulties of Persuasion,'" 171.

69. Cf. Lundahl, *Han Fei Zi*, 92–113.

70. *Han Feizi xin jiaozhu* 2.6.111 ("Youdu").

71. Cf. Pines, "From Historical Evolution to the End of History," 36.

72. *Han Feizi xin jiaozhu* 5.18.334 ("Nanmian").

73. *Han Feizi xin jiaozhu* 19.49.1085 ("Wudu").

74. E.g., *Han Feizi xin jiaozhu* 5.19.359 ("Shixie" 飾邪).

75. E.g., *Han Feizi xin jiaozhu* 6.20.400 ("Jie Lao" 解老).

76. *Shiji* 63.2146.

77. The name Huang-Lao is explained in *Lunheng jiaoshi* 18.54.781 ("Ziran" 自然). Frustratingly, it was used by different authors to mean different things (Emmerich, "Bemerkungen zu Huang und Lao in der frühen Han-Zeit").

78. Qiu, *Wenshi conggao*, 81–89, trenchantly objects to the widespread identification of the Huang-Lao manuscripts from Mawangdui as the lost classical text called *The Four Canons of Huang-Lao* (*Huang-Lao sijing* 黄老四經). But he does not challenge the consensus that they exemplify the *philosophy* of Huang-Lao.

79. Peerenboom, *Law and Morality in Ancient China*, 27.

80. *Han Feizi xin jiaozhu* 1.5.66 ("Zhudao").

81. The most famous example is probably *Xunzi jijie* 11.17.306 ("Tianlun"): "There is a constancy to Heaven's processes" 天行有常 (see pp. 182–83). Another illustrative line comes from the Guodian manuscripts: "Heaven lays down a great constancy with which to rationalize human relations" 天降大常，以理人倫 (Cook, *Bamboo Texts of Guodian*, 2:622); in context, it is clear that this "great constancy" is the *dao* (Goldin, *After Confucius*, 44).

82. "Zhudao" can also mean "Making the *dao* One's Chief Concern."

83. *Shiji* 63.2147.

84. Yang Yi, *Han Feizi huanyuan*, 18–26, argues for the latter.

85. Cf. Pines, "Submerged by Absolute Power," 70–71.

86. *Han Feizi xin jiaozhu* 1.5.66 ("Zhudao").

87. *Han Feizi xin jiaozhu* 2.8.145 ("Yangquan").

88. For the case of *Huainanzi*, see Major et al., *Huainanzi*, 13–22. Similarly, *Zhuangzi jishi* 7B.21.714 ("Tian Zifang"), states that beasts that have attained perfect equanimity "may make small changes but do not lose their great constancy" 行小變而不失其大常 也, i.e., their most basic patterns of behavior. (As above, "great constancy" can also refer to the *dao*.)

## APPENDIX. WHAT IS *QI* 氣 AND WHY WAS IT A GOOD IDEA?

1. For a good overview, see Li Cunshan, "Differentiation of the Meaning of '*qi*' on Several Levels"; also Takeda Kenji, "Zhanguo shidai de qi gainian."

2. Etymology refers to the history of a *word*, reconstructed according to linguistic principles, not a set of speculations about the *graphic components used to represent that word* in the writing system (a common misconception in Chinese studies). Schuessler, *ABC Etymological Dictionary of Old Chinese*, 1–28, is a succinct and authoritative discussion.

3. Gardner, *Learning to Be a Sage*, esp. 50.

4. In phrases like "flood-like *qi*" (*haoran zhi qi* 浩然之氣, *Mencius* 2A.2), we could be dealing with either of the two.

5. Baxter and Sagart, *Old Chinese*, 43–46, building on earlier suggestions by Pan Wuyun, "Houyin kao."

6. Two rarer words are easily recognized as cognates: *kai* 嘅/慨 (*C.qʰˤəp-s), "to sigh," and *kai* 愾 (*qʰˤəp-s), "to sigh, to grow angry."

7. For example, Schuessler, *ABC Etymological Dictionary of Old Chinese*, reconstructed (s.vv.) *qi* 氣 as *kə(t)s [*sic*] and *xi* 吸 as *həp, because his system does not include a uvular series. More recently (private communication), he has reinterpreted *qi* as *khəps, i.e., *xi* with a *k- prefix and *-s suffix. He also regards the aspirated initial as an indication that the whole word family is sound-symbolic for breathing; cf. his "Tenues aspiratae im Altchinesischen," 160.

8. For example, Needham et al., *Science and Civilisation in China*, 2:228, like so many others, follows the opinion of Xu Shen 許慎 (d. after AD 120) that 气 is a pictograph of vapor (*Shuowen jiezi jizhu* 1A.77). Perhaps Xu Shen was right; this still does not tell us anything about the *word*. A fair account of palaeographic evidence (though without any consideration of linguistics) is Maekawa, "Kōkotsubun, kimbun ni mieru ki," esp. 14–17.

9. Ma Jixing, *Mawangdui gu yishu kaoshi*, 1039.

10. Such techniques were branded as "sexual vampirism" by Van Gulik (*Erotic Colour Prints of the Ming Period*, 2:12). See the discussion in Goldin, "Introduction," in Van Gulik, *Sexual Life in Ancient China*, xxi–xxii.; more recently, Goldin, "Cultural and Religious Background of Sexual Vampirism in Ancient China"; Sakade and Umekawa, "*Ki*" *no shisō kara miru Dōkyō no bōchūjutsu*; and Li Jianmin, *Fangshu, yixue, lishi*, 66–80.

11. The unaspirated doublet *yi'ai* 唈僾 (*qˤəp qˤəp-s), meaning "to breathe uncom-

fortably," is attested in *Xunzi jijie* 13.19.376 ("Lilun"); see also *Mao-Shi zhengyi* 18B.559a ("Sangrou" 桑柔); and *Erya zhushu* 3.2528b ("Shi yan" 釋言). I cannot explain why *xiqi* 翕氣 is aspirated and *yi'ai* is not, but once again Schuessler may be right that all these words are onomatopoeic ("Tenues aspiratae im Altchinesischen," 160).

12. *Lunyu jishi* 15.520.

13. *Lunyu jishi* 19.651.

14. *Lunyu jishi* 20.694.

15. *Mozi jiaozhu* 1.6.46 ("Ciguo" 辭過). Compare *Mozi jiaozhu* 6.21.249 ("Jieyong zhong" 節用中): "When it is enough to fill the emptiness and sustain the *qi*, to strengthen the thighs and forearms, and to make the ears and eyes keen of hearing and keen of sight, stop [eating]" 足以充虛繼氣，強股肱，使耳目聰明，則止.

16. *Yanzi chunqiu jishi* 3.142 ("Jinggong wen yu shan Qiguo zhi zheng yi gan bawang Yanzi dui yi guan wei ju" 景公問欲善齊國之政以干霸王晏子對以官未具).

17. *Guanzi jiaozhu* 13.37.778 ("Xinshu xia" 心術下). Compare *Huainanzi jishi* 1.82 ("Yuandao" 原道): "*Qi* is what fills living things" 氣者生之充也.

18. *Zhuangzi jishi* 7B.22.733 ("Zhi bei you" 知北遊).

19. *Mengzi zhengyi* 27.933.

20. *Liji zhengyi* 47.1594a (Jiyi" 祭義).

21. *Shiji* 118.3090.

22. *Chunqiu fanlu yizheng* 16.77.447–48 ("Xun tian zhi dao" 循天之道).

23. The three most detailed studies (in any language) come to similar general conclusions: Loewe, *Dong Zhongshu*, 191–224; Queen, *From Chronicle to Canon*, 39–112; and Arbuckle, "Restoring Dong Zhongshu," 315–542.

24. Queen and Major, *Luxuriant Gems of the Spring and Autumn*, 27–28, list this section of the chapter under "Works by Dong Zhongshu or members of his immediate circle, including first-generation disciples (ca. 130–100 B.C.E.)," but I do not see any grounds for such certitude.

25. *Hanshu* 30.1725. Cf. Xu Jianwei, Shuoyuan *yanjiu*, 24–25.

26. For possible connections between Gongsun Nizi and the recently discovered Guodian manuscripts (with references to further information about Gongsun Nizi's identity, which need not be repeated here), see Goldin, *After Confucius*, 56–57.

27. *Liji zhengyi* 52.1625b: "If one brings about equilibrium and harmony, Heaven and Earth will attain their respective positions and the Myriad Creatures will be nourished thereby" 致中和，天地位焉，萬物育焉. It may be significant that the extant "Record of Music" ("Yueji" 樂記) uses the phrase as well (*Liji zhengyi* 39.1545a), because some commentators state that Gongsun Nizi was the compiler of a text by this name: e.g., Zhang Shoujie 張守節 (fl. AD 737) in his commentary to *Shiji* 24.1234n11. Cf. Cook, "Yue ji," 3–7.

28. As in texts like *Heguanzi huijiao jizhu* 5.73 ("Huanliu" 環流): "There is nothing that does not emerge from *qi*" 莫不發於氣.

29. E.g., *Lüshi chunqiu xin jiaoshi* 20.1382 ("Dayu" 達鬱): "It is desirable that the refined *qi* circulate" 精氣欲其行也. One of the most important palaeographic sources for the notion of circulating *qi* is an inscribed jade that has been called *Xingqi yuming* 行氣玉銘; see, e.g., Chen Banghuai, *Yide ji*, 128–37.

30. *Lüshi chunqiu xin jiaoshi* 3.174 ("Huandao" 圜道).

31. E.g., Aihe Wang, *Cosmology and Political Culture in Early China*; Major, *Heaven*

*and Earth in Early Han Thought*; Sivin, *Traditional Medicine in Contemporary China*; and Porkert, *Theoretical Foundations of Chinese Medicine*. Gu Jiegang, "Wude zhongshi shuo xia de zhengzhi he lishi," is still relevant.

32. There were others as well; for example, the normal progression of the seasons—Wood, Fire, Metal, and Water, with Earth remaining in the center—does not conform to either the *xiangsheng* or *xiangke* sequences. For more on the various attested sequences, see Eberhard, "Beiträge zur kosmologischen Spekulation Chinas in der Han-Zeit."

33. The difficulty that most of China, then as now, goes through four natural seasons (spring 春, summer 夏, autumn 秋, and winter 冬), rather than five, was overcome in some texts by the insertion of a factitious fifth season, as mandated by theory. See Rickett, *Guanzi*, 1:151–66.

34. For the example of economic cycles based on phases of *qi*, see my "Economic Cycles and Price Theory in Early Chinese Texts."

35. Cf. Li Jingwei and Zhang Zhibin, *Zhongyixue sixiangshi*, 12–14.

36. Guo Moruo et al., *Jiaguwen heji*, no. 822a.

37. Guo Moruo et al., *Jiaguwen heji*, no. 2235a1.

38. For another example (from *Zhuangzi*), see Leder, "Ein geistreicher Exorzismus im *Zhuangzi* 19,6."

39. The episode is dated to 581 BC, but the text is probably from the fourth century. I have discussed the date of the *Zuozhuan* in "Hermeneutics of Emmentaler." An evenhanded survey of the issue is Wai-yee Li, *Readability of the Past in Early Chinese Historiography*, 33–59.

40. *Chunqiu Zuozhuan zhu*, 2:849–50 (Cheng 成 10 = 581 BC).

41. Cf. Unschuld, "Die Anfänge der chinesischen Medizin," 149–52; Zhu Jianping, *Zhongguo yixueshi yanjiu*, 70–72; and Li Jingwei and Zhang Zhibin, *Zhongyixue sixiangshi*, 62–83.

42. *Chunqiu Zuozhuan zhu*, 4:1222 (Zhao 昭 1 = 541 BC).

43. The Five Measures are variously construed as either the five tones of the pentatonic scale or five fifths of the calendar year.

44. Contrast the scheme in *Lingshu jiangyi* 4.8.199ff. ("Benshen" 本神), where disorder can be the result of either abnormal "fullness" (*shi* 實) or "emptiness" (*xu* 虛), i.e., not simply excess.

45. *Suwen cizhu jishu* 1.1.20–22 ("Shanggu tianzhen lun" 上古天真論).

46. Compare the translations in Unschuld and Tessenow, *Huang Di nei jing su wen*, 1:32–33; and Sivin, *Traditional Medicine in Contemporary China*, 98.

47. *Lingshu jiangyi* 19.66.886 ("Baibing shi sheng" 百病始生).

48. On this figure, see, e.g., Zhu Jianping, *Zhongguo yixueshi yanjiu*, 1–8.

49. Compare the translations in Unschuld, *Huang Di Nei Jing Ling Shu*, 604; and Sivin, *Traditional Medicine in Contemporary China*, 100; see also Sivin's reasoning for the punctuation followed here (101n9).

50. E.g., *Lüshi chunqiu xin jiaoshi* 3.146 ("Xianji" 先己): "By renewing the refined *qi* every day and completely expelling deviant *qi*, one will attain one's Heaven-allotted years" 精氣日新，邪氣盡去，及其天年.

51. Kuriyama, *Expressiveness of the Body and the Divergence of Greek and Chinese Medicine*, 236, writes that wind and *qi* "were frequently interchangeable," but this is misleading; a more accurate statement would be that wind is (sometimes) construed as one type of *qi*. Simplifications and misrepresentations of this kind undermine Kuriyama's

book. For a fuller account of the relationship between *qi* and wind, see Lewis, *Sanctioned Violence in Early China*, 214–21.

52. *Ke* is the standard term for an invading force in military manuals; e.g., *Shiyi jia zhu Sunzi jiaoli* C.246ff. ("Jiudi").

53. I hesitate to attribute the diagnosis to Chunyu Yi personally because of recent analyses of the text demonstrating its composite origin. See esp. Elisabeth Hsu, *Pulse Diagnosis in Early Chinese Medicine*, 49–61; also Brown, *Art of Medicine in Early China*, 70–83. For the purposes of this paper, the idea itself is more important than the identity of its author.

54. *Shiji* 105.2812.

55. *Lunheng jiaoshi* 20.62.871 ("Lunsi" 論死).

56. Cf. Goldin, "Consciousness of the Dead as a Philosophical Problem in Ancient China," 81–82.

57. Cf. Raphals, *Divination and Prediction in Early China and Ancient Greece*, 317–21. Illness is construed straightforwardly as the intervention of ghosts (justified or otherwise) in diverse Warring States texts, including *Mozi jiaozhu* 7.27.297–98 ("Tianzhi zhong"); and *Han Feizi xin jiaozhu* 6.20.402–3 ("Jie Lao").

58. See Strickmann, *Chinese Magical Medicine*, 23–39; Li Jianmin, "Contagion and Its Consequences"; and Sivin, *Traditional Medicine in Contemporary China*, 102–6.

59. Ōfuchi Ninji, *Shoki no Dōkyō*, 87–98, remains crucial.

60. Cf. Strickmann, *Chinese Magical Medicine*, 72ff.; also Mollier, "Visions of Evil," 75. Consider also *Chunqiu Zuozhuan zhu*, 1:196–97 (Zhuang 莊 14 = 680 BC), where monsters such as serpents are explained as the product of people's fearful *qi*.

61. Ma Jixing, *Mawangdui gu yishu kaoshi*, 361.

62. Ma Jixing, *Mawangdui gu yishu kaoshi*, 414.

63. On the Pace of Yu, both Schafer, *Pacing the Void*, 238–42; and Granet, *Danses et légendes de la Chine ancienne*, 549–69, are still useful, even though neither could have known about the Mawangdui manuscripts.

64. On this concept, see, e.g., Luo Xinhui, "Zhoudai tianming guannian de fazhan yu shanbian"; Deng Peiling, *Tianming, guishen yu zhudao*, 30–48; Shaughnessy, "Western Zhou History," 313–17; and Kominami, "Temmei to toku." The discussion in Creel, *Origins of Statecraft in China*, 93–100, is marred by his conception of the political system as feudalistic.

65. *Shangshu jiaoshi yilun*, 3:1512.

66. For this term, see, e.g., Takeuchi, "Sei Shū kimbun chū no 'tenshi' ni tsuite."

67. For example, An Zuozhang and Meng Xiangcai, *Qin shihuangdi dazhuan*, 432ff., discuss the First Emperor's cosmological views, which do not seem to have been centered on a notion of Heaven's Mandate.

68. *Lüshi chunqiu xin jiaoshi* 13.682–83 ("Yingtong" 應同).

69. *Shiji* 6.237.

70. Cf. Louton, "Concepts of Comprehensiveness and Historical Change in the *Lü-shih ch'un-ch'iu*," 106ff.; and He Lingxu, *Lüshi chunqiu de zhengzhi lilun*, 156–63. The final line ("the sequence will come full circle and shift back to Earth") would seem to contradict Puett's suggestion "that the first emperor believed that, having attained the fifth and final power, the Qin marked the end of the era begun by Huangdi [黃帝]. There would, then, never be a return to the power of earth" (*Ambivalence of Creation*, 144). Pines, "Messianic Emperor," 271, endorses Puett's opinion.

71. *Guanzi jiaozhu* 16.49.931.

72. *Guanzi jiaozhu* 16.49.937.

73. Cf. Graziani, "Subject and the Sovereign"; and Puett, *To Become a God*. The first great study in any Western language was Maspero, *Taoism and Chinese Religion*. Qiu, *Wenshi conggao*, 43–44, argues that such systems cannot be purely materialistic. I disagree and read *Neiye* as arguing that rectifying the material substance of the body leads to improved sensory and cognitive functioning (which only *appear* magical to those who do not comprehend the basis).

74. This is the vigorous contention of Roth, *Original Tao*, 109–23.

75. For an introduction to this immense field, see Needham et al., *Science and Civilisation in China*, 5:142–81; also Kohn with Yoshinobu Sakade, *Taoist Meditation and Longevity Techniques*.

76. Sivin has analyzed the few surviving fragments in his *Medicine, Philosophy and Religion in Ancient China*, chap. 4 ("The Myth of the Naturalists"). He adds the insight that the Qin model, whereby Water *qi* must replace the Fire *qi* of Zhou (examined above), is borrowed from Zou Yan.

77. *Shiji* 74.2344.

78. Cf. Needham et al., *Science and Civilisation in China*, 4.1:134–41. Not surprisingly, the five tones of the pentatonic scale were eventually associated with the Five Phases (e.g., Pokora, *Hsin-lun (New Treatise) and Other Writings by Huan T'an*, fragment 124). Cf. DeWoskin, *Song for One or Two*, 67ff. Just as there were various sequences of the Five Phases, there were at least three different systems of spatial associations for the Five Tones: see Yan, "Cong chutu wenxian kan xian-Qin zhuzi de wuyin peizhi."

79. Cf. DeWoskin, *Song for One or Two*, 72ff.; also Major and So, "Music in Late Bronze Age China," 29–30.

80. *Huainanzi jishi* 9.618 ("Zhushu" 主術).

81. See Ames, *Art of Rulership*, 242nn40–41, for classical sources of these two anecdotes. Cf. also Yimin Jiang, "*Große Musik is tonlos*," 45ff.

82. Cf. Goldin, *After Confucius*, 105ff.

83. *Shiji* 74.2344.

84. Wang Chong, on this basis, constructed one of the most devastating critiques of Five Phases speculation in the entire literature (even though he was a firm believer in *qi* himself): *Lunheng jiaoshi* 3.14.146–52 ("Wushi" 物勢). Cf. Zufferey, *Wang Chong*, 280–85.

85. The literature is too large to cite in a single note; I have benefited in particular from Perrin, "Chemical Revolution."

86. Humanists sometimes balk at the notion of obsolete paradigms (as though all scientific paradigms were equally valid), but here I follow Weinberg, *To Explain the World*, 28–29; and, more fully, "Eye on the Present." This is not to say that I generally endorse Whig historiography or other modes of presentism, but if, say, electrons are natural particles rather than simply convenient human constructions, then inevitably some scientific paradigms will prove superior to others.

87. For example, in the cosmogony that opens the "Tianwen" 天文 chapter of *Huainanzi*, *qi* is said to have split into "clear and bright" (*qingyang* 清陽) and "heavy and turbid" (*zhongzhuo* 重濁), which became Heaven and Earth, respectively (*Huainanzi jishi* 3.166). Once again, there is no explanation for this fission.

88. Readers probably assumed that the target of Wang's criticism was Dong Zhong-shu, who was well known for using the term *qian'gao*: e.g., *Hanshu* 65.2498.

89. *Lunheng jiaoshi* 18.54.785 ("Ziran" 自然).

90. See also *Lunheng jiaoshi* 14.42.634–48 ("Qian'gao").

91. Cf. Needham et al., *Science and Civilisation in China*, 2:386.

92. Tolstoy mercilessly exposed this fallacy: "Peasants having no clear idea of the cause of rain, say, according to whether they want rain or fine weather: 'The wind has blown the clouds away,' or, 'The wind has brought up the clouds'" (*War and Peace*, 1048).

93. For this concept, see, e.g., Popper, *Logic of Scientific Discovery*.

94. Peierls, "Wolfgang Ernst Pauli."

95. See, e.g., Peng, *Zhongguo yishuxue*, 424–57; also Li Zehou, *Chinese Aesthetic Tradition*, 62ff. For *qi* in literature, see, e.g., Pollard, "*Ch'i* in Chinese Literary Theory."

96. See, e.g., Bruun, *Introduction to feng shui*, 106–10; and Needham et al., *Science and Civilisation in China*, 2:359–6

# Bibliography

## PRE-TANG CHINESE TEXTS (CITED BY TITLE)

### *Baihu tong* 白虎通

Chen Li 陳立 (1809–69). *Baihu tong shuzheng* 白虎通疏證. Edited by Wu Zeyu 吳則虞. Xinbian Zhuzi jicheng. Beijing: Zhonghua, 1994.

### *Baopuzi* 抱朴子

Yang Mingzhao 楊明照. *Baopuzi waipian jiaojian* 抱朴子外篇校箋. Xinbian Zhuzi jicheng. Beijing: Zhonghua, 1991.

### *Chunqiu fanlu* 春秋繁露

Su Yu 蘇輿 (d. 1914). *Chunqiu fanlu yizheng* 春秋繁露義證. Edited by Zhong Zhe 鍾哲. Xinbian Zhuzi jicheng. Beijing: Zhonghua, 1992.

### *Erya* 爾雅

Erya zhushu 爾雅注疏. Shisan jing zhushu 十三經注疏.

### *Gongsun Longzi* 公孫龍子

Tan Jiefu 譚戒甫. *Gongsun Longzi xingming fawei* 公孫龍子形名發微. Xinbian Zhuzi jicheng. Beijing: Zhonghua, 1963.

### *Guanzi* 管子

Li Xiangfeng 黎翔鳳. *Guanzi jiaozhu* 管子校注. Edited by Liang Yunhua 梁運華. Xinbian Zhuzi jicheng. Beijing: Zhonghua, 2004.

### *Guoyu* 國語

Xu Yuangao 徐元誥 (1876–1955). *Guoyu jijie* 國語集解. Edited by Wang Shumin 王樹民 and Shen Changyun 沈長雲. Beijing: Zhonghua, 2002.

### *Han Feizi* 韓非子

Chen Qiyou 陳奇猷. *Han Feizi xin jiaozhu* 韓非子新校注. 2 vols. Shanghai: Guji, 2000.

*Hanshu* 漢書

*Hanshu*. Beijing: Zhonghua, 1962.

*Heguanzi* 鶡冠子

Huang Huaixin 黃懷信. *Heguanzi huijiao jizhu* 鶡冠子彙校集注. Beijing: Zhonghua, 2004.

*Huainanzi* 淮南子

He Ning 何寧. *Huainanzi jishi* 淮南子集釋. Xinbian Zhuzi jicheng. Beijing: Zhonghua, 1998.

*Huangdi neijing: Lingshu* 黃帝內經・靈樞

Shibue Chūsai 澀江抽齋 (1805–58). *Lingshu jiangyi* 靈樞講義. Edited by Cui Zhongping 崔仲平 et al. Zhong yiyao dianji yu xueshu liupai yanjiu congshu. Beijing: Xueyuan, 2003.

*Huangdi neijing: Suwen* 黃帝內經・素問

Yamada Gyōkō 山田業廣 (1808–81). *Suwen cizhu jishu* 素問次注集疏. Edited by Cui Zhongping et al. Zhong yiyao dianji yu xueshu liupai yanjiu congshu. Beijing: Xueyuan, 2004.

*Kongzi jiayu* 孔子家語

Yang Zhaoming 楊朝明 and Song Lilin 宋立林. *Kongzi jiayu tongjie* 孔子家語通解. Ji'nan: Qi-Lu, 2013.

*Laozi* 老子

Gao Ming 高明. *Boshu Laozi jiaozhu* 帛書老子校注. Xinbian Zhuzi jicheng. Beijing: Zhonghua, 1996.
Lou Yulie 樓宇烈. *Wang Bi ji jiaoshi* 王弼集校釋. Beijing: Zhonghua, 1980.
Rao Zongyi 饒宗頤. *Laozi Xiang'er zhu jiaojian* 老子想爾注校箋. Hong Kong: Tong Nam, 1956.

*Liji* 禮記

*Liji zhengyi* 禮記正義. Shisan jing zhushu.

*Lunheng* 論衡

Huang Hui 黃暉. *Lunheng jiaoshi (fu Liu Pansui jijie)* 論衡校釋（附劉盼遂集解）. 4 vols. Xinbian Zhuzi jicheng. Beijing: Zhonghua, 1990.

*Lunyu* 論語

Cheng Shude 程樹德 (1877–1944). *Lunyu jishi* 論語集釋. Edited by Cheng Junying 程俊英 and Jiang Jianyuan 蔣見元. 4 vols. Xinbian zhuzi jicheng. Beijing: Zhonghua, 1990.

*Lüshi chunqiu* 呂氏春秋

Chen Qiyou. *Lüshi chunqiu xin jiaoshi* 呂氏春秋新校釋. Shanghai: Guji, 2002.

*Mao-Shi* 毛詩

*Mao-Shi zhengyi* 毛詩正義. Shisan jing zhushu.

*Mengzi* 孟子

Jiao Xun 焦循 (1763–1820). *Mengzi zhengyi* 孟子正義. Edited by Shen Wenzhuo 沈文倬. 2 vols. Xinbian Zhuzi jicheng. Beijing: Zhonghua, 1987.

*Mozi* 墨子

Wu Yujiang 吳毓江. *Mozi jiaozhu* 墨子校注. Edited by Sun Qizhi 孫啟治. 2nd ed. Xinbian Zhuzi jicheng. Beijing: Zhonghua, 2006. [N.b.: The pagination of this second edition is not identical to that of the first.]

*Shangjun shu* 商君書

Jiang Lihong 蔣禮鴻. *Shangjun shu zhuizhi* 商君書錐指. Xinbian Zhuzi jicheng. Beijing: Zhonghua, 1986.

*Shangqing housheng daojun lieji* 上清後聖道君列紀

*Shangqing housheng daojun lieji*. Daozang 道藏, HY 442.

*Shangshu* 尚書

Gu Jiegang 顧頡剛 (1893–1980) and Liu Qiyu 劉起釪. *Shangshu jiaoshi yilun* 尚書校釋譯論. 4 vols. Beijing: Zhonghua, 2005.

*Shenxian zhuan* 神仙傳

Hu Shouwei 胡守為. *Shenxian zhuan jiaoshi* 神仙傳校釋. Daojiao dianji xuankan. Beijing: Zhonghua, 2010.

*Shiji* 史記

*Shiji*. Beijing: Zhonghua, 1959.

Takigawa Kametarō 瀧川龜太郎 (1865–1946). *Shiki kaichū kōshō* 史記會注考證. 2nd ed. Tokyo, 1957–59.

*Shuowen jiezi* 說文解字

Jiang Renjie 蔣人傑. *Shuowen jiezi jizhu* 說文解字集注. Edited by Liu Rui 劉銳. Shanghai: Guji, 1996.

*Sunzi* 孫子

Yang Bing'an 楊丙安, ed. *Shiyi jia zhu Sunzi jiaoli* 十一家注孫子校理. Xinbian Zhuzi jicheng. Beijing: Zhonghua, 1999.

*Taixuan jing* 太玄經

Sima Guang 司馬光 (1019–86). *Taixuan jizhu* 太玄集注. Edited by Liu Shaojun 劉韶軍. Xinbian Zhuzi jicheng. Beijing: Zhonghua, 1998.

*Weimojie suoshuo jing* 維摩詰所說經

*Weimojie suoshuo jing*. *Taishō shinshū daizōkyō* 大正新脩大藏經 XIV.475.

*Xinshu* 新書

Yan Zhenyi 閻振益 and Zhong Xia 鍾夏. *Xinshu jiaozhu* 新書校注. Xinbian Zhuzi jicheng. Beijing: Zhonghua, 2000.

*Xunzi* 荀子

Wang Xianqian. *Xunzi jijie* 荀子集解. Edited by Shen Xiaohuan 沈嘯寰 and Wang Xingxian 王星賢. 2 vols. Xinbian Zhuzi jicheng. Beijing: Zhonghua, 1988.

*Yanzi chunqiu* 晏子春秋

Wu Zeyu 吳則虞. *Yanzi chunqiu jishi* 晏子春秋集釋. Edited by Wu Shouju 吳受琚 and Yu Zhen 俞震. Rev. ed. Beijing: Guojia Tushuguan, 2011.

*Yuejue shu* 越絕書

Li Bujia 李步嘉. *Yuejue shu jiaoshi* 越絕書校釋. Zhongguo shixue jiben dianji congkan. Beijing: Zhonghua, 2013.

*Zhanguo ce* 戰國策

He Jianzhang 何建章. *Zhanguo ce zhushi* 戰國策注釋. Beijing: Zhonghua, 1990.

*Zhuangzi* 莊子

Guo Qingfan 郭慶藩 (1844–96). *Zhuangzi jishi* 莊子集釋. Edited by Wang Xiaoyu 王孝
魚. 4 vols. Xinbian Zhuzi jicheng. Beijing: Zhonghua, 1961.

*Zhushu jinian* 竹書紀年

*Zhushu jinian* 竹書紀年. Sibu beiyao 四部備要.

*Zuozhuan* 左傳

Yang Bojun 楊伯峻. *Chunqiu Zuozhuan zhu* 春秋左傳注. 2nd ed. Zhongguo gudian
mingzhu yizhu congshu. Beijing: Zhonghua, 1990.

## CHINESE TEXTS FROM THE TANG AND LATER, AND WORKS
## IN ALL OTHER LANGUAGES (CITED BY AUTHOR AND TITLE)

Allan, Sarah. "The Great One, Water, and the *Laozi*: New Light from Guodian." *T'oung
Pao* 89.4–5 (2003): 237–85.

———. *The Way of Water and Sprouts of Virtue*. SUNY Series in Chinese Philosophy and
Culture. Albany: State University of New York Press, 1997.

Allen, Barry. *Vanishing into Things: Knowledge in Chinese Tradition*. Cambridge, MA:
Harvard University Press, 2015.

Allen, Joseph Roe, III. "An Introductory Study of Narrative Structure in *Shiji*." *Chinese
Literature: Essays, Articles, Reviews* 3.1 (1981): 31–66.

Allinson, Robert Elliott. "How Metaphor Functions in the *Zhuangzi*: The Case of the
Unlikely Messenger." In *New Visions of the* Zhuangzi, edited by Livia Kohn, 95–116.
St. Petersburg, FL: Three Pines, 2015.

Ames, Roger T. *The Art of Rulership: A Study of Ancient Chinese Political Thought*. Honolulu: University of Hawaii Press, 1983. Reprint, Albany: State University of New
York Press, 1994.

———. "Death as Transformation in Classical Daoism." In *Death and Philosophy*, edited
by Jeff Malpas and Robert C. Solomon, 57–70. London: Routledge, 1998.

———. "The Mencian Conception of *Ren xing* 人性: Does It Mean 'Human Nature'?" In
Rosemont, *Chinese Texts and Philosophical Contexts*, 143–75.

———. "Observing Ritual 'Propriety' (*li* 禮) as Focusing the 'Familiar' in the Affairs of
the Day." *Dao* 1.2 (2002): 143–56.

———. "Paronomasia: A Confucian Way of Making Meaning." In Jones, *Confucius Now*,
37–48.

———, ed. *Wandering at Ease in the* Zhuangzi. SUNY Series in Chinese Philosophy and
Culture. Albany: State University of New York Press, 1998.

———. "What Ever Happened to 'Wisdom'? Confucian Philosophy of Process and
'Human Becomings.'" *Asia Major*, 3rd ser., 21.1 (2008): 45–68.

Andreini, Attilio. *Il pensiero di Yang Zhu (IV secolo a.C.) attraverso un esame delle fonti
cinesi classiche*. Trieste: Edizioni Università di Trieste, 2000.

Angell, Marcia. *The Truth about Drug Companies: How They Deceive Us and What to Do
about It*. Rev. ed. New York: Random House, 2005.

An Zuozhang 安作璋 and Meng Xiangcai 孟祥才. *Qin shihuangdi dazhuan* 秦始皇帝大傳. Beijing: Zhonghua, 2005.

Arbuckle, Gary. "Restoring Dong Zhongshu (BCE 195–115): An Experiment in Historical and Philosophical Reconstruction." PhD diss., University of British Columbia, 1991.

Arendt, Hannah. *The Origins of Totalitarianism.* New York: Schocken, 2004.

Arthur, Shawn. *Early Daoist Dietary Practices: Examining Ways to Health and Longevity.* Studies in Body and Religion. Lanham, MD: Lexington, 2013.

*The Art of War: The Denma Translation.* Boston: Shambhala, 2001.

Balazs, Etienne. *Chinese Civilization and Bureaucracy: Variations on a Theme.* Translated by H. M. Wright. Edited by Arthur F. Wright. New Haven, CT: Yale University Press, 1964.

Barnes, Jonathan. "Aristotle." In *Founders of Thought,* 85–189. Oxford: Oxford University Press, 1991.

———, ed. *The Complete Works of Aristotle: The Revised Oxford Translation.* 2 vols. Bollingen Series 71.2. Princeton, NJ: Princeton University Press, 1984.

Bauer, Wolfgang. "Das Stirnrunzeln des Totenkopfes: Über die Paradoxie des Todes in der frühen chinesischen Philosophie." In *Der Tod in den Weltkulturen und Weltreligionen,* edited by Constantin von Barloewen, 247–81. Munich: Diederichs, 1996.

Baxter, William H., and Laurent Sagart. *Old Chinese: A New Reconstruction.* Oxford: Oxford University Press, 2014.

Beardsley, Monroe C. *Aesthetics: Problems in the Philosophy of Criticism.* 2nd ed. Indianapolis: Hackett, 1981.

Beecroft, Alexander. *Authorship and Cultural Identity in Early Greece and China: Patterns of Literary Circulation.* Cambridge: Cambridge University Press, 2010.

Behr, Wolfgang. "Der gegenwärtige Forschungsstand zur Etymologie von *rén* 仁 im Überblick." *Bochumer Jahrbuch zur Ostasienforschung* 38 (2015): 199–224.

Bentham, Jeremy (1748–1832). *Bentham's Handbook of Political Fallacies.* Edited by Harold A. Larrabee. Baltimore: Johns Hopkins University Press, 1952.

———. *An Introduction to the Principles of Morals and Legislation.* Edited by J. H. Burns and H.L.A. Hart. 2nd ed. Collected Works of Jeremy Bentham. Oxford: Oxford University Press, 1996.

Berling, Judith. "Self and Whole in Chuang Tzu." In Munro, *Individualism and Holism,* 101–20.

Bhattacharya, Ramkrishna. "What the Cārvākas Originally Meant: More on the Commentators on the *Cārvākasūtra.*" *Journal of Indian Philosophy* 38.6 (2010): 529–42.

Billeter, Jean François. *Études sur Tchouang-Tseu.* Rev. ed. Paris: Allia, 2006.

Bloom, Irene. "Mencian Arguments on Human Nature (*jen-hsing*)." *Philosophy East and West* 44.1 (1994): 19–53. Reprinted in Liu and Ivanhoe, *Essays on the Moral Philosophy of Mengzi,* 64–100.

———. "On the Matter of the Mind: The Metaphysical Basis of the Expanded Self." In Munro, *Individualism and Holism,* 293–330.

Boaz, David. *The Libertarian Reader: Classic and Contemporary Writings from Lao-tzu to Milton Friedman.* New York: Free Press, 1997.

Bodde, Derk. *China's First Unifier: A Study of the Ch'in Dynasty as Seen in the Life of Li Ssu.* Sinica Leidensia 3. Leiden: E. J. Brill, 1938.

Bodde, Derk, and Clarence Morris. *Law in Imperial China: Exemplified by 190 Ch'ing Dynasty Cases.* Philadelphia: University of Pennsylvania Press, 1967.

Bokenkamp, Stephen R. *Early Daoist Scriptures*. Taoist Classics 1. Berkeley: University of California Press, 1997.

Boltz, William G. "The Composite Nature of Early Chinese Texts." In *Text and Ritual in Early China*, edited by Martin Kern, 50–78. Seattle: University of Washington Press, 2005.

———. "Why So Many *Laozi*-s?" In *Studies in Chinese Manuscripts: From the Warring States Period to the 20th Century*, edited by Imre Galambos, 1–31. Budapest Monographs in East Asian Studies. Budapest: Institute of East Asian Studies, Eötvös Loránd University, 2013.

Boyce, Christopher J., et al. "Money and Happiness: Rank of Income, Not Income, Affects Life Satisfaction." *Psychological Science* 21.4 (2010): 471–75.

Brashier, K. E. *Ancestral Memory in Early China*. Harvard-Yenching Institute Monograph Series 72. Cambridge, MA: Harvard University Asia Center, 2011.

Brecht, Bertolt (1898–1956). *Die Dreigroschenoper*. Edition Suhrkamp 229. Berlin: Suhrkamp, 1968.

Brindley, Erica [Fox]. "Human Agency and the Ideal of *shang tong* (Upward Conformity) in Early Mohist Writings." *Journal of Chinese Philosophy* 34.3 (2007): 409–25.

———. *Individualism in Early China: Human Agency and the Self in Thought and Politics*. Honolulu: University of Hawaii Press, 2010.

Brockington, John. *The Sanskrit Epics*. Handbuch der Orientalistik II.12. Leiden: Brill, 1998.

Brooks, E. Bruce, and A. Taeko Brooks. *The Emergence of China: From Confucius to the Empire*. Ancient China in Context. Amherst, MA: Warring States Project, 2015.

———. *The Original Analects: Sayings of Confucius and His Successors*. Translations from the Asian Classics. New York: Columbia University Press, 1998.

Brown, Miranda. *The Art of Medicine in Early China: The Ancient and Medieval Origins of a Modern Archive*. Cambridge: Cambridge University Press, 2015.

Bruun, Ole. *An Introduction to feng shui*. Cambridge: Cambridge University Press, 2008.

Bumbacher, Stephan Peter. "Ge Hong's *Zhuang zi*." *Asiatische Studien* 72.4 (2018): 1021–58.

———. "On the *Shenxian zhuan*." *Asiatische Studien* 54.4 (2000): 729–814.

———. "Reconstructing the *Zhuang zi*: Preliminary Considerations." *Asiatische Studien* 70.3 (2016): 611–74.

Burke, Peter. *What Is Cultural History?* 2nd ed. Cambridge, MA: Polity, 2008.

Cai Renhou 蔡仁厚. *Mojia zhexue* 墨家哲學. Canghai congkan. Taipei: Dongda, 1983.

Campany, Robert Ford. *Making Transcendents: Ascetics and Social Memory in Early Medieval China*. Honolulu: University of Hawaii Press, 2009.

———, trans. *To Live as Long as Heaven and Earth: A Translation and Study of Ge Hong's Traditions of Divine Transcendents*. Daoist Classics 2. Berkeley: University of California Press, 2002.

———. "Xunzi and Durkheim as Theorists of Ritual Practice." In *Discourse and Practice*, edited by Frank Reynolds and David Tracy, 197–231. SUNY Series: Toward a Comparative Philosophy of Religions. Albany: State University of New York Press, 1992.

Cao Minggang 曹明綱. *Liu Zongyuan quanji* 柳宗元全集. Shanghai: Guji, 1997.

Cao Shengqiang 曹勝強 and Sun Zhuocai 孫卓彩, eds. *Mozi yanjiu* 墨子研究. Beijing: Zhongguo shehui kexue, 2008.

Carmichael, Lucas. "The *Daode jing* as American Scripture: Text, Tradition, and Translation." PhD diss., University of Chicago, 2017.

Caro, Mike. *Caro's Book of Poker Tells: The Psychology and Body Language of Poker*. New York: Cardoza, 2003.

Chan, Alan K. L. "A Matter of Taste: *Qi* (Vital Energy) and the Tending of the Heart (*xin*) in *Mencius* 2A.2." In *Mencius: Contexts and Interpretations*, edited by Alan K. L. Chan, 42–71. Honolulu: University of Hawaii Press, 2002.

Chan, Sin Yee. "Disputes on the One Thread of *Chung-Shu*." *Journal of Chinese Philosophy* 26.2 (1999): 165–86.

Chan, Wing-tsit. "The Neo-Confucian Solution of the Problem of Evil." *Qingzhu Hu Shi xiansheng liushiwu sui lunwenji* 慶祝胡適先生六十五歲論文集. *Zhongyang Yanjiuyuan Lishi Yuyan Yanjiusuo jikan* 中央研究院歷史語言研究所集刊 28 (1957): 773–91.

Chang, Carsun. *The Development of Neo-Confucian Thought*. 2 vols. New York: Bookman, 1957–62.

Chang, Chun-shu. *The Rise of the Chinese Empire*. 2 vols. Ann Arbor: University of Michigan Press, 2007.

Chang, Hao. *Liang Ch'i-ch'ao and Intellectual Transition in China, 1890–1907*. Harvard East Asian Series 64. Cambridge, MA: Harvard University Press, 1971.

Chang Tsung-tung. *Der Kult der Shang-Dynastie im Spiegel der Orakelinschriften: Eine paläographische Studie zur Religion im archaischen China*. Wiesbaden: Otto Harrassowitz, 1970.

Chan Sin-wai. *An Exposition of Benevolence: The* Jen-hsüeh *of T'an Ssu-t'ung*. Institute of Chinese Studies Monograph Series 6. Hong Kong: Chinese University Press, 1984.

Chen Banghuai 陳邦懷 (1897–1986). *Yide ji* 一得集. Ji'nan: Qi-Lu, 1989.

Chen, Ellen Marie. "Is There a Doctrine of Physical Immortality in the *Tao Te Ching*?" *History of Religions* 12.3 (1973): 231–49.

Chen, Jack W., and David Schaberg, eds. *Idle Talk: Gossip and Anecdote in Traditional China*. New Perspectives on Chinese Culture and Society 5. Berkeley: University of California Press, 2014.

Chen, Ning. "The Concept of Fate in *Mencius*." *Philosophy East and West* 47.4 (1997): 495–520.

———. "Problem of Theodicy in Ancient China." *Journal of Chinese Religions* 22 (1994): 51–74.

Cheng, François. "*Bi* 比 et *xing* 興." *Cahiers de linguistique: Asie orientale* 6 (1979): 63–74.

Cheng Shuijin 程水金 and Feng Yiming 馮一鳴. "*Liezi* kaobian shuping yu *Liezi* weishu xinzheng" 《列子》考辨述評與《列子》偽書新證. *Zhongguo zhexueshi* 中國哲學史 2007.2:40–48.

Chen Guying 陳鼓應. *Daojia de renwen jingshen* 道家的人文精神. Beijing: Zhonghua, 2012.

Chen Ruigeng 陳瑞庚. *Yanzi chunqiu kaobian* 晏子春秋考辨. Taipei: Chang'an, 1980.

Chen Shaoming 陳少明. "*Qiwulun*" jiqi yingxiang 《齊物論》及其影響. Xueshushi congshu. Beijing: Beijing Daxue, 2004.

Chen Zhibin 陳之斌. "Lun Zhuangzi zhexue de benyu: Hundun" 論莊子哲學的本喻: 渾沌. *Zhongguo zhexueshi* 中國哲學史 2016.3:25–32.

Chin, Tamara T. *Savage Exchange: Han Imperialism, Chinese Literary Style, and the Impe-*

*rial Imagination*. Harvard-Yenching Institute Monograph Series 94. Cambridge, MA: Harvard University Press, 2014.

Chmielewski, Janusz. "Concerning the Problem of Analogic Reasoning in Ancient China." *Rocznik orientalisticzny* 40.2 (1979): 65–78.

Chow, Kai-wing. *The Rise of Confucian Ritualism in Late Imperial China: Ethics, Classics, and Lineage Discourse*. Stanford, CA: Stanford University Press, 1994.

Chow Tse-tsung. "The Early History of the Chinese Word *shih* (Poetry)." In Chow Tse-tsung, *Wen-lin*, 1:151–209.

———. "A New Theory on the Origins of Mohism." In Chow Tse-tsung, *Wen-lin*, 2:123–51.

———, ed. *Wen-lin: Studies in the Chinese Humanities*. 2 vols. Vol. 1: Madison: University of Wisconsin Press, 1968; Vol. 2: Madison: Department of East Asian Languages and Literatures, University of Wisconsin, 1989.

Ch'ü, T'ung-tsu. *Law and Society in Traditional China*. Le monde d'outre-mer passé et présent, Première série: Études 4. Paris: Mouton, 1961.

Cikoski, John S. "On Standards of Analogic Reasoning in the Late Chou." *Journal of Chinese Philosophy* 2.3 (1975): 325–57.

Clark, Kelly James, and Robin R. Wang. "A Confucian Defense of Gender Equity." *Journal of the American Academy of Religion* 72.2 (2004): 395–422.

Clarke, J. J. *Oriental Enlightenment: The Encounter between Asian and Western Thought*. London: Routledge, 1997.

Cook, Scott. *The Bamboo Texts of Guodian: A Study and Complete Translation*. 2 vols. Cornell East Asia Series 164–65. Ithaca, NY: Cornell University Press, 2012.

———. "The Changing Role of the Minister in the Warring States: Evidence from the *Yanzi chunqiu* 晏子春秋." In *Ideology of Power and Power of Ideology in Early China*, edited by Yuri Pines et al., 181–210. Sinica Leidensia 124. Leiden: Brill, 2015.

———, ed. *Hiding the World in the World: Uneven Discourses on the Zhuangzi*. SUNY Series in Chinese Philosophy and Culture. Albany: State University of New York Press, 2003.

———. "Xun Zi on Ritual and Music." *Monumenta Serica* 45 (1997): 1–38.

———. "*Yue ji*—Record of Music: Introduction, Translation, Notes, and Commentary." *Asian Music* 26.2 (1995): 1–96.

———. "Zhuang Zi and His Carving of the Confucian Ox." *Philosophy East and West* 47.4 (1997): 521–53.

Coutinho, Steve. *Zhuangzi and Early Chinese Philosophy: Vagueness, Transformation, and Paradox*. Ashgate World Philosophies Series. Aldershot, UK: Ashgate, 2004.

Creel, Herrlee G. *Chinese Thought from Confucius to Mao Tse-tung*. Chicago: University of Chicago Press, 1953.

———. *Confucius and the Chinese Way*. New York: Harper and Row, 1960.

———. *The Origins of Statecraft in China*. Chicago: University of Chicago Press, 1970.

———. *Shen Pu-hai: A Chinese Political Philosopher of the Fourth Century B.C.* Chicago: University of Chicago Press, 1974.

Csikszentmihalyi, Mark. "Confucius." In *The Rivers of Paradise: Moses, Buddha, Confucius, Jesus, and Muhammad as Religious Founders*, edited by David Noel Freedman and Michael J. McClymond, 233–308. Grand Rapids, MI: William B. Eerdmans, 2001.

Csikszentmihalyi, Mark, and Philip J. Ivanhoe, eds. *Religious and Philosophical Aspects of the* Laozi. SUNY Series in Chinese Philosophy and Culture. Albany: State University of New York Press, 1999.

Cua, Antonio S. *Human Nature, Ritual, and History: Studies in Xunzi and Chinese Philosophy*. Studies in Philosophy and the History of Philosophy 43. Washington, DC: Catholic University of America Press, 2005.

Cui Dahua 崔大華. *Zhuangxue yanjiu—Zhongguo zhexue yige guannian yuanyuan de lishi kaocha* 莊學研究—中國哲學一個觀念淵源的歷史考察. Beijing: Renmin, 1992.

Dai Junren 戴君仁. *Meiyuan lunxue ji* 梅園論學集. Taipei: Kaiming, 1970.

———. *Meiyuan lunxue xuji* 梅園論學續集. Taipei: Yiwen, 1974.

Dalby, Michael. "Revenge and the Law in Traditional China." *American Journal of Legal History* 25.4 (1981): 267–307.

Defoort, Carine. "Is 'Chinese Philosophy' a Proper Name? A Response to Rein Raud." *Philosophy East and West* 56.4 (2006): 625–60.

———. "Is There Such a Thing as Chinese Philosophy? Arguments of an Implicit Debate." *Philosophy East and West* 51.3 (2001): 393–413.

———. "The Profit That Does Not Profit: Paradoxes with *li* in Early Chinese Texts." *Asia Major*, 3rd ser., 21.1 (2008): 153–81.

———. "Unfounded and Unfollowed: Mencius's Portrayal of Yang Zhu and Mo Di." In Defoort and Ames, *Having a Word with Angus Graham*, 165–84.

Defoort, Carine, and Roger T. Ames, eds. *Having a Word with Angus Graham: At Twenty-Five Years into His Immortality*. SUNY Series in Chinese Philosophy and Culture. Albany: State University of New York Press, 2018.

Defoort, Carine, and Nicolas Standaert, eds. *The* Mozi *as an Evolving Text: Different Voices in Early Chinese Thought*. Studies in the History of Chinese Texts 4. Leiden: Brill, 2013.

Denecke, Wiebke. *The Dynamics of Masters Literature: Early Chinese Thought from Confucius to Han Feizi*. Harvard-Yenching Institute Monograph Series 74. Cambridge, MA: Harvard University Press, 2010.

Deng Junjie 鄧駿捷. *Liu Xiang jiaoshu kaolun* 劉向校書考論. Beijing: Renmin, 2012.

Deng Peiling 鄧佩玲. *Tianming, guishen yu zhudao: Dong-Zhou jinwen guci tanlun* 天命、鬼神與祝禱: 東周金文嘏辭探論. Taipei: Yiwen, 2011.

Deng Ruiquan 鄧瑞全 and Wang Guanying 王冠英. *Zhongguo weishu zongkao* 中國偽書綜考. Hefei: Huangshan, 1998.

De Reu, Wim. "A Ragbag of Odds and Ends?" In Gentz and Meyer, 243–96.

———. "Right Words Seem Wrong: Neglected Paradoxes in Early Chinese Texts." *Philosophy East and West* 56.2 (2006): 281–300.

Descartes, René (1596–1650). *Œuvres de Descartes*, edited by Victor Cousin. 11 vols. Paris: F. G. Levrault, 1824.

Despeux, Catherine. "La gymnastique *daoyin* 導引 dans la Chine ancienne." *Études chinoises* 23 (2004): 45–85.

DeWoskin, Kenneth J. *A Song for One or Two: Music and the Concept of Art in Early China*. Michigan Papers in Chinese Studies 42. Ann Arbor: University of Michigan Press, 1982.

Ding Sixin 丁四新. "Lun *Mozi* 'Moyu' Mojia houxue zhi guishenguan" 論《墨子 • 墨語》墨家後學之鬼神觀. *Anhui Daxue xuebao (Zhexue shehui kexue ban)* 安徽大學學報（哲學社會科學版）2011.2:7–9.

Durrant, Stephen W. "The Taoist Apotheosis of Mo Ti." *Journal of the American Oriental Society* 97.4 (1977): 540–46.

Dworkin, Ronald. *Law's Empire*. Cambridge, MA: Belknap Press of Harvard University Press, 1986.

Eberhard, Wolfram. "Beiträge zur kosmologischen Spekulation Chinas in der Han-Zeit." *Baessler Archiv* 16.1 (1933): 1–100.

———. *The Local Cultures of South and East China*. Translated by Alide Eberhard. Leiden: E. J. Brill, 1968.

Ebrey, Patricia Buckley. *Confucianism and Family Rituals in Imperial China: A Social History of Writing about Rites*. Princeton, NJ: Princeton University Press, 1991.

Eco, Umberto. *Interpretation and Overinterpretation*. Edited by Stefan Collini. Cambridge: Cambridge University Press, 1992.

Emmerich, Reinhard. "Bemerkungen zu Huang und Lao in der frühen Han-Zeit: Erkenntnisse aus *Shiji* und *Hanshu*." *Monumenta Serica* 43 (1995): 53–140.

———. "Religiöse Einstellungen der Mohisten." In *Chinesische Religion und Philosophie: Konfuzianismus—Mohismus—Daoismus—Buddhismus*, edited by Konrad Meisig, 35–52. Interkulturelle Ostasienstudien 1. Wiesbaden: Harrassowitz, 2005.

Emmerich, Reinhard, et al., eds. *Und folge nun dem, was mein Herz begehrt: Festschrift für Ulrich Unger zum 70. Geburtstag*. 2 vols. Hamburger Sinologische Schriften 8. Hamburg: Hamburger Sinologische Gesellschaft, 2002.

Engelhardt, Ute. "*Daoyin tu* und *Yinshu*: Neue Erkenntnisse über die Übungen zur Lebenspflege in der frühen Han-Zeit." *Monumenta Serica* 49 (2001): 213–26.

Eno, Robert. "The Background of the Kong Family of Lu and the Origins of Ruism." *Early China* 28 (2003): 1–41.

———. "Cook Ding's Dao and the Limits of Philosophy." In Kjellberg and Ivanhoe, *Essays on Skepticism*, 127–51.

Eskildsen, Stephen. *Asceticism in Early Taoist Thought*. SUNY Series in Chinese Philosophy and Culture. Albany: State University of New York Press, 1998.

———. *Daoism, Meditation, and the Wonders of Serenity: From the Latter Han Dynasty (25–220) to the Tang Dynasty (618–907)*. SUNY Series in Chinese Philosophy and Culture. Albany: State University of New York Press, 2015.

Fang Shouchu 方授楚. *Moxue yuanliu* 墨學源流. 2nd ed. Shanghai: Zhonghua, 1940.

Feng Mengzhen 馮夢禎 (1548–1605). *Kuaixuetang ji* 快雪堂集. 1616.

Fields, Dorothy, et al. *Seesaw: A Musical*. New York: Samuel French, 1975.

Fingarette, Herbert. *Confucius—the Secular as Sacred*. Harper Torchbooks. New York: Harper and Row, 1972.

Fischer, Paul. "Authentication Studies (辨偽學) Methodology and the Polymorphous Text Paradigm." *Early China* 32 (2008–9): 1–43.

Fleming, Jesse. "On Translation of Taoist Philosophical Texts: Preservation of Ambiguity and Contradiction." *Journal of Chinese Philosophy* 25.1 (1998): 147–56.

Forke, A[lfred] (1867–1944). "The Chinese Sophists." *Journal of the North China Branch of the Royal Asiatic Society* 34.1 (1901–2): 1–100.

———. *Geschichte der alten chinesischen Philosophie*. Universität Hamburg: Abhandlungen aus dem Gebiet der Auslandskunde 25; Reihe B., Völkerkunde, Kulturgeschichte und Sprachen 14. Hamburg: Friederichsen, 1927.

———, trans. *Mê Ti des Sozialethikers und seiner Schüler philosophische Werke*. Mitteilungen des Seminars für Orientalische Sprachen, Beiband zum Jahrgang 23/25. Berlin: Kommissionsverlag der Vereinigung wissenschaftlicher Verleger, 1922.

Fox, Alan. "Reflex and Reflectivity: *Wuwei* in the *Zhuangzi*." In Cook, *Hiding the World in the World*, 207–25.

Fraser, Chris. "Language and Logic in the *Xunzi*." In Hutton, *Dao Companion to the Philosophy of Xunzi*, 291–321.

———. *The Philosophy of the* Mòz ĭ : *The First Consequentialists*. New York: Columbia University Press, 2016.

Fu, Zhengyuan. *China's Legalists: The Earliest Totalitarians and Their Art of Ruling*. Armonk, NY: M. E. Sharpe, 1996.

Fuehrer, Bernhard. "*Mencius* for Han Readers: Commentarial Features and Hermeneutical Strategies in Zhao Qi's Work on the *Mencius*." *Zeitschrift der Deutschen Morgenländischen Gesellschaft* 164.2 (2014): 501–26.

Fukui Shigemasa 福井重雅. *Kandai Jukyō no shiteki kenkyū—Jukyō no kangakuka o meguru teisetsu no saikentō* 漢代儒教の史的研究—儒教の官學化をめぐる定説の再檢討. Kyūko shōso 60. Tokyo: Kyūko, 2005.

———. "Zen Kan ni okeru Bokuka no saisei—Jukyō no kangakuka ni tsuite no isshiron" 前漢における墨家の再生—儒教の官学化についての一試論. *Tōhōgaku* 東方學 29 (1970): 1–18.

Fukunaga Mitsuji 福永光司. *Dōkyō shisōshi kenkyū* 道教思想史研究. Tokyo: Iwanami, 1987.

Fung, Yiu-ming. "A Logical Perspective on the Parallelism in Later Moism." *Journal of Chinese Philosophy* 39.3 (2012): 333–50.

Galvany, Albert. "Beyond the Rule of Rules: The Foundations of Sovereign Power in the *Han Feizi*." In Goldin, *Dao Companion to the Philosophy of Han Fei*, 87–106.

Gao Dalun 高大倫. *Zhangjiashan Hanmu* Yinshu *yanjiu* 張家山漢墓《引書》研究. Chengdu: Ba-Shu, 1995.

Gao Heng 高亨. *Chongding Laozi zhenggu* 重訂老子正詁. Beijing: Guji, 1956.

Gardner, Daniel K., trans. *Learning to Be a Sage: Selections from the* Conversations of Master Chu, Arranged Topically. Berkeley: University of California Press, 1990.

Gassmann, Robert H. "Die Bezeichnung *jun-zi*: Ansätze zur Chun-qiu-zeitlichen Kontextualisierung und zur Bedeutungsbestimmung im *Lun Yu*." In *Zurück zur Freude: Studien zur chinesichen Literatur und Lebenswelt und ihrer Rezeption in Ost und West: Festschrift für Wolfgang Kubin*, edited by Marc Hermann and Christian Schwermann, 411–36. Monumenta Serica Monograph Series 57. Sankt Augustin: Institut Monumenta Serica, 2007.

Gazdar, Gerald. *Pragmatics: Implicature, Presupposition, and Logical Form*. New York: Academic, 1979.

Geaney, Jane M. "A Critique of A. C. Graham's Reconstruction of the 'Neo-Mohist Canons.'" *Journal of the American Oriental Society* 119.1 (1999): 1–11.

Gentz, Joachim. "Defining Boundaries and Relations of Textual Units: Examples from the Literary Tool-Kit of Early Chinese Argumentation." In Gentz and Meyer, *Literary Forms of Argument in Early China*, 112–57.

———. "Mohist Traces in the Early *Chunqiu fanlu* Chapters." *Oriens Extremus* 48 (2009): 55–70.

Gentz, Joachim, and Dirk Meyer, eds. *Literary Forms of Argument in Early China*. Leiden: Brill, 2015.

Gewirth, Alan. "The Golden Rule Rationalized." *Midwest Studies in Philosophy* 3 (1978): 133–47.

———. *Reason and Morality*. Chicago: University of Chicago Press, 1981.

Gibas, Piotr. "Mozi and the Ghosts: The Concept of *ming* 明 in *Mozi*'s 'Ming gui' 明鬼." *Early China* 40 (2017): 89–123.

Girardot, N. J. *Myth and Meaning in Early Taoism: The Theme of Chaos (hun-tun)*. Hermeneutics: Studies in the History of Religion. Berkeley: University of California Press, 1983.

Giroud, Vincent, and Michael Kaye. *The Real* Tales of Hoffmann: *Origin, History, and Restoration of an Operatic Masterpiece*. Lanham, MD: Rowman and Littlefield, 2017.

Goldin, Paul R[akita]. *After Confucius: Studies in Early Chinese Philosophy*. Honolulu: University of Hawaii Press, 2005.

———. "Appeals to History in Early Chinese Philosophy and Rhetoric." *Journal of Chinese Philosophy* 35.1 (2008): 79–96.

———. *Confucianism*. Ancient Philosophies 9. Durham, UK: Acumen; Berkeley: University of California Press, 2011. Reprint, Abingdon, UK: Routledge, 2014.

———, ed. *A Concise Companion to Confucius*. Blackwell Companions to Philosophy 65. Oxford: John Wiley and Sons, 2017.

———. "Confucius and His Disciples in the *Lunyu*: The Basis for the Traditional View." In Hunter and Kern, *Confucius and the* Analects *Revisited*, 92–115.

———. "The Consciousness of the Dead as a Philosophical Problem in Ancient China." In *The Good Life and Conceptions of Life in Early China and Græco-Roman Antiquity*, edited by R.A.H. King, 59–92. Chinese-Western Discourse 3. Berlin: De Gruyter, 2015.

———. "The Cultural and Religious Background of Sexual Vampirism in Ancient China." *Theology and Sexuality* 12.3 (2006): 287–310.

———. *The Culture of Sex in Ancient China*. Honolulu: University of Hawaii Press, 2002.

———, ed. *Dao Companion to the Philosophy of Han Fei*. Dao Companions to Chinese Philosophy 2. Dordrecht, Netherlands: Springer, 2013.

———. "Economic Cycles and Price Theory in Early Chinese Texts." In "Between Command and Market: Economic Thought and Practice in Early China," edited by Elisa Sabattini and Christian Schwermann. Unpublished manuscript.

———. "The Hermeneutics of Emmentaler." *Warring States Papers* 1 (2010): 75–78.

———. "Hsiao Kung-chuan on Mencian Populism." *Xiao Gongquan xueji* 蕭公權學記, edited by Wang Rongzu 汪榮祖 and Huang Junjie 黃俊傑, 249–63. Dong-Ya wenming yanjiu ziliao congkan 8. Taipei: National Taiwan University Press, 2009.

———. "A Mind-Body Problem in the *Zhuangzi*?" In Cook, *Hiding the World in the World*, 226–47.

———. "Persistent Misconceptions about Chinese 'Legalism.'" *Journal of Chinese Philosophy* 38.1 (2011): 88–104.

———. Review of A. C. Graham, trans., *Chuang-tzu: The Inner Chapters*, and Harold D. Roth, *A Companion to Angus C. Graham's* Chuang-tzu: The Inner Chapters. *Early China* 28 (2003): 201–14.

———. Review of Eske Møllgaard, *An Introduction to Daoist Thought: Action, Language, and Ethics in Zhuangzi. Journal of Chinese Religions* 35 (2007): 176–78.

———. Review of Roger T. Ames, ed., *Wandering at Ease in the Zhuangzi. Journal of the American Oriental Society* 120.3:474–77.

———. *Rituals of the Way: The Philosophy of Xunzi*. Chicago: Open Court, 1999.

———. "Some Shang Antecedents of Later Chinese Ideology and Culture." *Journal of the American Oriental Society* 137.1 (2017): 121–27.

———. "The Theme of the Primacy of the Situation in Classical Chinese Philosophy and Rhetoric." *Asia Major*, 3rd ser., 18.2 (2005): 1–25.

———. "When *zhong* 忠 Does Not Mean 'Loyalty.'" *Dao* 7.2 (2008): 165–74.

Goldin, Paul R[akita]. "Why Daoism Is Not Environmentalism." *Journal of Chinese Philosophy* 32.1 (2005): 75–87.

———. "Why *Mozi* Is Included in the Daoist Canon—or, Why There Is More to Mohism Than Utilitarian Ethics." In *How Should One Live? Comparing Ethics in Ancient China and Greco-Roman Antiquity*, edited by R.A.H. King and Dennis Schilling, 63–91. Berlin: De Gruyter, 2011.

———. "Xunzi and Early Han Philosophy." *Harvard Journal of Asiatic Studies* 67.1 (2007): 135–66.

Goldstein, Phil. *Verbal Control: A Treatise on the Under-explored Art of Equivoque*. N.p.: n.p., 1976.

Graham, A. C., trans. *Chuang-tzŭ: The Inner Chapters*. London: George Allen and Unwin, 1981. Reprint, Indianapolis: Hackett, 2001.

———. *Disputers of the Tao: Philosophical Argument in Ancient China*. La Salle, IL: Open Court, 1989.

———. *Divisions in Early Mohism Reflected in the Core Chapters of Mo-tzu*. Institute of East Asian Philosophies Occasional Paper and Monograph Series 1. Singapore: Institute of East Asian Philosophies, 1985.

———. *Later Mohist Logic, Ethics and Science*. Hong Kong: Chinese University Press, 1978.

———. *Studies in Chinese Philosophy and Philosophical Literature*. SUNY Series in Chinese Philosophy and Culture. Albany: State University of New York Press, 1990.

Granet, Marcel (1884–1940). *Danses et légendes de la Chine ancienne*. Edited by Rémi Mathieu. 3rd ed. 2 volumes. Orientales. Paris: Presses Universitaires de France, 1994.

———. *La pensée chinoise*. Bibliothèque de "L'Évolution de l'Humanité." Paris: La Renaissance du Livre, 1934.

Gray, Richard M. "Psychopathy and Will to Power: Ted Bundy and Dennis Rader." In *Serial Killers*, edited by S. Waller, 191–205. Philosophy for Everyone. Chichester, UK: Wiley-Blackwell, 2010.

Graziani, Romain. "Of Words and Swords: Therapeutic Imagination in Action—a Study of Chapter 30 of the *Zhuangzi*, 'Shuo jian' 說劍." *Philosophy East and West* 64.2 (2014): 375–403.

———. "The Subject and the Sovereign: Exploring the Self in Early Chinese Self-Cultivation." In *Early Chinese Religion, Part One: Shang through Han (1250 BC–220 AD)*, edited by John Lagerwey and Marc Kalinowski, 1:459–517. Handbuch der Orientalistik IV.21–1. Leiden: Brill, 2009.

Graziosi, Barbara. *Inventing Homer: The Early Reception of Epic*. Cambridge Classical Studies. Cambridge: Cambridge University Press, 2002.

Grice, Paul. *Studies in the Way of Words*. Cambridge, MA: Harvard University Press, 1989.

Griffioen, Sander. "Hegel on Chinese Religion." In *Hegel's Philosophy of the Historical Religions*, edited by Bart Labuschagne and Timo Slootweg, 21–30. Critical Studies in German Idealism 6. Leiden: Brill, 2012.

Griffith, Samuel B., trans. *Sun Tzu: The Art of War*. Oxford: Clarendon, 1963.

Gu, Ming Dong. "*Fu-bi-xing*: A Metatheory of Poetry-Making." *Chinese Literature: Essays, Articles, Reviews* 19 (1997): 1–22.

Guan Feng 關鋒. *Zhuangzi neipian yijie he pipan* 莊子內篇譯解和批判. Beijing: Zhonghua, 1961.

Gu Jiegang. "Chunqiu shi de Kongzi he Handai de Kongzi" 春秋時的孔子和漢代的孔子. In Gu Jiegang et al., *Gushi bian*, 2:130–39.

———. "Wude zhongshi shuo xia de zhengzhi he lishi" 五德終始說下的政治和歷史. In Gu Jiegang et al., *Gushi bian*, 5:404–617.

Gu Jiegang et al., eds. *Gushi bian* 古史辨. 7 vols. Reprint, Shanghai: Guji, 1982.

Guo Moruo 郭沫若 (1892–1978) et al., eds. *Jiaguwen heji* 甲骨文合集. 13 vols. Beijing: Zhonghua, 1979–83.

Gu Shikao 顧史考 (i.e., Scott Cook, q.v.). "Yi Zhanguo zhushu chongdu *Gushu tongli*" 以戰國竹書重讀《古書通例》. *Jianbo* 簡帛 4 (2009): 425–42.

Hagen, Kurtis. *The Philosophy of Xunzi: A Reconstruction*. Chicago: Open Court, 2007.

Hammer, Ben. "Confucian Thought and China's Moral Crisis." *International Communication of Chinese Culture* 4.4 (2017): 481–92.

Hansen, Chad. *A Daoist Theory of Chinese Thought: A Philosophical Interpretation*. Oxford: Oxford University Press, 1992.

Han Yu 韓愈 (768–824). *Han Changli wenji jiaozhu* 韓昌黎文集校注. Edited by Ma Tongbo 馬通伯. Beijing: Zhonghua, 1972.

Harbsmeier, Christoph. "Authorial Presence in Some Pre-Buddhist Chinese Texts." In *De l'un au multiple: Traductions du chinois vers les langues européenes*, edited by Viviane Alleton and Michael Lackner, 219–50. Paris: Maison des sciences de l'homme, 1999.

———. "The Birth of Confucianism from Competition with Organized Mohism." *Journal of Chinese Studies* 56 (2013): 1–19.

———. *Language and Logic in Traditional China*, edited by Kenneth Robinson. In Needham et al., *Science and Civilisation in China*, 7:1.

———. "The Mass Noun Hypothesis and the Part-Whole Analysis of the White Horse Dialogue." In Rosemont, *Chinese Texts and Philosophical Contexts*, 49–66.

———. "On the Nature of Early Confucian Classical Chinese Discourse on Ethical Norms." *Journal of Value Inquiry* 49.4 (2015): 517–41.

Hardy, Grant. *Worlds of Bronze and Bamboo: Sima Qian's Conquest of History*. New York: Columbia University Press, 1999.

Harper, Donald. "The Bellows Analogy in *Laozi* V and Warring States Macrobiotic Hygiene." *Early China* 20 (1995): 381–91.

———. *Early Chinese Medical Literature: The Mawangdui Medical Manuscripts*. Sir Henry Wellcome Asian Series 2. London: Kegan Paul International, 1998.

Harris, Eirik Lang, trans. *The Shenzi Fragments: A Philosophical Analysis and Translation*. Translations from the Asian Classics. New York: Columbia University Press, 2016.

Hartman, Charles. *Han Yü and the T'ang Search for Unity*. Princeton, NJ: Princeton University Press, 1986.

Hartwell, Robert M. "Historical Analogism, Public Policy, and Social Science in Eleventh- and Twelfth-Century China." *American Historical Review* 76.3 (1971): 690–727.

Hattori, U. "Confucius' Conviction of His Heavenly Mission." Translated by S. Elisséeff. *Harvard Journal of Asiatic Studies* 1.1 (1936): 96–108.

He Bingdi 何炳棣. *He Bingdi sixiang zhidushi lun* 何炳棣思想制度史論. Edited by Fan Yijun 范毅軍 and He Hanwei 何漢威. Yuanshi congshu. Taipei: Lianjing, 2013.

He Lingxu 賀凌虛. *Lüshi chunqiu de zhengzhi lilun* 呂氏春秋的政治理論. Taipei: Shangwu, 1970.

Henry, Eric. "The Motif of Recognition in Early China." *Harvard Journal of Asiatic Studies* 47.1 (1987): 5–30.

Heuer, Richards J., Jr. *Psychology of Intelligence Analysis*. [Washington, DC]: Center for the Study of Intelligence, Central Intelligence Agency, 1999.

Ho, Wing-chung. *The Transition Study of Postsocialist China: An Ethnographic Study of a Model Community*. Singapore: World Scientific, 2010.

Holzer, Rainer. *Yen-tzu und das Yen-tzu ch'un-ch'iu*. Würzburger Sino-Japonica 10. Frankfurt: Peter Lang, 1983.

Hsiao, Kung-chuan. *A Modern China and a New World: K'ang Yu-wei, Reformer and Utopian, 1858–1927*. Publications on Asia of the Institute for Comparative and Foreign Area Studies 25. Seattle: University of Washington Press, 1975.

Hsu, Cho-yun. *Ancient China in Transition: An Analysis of Social Mobility, 722–222 B.C.* Stanford Studies in the Civilizations of Eastern Asia. Stanford, CA: Stanford University Press, 1965.

Hsu, Elisabeth. *Pulse Diagnosis in Early Chinese Medicine: The Telling Touch*. University of Cambridge Oriental Publications 68. Cambridge: Cambridge University Press, 2010.

Huang, Chun-chieh. *Mencian Hermeneutics: A History of Interpretations in China*. New Brunswick: Transaction, 2001.

Hunter, Michael. *Confucius beyond the* Analects. Studies in the History of Chinese Texts. Leiden: Brill, 2017.

———. "Did Mencius Know the *Analects*?" *T'oung Pao* 100.1–3 (2014): 33–79.

———. "The Difficulty with 'The Difficulties of Persuasion' ('Shuinan' 說難)." In Goldin, *Dao Companion to the Philosophy of Han Fei*, 169–95.

Hunter, Michael, and Michael Kern, eds. *Confucius and the* Analects *Revisited: New Perspectives on Composition, Dating, and Authorship*. Studies in the History of Chinese Texts 11. Leiden: Brill, 2018.

Huntington, Samuel P. *The Third Wave: Democratization in the Late Twentieth Century*. Julian J. Rothbaum Distinguished Lecture Series 4. Norman: University of Oklahoma Press, 1991.

Hu Pingsheng 胡平生. "Fuyang Shuanggudui Hanjian *Zhuangzi*" 阜陽雙古堆漢簡《莊子》. *Chutu wenxian yanjiu* 出土文獻研究 12 (2013): 188–201.

Hu Shi 胡適 (1891–1962). *Zhongguo zhexueshi dagang* 中國哲學史大綱. Beijing: Dongfang, 1996.

Hu Shih (i.e., Hu Shi, q.v.). *The Development of the Logical Method in Ancient China*. Shanghai: Oriental Book, 1928.

Hutton, Eric L., ed. *Dao Companion to the Philosophy of Xunzi*. Dao Companions to Chinese Philosophy 7. Dordrecht, Netherlands: Springer, 2016.

———. "Does Xunzi Have a Consistent Theory of Human Nature?" In Kline and Ivanhoe, *Virtue, Nature, and Moral Agency*, 220–36.

———. "Ethics in the *Xunzi*." In Hutton, *Dao Companion to the Philosophy of Xunzi*, 67–93.

———. "Moral Connoisseurship in Mengzi." In Liu and Ivanhoe, *Essays on the Moral Philosophy of Mengzi*, 163–86.

———, trans. *Xunzi: The Complete Text*. Princeton, NJ: Princeton University Press, 2014.

Hu Zizong 胡子宗 et al. *Mozi sixiang yanjiu* 墨子思想研究. Beijing: Renmin, 2007.

Iaccino, Ludovica. "Kim Young-Il Fled North Korea as a Young Soldier—Now He Helps Others Who Escape." *International Business Times*, August 23, 2017; revised August 24, 2017. https://www.ibtimes.co.uk/harrowing-story-north-korean-soldiers-defection-brutal-kim-regime-1636336.

Itō, Michiharu, and Ken-ichi Takashima. *Studies in Early Chinese Civilization: Religion,*

*Society, Language, and Palaeography.* Edited by Gary F. Arbuckle. 2 vols. Osaka: Intercultural Research Institute, Kansai Gaidai University, 1996.

Ivanhoe, Philip J. "Confucian Self Cultivation and Mengzi's Notion of Extension." In Liu and Ivanhoe, *Essays on the Moral Philosophy of Mengzi*, 221–41.

———. "The Concept of *de* ('Virtue') in the *Laozi*." In Csikszentmihalyi and Ivanhoe, *Religious and Philosophical Aspects of the* Laozi, 239–57.

———. "The 'Golden Rule' in the *Analects*." In Jones, *Confucius Now*, 81–107.

———. "A Happy Symmetry: Xunzi's Ethical Thought." *Journal of the American Academy of Religion* 59.2 (1991): 309–22. Reprinted in Kline and Tiwald, *Ritual and Religion in the* Xunzi, 43–60.

———. "McDowell, Wang Yangming, and Mengzi's Contribution to Understanding Moral Perception." *Dao* 10.3 (2011): 273–90.

———. "Was Zhuangzi a Relativist?" In Kjellberg and Ivanhoe, *Essays on Skepticism, Relativism, and Ethics*, 196–214.

———. "Whose Confucius? Which *Analects*?" In Van Norden, *Confucius and the* Analects, 119–33.

Jäger, F. (1886–1957). "Die Biographie des Wu Tzu-hsü." *Oriens Extremus* 7 (1960): 1–16.

Jiang, Yimin. *"Große Musik is tonlos": Eine historische Darstellung der frühen philosophisch-daoistischen Musikästhetik.* Europäische Hochschulschriften 36.135. Frankfurt: Peter Lang, 1995.

Jiang Shanguo 蔣善國 (1898–1986). *Shangshu zongshu* 尚書綜述. Shanghai: Guji, 1988.

Johnson, David. "Epic and History in Early China: The Matter of Wu Tzu-hsü." *Journal of Asian Studies* 40.2 (1981): 255–71.

———. "The Wu Tzu-hsü *pien-wen* and Its Sources." *Harvard Journal of Asiatic Studies* 40.1 (1980): 93–156; 40.2 (1980): 465–505.

Jones, David, ed. *Confucius Now: Contemporary Encounters with the* Analects. Chicago: Open Court, 2008.

Jullien, François. *The Propensity of Things: Toward a History of Efficacy in China.* Translated by Janet Lloyd. New York: Zone Books, 1995.

Kahneman, Daniel, and Amos Tversky. "On the Reality of Cognitive Illusions." *Psychological Review* 103.3 (1996): 582–91.

Kaizuka, Shigeki. *Confucius.* Translated by Geoffrey Bownas. Ethical and Religious Classics of East and West 17. New York: Macmillan, 1956.

Kaltenmark, Max. *Lao Tzu and Taoism.* Translated by Roger Greaves. Stanford, CA: Stanford University Press, 1969.

Kanaya Osamu 金谷治. *Kanaya Osamu Chūgoku shisō ronshū* 金谷治中國思想論集. 3 vols. Tokyo: Hirakawa, 1997.

Kao, Karl S. Y. "Comparative Literature and the Ideology of Metaphor, East and West." In *Comparative Literature and Comparative Cultural Studies*, edited by Steven Tötösy de Zepetnek, 97–110. Comparative Cultural Studies 2. West Lafayette, IN.: Purdue University Press, 2003.

Kasoff, Ira E. *The Thought of Chang Tsai (1020–1077).* Cambridge Studies in Chinese History, Literature and Institutions. Cambridge: Cambridge University Press, 1984.

Keane, John. "More Theses on the Philosophy of History." In *Meaning and Context: Quentin Skinner and His Critics*, edited by James Tully, 204–17. Princeton, NJ: Princeton University Press, 1988.

Keightley, David N. *The Ancestral Landscape: Time, Space, and Community in Late Shang*

*China (ca. 1200–1045 B.C.)*. China Research Monograph 53. Berkeley: Institute of East Asian Studies, 2000.

Ke Mading 柯馬丁 (i.e., Martin Kern, q.v.). "*Shiji* li de 'zuozhe' gainian" 《史記》裡的「作者」概念. Translated by Yang Zhiyi 楊治宜 and Fu Su 付蘇. In *Shiji xue yu shijie Hanxue lunji xubian* 史記學與世界漢學論集續編, edited by Ke Mading and Li Jixiang 李紀祥, 23–61. Taipei: Tangshan, 2016.

Kern, Martin. "Kongzi as Author in the Han." In Hunter and Kern, *Confucius and the Analects Revisited*, 268–307.

———. "The 'Masters' in the *Shiji*." *T'oung Pao* 101.4–5 (2015): 335–62.

———. "Methodological Reflections on the Analysis of Textual Variants and the Modes of Manuscript Production in Early China." *Journal of East Asian Archaeology* 4 (2002): 143–81.

———. "The Performance of Writing in Western Zhou China." In *The Poetics of Grammar and the Metaphysics of Sound and Sign*, edited by S. La Porta and D. Shulman, 109–75. Jerusalem Studies in Religion and Culture 6. Leiden: Brill, 2007.

———. "Speaking of Poetry: Pattern and Argument in the 'Kongzi Shilun.'" In Gentz and Meyer, *Literary Forms of Argument in Early China*, 175–200.

———. "Style and Poetic Diction in the *Xunzi*." In Hutton, *Dao Companion to the Philosophy of Xunzi*, 1–33.

Kern, Martin, and Dirk Meyer, eds. *Origins of Chinese Political Philosophy: Studies in the Composition and Thought of the* Shangshu *(Classic of Documents)*. Studies in the History of Chinese Texts 8. Leiden: Brill, 2017.

Kim, Tae Hyun. "Other *Laozi* Parallels in the *Hanfeizi*: An Alternative Approach to the Textual History of the *Laozi* and Early Chinese Thought." *Sino-Platonic Papers* 199 (2010).

Kimura Eiichi 木村英一. *Chūgoku tetsugaku no tankyū* 中國哲學の探究. Tōyōgaku sōsho 22. Tokyo: Sōbunsha, 1981.

Kirkland, Russell. "Hermeneutics and Pedagogy: Methodological Issues in Teaching the *Daode jing*." In *Teaching the Daode jing*, edited by Gary D. DeAngelis and Warren G. Frisina, 145–65. AAR Teaching Religious Studies Series. Oxford: Oxford University Press, 2008.

———. *Taoism: The Enduring Tradition*. New York: Routledge, 2004.

Kjellberg, Paul, and Philip J. Ivanhoe, eds. *Essays on Skepticism, Relativism, and Ethics in the* Zhuangzi. SUNY Series in Chinese Philosophy and Culture. Albany: State University of New York Press, 1996.

Klein, Esther Sunkyung. *Reading Sima Qian from Han to Song: The Father of History in Pre-modern China*. Studies in the History of Chinese Texts 10. Leiden: Brill, 2018.

———. "Reading the *Zhuangzi* Anthology." In Defoort and Ames, *Having a Word with Angus Graham*, 11–26.

———. "Were There 'Inner Chapters' in the Warring States? A New Examination of Evidence about the *Zhuangzi*." *T'oung Pao* 96.4–5 (2010): 299–369.

Kline, T. C., III, and Philip J. Ivanhoe, eds. *Virtue, Nature, and Moral Agency in the* Xunzi. Indianapolis: Hackett, 2000.

Kline, T. C., III, and Justin Tiwald, eds. *Ritual and Religion in the* Xunzi. SUNY Series in Chinese Philosophy and Culture. Albany: State University of New York Press, 2014.

Kneale, William, and Martha Kneale. *The Development of Logic*. Oxford: Clarendon, 1962.

Knechtges, David R. "Riddles as Poetry: The 'Fu' Chapter of the *Hsün-tzu*." In Chow Tse-tsung, *Wen-lin*, 2:1–31.

Knoblock, John, trans. *Xunzi: A Translation and Study of the Complete Works*. 3 vols. Stanford, CA: Stanford University Press, 1988–94.

Kobayashi Masayoshi 小林正美. *Rikuchō Dōkyō shi kenkyū* 六朝道教史研究. Tōyōgaku sōsho 37. Tokyo: Sōbunsha, 1990.

Kohn, Livia. "The Lao-tzu Myth." In *Lao-tzu and the* Tao-te-ching, edited by Livia Kohn and Michael LaFargue, 41–62. SUNY Series in Chinese Philosophy and Culture. Albany: State University of New York Press, 1998.

———. *Zhuangzi: Text and Context*. St. Petersburg, FL: Three Pines, 2014.

Kohn, Livia, ed., in cooperation with Yoshinobu Sakade. *Taoist Meditation and Longevity Techniques*. Michigan Monographs in Chinese Studies 61. Ann Arbor: University of Michigan Press, 1989.

Kominami Ichirō 小南一郎. "Temmei to toku" 天命と德. *Tōhō gakuhō* 東方學報 64 (1992): 1–59.

Kramers, R. P., trans. *K'ung tzu chia yu: The School Sayings of Confucius*. Sinica Leidensia 7. Leiden: E. J. Brill, 1950.

[Ku Chieh-kang] (i.e., Gu Jiegang, q.v.). *Autobiography of a Chinese Historian: Being the Preface to a Symposium on Ancient Chinese History* (Ku shih pien). Translated by Arthur W. Hummel. Sinica Leidensia 1. Leiden: E. J. Brill, 1931.

Kuriyama, Shigehisa. *The Expressiveness of the Body and the Divergence of Greek and Chinese Medicine*. New York: Zone, 1999.

Kurtz, Joachim. *The Discovery of Chinese Logic*. Modern Chinese Philosophy 1. Leiden: Brill, 2011.

Lai, Karyn. "*Li* in the *Analects*: Training in Moral Competence and the Question of Flexibility." *Philosophy East and West* 56.1 (2006): 69–83.

Lai, Karyn, and Wai Wai Chiu, eds. *Skill and Mastery: Philosophical Stories from the Zhuangzi*. East Asian Comparative Ethics, Politics and Philosophy of Law. London: Rowman and Littlefield, 2019.

Lau, D. C., trans. *Confucius: The Analects*. 2nd ed. Hong Kong: Chinese University Press, 1992.

———, trans. *Mencius: A Bilingual Edition*. Rev. ed. Hong Kong: Chinese University Press, 2003.

Leder, Alfred. "Ein geistreicher Exorzismus im *Zhuangzi* 19,6." *Asiatische Studien* 67.1 (2013): 75–85.

Lee, Janghee. *Xunzi and Early Chinese Naturalism*. SUNY Series in Chinese Philosophy and Culture. Albany: State University of New York Press, 2004.

Lee, Ting-mien. "'Benevolence-Righteousness' as Strategic Terminology: Reading Mengzi's '*ren-yi*' through Strategic Manuals." *Dao* 16.1 (2017): 15–34.

———. "Mozi as a Daoist Sage? An Intertextual Analysis of the 'Gongshu' Anecdote in the *Mozi*." In *Between History and Philosophy: Anecdotes in Early China*, edited by Paul van Els and Sarah A. Queen, 93–112. SUNY Series in Chinese Philosophy and Culture. Albany: State University of New York Press, 2017.

Lee Hur-Li. *Intellectual Activism in Knowledge Organization: A Hermeneutic Study of the Seven Epitomes*. Taipei: National Taiwan University Press, 2016.

Legge, James (1815–97), trans. *The Chinese Classics*. 2nd ed. Oxford: Clarendon, 1893–95.

Levenson, Joseph R. *Liang Ch'i-ch'ao and the Mind of Modern China*. [Rev. ed.] Harvard Historical Monographs 26. Cambridge, MA: Harvard University Press, 1959.

Lévi [Levi], Jean. *Confucius*. Chemins d'Éternité. Paris: Pygmalion/Gérard Watelet, 2002.

———. "L'abstinence des céréales chez les taoïstes." *Études chinoises* 1 (1982): 3–47.

———, trans. *Les sept traités de la guerre*. Grand Pluriel. Paris: Hachette Littératures, 2008.

Levinson, Stephen C. *Pragmatics*. Cambridge: Cambridge University Press, 1983.

Lewis, Mark Edward. *Sanctioned Violence in Early China*. SUNY Series in Chinese Philosophy and Culture. Albany: State University of New York Press, 1990.

———. *Writing and Authority in Early China*. SUNY Series in Chinese Philosophy and Culture. Albany: State University of New York Press, 1999.

Li, Wai-yee. "Concepts of Authorship." In *The Oxford Handbook of Classical Chinese Literature (1000 BCE–900 CE)*, edited by Wiebke Denecke et al., 360–76. Oxford: Oxford University Press, 2017.

———. *The Readability of the Past in Early Chinese Historiography*. Harvard East Asian Monographs 253. Cambridge, MA: Harvard University Press, 2007.

———. "Riddles, Concealment, and Rhetoric in Early China." In *Facing the Monarch: Modes of Advice in the Early Chinese Court*, edited by Garrett P. S. Olberding, 100–132. Harvard East Asian Monographs 359. Cambridge, MA: Harvard University Press, 2013.

Liang Qichao 梁啓超 (1873–1929). *Mozi xue'an* 墨子學案. 4th ed. Zheren zhuanji congshu. Shanghai: Shangwu, 1926.

Li Cunshan 李存山. "A Differentiation of the Meaning of '*qi*' on Several Levels." Translated by Yan Xin. *Frontiers of Philosophy in China* 3.2 (2008): 194–212.

———. "Dui Zhongguo wenhua minben sixiang de zai renshi" 對中國文化民本思想的再認識. *Kongzi yanjiu* 孔子研究 2016.6:5–15.

Li Guisheng 李桂生. *Zhuzi wenhua yu xian-Qin bingjia* 諸子文化與先秦兵家. Yuelu xueshu wencong. Changsha: Yuelu, 2009.

Li Jianmin 李建民. "Contagion and Its Consequences: The Problem of Death Pollution in Ancient China." In *Medicine and the History of the Body: Proceedings of the 20th, 21st and 22nd International Symposium on the Comparative History of Medicine—East and West*, edited by Yasuo Otsuko et al., 201–22. Tokyo: Ishiyaku EuroAmerica, 1999.

———. *Fangshu, yixue, lishi* 方術醫學歷史. Taipei: Nantian, 2000.

Li Jingde 黎靖德 (fl. 1263). *Zhuzi yulei* 朱子語類. Edited by Wang Xingxian 王星賢. Lixue congshu. Beijing: Zhonghua, 1985.

Li Jingwei 李經緯 and Zhang Zhibin 張志斌. *Zhongyixue sixiangshi* 中醫學思想史. Xueke sixiangshi congshu. Changsha: Hunan jiaoyu, 2003.

Lightbody, Brian, and Michael Berman. "The Metaphoric Fallacy to a Deductive Inference." *Informal Logic* 30.2 (2010): 185–93.

Li Linhao 李林浩 and Chen Sufang 陳蘇方. "Shixi yuan zi *Han Feizi* de chengyu" 試析源自《韓非子》的成語. *Mudanjiang Daxue xuebao* 牡丹江大學學報 2009.10: 46–48.

Li Ling 李零. *Jianbo gushu yu xueshu yuanliu* 簡帛古書與學術源流. Rev. ed. Beijing: Sanlian, 2008.

———. *Sunzi shisan pian zonghe yanjiu*《孫子》十三篇綜合研究. Beijing: Zhonghua, 2006.

Lin Tongqi et al. "Chinese Philosophy: A Philosophical Essay on the 'State-of-the-Art.'" *Journal of Asian Studies* 54.3 (1995): 727–58.

Li Rui 李鋭. *Zhanguo Qin Han shiqi de xuepai wenti yanjiu* 戰國秦漢時期的學派問題研究. Beijing: Beijing Shifan Daxue, 2011.

Littlejohn, Ronnie. "Kongzi in the *Zhuangzi*." In *Experimental Essays on Zhuangzi*, edited by Victor H. Mair, 177–94. 2nd ed. Dunedin, FL: Three Pines, 2010.

Liu, Xiusheng, and Philip J. Ivanhoe, eds. *Essays on the Moral Philosophy of Mengzi*. Indianapolis: Hackett, 2002.

Liu Rongxian 劉榮賢. *Zhuangzi waizapian yanjiu* 莊子外雜篇研究. Taipei: Lianjing, 2004.

Liu Wenbin 劉文斌. Yanzi chunqiu *yanjiu shi* 《晏子春秋》研究史. Beijing: Renmin wenxue, 2014.

Liu Xiaogan. *Classifying the* Zhuangzi *Chapters*. [Translated by William E. Savage.] Michigan Monographs in Chinese Studies 65. Ann Arbor: University of Michigan Press, 1994.

Liu Yuan 劉源. *Shang Zhou jizuli yanjiu* 商周祭祖禮研究. Zhongguo Shehui Kexue Yuan Lishi Yanjiu Suo zhuankan A.4. Beijing: Shangwu, 2004.

Li Xueqin. "Looking at the 'Qu qie' Chapter of the *Zhuangzi* from the Guodian *Yucong IV Bamboo Slip Manuscript." Translated by Kim Tae Hyun. *Bamboo and Silk* 1.2 (2018): 337–46.

Li Zehou. *The Chinese Aesthetic Tradition*. Translated by Maija Bell Samei. Honolulu: University of Hawaii Press, 2010.

Lloyd, G[eoffrey] E. R. *Analogical Investigations: Historical and Cross-Cultural Perspectives on Human Reasoning*. Cambridge: Cambridge University Press, 2015.

Lloyd, Geoffrey [E. R.], and Nathan Sivin. *The Way and the Word: Science and Medicine in Early Greece and China*. New Haven, CT: Yale University Press, 2002.

Lo, Yuet Keung. "From a Dual Soul to a Unitary Soul: The Babel of Soul Terminologies in Early China." *Monumenta Serica* 56 (2008): 1–22.

———. "From Analogy to Proof: An Inquiry into the Chinese Mode of Knowledge." *Monumenta Serica* 43 (1995): 141–58.

Loewe, Michael. *Dong Zhongshu, a "Confucian" Heritage and the* Chunqiu fanlu. China Studies 20. Leiden: Brill, 2011.

Loewe, Michael, and Edward L. Shaughnessy, eds. *The Cambridge History of Ancient China: From the Origins of Civilization to 221 B.C.* Cambridge: Cambridge University Press, 1999.

Louie, Kam. *Inheriting Tradition: Interpretations of the Classical Philosophers in Communist China, 1949–1966*. Oxford: Oxford University Press, 1986.

Louton, John. "Concepts of Comprehensiveness and Historical Change in the *Lü-shih ch'un-ch'iu*." In *Explorations in Early Chinese Cosmology: Papers Presented at the Workshop on Classical Chinese Thought Held at Harvard University, August 1976*, edited by Henry Rosemont Jr., 105–17. Journal of the American Academy of Religion Thematic Studies 50.2. Chico, CA: Scholars, 1984.

Lowe, Scott. *Mo Tzu's Religious Blueprint for a Chinese Utopia: The Will and the Way*. Lewiston, NY: Edwin Mellen, 1992.

Loy Hui-chieh. "*Analects* 13.3 and the Doctrine of 'Correcting Names.'" In Jones *Confucius Now*, 223–42.

Loy Hui-chieh. "Justification and Debate: Thoughts on Moist Moral Epistemology." *Journal of Chinese Philosophy* 35.3 (2008): 455–71.

Lundahl, Bertil. *Han Fei Zi: The Man and the Work*. Stockholm East Asian Monographs 4. Stockholm: Institute of Oriental Languages, Stockholm University, 1992.

Luo Genze 羅根澤. *Zhuzi kaosuo* 諸子考索. Beijing: Renmin, 1958.

Luo Xinhui 羅新慧. "Zhoudai tianming guannian de fazhan yu shanbian" 周代天命觀念的發展與嬗變. *Lishi yanjiu* 歷史研究 5 (2012): 4–18.

Lü Shaoyu 呂紹虞. *Zhongguo muluxue shi gao* 中國目錄學史稿. Hefei: Anhui jiaoyu, 1984.

Lü Shihao 呂世浩. *Cong Shiji dao* Hanshu—*Zhuanzhe guocheng yu lishi yiyi* 從《史記》到《漢書》—轉折過程與歷史意義. Guoli Taiwan Daxue wenshi congkan 138. Taipei: Taiwan da chuban zhongxin, 2009.

Lu Shiyi 陸世儀 (1611–72). *Lu Futing Sibian lu jiyao* 陸桴亭思辨錄輯要. Edited by Zhang Boxing 張伯行 (1651–1725). *Baibu Congshu jicheng* 百部叢書集成.

Lu Xun 魯迅 (1881–1936). *Nahan* 吶喊. Beijing: Renmin wenxue, 1976.

MacCormack, Geoffrey. *The Spirit of Traditional Chinese Law*. Spirit of the Laws. Athens: University of Georgia Press, 1996.

Machle, Edward J. *Nature and Heaven in the* Xunzi: *A Study of the Tian lun*. SUNY Series in Chinese Philosophy and Culture. Albany: State University of New York Press, 1993.

Maeder, Erik W. "Some Observations on the Composition of the 'Core Chapters' of the *Mozi*." *Early China* 17 (1992): 27–82.

Maekawa Shōzō 前川捷三. "Kōkotsubun, kimbun ni mieru ki" 甲骨文・金文に見える氣. in *Ki no shisō: Chūgoku ni okeru shizenkan to ningenkan no tenkai* 氣の思想: 中國における自然觀と人間觀の展開, edited by Onozawa Seiichi 小野澤一 et al., 13–29. Tokyo: Tōkyō Daigaku, 1978.

Mair, Victor H., trans. *The Art of War: Sun Zi's Military Methods*. Translations from the Asian Classics. New York: Columbia University Press, 2007.

———, trans. *Wandering on the Way: Early Taoist Tales and Parables of Chuang Tzu*. New York: Bantam, 1994.

Ma Jixing 馬繼興. *Mawangdui gu yishu kaoshi* 馬王堆古醫書考釋. Changsha: Hunan kexue jishu, 1992.

Major, John S. "The Efficacy of Uselessness: A Chuang-tzu Motif." *Philosophy East and West* 25.3 (1975): 265–79.

———. *Heaven and Earth in Early Han Thought: Chapters Three, Four, and Five of the Huainanzi*. SUNY Series in Chinese Philosophy and Culture. Albany: State University of New York Press, 1993.

Major, John S., and Jenny F. So. "Music in Late Bronze Age China." In *Music in the Age of Confucius*, edited by Jenny F. So, 13–33. Washington, DC: Freer Gallery of Art and Arthur M. Sackler Gallery, Smithsonian Institution, 2000.

Major, John S., et al., trans. *The Huainanzi: A Guide to the Theory and Practice of Government in Early Han China*. Translations from the Asian Classics. New York: Columbia University Press, 2010.

Makeham, John. "Between Chen and Cai: *Zhuangzi* and the *Analects*." In Ames, *Wandering at Ease in the* Zhuangzi, 75–100.

———. *Transmitters and Creators: Chinese Commentators and Commentaries on the Analects*. Harvard East Asian Monographs 228. Cambridge, MA: Harvard University Press, 2003.

Mansvelt Beck, Burchard J. " 'Ik' zei de gek, 'I' Mencius, 'I' Laozi, 'Zhuang Zhou' Zhuangzi." In *Linked Faiths: Essays on Chinese Religions and Traditional Culture in Honour of Kristofer Schipper*, edited by Jan A. M. de Meyer and Peter M. Engelfriet, 7–17. Sinica Leidensia 46. Leiden: Brill, 2000.

Maspero, Henri (1883–1945). *Taoism and Chinese Religion*. Translated by Frank A. Kierman Jr. Amherst: University of Massachusetts Press, 1981.

Mattice, Sarah A. *Metaphor and Metaphilosophy: Philosophy as Combat, Play, and Aesthetic Experience*. Studies in Comparative Philosophy and Religion. Lanham, MD: Lexington, 2014.

*Mawangdui Hanmu boshu* 馬王堆漢墓帛書. 4 vols. Beijing: Wenwu, 1985.

Max, D. T. "The Prince's Gambit." *New Yorker* 87.5 (March 21, 2011). https://www.new yorker.com/magazine/2011/03/21/the-princes-gambit, dated March 14, 2011.

Ma Xulun 馬敘倫 (1884–1970). *Laozi jiaogu* 老子校詁. Beijing: Zhonghua, 1974.

McLeod, Alexus. *The Philosophical Thought of Wang Chong*. Cham, Switzerland: Springer Nature, Palgrave Macmillan, 2018.

———. *Theories of Truth in Chinese Philosophy: A Comparative Approach*. Critical Inquiries in Comparative Philosophy. Lanham, MD: Rowman and Littlefield, 2016.

Mei, Yi-pao. *Motse, the Neglected Rival of Confucius*. Probsthain's Oriental Series 20. London: Arthur Probsthain, 1934.

Meng Wentong 蒙文通 (1894–1968). *Zhongguo zhexue sixiang tanyuan* 中國哲學思想探原. Taipei: Taiwan guji, 1997.

Metzger, Thomas A. "Some Ancient Roots of Ancient Chinese Thought: This-Worldliness, Epistemological Optimism, Doctrinality, and the Emergence of Reflexivity in the Eastern Chou." *Early China* 11–12 (1985–87): 61–117.

Meyer, Andrew. " 'The Altars of the Soil and Grain Are Closer Than Kin' 社稷咸於親: The Qi 齊 Model of Intellectual Participation and the Jixia 稷下 Patronage Community." *Early China* 33–34 (2010–11): 37–99.

———. "Reading 'Sunzi' as a Master." *Asia Major*, 3rd ser., 30.1 (2017): 1–24.

Meyer, Andrew, and Andrew Wilson. "*Sunzi Bingfa* as History and Theory." In *Strategic Logic and Political Rationality: Essays in Honor of Michael I. Handel*, edited by Bradford A. Lee and Karl F. Walling, 99–118. London: Frank Cass, 2003.

Michael, Thomas. *The Pristine Dao: Metaphysics in Early Daoist Discourse*. SUNY Series in Chinese Philosophy and Culture. Albany: State University of New York Press, 2005.

Milburn, Olivia, trans. *The Spring and Autumn Annals of Master Yan*. Sinica Leidensia 128. Leiden: Brill, 2016.

Mill, John Stuart (1806–73). *Collected Works of John Stuart Mill*. Vol. 10, *Essays on Ethics, Religion and Society*, edited by J. M. Robson. Toronto: University of Toronto Press, 1969.

Modrak, Deborah K. W. *Aristotle: The Power of Perception*. Chicago: University of Chicago Press, 1987.

Moeller, Hans-Georg. *Daoism Explained: From the Dream of the Butterfly to the Fishnet Allegory*. Ideas Explained 1. Chicago: Open Court, 2004.

———. "The Naked Scribe: The Skill of Dissociation in Society." In Lai and Chiu, *Skill and Mastery*, 243–58.

———. *The Philosophy of the* Daodejing. New York: Columbia University Press, 2006.

———. "Rambling without Destination: On Daoist '*you*-ing' in the World." Zhuangzi *and the Happy Fish*, edited by Roger T. Ames and Takahiro Nakajima, 248–60. Honolulu: University of Hawaii Press, 2015.

Møllgaard, Eske. *An Introduction to Daoist Thought: Action, Language, and Ethics in Zhuangzi.* Routledge Studies in Asian Religion and Philosophy. London: Routledge, 2007.

Mollier, Christine. "Visions of Evil: Demonology and Orthodoxy in Early Daoism." In *Daoism in History: Essays in Honour of Liu Ts'un-yan*, edited by Benjamin Penny, 74–100. Routledge Studies in Taoism. London: Routledge, 2006.

Momand, Pop (1886–1987). *Keeping Up with the Joneses.* New York: Cupples and Leon, 1920.

Montaigne, Michel de (1533–92). *Les essais.* Edited by Pierre Villey (1879–1933). Revised by V.-L. Saulnier. Rev. ed. Quadriges: Grands Textes. Paris: Presses Universitaires de France, 2004.

Moore, John A. *Science as a Way of Knowing: The Foundations of Modern Biology.* Cambridge, MA: Harvard University Press, 1993.

Most, Glenn W. "What Is a Critical Edition?" In *Ars Edendi: Lecture Series*, vol. 4, edited by Barbara Crostini et al., 162–80. Studia Latina Stockholmiensia 62. Stockholm: Stockholm University Press, 2016.

Mote, Frederick W. *Intellectual Foundations of China.* 2nd ed. New York: Knopf, 1989.

Mou, Bo. "Quine's Naturalized Epistemology and Zhuangzi's Daoist Naturalism: How This Constructive Engagement Is Possible." In *The Philosophical Challenge from China*, edited by Brian Bruya, 303–37. Cambridge, MA: MIT Press, 2015.

———. "A Reexamination of the Structure and Content of Confucius' Version of the Golden Rule." *Philosophy East and West* 54.2 (2004): 218–48.

Mou Zongsan 牟宗三. *Mingjia yu Xunzi* 名家與荀子. Xinya Yanjiusuo congkan. Taipei: Xuesheng, 1979.

Mungello, D. E. *Curious Land: Jesuit Accommodation and the Origins of Sinology.* Wiesbaden: Franz Steiner, 1985.

Munro, Donald J. *A Chinese Ethics for the New Century: The Ch'ien Mu Lectures in History and Culture, and Other Essays on Science and Confucian Ethics.* Hong Kong: Chinese University Press, 2005.

———. *The Concept of Man in Early China.* Stanford, CA: Stanford University Press, 1969.

———, ed. *Individualism and Holism: Studies in Confucian and Taoist Values.* Michigan Monographs in Chinese Studies 52. Ann Arbor: University of Michigan Press, 1985.

Nagy, Gregory. "Hesiod and the Ancient Biographical Traditions." *Brill's Companion to Hesiod*, edited by Franco Montanari et al., 271–311. Leiden, 2009.

Needham, Joseph, and Krzysztof Gawlikowski, "Chinese Literature on the Art of War." In Needham et al., *Science and Civilisation in China*, 6:10–66.

Needham, Joseph, et al., eds. *Science and Civilisation in China.* 7 volumes projected. Cambridge: Cambridge University Press, 1954–.

Nisbett, Richard E. *The Geography of Thought: How Asians and Westerners Think Differently.* New York: Free Press, 2003.

Nivison, David S. "The Classical Philosophical Writings." In Loewe and Shaughnessy, *Cambridge History of Ancient China*, 745–812.

———. *The Ways of Confucianism: Investigations in Chinese Philosophy.* Edited by Bryan W. Van Norden. Chicago: Open Court, 1996.

Nussbaum, Martha. "Golden Rule Arguments: A Missing Thought?" *The Moral Circle and the Self: Chinese and Western Approaches*, edited by Kim-chong Chong et al., 3–16. Chicago: Open Court, 2003.

Nylan, Michael. *The Chinese Pleasure Book*. New York: Zone, 2018.

———. "Kongzi and Mozi, the Classicists (Ru 儒) and the Mohists (Mo 墨) in Classical-Era Thinking." *Oriens Extremus* 48 (2009): 1–20.

———. "Lots of Pleasure but Little Happiness." *Philosophy East and West* 65.1 (2015): 196–226.

———. *Yang Xiong and the Pleasures of Reading and Classical Learning in China*. American Oriental Series 94. New Haven, CT: Yale University Press, 2011.

Nylan, Michael, and Thomas Wilson. *Lives of Confucius: Civilization's Greatest Sage through the Ages*. New York: Doubleday Religion, 2010.

Ôfuchi Ninji 大淵忍爾. *Shoki no Dōkyō* 初期の道教. Tōyōgaku sōsho 38. Tokyo: Sōbunsha, 1991.

Olberding, Amy. *Moral Exemplars in the* Analects: *The Good Person Is That*. Routledge Studies in Ethics and Moral Theory 15. New York: Routledge, 2012.

Oliver, Robert T. *Communication and Culture in Ancient India and China*. Syracuse, NY: Syracuse University Press, 1971.

Ommerborn, Wolfgang. "Einflüsse des Menzius und seiner Theorie der Politik der Menschlichkeit (*renzheng*) in der Zeit vom 3. Jh. bis zum Ende der Tang-Zeit." *Archiv Orientální* 73 (2005): 111–39.

Owen, Stephen. *Readings in Chinese Literary Thought*. Harvard-Yenching Institute Monograph Series 30. Cambridge, MA: Harvard University Press, 1992.

Pan Wuyun 潘悟雲. "Houyin kao" 喉音考. *Minzu yuwen* 民族語文 1997.5:10–24.

Parks, Tim. "The Rabelais of Naples." *New York Review of Books*, May 9, 2019. https://www.nybooks.com/articles/2019/05/09/giambattista-basile-rabelais-naples/.

Patt-Shamir, Galia. "To Live a Riddle: The Transformative Aspect of the *Laozi* 《老子》." *Journal of Chinese Philosophy* 36.3 (2009): 408–23.

Peerenboom, R. P. *Law and Morality in Ancient China: The Silk Manuscripts of Huang-Lao*. SUNY Series in Chinese Philosophy and Culture. Albany: State University of New York Press, 1993.

Peierls, R. E. "Wolfgang Ernst Pauli, 1900–1958." *Biographical Memoirs of Fellows of the Royal Society* 5 (1960): 186.

Peng Jixiang 彭吉象. *Zhongguo yishuxue* 中國藝術學. Beijing: Beijing Daxue, 2007.

Penny, Benjamin. "Immortality and Transcendence." In *Daoism Handbook*, edited by Livia Kohn, 109–33. Handbuch der Orientalistik IV.14. Leiden: Brill, 2000.

———. "The Text and Authorship of *Shen xian zhuan*." *Journal of Oriental Studies* 34.2 (1996): 165–209.

Perkins, Franklin. *Heaven and Earth Are Not Humane: The Problem of Evil in Classical Chinese Philosophy*. World Philosophies. Bloomington: Indiana University Press, 2014.

Perrin, Carleton E. "The Chemical Revolution." In *Companion to the History of Modern Science*, edited by R. C. Olby et al., 264–77. London: Routledge, 1990.

Petersen, Jens Østergård. "What's in a Name? On the Sources concerning Sun Wu." *Asia Major*, 3rd ser., 5.1 (1992): 1–31.

Peterson, Willard J. "Squares and Circles: Mapping the History of Chinese Thought." *Journal of the History of Ideas* 49.1 (1988): 47–60.

Pian Yuqian 駢宇騫. *Jianbo wenxian gangyao* 簡帛文獻綱要. Beijing: Beijing Daxue, 2015.

Pines, Yuri, trans. *The Book of Lord Shang: Apologetics of State Power in Early China*. Translations from the Asian Classics. New York: Columbia University Press, 2017.

———. "Confucius' Elitism: The Concepts of *junzi* and *xiaoren* Revisited." In Goldin, *Concise Companion to Confucius*, 164–84.

———. "Disputers of Abdication: Zhanguo Egalitarianism and the Sovereign's Power." *T'oung Pao* 91.4–5 (2005): 243–300.

———. *Envisioning Eternal Empire: Chinese Political Thought of the Warring States Era*. Honolulu: University of Hawaii Press, 2009.

———. "From Historical Evolution to the End of History: Past, Present and Future from Shang Yang to the First Emperor." In Goldin, *Dao Companion to the Philosophy of Han Fei*, 25–45.

———. "Lexical Changes in Zhanguo Texts." *Journal of the American Oriental Society* 122.4 (2002): 691–705.

———. "The Messianic Emperor: A New Look at Qin's Place in China's History." *Birth of an Empire: The State of Qin Revisited*, edited by Yuri Pines et al., 258–79. Global, Area, and International Archive. Berkeley: University of California Press, 2014.

———. "Submerged by Absolute Power: The Ruler's Predicament in the *Han Feizi*." In Goldin, *Dao Companion to the Philosophy of Han Fei*, 67–86.

Pokora, Timoteus. *Hsin-lun (New Treatise) and Other Writings by Huan T'an*. Michigan Papers in Chinese Studies 20. Ann Arbor: University of Michigan Press, 1974.

Pollard, David. *"Ch'i* in Chinese Literary Theory." *Chinese Approaches to Literature from Confucius to Liang Ch'i-ch'ao*, edited by Adele Austin Rickett, 43–66. Princeton, NJ: Princeton University Press, 1978.

Popper, Karl R. *The Logic of Scientific Discovery*. 3rd ed. London: Hutchinson, 1968.

Porkert, Manfred. *The Theoretical Foundations of Chinese Medicine: Systems of Correspondence*. MIT East Asian Science Series 3. Cambridge, MA: MIT Press, 1974.

Powers, Lawrence H. "Equivocation." *Fallacies: Classical and Contemporary Readings*, edited by Hans V. Hansen and Robert C. Pinto, 287–301. University Park: Pennsylvania State University Press, 1995.

Powers, Martin J. *Pattern and Person: Ornament, Society, and Self in Classical China*. Harvard East Asian Monographs 262. Cambridge, MA: Harvard University Press, 2006.

Puett, Michael J. *The Ambivalence of Creation: Debates concerning Innovation and Artifice in Early China*. Stanford, CA: Stanford University Press, 2001.

———. "Forming Spirits for the Way: The Cosmology of the *Xiang'er* Commentary to the *Laozi*." *Journal of Chinese Religions* 32 (2004): 1–28.

———. *To Become a God: Cosmology, Sacrifice, and Self-Divinization in Early China*. Harvard-Yenching Institute Monograph Series 57. Cambridge, MA: Harvard University Press 2002.

Qian Mu 錢穆. *Xian-Qin zhuzi xinian* 先秦諸子繫年. 2nd ed. Hong Kong: Hong Kong University Press, 1956.

Qian Zhongshu 錢鍾書. *Guanzhui bian* 管錐編. 2nd ed. 4 vols. Beijing: Zhonghua, 1986.

Qing Xitai 卿希泰. *Zhongguo Daojiao sixiangshi gang* 中國道教思想史綱. 2 vols. Chengdu: Sichuan renmin, 1980–85.

Qin Yanshi 秦彥士. *Gudai fangyu junshi yu Mojia heping zhuyi*—Mozi *"Bei chengmen" zonghe yanjiu* 古代防禦軍事與墨家和平主義—《墨子·備城門》綜合研究. Beijing: Renmin, 2008.

———. *Mozi kaolun* 墨子考論. Sichuan Shifan Daxue Wenxue Yuan xueshu congshu. Chengdu: Ba-Shu, 2002.

Qiu Xigui 裘錫珪. *Wenshi conggao: Shanggu sixiang, minsu yu guwenzixue shi* 文史叢稿: 上古思想、民俗與古文字學史. Xueshu jilin congshu 7. Shanghai: Yuandong, 1996.

Queen, Sarah [A.] *From Chronicle to Canon: The Hermeneutics of the* Spring and Autumn, *According to Tung Chung-shu*. Cambridge Studies in Chinese History, Literature and Institutions. Cambridge: Cambridge University Press, 1996.

———. "*Han Feizi* and the Old Master: A Comparative Analysis and Translation of *Han Feizi* Chapter 20, 'Jie Lao,' and Chapter 21, 'Yu Lao.'" In Goldin, *Dao Companion to the Philosophy of Han Fei*, 197–256.

Queen, Sarah A., and John S. Major, trans. *Luxuriant Gems of the Spring and Autumn, Attributed to Dong Zhongshu*. Translations from the Asian Classics. New York: Columbia University Press, 2016.

Quine, W[illard] V[an Orman]. *Methods of Logic*. 4th ed. Cambridge, MA: Harvard University Press, 1982.

———. *The Ways of Paradox and Other Essays*. Rev. ed. Cambridge, MA: Harvard University Press, 1976.

———. *Word and Object*. Cambridge, MA: MIT Press, 1960.

Quinton, Anthony. *Utilitarian Ethics*. 2nd ed. London: Duckworth, 1989.

Radcliffe-Brown, A. R. (1881–1955). *Structure and Function in Primitive Society: Essays and Addresses*. New York: Free Press, 1968.

Rainey, Lee. "Mencius and His Vast, Overflowing *qi* (*haoran zhi qi*)." *Monumenta Serica* 46 (1998): 91–104.

Ralph, Philip L. "Mo Ti and the English Utilitarians." *Far Eastern Quarterly* 9.1 (1949): 42–62.

Rand, Christopher C. *Military Thought in Early China*. Albany: State University of New York Press, 2017.

Raphals, Lisa. "Body and Mind in Early China and Greece." *Journal of Cognitive Historiography* 2.2 (2015): 132–82.

———. *Divination and Prediction in Early China and Ancient Greece*. Cambridge: Cambridge University Press, 2013.

———. "Human and Animal in Early China and Greece." In *Ancient Greece and China Compared*, edited by G.E.R. Lloyd and Jingyi Jenny Zhao, in collaboration with Qiaosheng Dong, 131–59. Cambridge: Cambridge University Press, 2018.

———. "On Hui Shi." In Ames, *Wandering at Ease in the* Zhuangzi, 143–61.

———. "*Sunzi* versus *Xunzi*: Two Views of Deception and Indirection." *Early China* 39 (2016): 185–229.

———. "Wheelwright Bian: A Difficult *dao*." In Lai and Chiu, *Skill and Mastery*, 129–42.

Raz, Gil. *The Emergence of Daoism: Creation of Tradition*. Routledge Studies in Taoism 3. London: Routledge, 2011.

Reding, Jean-Paul. *Comparative Essays in Early Greek and Chinese Rational Thinking*. Aldershot, UK: Ashgate, 2004.

———. *Les fondements philosophiques de la rhétorique chez les sophistes grecs et chez les sophistes chinois*. Berne: Peter Lang, 1985.

Ren Jiyu 任繼愈. *Zhongguo zhexueshi* 中國哲學史. Rev. ed. 2 vols. Daxue zhexue cong-shu. Beijing: Renmin, 2003.

Richter, Matthias L. *The Embodied Text: Establishing Textual Identity in Early Chinese Manuscripts*. Studies in the History of Chinese Texts 3. Leiden: Brill, 2013.

———. *Guan ren: Texte der altchinesischen Literatur zur Charakterkunde und Beamten-rekrutierung*. Welten Ostasiens 3. Bern: Peter Lang, 2005.

———. "Roots of Ru 儒 Ethics in *shi* 士 Status Anxiety." *Journal of the American Oriental Society* 137.3 (2017): 449–71.

Rickett, W. Allyn, trans. *Guanzi: Political, Economic, and Philosophical Essays from Early China*. 2 vols. Princeton Library of Asian Translations. Princeton, NJ: Princeton University Press, 1985–98. Rev. ed., C & T Asian Translation Series. Boston: Cheng and Tsui, 2001. [The revised edition includes vol. 1 only.]

Robinet, Isabelle. "The Diverse Interpretations of the *Laozi*." In Csikszentmihalyi and Ivanhoe, 127–59.

———. *Les commentaires du Tao Tö King jusqu'au VIIᵉ siècle*. Mémoires de l'Institut des Hautes Études Chinoises 5. Paris: l'Institut des Hautes Études Chinoises, 1977.

Robson, James. "Ritual and Tradition in Xunzi and Dōgen." In Kline and Tiwald, *Ritual and Religion in the Xunzi*, 135–57.

Roetz, Heiner. *Konfuzius*. Beck'sche Reihe "Denker" 529. 2nd ed. Munich, 1998.

Rong Zhaozu 容肇祖 (1897–1994). *Han Feizi kaozheng* 韓非子考證. Shanghai: Shangwu, 1936.

Rosemont, Henry, Jr., ed. *Chinese Texts and Philosophical Contexts: Essays Dedicated to Angus C. Graham*. Critics and Their Critics 1. La Salle, IL: Open Court, 1991.

Roth, Harold D. *A Companion to Angus C. Graham's Chuang-tzu: The Inner Chapters*. Monographs of the Society for Asian and Comparative Philosophy 20. Honolulu: University of Hawaii Press, 2003.

———. *Original Tao: Inward Training and the Foundations of Taoist Mysticism*. Translations from the Asian Classics. New York: Columbia University Press, 1999.

———. "Who Compiled the *Chuang Tzu*?" In Rosemont, *Chinese Texts and Philosophical Contexts*, 79–128.

Rothbard, Murray N. *An Austrian Perspective on the History of Economic Thought*. 2 vols. Cheltenham, UK: Edward Elgar, 1995.

Rule, Paul A. *K'ung-tzu or Confucius? The Jesuit Interpretation of Confucianism*. Sydney: Allen and Unwin, 1986.

Said, Edward W. *Orientalism*. New York: Vintage, 1978.

Sakade Yoshinobu 坂出祥伸 and Umekawa Sumiyo 梅川純代. *"Ki" no shisō kara miru Dōkyō no bōchūjutsu: Ima ni ikiru kodai Chūgoku no seiai chōjuhō* 「氣」の思想から見る道教の房中術: いまに生きる古代中國の性愛長壽法. Kokoro to kyōyō shirīzu 3. Tokyo: Goyō shobō, 2003.

Sanft, Charles. "Evaluating Swords: Introduction and Translation of a How-to Guide from the Han-Xin Period." *Early China* 39 (2016): 231–53.

Santangelo, Paolo. "Emotions and the Origin of Evil in Neo-Confucian Thought." In *Minds and Mentalities in Traditional Chinese Literature*, edited by Halvor Eifring, 184–316. Studies of Chinese Literature and Psychology 1. Beijing: Culture and Art, 1999.

Sato, Masayuki. *The Confucian Quest for Order: The Origin and Formation of the Political Thought of Xun Zi*. Sinica Leidensia 58. Leiden: Brill, 2003.

Saussy, Haun. *Great Walls of Discourse and Other Adventures in Cultural China*. Harvard East Asian Monographs 212. Cambridge, MA: Harvard University Press 2001.

Sawyer, Ralph D., trans. *The Seven Military Classics of Ancient China*. History and Warfare. Boulder, CO: Westview, 1993.

Sawyer, Ralph D., with the collaboration of Mei-chün Lee Sawyer. *The Tao of Deception: Unorthodox Warfare in Historic and Modern China*. Cambridge, MA: Basic Books, 2007.

———. *The Tao of Spycraft: Intelligence Theory and Practice in Traditional China*. Boulder, CO: Westview, 1998.

Scarre, Geoffrey. *Utilitarianism*. Problems of Philosophy. London: Routledge, 1996.

Schaberg, David. "Chinese History and Philosophy." In *The Oxford History of Historical Writing*, vol. 1, *Beginnings to AD 600*, edited by Andrew Feldherr and Grant Hardy, 394–414. Oxford: Oxford University Press, 2011.

———. "Command and the Content of Tradition." In *The Magnitude of Ming: Command, Allotment, and Fate in Chinese Culture*, edited by Christopher Lupke, 23–48. Honolulu: University of Hawaii Press, 2005.

———. *A Patterned Past: Form and Thought in Early Chinese Historiography*. Harvard East Asian Monographs 205. Cambridge, MA: Harvard University Press, 2001.

———. "'Sell It! Sell It!': Recent Translations of *Lunyu*." *Chinese Literature: Essays, Articles, Reviews* 23 (2001): 115–39.

———. "Speaking of Documents: *Shu* Citations in Warring States Texts." In Kern and Meyer, *Origins of Chinese Political Philosophy*, 320–59.

Schafer, Edward H. *Pacing the Void: T'ang Approaches to the Stars*. Berkeley: University of California Press, 1977.

Schipper, Kristofer. "Chiens de paille et tigres en papier: Une pratique rituelle et ses gloses au cours de la tradition chinoise." *Extrême-Orient Extrême-Occident* 6 (1985): 83–94.

Schuessler, Axel. *ABC Etymological Dictionary of Old Chinese*. Honolulu: University of Hawaii Press, 2007.

———. "Tenues aspiratae im Altchinesischen." In Emmerich et al., *Und folge nun dem, was mein Herz begehrt*, 1:155–64.

Schwartz, Benjamin I. *The World of Thought in Ancient China*. Cambridge, MA: Belknap Press of Harvard University Press, 1985.

Schwermann, Christian. "Composite Authorship in Western Zhou Bronze Inscriptions: The Case of the 'Tiānwáng *guǐ* 天亡簋 Inscription." In *That Wonderful Composite Called Author: Authorship in East Asian Literatures from the Beginnings to the Seventeenth Century*, edited by Christian Schwermann and Raji C. Steineck, 30–57. East Asian Comparative Literature and Culture 4. Leiden: Brill, 2014.

Seidel, Anna K. *La divination de Lao tseu dans le taoïsme des Han*. Publications de l'École Française d'Extrême-Orient 71. Paris, 1969.

Selby, Stephen. *Chinese Archery*. Hong Kong: Hong Kong University Press, 2000.

Sellmann, James D. "Butcher Ding: A Meditation in Flow." In Lai and Chiu, *Skill and Mastery*, 111–27.

Shackleton Bailey, D. R. *Philippics 7–14*. Edited by John T. Ramsey. Loeb Classical Library 507. Cambridge, MA: Harvard University Press, 2010.

Shariff, Azim F., and Kathleen D. Vohs. "The World without Free Will: What Happens to a Society That Believes People Have No Conscious Control over Their Actions?" *Scientific American* 310.6 (2014): 76–79.

Shaughnessy, Edward L. "Of Trees, a Son, and Kingship: Recovering an Ancient Chinese Dream." *Journal of Asian Studies* 77.3 (2018): 593–609.

———. *Rewriting Early Chinese Texts*. SUNY Series in Chinese Philosophy and Culture. Albany: State University of New York Press, 2006.

———. *Unearthing the* Changes: *Recently Discovered Manuscripts of the* Yi jing *(I ching) and Related Texts*. Translations from the Asian Classics. New York: Columbia University Press, 2014.

———. "Western Zhou History." In Loewe and Shaughnessy, *Cambridge History of Ancient China*, 292–351.

Shklovsky, Viktor (1893–1984). *Theory of Prose*. Translated by Benjamin Sher. Champaign, IL: Dalkey Archive, 1990.

Shun, Kwong-loi. "*Le* in the *Analects*." In Goldin, *Concise Companion to Confucius*, 133–47.

———. *Mencius and Early Chinese Thought*. Stanford, CA: Stanford University Press, 1997.

———. "*Rén* and *lǐ* in the *Analects*." In Van Norden, *Confucius and the* Analects, 53–72.

Sivin, Nathan. *Medicine, Philosophy and Religion in Ancient China: Researches and Reflections*. Variorum Collected Studies Series CS512. Aldershot, UK: Ashgate, 1995.

———. *Traditional Medicine in Contemporary China*. Science, Medicine, and Technology in East Asia 2. Ann Arbor: Center for Chinese Studies, University of Michigan, 1987.

Slingerland, Edward. "Metaphor and Meaning in Early China." *Dao* 10.1 (2011): 1–30.

———. *Trying Not to Try: The Art and Science of Spontaneity*. New York: Crown, 2014.

Small, Sharon. "A Daoist Exploration of *shenming*." *Journal of Daoist Studies* 11 (2018): 1–20.

Solomon, Bernard S. *On the School of Names in Ancient China*. Monumenta Serica Monograph Series 64. Sankt Augustin, 2013.

Stalnaker, Aaron. "Aspects of Xunzi's Engagement with Early Daoism." *Philosophy East and West* 53.1 (2003): 87–129.

———. *Overcoming Our Evil: Human Nature and Spiritual Exercises in Xunzi and Augustine*. Moral Traditions Series. Washington, DC: Georgetown University Press, 2006.

Sterckx, Roel. *Chinese Thought: From Confucius to Cook Ding*. London: Pelican, 2019.

———. "*Mozi* 31: Explaining Ghosts, Again." In Defoort and Standaert, *The* Mozi *as an Evolving Text*, 95–141.

Sternberg, Meir. *The Poetics of Biblical Narrative: Ideological Literature and the Drama of Reading*. Indiana Literary Biblical Series. Bloomington: Indiana University Press, 1985.

Strickmann, Michel. *Chinese Magical Medicine*. Edited by Bernard Faure. Stanford, CA: Stanford University Press, 2002.

Stumpfeldt, Hans. "Ein Diener vieler Herren: Einige Bemerkungen zum *Yen-tzu ch'unch'iu*." In Emmerich et al., *Und folge nun dem, was mein Herz begehrt*, 1:183–208.

Sun Xiaochun and Jacob Kistemaker. *The Chinese Sky during the Han: Constellating Stars and Society*. Sinica Leidensia 38. Leiden: E. J. Brill, 1997.

Sun Zhuocai 孫卓彩. *Moxue gaiyao* 墨學概要. Ji'nan: Qi-Lu, 2007.

Svarverud, Rune. "The Usefulness of Uselessness: The Realm of Useless Trees According to Zhuāngzǐ." In *Studies in Chinese Language and Culture: Festschrift in Honour of*

*Christoph Harbsmeier on the Occasion of His 60th Birthday*, edited by Christoph Anderl and Halvor Eifring, 157–68. Oslo: Hermes, 2006.

Szabłowski, Witold. *Dancing Bears: True Stories of People Nostalgic for Life under Tyranny*. Translated by Antonia Lloyd-Jones. New York: Random House, Penguin Books, 2014.

Szabó, Sándor P. "The Term *shenming*—Its Meaning in the Ancient Chinese Thought and in a Recently Discovered Manuscript." *Acta Orientalia* 56.2–4 (2003): 251–74.

Takeda Kenji 竹田健二. "Zhanguo shidai de qi gainian—Yi chutu wenxian wei zhongxin" 戰國時代的氣概念—以出土文獻為中心. *Journal of the History of Ideas in East Asia* 東亞觀念史集刊 11 (2016): 23–59.

Takeuchi Yasuhiro 內竹康浩. "Sei Shū kimbun chū no 'tenshi' ni tsuite" 西周金文中の《天子》について. In *Ronshū Chūgoku kodai no moji to bunka* 論集中國古代の文字と文化, 105–30. Tokyo: Kyūko, 1999.

Tan, Sor-hoon. "Three Corners for One: Tradition and Creativity in the *Analects*." In Jones, *Confucius Now*, 59–77.

Tang, Siufu. *Self-Realization through Confucian Learning: A Contemporary Reconstruction of Xunzi's Ethics*. SUNY Series in Chinese Philosophy and Culture. Albany: State University of New York Press, 2016.

Tang Minggui 唐明貴. "Zhao Qi *Mengzi zhangju* de quanshi tese" 趙岐《孟子章句》的詮釋特色. *Guoxue xuekan* 國學學刊 2017.1:44–65.

Tang Yijie 唐一介. *Guo Xiang yu Wei Jin xuanxue* 郭象與魏晉玄學. Rev. ed. Beida mingjia mingzhu wencong. Beijing: Beijing Daxue, 2000.

Taniguchi Hiroshi 谷口洋. "Fu ni jijo o tsukeru koto: Ryō Kan no kō ni okeru 'sakusha' no mezame" 賦に自序をつけること: 兩漢の交における「作者」のめざめ. *Tōhōgaku* 東方學 119 (2010): 22–39.

Tan Jiajian 譚家健. *Mozi yanjiu* 墨子研究. Guiyang: Guizhou jiaoyu, 1995.

Tashima, Pauli. "Fragments Speak: Reexamining the Rejected Pre-Du Yu Commentaries on the *Zuozhuan*." *Chinese Literature: Essays, Articles, Reviews* 38 (2016): 1–39.

Thompson, P. M. *The* Shen tzu *Fragments*. London Oriental Series 29. Oxford: Oxford University Press, 1979.

Timpanaro, Sebastiano. *The Genesis of Lachmann's Method*. Translated by Glenn W. Most. Chicago: University of Chicago Press, 2005.

Tiwald, Justin. "A Right of Rebellion in the *Mengzi*?" *Dao* 7.3 (2008): 269–82.

Tolstoy, Leo (1828–1910). *War and Peace: The Maude Translation*. Edited by George Gibian. 2nd ed. New York: W. W. Norton, 1996.

Tong Shuye 童書業. *Tong Shuye shiji kaozheng lunji* 童書業史籍考證論集. Edited by Tong Jiaoying 童教英. 2 vols. Xiandai shixuejia wencong. Beijing: Zhonghua, 2005.

Tsuda Sōkichi 津田左右吉 (1873–1961). *Rongo to Kōshi no shisō* 論語と孔子の思想. Tokyo: Iwanami, 1946.

Tu Wei-ming. *Centrality and Commonality: An Essay on Confucian Religiousness*. SUNY Series in Chinese Philosophy and Culture. Rev. ed. Albany: State University of New York Press, 1989.

Ullman, Harlan K., et al. *Shock and Awe: Achieving Rapid Dominance*. Washington, DC: Center for Advanced Concepts and Technology, [1996].

Unschuld, Paul U. "Die Anfänge der chinesischen Medizin: Säkulare Naturwissenschaft als Möglichkeit existentieller Selbstbestimmung." In *Rooted in Hope: China—Religion—Christianity: Festschrift in Honor of Roman Malek S.V.D. on the Occasion of His*

*65th Birthday*, edited by Barbara Hoster et al., 1:137–52. Monumenta Serica Monograph Series 68. Abingdon, UK: Routledge, 2017.

———, trans. *Huang Di Nei Jing Ling Shu: The Ancient Classic on Needle Therapy*. Oakland: University of California Press, 2016.

Unschuld, Paul U., and Hermann Tessenow, trans., in collaboration with Zhang Jinsheng. *Huang Di nei jing su wen: An Annotated Translation of Huang Di's Inner Classic—Basic Questions*. 2 vols. Berkeley: University of California Press, 2011.

Van der Loon, Piet. "On the Transmission of the *Kuan-tzŭ*." *T'oung Pao* 41.4–5 (1952): 357–93.

Van Ess, Hans. "Die Idee des Zyklus von fünfhundert Jahren bei *Mengzi*, Sima Qian und einigen anderen Denkern der Han." In *Dem Text ein Freund: Erkundungen des chinesischen Altertums: Robert H. Gassmann gewidmet*, edited by Roland Altenburger et al., 57–75. Bern: Peter Lang, 2009.

———. "Einige Anmerkungen zur Biographie des Konfuzius im *Shih-chi* und vergleichbaren Stellen im *K'ung-tzu chia-yü*." *Oriens Extremus* 50 (2011): 157–80; 52 (2013): 215–62.

Van Gulik, R. H. *Erotic Colour Prints of the Ming Period: With an Essay on Chinese Sex Life from the Han to the Ch'ing Dynasty, B.C. 206–A.D. 1644*. [Typeset ed.] 2 vols. Sinica Leidensia 62. Leiden: Brill, 2004.

———. *Sexual Life in Ancient China: A Preliminary Survey of Chinese Sex and Society from ca. 1500 B.C. till 1644 A.D.* Rev. ed. Sinica Leidensia 57. Leiden: Brill, 2003.

Vankeerberghen, Griet. "Choosing Balance: Weighing (*quan*) as a Metaphor for Action in Early Chinese Texts." *Early China* 30 (2005–6): 47–89.

———. "Texts and Authors in the *Shiji*." In *China's Early Empires: A Re-appraisal*, edited by Michael Nylan and Michael Loewe, 461–79. University of Cambridge Oriental Publications 67. Cambridge: Cambridge University Press, 2010.

Van Norden, Bryan W., ed. *Confucius and the* Analects: *New Essays*. Oxford: Oxford University Press, 2002.

———. "Han Fei and Confucianism: Toward a Synthesis." In Goldin, *Dao Companion to the Philosophy of Han Fei*, 135–45.

———. "Method in the Madness of the *Laozi*." In *Religious and Philosophical Aspects of the* Laozi, edited by Mark Csikszentmihalyi and Philip J. Ivanhoe, 187–210. SUNY Series in Chinese Philosophy and Culture. Albany: State University of New York Press, 1999.

———. "Unweaving the 'One Thread' of *Analects* 4:15." In Van Norden, *Confucius and the* Analects, 216–36.

———. *Virtue Ethics and Consequentialism in Early Chinese Philosophy*. Cambridge: Cambridge University Press, 2007.

———. "What Should Western Philosophy Learn from Chinese Philosophy?" In *Chinese Language, Thought, and Culture: Nivison and His Critics*, edited by Philip J. Ivanhoe, 224–49. Critics and Their Critics 3. Chicago: Open Court, 1996.

Villaver, Ranie. "Does *guiji* Mean Egoism? Yang Zhu's Conception of Self." *Asian Philosophy* 25.2 (2015): 216–23.

Vogelsang, Kai. "Beyond Confucius: A Socio-historical Reading of the *Lunyu*." *Oriens Extremus* 49 (2010): 29–61.

Volkov, Alexeï. "Analogical Reasoning in Ancient China: Some Examples." *Extrême-Orient, Extrême-Occident* 14 (1992): 15–48.

Voltaire [i.e., François-Marie Arouet, 1694–1778]. *Dictionnaire philosophique, portratif.* London: N.p., 1764.

Von Glahn, Richard. *The Sinister Way: The Divine and the Demonic in Chinese Religious Culture.* Berkeley: University of California Press, 2004.

Wagner, Rudolf G., trans. *A Chinese Reading of the* Daodejing: *Wang Bi's Commentary on the* Laozi *with Critical Text and Translation.* SUNY Series in Chinese Philosophy and Culture. Albany: State University of New York Press, 2003.

Waley, Arthur (1889–1966), trans. *The Analects of Confucius.* London: George Allen and Unwin, 1938.

———. *Three Ways of Thought in Ancient China.* London: George Allen and Unwin, 1939.

Wang, Aihe. *Cosmology and Political Culture in Early China.* Cambridge Studies in Chinese History, Literature and Institutions. Cambridge: Cambridge University Press, 2000.

Wang, William S-Y. "Language in China: A Chapter in the History of Linguistics." *Journal of Chinese Linguistics* 17.2 (1989): 183–222.

Wang Bo 王博. *Zhuangzi zhexue* 莊子哲學. 2nd ed. Shafa tushuguan: Renjian shi. Beijing: Beijing Daxue, 2013.

Wang Jianwen 王健文. "Guojun yiti—Gudai Zhongguo guojia gainian de yige mianxiang" 國君一體—古代中國國家概念的一個面向. In *Zhongguo gudai sixiang zhong de qilun ji shentiguan* 中國古代思想中的氣論及身體觀, edited by Yang Rubin 楊儒賓, 227–60. Taipei: Juliu, 1993.

Wang Li 王力. *Tongyuan zidian* 同源字典. Beijing: Shangwu, 1982.

Wang Ming 王明. *Daojia he Daojiao sixiang yanjiu* 道教和道教思想研究. Beijing: Zhongguo shehui kexue, 1984.

Wang Qing 王青. *Yang Xiong pingzhuan* 揚雄評傳. Zhongguo sixiangjia pingzhuan congshu. Nanjing: Nanjing Daxue, 2000.

Wang Shouren 王守仁 (1472–1529). *Wang Yangming quanji* 王陽明全集. Edited by Wu Guang 吳光 et al. Shanghai: Guji, 2011.

Wang Shumin 王叔岷. *Zhuangzi guankui* 莊子管闚. Wang Shumin zhuzuo ji. Beijing: Zhonghua, 2007.

Wang Yu'an 王裕安. "Mozi 'guiyi' xinxi" 墨子"貴義"新析. In Cao Shengqiang and Sun, *Mozi yanjiu*, 46–53.

Wang Zhongjiang 王中江. *Daojia xueshuo de guannianshi yanjiu* 道家學說的觀念史研究. Guoxue luncong. Beijing: Zhonghua, 2015.

———. *Daoism Excavated: Cosmos and Humanity in Early Manuscripts.* Translated by Livia Kohn. Contemporary Chinese Scholarship in Daoist Studies. St. Petersburg, FL: Three Pines, 2015.

*Warfighting.* Fleet Marine Force Manual 1. [Washington, DC]: US Marine Corps, [1989].

Warnke, Georgia. *Justice and Interpretation.* Cambridge: Polity, 1992.

Watanabe Takashi 渡邊卓. *Kodai Chūgoku shisō no kenkyū—"Kōshiden no keisei" to Ju Boku shūdan no shisō kōdō* 古代中國思想の研究—〈孔子傳の形成〉と儒墨集團の思想行動. Tōyōgaku sōsho 7. Tokyo: Sōbunsha, 1973.

Watson, Burton, trans. *Han Feizi: Basic Writings.* Translations from the Asian Classics. New York: Columbia University Press, 2003.

———, trans. *Mozi: Basic Writings.* Translations from the Asian Classics. New York: Columbia University Press, 2003.

Weinberg, Steven. "Eye on the Present—the Whig History of Science." *New York Review of Books* 62.20 (December 17, 2015).

———. *To Explain the World: The Discovery of Modern Science*. New York: Harper, 2015.

Weingarten, Oliver. "Chunyu Kun: Motifs, Narratives, and Personas in Early Chinese Anecdotal Literature." *Journal of the Royal Asiatic Society* 27.3 (2017): 501–21.

Wei Qipeng 魏啓鵬. *Mawangdui Hanmu boshu* Huangdi shu *jianzheng* 馬王堆漢墓帛書《黃帝四書》箋證. Ershi shiji chutu jianbo wenxian jiaoshi ji yanjiu congshu. Beijing: Zhonghua, 2004.

Wilde, Oscar (1854–1900). *Complete Works of Oscar Wilde*. London: Collins, 1966.

Wilhelm, Richard (1873–1930). *Confucius and Confucianism*. Translated by George H. Danton and Annina Periam Danton. Harvest Book 216. New York: Harcourt Brace, 1931.

Williams, Paul. *Mahāyāna Buddhism: The Doctrinal Foundations*. Library of Religious Beliefs and Practices. London: Routledge, 1989.

Winter, Marc. "Suggestions for a Re-interpretation of the Concept of *Wu xing* in the *Sunzi bingfa*." *Bulletin of the Museum of Far Eastern Antiquities* 76 (2004): 147–80.

Wohlleben, Peter. *Das geheime Leben der Bäume: Was sie fühlen, wie sie kommunizieren*. Munich: Ludwig, 2015.

Wong, Benjamin, and Hui-chieh Loy. "War and Ghosts in Mozi's Political Philosophy." *Philosophy East and West* 54.3 (2004): 343–63.

Wong, David B. "Reasons and Analogical Reasoning in Mengzi." In Liu and Ivanhoe, *Essays on the Moral Philosophy of Mengzi*, 187–220.

———. "Xunzi's Metaethics." In Hutton, *Dao Companion to the Philosophy of Xunzi*, 139–64.

Wyatt, Don J. *The Recluse of Loyang: Shao Yung and the Moral Evolution of Early Sung Thought*. Honolulu: University of Hawaii Press, 1996.

Xie Wenchao 解文超. *Xian-Qin bingshu yanjiu* 先秦兵書研究. Wenshizhe yanjiu congshu. Shanghai: Guji, 2007.

Xiong Tieji 熊鐵基 et al. *Zhongguo Zhuangxue shi* 中國莊學史. Xuehai yiniu ming. Changsha: Hunan renmin, 2003.

Xu Fuguan 徐復觀. *Zhongguo renxinglun shi: Xian-Qin pian* 中國人性論史: 先秦篇. Taipei: Shangwu, 1969.

Xu Jianwei 徐建委. *Shuoyuan yanjiu: Yi Zhanguo Qin Han zhi jian de wenxian leiji yu xueshushi wei zhongxin* 《說苑》研究:以戰國秦漢之間的文獻纍積與學術史爲中心. Guoxue yanjiu congkan. Beijing: Peking University Press, 2011.

Xu Keqian 徐克謙. *Xian-Qin sixiang wenhua lunzha* 先秦思想文化論札. Suiyuan wenshi yanjiu congkan. Beijing: Zhonghua, 2007.

———. *Zhuangzi zhexue xintan: Dao, yan, ziyou yu mei* 莊子哲學新探: 道·言·自由與美. Beijing: Zhonghua, 2005.

Xu Zhengying 徐正英. *Xian-Tang wenxue yu wenxue sixiang kaolun* 先唐文學與文學思想考論. Zhongguo Renmin Daxue gudai wenxue yu wenxianxue yanjiu congshu. Shanghai: Guji, 2015.

Yamada, Makiko, and Hidehiko Takahashi. "Happiness Is a Matter of Social Comparison." *Psychologia* 54 (2011): 252–60.

Yan Changgui 晏昌貴. "Cong chutu wenxian kan xian-Qin zhuzi de wuyin peizhi" 從出

土文獻看先秦諸子的五音配置. *Zhongyuan wenhua yanjiu* 中原文化研究 2015.3:86–90.

Yang, Lien-sheng. "The Concept of *pao* as a Basis for Social Relations in China." In *Chinese Thought and Institutions*, edited by John K. Fairbank, 291–309. Chicago: University of Chicago Press, 1957.

———. *Studies in Chinese Institutional History*. Harvard-Yenching Institute Studies 20. Cambridge, MA: Harvard University Press, 1961.

Yang Guorong 楊國榮. *Zhuangzi de sixiang shijie* 莊子的思想世界. Yang Guorong zhuzuo ji. Shanghai: Huadong Shifan Daxue, 2009.

Yang Junguang 楊俊光. *Mojing yanjiu* 墨經研究. Xin xueheng shulin. Nanjing: Nanjing Daxue, 2002.

Yang Kuan 楊寬. *Zhanguo shiliao biannian jizheng* 戰國史料編年輯證. Shanghai: Renmin, 2001.

Yang Rongguo 楊榮國. *Zhongguo gudai sixiangshi* 中國古代思想史. 2nd ed. Beijing: Renmin, 1973.

Yang Shanqun 楊善群. *Sunzi pingzhuan* 孫子評傳. Zhongguo sixiangjia pingzhuan congshu. Nanjing: Nanjing Daxue, 1995.

Yang Yi 楊義. *Han Feizi huanyuan* 韓非子還原. Beijing: Zhonghua, 2011.

———. *Laozi huanyuan* 老子還原. Beijing: Zhonghua, 2011.

———. *Mozi huanyuan* 墨子還原. Beijing: Zhonghua, 2011.

———. *Zhuangzi huanyuan* 莊子還原. Beijing: Zhonghua, 2011.

Yao Mingda 姚名達. *Zhongguo muluxue shi* 中國目錄學史. Zhongguo wenhuashi congshu. Changsha: Shangwu, 1938.

Yates, Robin D. S. "Early Poliorcetics: The Mohists to the Sung." In Needham et al., *Science and Civilisation in China*, 6:241–485.

Yearley, Lee H. "Hsün Tzu on the Mind: His Attempted Synthesis of Confucianism and Taoism." *Journal of Asian Studies* 39.3 (1980): 465–80.

———. "Xunzi: Ritualization as Humanization." In Kline and Tiwald, *Ritual and Religion in the Xunzi*, 81–106.

Ye Shuxian 葉舒憲. *Zhuangzi de wenhua jiexi* 莊子的文化解析. Xi'an: Shaanxi renmin, 2004.

*Yinqueshan Hanmu zhujian* 銀雀山漢墓竹簡. 2 vols. to date. Beijing: Wenwu, 1985–.

Yin Zhenhuan 尹振環. *Chongshi Laozi yu* Laozi—*Qiren qishu qishu qi yanbian* 重識老子與《老子》—其人其書其術其演變. Guojia sheke jijin chengguo wenku. Beijing: Shangwu, 2008.

Yoshinaga Shinjirō 吉永慎二郎. *Sengoku shisōshi kenkyū: Juka to Bokuka no shisōshiteki kōshō* 戰國思想史研究: 儒家と墨家の思想史的交涉. Kyoto: Hōyū, 2004.

Yu, Pauline. *The Reading of Imagery in the Chinese Poetic Tradition*. Princeton, NJ: Princeton University Press, 1987.

Yu Jiaxi 余嘉錫 (1884–1955). *Yu Jiaxi shuo wenxianxue* 余嘉錫說文獻學. Mingjia shuo—"Shanggu" xueshu cuibian. Shanghai: Guji, 2001.

Yu Yingshi 余英時. *Lishi yu sixiang* 歷史與思想. Taipei: Lianjing, 1976.

Zhang, Hanmo. *Authorship and Text-Making in Early China*. Library of Sinology 2. Boston: De Gruyter, 2018.

Zhang, Qianfan. "Human Dignity in Classical Chinese Philosophy: Reinterpreting Mohism." *Journal of Chinese Philosophy* 34.2 (2007): 239–55.

Zhang Dake 張大可. *Shiji yanjiu* 史記研究. Beijing: Huawen, 2002.

Zhang Duansui 張端穗. *Xi-Han Gongyangxue yanjiu* 西漢公羊學研究. Wenshizhe daxi 187. Taipei: Wenjin, 2005.

*Zhangjiashan Hanmu zhujian (Ersiqi hao mu)* 張家山漢墓竹簡 (二四七號墓). Beijing: Wenwu, 2001.

Zhang Longxi. "Qian Zhongshu on Philosophical and Mystical Paradoxes in the *Laozi*." In Csikszentmihalyi and Ivanhoe, *Religious and Philosophical Aspects of the* Laozi, 97–126.

Zhang Songhui 張松輝. *Laozi yanjiu* 老子研究. Zongjiao yu shehui yanjiu congshu. Beijing: Renmin, 2009.

———. *Zhuangzi yanjiu* 莊子研究. Zongjiao yu shehui yanjiu congshu. Beijing: Renmin, 2009.

Zhang Wenxiu 張文修. "Zhongguo zhexue zhong de zhengming wenti" 中國哲學中的證明問題. *Wen shi zhe* 文史哲 2015.4:136–50.

Zhang Xifeng 張西峰. "Lun Moxue shuailuo de yuanyin" 論墨學衰落的原因. In Cao Shengqiang and Sun, *Mozi yanjiu*, 329–38.

Zhang Youlin 張幼林 and Zhang Xiyu 張布宇. "*Mozi* zhongyao banben de chuancheng guanxi kaolüe"《墨子》重要版本的傳承關係考略. In Cao Shengqiang and Sun, *Mozi yanjiu*, 146–55.

Zhan Jianfeng 詹劍峰. *Mojia de xingshi luoji* 墨家的形式邏輯. 2nd ed. Wuhan: Hubei renmin, 1979.

Zheng Jiewen 鄭傑文. *Zhongguo Moxue tongshi* 中國墨學通史. Guojia sheke jijin chengguo wenku. Beijing: Renmin, 2006.

Zheng Liangshu 鄭良樹. *Han Fei zhi zhushu ji sixiang* 韓非之著書及思想. Taipei: Xuesheng, 1993.

———. *Zhuzi zhuzuo niandai kao* 諸子著作年代考. Beijing: Beijing Tushuguan, 2001.

Zhong Zhaopeng 鐘肇鵬 and Zhou Guidian 周桂鈿. *Huan Tan Wang Chong pingzhuan* 桓譚王充評傳. Zhongguo sixiangjia pingzhuan congshu. Nanjing: Nanjing Daxue, 1993.

Zhou Fumei 周富美. *Mozi jiajiezi jizheng* 墨子假借字集證. 2nd ed. Wenshi congkan 6. Taipei: Guoli Taiwan Daxue, 1965.

Zhu Fenghan 朱鳳瀚. "Zuoce Ban yuan tanxi" 作冊般黿探析. *Zhongguo lishi wenwu* 中國歷史文物 1 (2005): 6–10.

Zhu Jianping 朱建平. *Zhongguo yixueshi yanjiu* 中國醫學史研究. Beijing: Zhongyi guji, 2003.

Zhu Xi 朱熹 (1130–1200). *Chuci houyu* 楚辭後語. *Siku quanshu* 四庫全書.

———. *Sishu zhangju jizhu* 四書章句集注. Xinbian Zhuzi jicheng. Beijing: Zhonghua, 1983.

Zhu Ziqing 朱自清 (1898–1948). *Shi yan zhi bian* 詩言志辨. Kaiming wenshi congkan. Shanghai, 1947.

Ziporyn, Brook. "How Many Are the Ten Thousand Things and I? Relativism, Mysticism, and the Privileging of Oneness in the 'Inner Chapters.'" In Cook, *Hiding the World in the World*, 33–63.

———. *The Penumbra Unbound: The Neo-Taoist Philosophy of Guo Xiang*. SUNY Series in Chinese Philosophy and Culture. Albany: State University of New York Press, 2003.

Zufferey, Nicolas. *To the Origins of Confucianism: The* ru *in Pre-Qin Times and during the*

*Early Han Dynasty.* Schweizer Asiatische Studien: Monographien 43. Bern: Peter Lang, 2003.

———. *Wang Chong (27–97?): Connaisance, politique et vérité en Chine ancienne.* [Schweizer Asiatische Studien: Monographien 19.] Berne: Peter Lang, 1995.

Zürcher, E. *The Buddhist Conquest of China: The Spread and Adaptation of Buddhism in Early Medieval China.* 2 vols. Sinica Leidensia 11. Leiden: E. J. Brill, 1972.

# General Index

# Index Locorum

N.b.: Texts with standard sequences are cited by chapter number; others are cited by chapter title.